Joe Gans

Joe Gans

*A Biography of
the First African American
World Boxing Champion*

COLLEEN AYCOCK *and*
MARK SCOTT

McFarland & Company, Inc., Publishers
Jefferson, North Carolina, and London

LIBRARY OF CONGRESS CATALOGUING-IN-PUBLICATION DATA

Aycock, Colleen.
Joe Gans : a biography of the first African American world
boxing champion / Colleen Aycock and Mark Scott.
   p.   cm.
Includes bibliographical references and index.

ISBN 978-0-7864-3994-2
softcover : 50# alkaline paper ∞

1. Gans, Joe.   2. Boxers (Sports)— United States—
Biography.   3. African American boxers— Biography.
I. Scott, Mark.   II. Title.
GV1132.G33A93   2008
796.83092 — dc22[B]   2008038572

British Library cataloguing data are available

On the cover: Joe Gans, 1898 (From the supplement to
The National Police Gazette, Vol. LXXIII, No. 1098)

Manufactured in the United States of America

McFarland & Company, Inc., Publishers
Box 611, Jefferson, North Carolina 28640
www.mcfarlandpub.com

Acknowledgments

Our deepest gratitude to the following people and institutions: Dave Wallace, Colleen's husband, for his technical help and the many trips he made to Baltimore; Vincent Fitzpatrick, curator of the H.L. Mencken Collection and the wonderful staff in the Maryland Room and the newspaper archives at the Enoch Pratt Free Library, Baltimore, Maryland; Archivist Ryan Flahive of the Sharlot Hall Museum in Prescott, Arizona; Francis P. O'Neill of the Maryland Historical Society; Karla Lund of Miles City, Montana; Stephanie Jacqueney and Daria Fessack of Madison Square Garden; Erin Tikovitsch of the Chicago History Museum; Jacquie Greff of Baltimore; Angela Haag, Allen Metscher and Eva La Rue of the Central Nevada Museum; Sgt. Micki Knight of Esmeralda County, Nevada; the Reginald F. Lewis Museum of Maryland African American History; boxing historians, Monte Cox, Tracy Callis, Thomas Scharf, Harry Shaffer and Dan Somrack. Your research, your insights, and your valuable time made this project possible.

Quotations from the writing of H. L. Mencken on Joe Gans used by permission of the Enoch Pratt Free Library, Baltimore, in accordance with the terms of Mr. Mencken's literary bequest to that library.

Table of Contents

Preface

Here we take the bold and willing reader into the life and times of Joe Gans, the first black American sports champion and the greatest boxer who ever lived. When the idea of a biography about the man called the "Old Master" surfaced, we were surprised that one had not already been written.

We had worked together in business and as co-authors in several offbeat fiction-writing ventures before we began research on this heartfelt subject. Both of us had a tremendous respect for the practitioners of the manly art. Mark achieved notice as a silver and golden glover in his younger days, and Colleen's father was a professional fighter in the hardscrabble days of the Depression. The time in which Gans fought, the Gay Nineties and Ragtime eras, considered the golden age of pugilism by the old boxers, held a special allure for us.

With the popularity of sport biographies, especially those of record-setting athletes, we wondered why there were no modern accounts of Joe Gans. Nat Fleischer, boxing historian emeritus and founder of *The Ring* magazine, had written in the 1930s an account of Gans along with other black boxers' ring exploits in *Black Dynamite,* but so many questions about Gans' life remained a mystery. When someone talks of "straight hitting" or "bringing home the bacon" they are using phrases coined by the Old Master, yet hardly anyone today recognizes his name. The questions we kept asking ourselves initially were: Why was this all-time great boxer always relegated to the footnotes of history? Why is Gans' ring record so consistently misrepresented? And more importantly, what happened to make his story so invisible to the world today? With all the coverage of the great "fights of the century," there is little recognition for the first one, the epic Goldfield battle.

Gans' memory seemed a ghost haunting the lore of the fistic world for generations, with his name only associated with the great fixed-fight scandal that caused the banning of boxing in Chicago for a quarter century. Yet the truly great fighters throughout history all remembered Gans with a sense of awe. Jack Johnson, Sam Langford, even "The Greatest" himself, Muhammad

Ali, spoke in reverence of "the days of Joe Gans." John L. Sullivan himself remarked how "Gans could lick them all on their best days." A few months of initial research convinced us that bringing the incredible story of the Baltimore Marvel to light would benefit more than just boxing historians. His saga was an essential piece of Americana, and it deserved a better place in the annals of American history.

Joe Gans was a member of the first generation of champion boxers under the Marquis of Queensberry rules (the era following the bare-knuckles melees inherited from "auld England"). Gans' pugilistic career coincided with the heyday of more recognizable ring stars, such as John L. Sullivan, Jim Jeffries, and Kid McCoy, when the professional sport began in the late nineteenth century. Gans' name is seldom mentioned with this illustrious group. He was a "colored" fighter, the first American-born black to hold a world title of any sort, and his road to recognition was arduous.

We set Gans' amazing life story in the context of American culture when boxing was the most popular sport and its champions were the rock stars of the age, appearing in the ring, on the vaudeville stage, and even as the first movie stars. (Edison's first film was of a boxing match between two of Gans' contemporaries.) At the turn of the century, prizefighting was the world's richest sport. Gans' championship contest in 1906 in Goldfield was promoted as the "Fight of the Century" with the largest purse of its time, a match with racial overtones that pitted the world's best black boxer against a white champion. It was the longest gloved-championship bout in history, the longest ever captured by Edison's new invention, the motion picture, and the match that accelerated Gans' eventual decline in health. Yet few know anything about the famous fight that gave Tex Rickard his start (he was the promoter of "million-dollar-gate" fame who later turned Madison Square Garden into the boxing capital of the world).

Gans was orphaned at the age of four, took a menial job at the Baltimore Harbor, and was discovered when a gambler witnessed his boxing prowess in a "battle royal," a popular, brutal racist spectacle of the age. He spent 18 years boxing, working his way up the professional ladder against tremendous obstacles in Jim Crow America. Fighting his way out of total poverty, he survived physical assaults, a stolen title, bankruptcy, and numerous, well-orchestrated attempts to destroy his reputation. Even at death's doorstep, he fought to earn enough money to leave his family financially secure. With his purse from the "Greatest Fight of the Century" (which, because he was black, was less than that of the loser, who was white) he built the Goldfield Hotel in Baltimore, a precursor to the Cotton Club and the venue that gave the great Eubie Blake his musical start.

We have researched the accounts of his fights from turn-of-the-nineteenth-century newspapers in the cities where he fought and early twentieth-century books mentioning these events for their eyewitness reportage. The actual on-the-scene dispatches telegraphed during each of Gans' major fights are included in our book. We set these reports against the backdrop of the *fin de siècle* controversies that occasioned the Old Master's life: such as when Gans lost the fixed fight in Chicago that caused boxing to be banned in the state of Illinois and nearly ended his career; or his struggle when his title was stolen through a flim-flam typical of the era; or the greatest fight of his career that mesmerized the entire world, the 42-round fight at Goldfield, Nevada.

Because of Gans' amazing physical abilities, the number of his knockouts, championship wins, and mastery in three weight divisions, along with his gentlemanly character, he was touted well into the 1940s as the "greatest boxer ever" and one of the world's greatest athletes. Gans was the first athlete to break the color barrier and to destroy the myth about blacks and the "yellowstreak." As a pioneer for civil rights, he paved the way for other twentieth century black heroes. Philosophers and preachers (founders of the Niagara Movement, forerunner of the NAACP) held him up as an example of what talented black men could achieve.

The title of a biography printed recently on Sugar Ray Robinson calls Robinson the "First Celebrity Athlete." Gans in his day was a world-renowned champion and celebrity. The general public may know a little about the history of boxing from movies such as *Cinderella Man* and documentaries such as *Unforgivable Blackness*, but few know the history of boxing in its golden age as Gans lived it, or his rags-to-riches story. Most people believe Jack Johnson to be the first black title-holder. But Gans was already considered the "Old Master" when Johnson selected Gans as his trainer for his famous fight in Reno against Great White Hope, Jim Jeffries (facts that Johnson biographers do not note). Gans was so seriously ill that he missed the fight and died one month afterwards. In telling Gans' inspiring story, we hope to set the record straight and restore his rightful place in history.

A statue commemorates Gans today in Madison Square Garden. World famous artist George Bellows captured his right hook in a painting permanently displayed in the National Gallery, and Gans' ring techniques are still being taught in the boxing gyms today. Yet few people, other than dedicated boxing fans, have ever heard his name. In this book we hope to re-establish Gans' amazing legacy as the father of modern scientific boxing and the greatest fighter ever to lace on the gloves.

Albeit tragic, Gans' story is an American success story, and provides an insight into American history during an epoch when racism held dominion and the White Death of tuberculosis cut men down in the prime of their lives. It is impossible to understand the development of American character without knowing the man Joe Gans. It is our hope that this work will fill a void in the annals of sport and cultural history, in a time when prize fighters were the real-life heroes of the Wild West — the history of which lies hidden between the lines of old newspapers and has been passed down from generation to generation, mainly via word of mouth.

1

A Marvel of the Ring

Before Muhammad Ali, Sugar Ray, or Joe Louis, even before Jack Johnson's heavyweight reign inspired the "Great White Hope" hue and cry, there was the great Joe Gans. The first American born black to hold a world title, Gans paved the way for the many African-American sports champions of the twentieth century. In the Monumental City of Baltimore, during an epoch nestled between the American Civil War and the Great War of 1914, lived a gladiator whose equal the world has yet to see. He rose from nothing to become the greatest fighter ever to grace the ring, worthy of inclusion in the pantheon of immortal athletes. During his amazing career, Joe Gans was referred to reverentially by virtually all of the boxing community as the "Old Master." Yet this splendid athlete, the first to raise his sport to the level of true artistry, is all but forgotten today. In 1904 the newspapers lightheartedly complained that Gans was more famous and received more press coverage than Booker T. Washington and the other black leaders of the time, but by the second half of the twentieth century, Gans was virtually unknown, invisible to history.

During the years he reigned supreme in the world of boxing, he was perhaps the most famous athlete in the world. The great ebony warrior worked his way up the championship ladder, fighting for two decades during a golden age of boxing beginning in the Gay Nineties. The coming of the twentieth century was filled with promise, yet the decade still witnessed on average one lynching of American blacks every three days.[1] Life expectancy for a black male at the time was 34 years, 14 years less than for a white male.[2] Gans' brilliant life lasted only 35 years. He died four years after the first great "Fight of the Century," the story of which filled more news space in 1906 than the coverage of the San Francisco earthquake.

That year would host several pivotal events in American life and mark a turning point in American culture. The California earthquake of April 18, 1906, the murder of the nation's greatest architect, Stanford White, over the

5

girl in the red velvet swing, and the Atlanta Race Riot, the largest in Atlanta history, grabbed the headlines. *The Jungle* and *The Shame of the Cities*, exposing the deplorable conditions of the factories and overcrowded slums, topped the best-sellers' lists. Two brilliant thinkers with opposing views on how to achieve progress for black Americans were prominent in the world of ideas. Booker T. Washington espoused industrial education while W.E.B. Du Bois' book *The Souls of Black Folk* presented a poignant longing for basic rights.

Through his ring accomplishments, Gans put into action what others could only theorize. The articulation of the black quest for social equality reached large audiences through the pulpits, and the most authoritative sermons were published in newspapers and religious quarterlies. One of the most recognized and influential men of the cloth, the Reverend Francis J. Grimke of Washington, D.C., speaking in his famous discourse after the great "Fight of the Century" noted, "It is generally conceded ... that Booker T. Washington has done much good and will do much for the colored race for its uplifting, its education, for making its members citizens in a true sense of the word; but with all that, in the entire course of his life work he never did one-tenth to place the black man in the front rank as a gentleman as has been

Joe Gans, the "Old Master."

done by Joe Gans."[3] The famous fighter became more than a historic sports phenomenon that fateful year — he became a cultural icon.

On Labor Day 1906, despite a multitude of important events, the eyes and ears of the world were tuned to a boxing match in Goldfield, Nevada. An obscure promoter named Tex Rickard devised a scheme to help populate the nearly empty state of Nevada and infuse millions of dollars into the economy of the little known town of Goldfield. He would bring together a pit bull of a man, the Durable Dane, Battling Nelson, with a legendary ring warrior, the Old Master, Joe Gans.

Before the fight the Durable Dane boasted, "There will be crepe in Coontown on Labor Day while the Danish descendants are celebrating."[4] American industrial and political royalty, as well as the wealthy citizenry of San Francisco, displaced by the earthquake from their accustomed entertainment venues, would brave temperatures of over 100 degrees in the blistering high-desert sun to watch the most anticipated *mano a mano* since Achilles fought Hector the Trojan. The result captivated the nation in 1906.

Gans was no stranger to the spotlight. He had climbed a steep mountain since losing one of the most controversial fights in the history of pugilism in 1900, in his first title bout against the great lightweight champion of the time, Frank Erne. For eleven rounds the two fighters lashed out with lightning combinations, blocked and moved gracefully, the ebb and flow favoring first Erne, then Gans, who seemed in control going into the fateful 12th round.

In the years to come much would be written about the calamity that happened next and its far-reaching ramifications. About the Old Master one scribe would write, "His face carries the sorrow of his people, he has the saddest eyes."[5] Above his left eye could be seen the deep, wide scar from the wound he was about to receive.

For many fighters of Gans' day, their Sunday punch was really an elbow or head-butt. And so it was for Erne in this fight. Imagine the smooth upward arc of a professional bowler's throw, only instead of rolling the ten-pound ball down the lane, he crashes it into your eye socket at high speed. That is what it was like for Gans when Erne fouled him with a head-butt in the 12th round. So badly mangled was his ocular that the ringside doctor had to work frantically to replace his eye in its socket. But the "unkindest cuts of all" came from the journalists and later historians: "Black boy doesn't like the gaffe." "Gans quits."[6] In recent times Gans would either have won the title on a foul or on points if the head-butt were ruled an accident. Instead, he was accused of cowardice when the fight was stopped. What had brought Gans so close to the top of the mountain, and why were some so eager to knock him back down? More importantly, how did he finally ascend to greatness?

Joe Gans would realize his dream in the face of life's most merciless adversities: poor health, lack of opportunity, and a bullying system that seemed to want nothing more than to crush the spirit. Born into Reconstruction America and orphaned at the age of four, he grew up with nothing more to look forward to in life than shucking oysters at the Baltimore Harbor. When black men were lucky to have any job at all, he would one day sit among the most famous athletes in the world, own a hotel that helped give birth to the Jazz Age, and even coin the hugely popular expression "bring home the bacon" when he telegraphed news of his greatest ring triumph to his beloved foster mother.[7]

Gans' career began during his teens in a racist spectacle called a *battle royal* where up to ten young blacks were thrown into a ring (often blindfolded) and made to beat each other senseless until only one remained standing. These battles were of such brutality that they were outlawed in the Roman Empire, where feeding Christians to the lions was considered appropriate entertainment for the entire family. Yet from these inauspicious beginnings arose the world's greatest fighter.

Why was Gans such a marvel of the ring? Throughout this book, we will compare Gans to the other greats of boxing in terms of ring skills, accomplishments, and historical significance. Gans not only dominated the lightweight division in the early 1900s, he fought much bigger men and handled them easily. On a routine basis he would fight ring greats such as Sam Langford (a dominant light heavyweight of that time), in addition to defending his lightweight laurels. Langford was so impressed by Gans that thirty years later he would maintain that the lightweight champion was the best fighter ever to enter the ring.

A good boxer's hand and footwork comprise a highly calibrated and sophisticated balletic art in which every move by the opponent brings a quick and clever counter. Boxers work in milliseconds and every inch of height and pound of weight is critically important when the opponents are evenly matched in skill. If a 133-pound Joe Gans could fight the heavier top professionals of his day on equivalent terms, it was because of his superior skill.

Sugar Ray Robinson, a tall 160-pounder, wilted when he moved up in weight to 175 pounds to challenge the mediocre titlist Joey Maxim. Robinson is generally regarded as the greatest fighter ever, but in fact he was easy to hit compared to Gans. Even Jack Johnson, recognized by many as the greatest defensive fighter in history, often tipped his hat to friend and mentor Gans, saying that Gans' footwork gave the impression that he was on wheels in the ring. Johnson would arrange to have Gans train him for his famous bout in Reno with Jim Jeffries, feeling himself lucky, although he generally disdained trainers.

Gans fought for an incredible 18 years, until the age of 34, against the best fighters of his day, ducking no one. Because of racial prejudice it was difficult for him to get fights with many of the best white fighters at the time. When boxing matches were moved out of public domain and into private clubs, black spectators and many black fighters were prevented from attending most fights. But with determination and perseverance and after twelve years of fighting, Gans was in a position to make the reigning titleholder accept his challenge. After he won the lightweight crown from Erne in 1902, Gans defended it regularly, a practice other titleholders were reluctant to follow. When a world boxing title is at stake, the challenger throws everything in his soul into the fray, so high are the stakes. In Gans' day the stakes were even higher than they are today because there were fewer world boxing titles. Gans always took on the top challengers and never had his opponents cherry-picked for him. Yet even after meeting and defeating all challengers, he still had his title taken away, and he had to win it back under the blistering Nevada sun after agreeing to incredibly dangerous and unfair conditions.

In Gans' era, civilization was just encroaching on the Wild West. As Muhammad Ali himself stated in his autobiography, *The Greatest*, "I used to hang around the gym and hear the pros talk about famous old fighters and their feats [dating back to the days of Joe Gans], and it sounded more exciting and daring to me than any tales of the Wild West."[8] By the 1940s, Gans' fellow Baltimorean, H. L. Mencken, one of the most influential American writers of the twentieth century, would lament in championing Gans' memory, "Joe Gans himself, though he was probably the greatest boxer who ever lived and unquestionably one of the gamest, is mentioned only rarely by the sporting writers."[9]

In the movie *The Joe Louis Story*, the Jack Blackburn character mentions Joe Gans numerous times when teaching the young Louis the tricks of boxing. Blackburn clearly regarded Gans as history's greatest fighter. Gans was a true marvel of the ring. His punches, footwork, and movements were flawless. Gans was always in a position to block and counter punches. Louis sought to copy his style, but never succeeded in perfecting the Old Master's artistry, especially with respect to defense. Some today may criticize the way Gans kept his hands low. But fighters in his day, one must remember, had to conserve energy because they fought "finish fights," usually lasting longer than 20 rounds or until one or the other was knocked out. Gans' title-fight win against Battling Nelson, on Labor Day, September 3, 1906, was the longest ever filmed. "The Fight of the Century" lasted a historic 42 rounds.[10] Across

America, fight fans gathered at railroad stations or newspaper offices to listen to announcers with megaphones shouting round-by-round telegraph bulletins coming in from the "wires." Gans' victory was one many feared would instigate uncontrollable riots throughout the country. Instead, the referee was cheered when he gave the decision to Joe Gans.[11]

The 1930s witnessed a deterioration of Gans' memory, beginning with a book that ostensibly sought to honor the great fighter. Here we set out to rehabilitate the legacy of the Old Master, and bring back to light not only Gans but also the Golden Age of the art of self-defense. Boxers at the beginning of the twentieth century embodied all that is sublime in the American dream, from rugged individualism to the burning desire to carve out a place in the sun for self and family. No one better exemplified this than Joe Gans, the Old Master.

2

Battle Royal

Shoved into the middle of the makeshift boxing ring, blindfolded and bloody-mouthed, a twelve-year-old boy flails at the darkness while multiple assailants rain blows upon his head and torso with all their might, kicking his shins and groin. The thick smoke of tobaccos from Havana to North Carolina fills his lungs as pain shoots like daggers through his body. He steps gingerly around the ring. The sound of gloves smacking against flesh and the jeers of the crowd direct his moves. On this night the boy decks two others, much older and heavier than himself, with his work-hardened knuckles and his self-taught, straight–arm punch. When the referee calls "winnah" and takes off the last blindfold, he knows he has won more than a week's worth of harbor labor pay.

Such was the spectacle of the 1886 battle royal, the de facto boot camp for black boxers when Joe Gans had his first experience in the boxing ring. As winner, he left the stage that night, went home and proudly handed his mother a purse full of coins. It was, for him, the princely sum of five dollars.

The two greatest fighters of the early twentieth century, first Joe Gans, and then Jack Johnson, both got their starts in contests known as *battle royals*. Johnson would go on to provoke a generation of whites and bring forth a call for a "great white hope" to "wipe the golden smile from his face."[1] Gans would be declared "the greatest ring general and expert in the use of the human fist the world has ever known," and then become an invisible man in the latter part of the twentieth century.[2] Battle royals would eventually be outlawed.

Fifty years after Gans and Johnson reigned supreme, the memory of these "athletic events" was brought to mainstream American consciousness by Ralph Ellison in his first and only novel, *Invisible Man*. At that time, few other than boxing enthusiasts had ever heard of this racist form of entertainment and gambling event. Ellison's vivid depiction of a battle royal became the classic symbolic antithesis of the "good fight."

Joe Gans, and Jack Johnson a decade later, were able to rise above these humiliating exploitations of physical courage by parlaying their battle wins into careers. Ellison, however, paints a bleaker picture of one less fortunate. In his book the narrator is invited to an evening "smoker," ostensibly to declaim his graduation speech. But when he arrives at the fashionable hotel, the superintendent of schools announces to the club's august patrons: "'Bring up the shines, gentlemen! Bring up the little shines!'" The narrator says, "I could hear the bleary voices yelling insistently for the battle royal to begin."[3]

The narrator is then pushed upstairs, blindfolded and thrown into a melee with nine similarly benighted boys. "My saliva became like hot bitter glue. A glove connected with my head, filling my mouth with warm blood. It was everywhere. I could not tell if the moisture I felt upon my body was sweat or blood. A blow landed hard against the nape of my neck. I felt myself going over, my head hitting the floor. Streaks of blue light filled the black world behind the blindfold."[4]

Use of the blindfold at these bloody events was popular perhaps because it evoked the relationship a lynch-mob has with the victim. Hoods over a face during a lynching help to hide identities, dehumanizing the event. Ellison's metaphors of blindness and invisibility could not have been any more appropriate for the America in which Gans would achieve fame.

At the time when Ellison penned this depiction, the popularity of the battle royal was in its decline. The event had been popular for a half century, most likely evolving from contests (part of a Sunday's entertainment) held on large plantations prior to the Civil War. The melees provided a means of selecting and grooming young fighters for individual competitions later on with the slaves of other plantation owners. But by the late nineteenth century, why would men stoop to such lows in promoting these events, and why would men submit to such treatment? The simple answer — a quick buck. These chaotic events suited gambling interests and proved immensely profitable business pursuits and popular leisure entertainment to a particular social class during the Gay Nineties.

Boxing at the turn of the twentieth century was not just a sport; it became a fashionable "craze" that tipped the scales of traditional American values by putting athletics and moneymaking at odds with Victorian piety. Policymakers had to wrangle with new questions. Should the sport be of public or private interest; regulated or not? Was the vigorous sport beneficial or fundamentally unsafe, and who could participate? While not something everyone could do well, it was, nevertheless, something everyone could do. Even "enlightened" women in full corseted dress were encouraged, in the privacy of their homes, to engage in boxing exercises with other women. For them, it was considered a healthful activity. The public sport, dangerous and life-threatening, and associated as it was with other moral vices, was considered a man's domain.

For two centuries along the Eastern Seaboard, especially in Maryland and Virginia, sport had meant horse racing and fox hunting with their aristocratic heritages. The populist spirit of the late nineteenth century called for a popular sport, and boxing appealed to all social classes. Football and lacrosse were also gaining favor at that time, but they were team sports played primarily at colleges. Individual sports such as racing were popular, but only a wealthy person owned a sporting horse or a motorcar. Both baseball and boxing cut across racial and economic divides, but boxing was by far the more popular and lucrative sport of the day because of the large purses. Top prizefighters could earn rewards of several thousand dollars. However, there were no training facilities and few opportunities, other than the streets, for youth interested in learning the art and achieving notoriety.

Potential boxers needed to attract attention. For black boxers in particular, one way of getting noticed was to sign up for a battle royal. The reality of limited educational and professional opportunities at the time meant that boxing offered someone like Gans the rare opportunity to fight his way out of poverty and attain "visibility." Albeit a brutal competition, the purse for a battle of amateur fighters young or old was typically four or five dollars, a week's wage for a grown laborer and perhaps a month's pay for a working boy. Battle royals did more than just pay for the next meal, they could jumpstart a professional career.

Biographer Geoffrey C. Ward, in his brilliant biography of Jack Johnson, *Unforgivable Blackness,* tells how difficult it was for the young boxer to obtain a manager in the tightly knit white boxing community. Johnson broke into the fistic clan when he was finally noticed by Chicago referee George Siler in a battle royal in Springfield, Illinois, in 1899. (Siler would referee the infamous "Chicago fix" between Joe Gans and Terry McGovern in December of 1900.) Jack Johnson had been traveling from town to town hoping to use his boxing talent to pay for food and lodging, when he stopped in Springfield. There, Ward says, he "caught the eye of Johnny Conner, an ex-bantamweight who ran the Senate Bar, a favorite hangout of Illinois legislators. Connor put on boxing shows above his saloon twice a month."[5]

Promoters invested serious money in boxing events and looked for ways to generate a good return on their investment. Fearing that his main card wouldn't be very exciting, Connor needed to bank on staging a battle royal. Looking for black contenders, he invited Johnson to participate, promising him a meal, housing for the night and a dollar and a half if he won. On his trip back to Chicago, Siler commented to Jack Curley, "The big coon that won it looked pretty good to me."[6] Within a few weeks through word of mouth, Johnson had been noticed and was boxing John Haines, "the Klondike," in Chicago. The battle royal must have seemed natural in the scheme of boxing events to Johnson because, even after he had made a name for himself as a heavyweight, he refereed a battle royal at the Broadway Theater in New York on December 16, 1909, knocking out one of the boys who accidentally hit him during the contest.[7]

Unlike with Johnson, who wrote about his boxing life, no extant autobiographies have surfaced for Joe Gans. What we know about his inauspicious beginnings we know only from interviews and the accounts told about him by various journalists.

One Baltimore night as the gay nineties approached, a young boy named Joseph Gant (his name would later be changed by the press) finished his shift of shucking oysters at the fish market, jumped on the back of the trolley designated for black patrons, and headed to the Monumental Theatre on Baltimore Street on the east bank of Jones Falls. The normal bill of fare was opera, vaudeville acts, and local prizefights. This particular evening Gans would apply for a spot on the battle royal, the preliminary bout guaranteed to boost attendance for a lackluster main event. When questioned by the theater's manager, Gans admitted he had never been in a ring. After explaining the nature of the slugfest and that only the last one standing would be paid, James Lawrence Kernan accepted his application.[8] It would be the first in a long string of successful fights.

Gans had heard the boastful talk of sailors and bets being wagered on brawlers around the harbor. Excitement surrounded him in the busy marketplace with impetuous set-tos in the streets and highly anticipated bouts occurring upstairs in the enclosed meeting-house above the stalls where he worked. Caleb Bond, owner of the fish market, reportedly recognized Gans' enthusiasm for the sport and encouraged his participation by letting him wear a pair of gloves he kept at the stand.[9] Recognizing Gans' talent, his boss went so far as to buy a second pair of mitts to allow Gans to practice with contenders on the street.

At his first battle royal Gans proved himself a ring natural. His phenomenal stamina, agility, and powerful punch elevated him quickly above other boxers. Before he returned to win another battle, he studied the fighters from ringside, carefully analyzing their moves and figuring out what it would take to protect his body from the punishing blows. After winning his second battle royal, the young Gans was invited to participate in individual preliminary bouts. He never had a teacher. Gans learned from observation, studying, as

A battle royal held in 1919 on the quarter deck of a military troop transport. Such melees were so barbaric that they were outlawed in ancient Rome, but they were a stepping stone for pugilists in Gans' day. Boxing "smokers" were popular entertainment on U.S. Navy ships during the first half of the twentieth century.

he said, "the movements of such great boxers as Jack Dempsey and Jack McAuliffe."[10] He observed the local fights as a student, wanting to learn whatever skills he could glean, to improve his odds of winning.

He addressed his sport with the objectivity of a scientist: hypothesizing, measuring and testing pugilistic form, power, and pace. In German, "Gans" means whole or complete. And there never lived a more complete fighter than Gans. Beginning with the battle royals, he developed the style that would make him the master of all ring men. His innate sixth sense in the ring, which he possibly developed from experiences blindfolded in the battle royals, would later cause opponents to say he knew what they were going to do before they themselves knew.

One aspect of the battle royal that survives to this day is the anonymity of one's opponent. In the battle royals the fighters were often, but not always, blindfolded. In either case, with or without the benefit of sight, the event was chaotic and a boy was never fighting one specific opponent. This aspect of uncertainty continues today in Golden Gloves and other amateur tournaments, and even at "smokers," in that the amateur boxer usually does not know whom he will fight until hours before the bout. The psychological preparation for these anonymous tussles is critically important. Around the nation today, boxing coaches prepare their young fighters by telling them, "Your opponent puts his shoes on one at a time, just like you do." "Don't worry who the judges are, let your left hook be your referee." "Your job is to get in shape — it's your opponents' job to worry."

Gans' experience in the battle royal melees would serve him quite well in the ring wars that were to be his calling in the decades before and after 1900. Certain fundamentals of boxing would have been of paramount importance to a blindfolded battler in a battle royal. Keeping the hands up, chin down, and elbows in would have been a lesson quickly learned, lest one be knocked out in short order. Developing a keen sense of balance and spatial perception would have been vital to compensate for the blindfolded eyes. All of these attributes would become trademarks of the Old Master.

The boxing term "ring generalship" seems to have been invented with Gans in mind. In all his fights, he was lord of the ring, whether near the ropes or in ring center. His uncanny ability to dodge punches, sometimes by fractions of an inch and with a minimum of effort, allowed him to fight 10 rounds, 20 rounds, up to 42 rounds without showing signs of fatigue. The seeds of his greatness were reported in the Baltimore paper under the name "Gans" (given him by the press) and also noted by the keen eye of a Baltimore bookmaker and restaurateur by the name of Abraham Lincoln Herford, who sported the name Al.

Herford looked and sounded the quintessential circus impresario, replete with derby hat tilted atop a chubby face and a confident clever tongue. In an era of fraud and shady characters boasting of Tammany Hall, faked pretexts for war, and shameless corporate greed, no character had a shadier reputation than Al Herford. At the time when private social clubs were being formed to skirt public laws of prohibition, the bookmaker chartered the Eureka Athletic and Social Club, serving as president and treasurer and installing his brother as secretary, to promote lucrative boxing matches, all under his design and control.[11]

Herford's carnival-like boxing matches were crowd pleasers. His inventiveness carried over into the battle royal. In an essay about the infamous promoter originally published in *The New Yorker*, noted literary critic and Gans contemporary in Baltimore H. L. Mencken said sardonically, "(Al Herford) did not invent the battle royal, but I believe it is only just to say that he greatly developed it. One of his contributions was the scheme of dividing the four boys into three very small ones and one very tall one: this favored a brisk entertainment, for the dwarfs always ganged up on the giant and knocked him out, usually by blows behind the ear. Another of Al's improvements was the device of dressing the colored boys who fought in battles-royal, not in ordinary trunks, but in the billowy white drawers that women then wore. The blacker the boy, the more striking the effect."[12]

Herford wasn't the only club or theater owner to become inventive when it came to the battle royal. Black individuals were also used for degrading post-fight entertainment at the Monumental Theater. One event was the "barrel fight," described in the sporting pages of the *Baltimore Sun* on March 26, 1895. A barrel fight took place following a ten round sparring exhibition between Jack Daly Moriarity and Abe Ullman at the Monumental Amphitheater. "Four colored men fought in a big hogshead. The contestants were: George and Buck Washington, Joseph Washington and Buck Myers." At the end of four rounds, Buck Myers was declared the winner, Joe second, George third and Buck Washington the loser. Barrel fights occurred with regularity, but by far the more common entertainment was the battle royal. Oddly enough, Buck Washington's name would appear as a mainstay of the boxing scene in accounts of regional bouts for the next few years.[13]

While Gans had fought only a handful of individual bouts, he displayed such a knack for footwork and punching ability that Herford, watching in the audience at the Monumental Theater at one of Gans' early preliminary bouts, decided to make a real, professional fighter of him. When Herford approached Gans with the offer to become his manager, Gans modestly told Herford that he would be taking a big risk. The latter replied, "That's my funeral, not yours."[14] Herford held the purse strings for Gans for years to come, splitting both Gans' earnings and his own gambling debts, and demanding that Gans fight according to his instruction. Gans would be faithful to the gambler who had given him his start.

Herford ran a lucrative athletic club with the help of his stars, one of which he was proud to call himself. He relished the job of ring announcer and enjoyed introducing each new protégé, which he pronounced "pro-teege."[15] He was one of the first ring managers to realize the promotional advantage of naming boxers after known celebrities. He particularly liked to describe his boxers as "Young." One of his better fighters who frequently boxed on the under-card to Gans' main events and served as his corner man was the Young Peter Jackson, named after the heavyweight Peter Jackson from the West Indies. By 1900 fighters entertained with names such as "Young Corbett" or "Black Griffo." (The practice of taking the name of a ring great became extremely popular during Gans' reign and following his death, and his name was one of the most frequently adopted *noms du ring*.)[16] In one preliminary fight during his heyday, Herford brought out "Young Terry McGovern" of San Francisco and "Young Joe Gans of Australia." As Mencken liked to joke, local Baltimore fight fans clearly knew they were water boys from the

Pimlico horse track. But the attitude was all a part of Herford's brazen, the-atrical style.

In describing his ring management, H. L. Mencken noted how Herford shaped the rules to suit the interest of showmanship. "When two boys sailed into each other with unusual vehemence and the members began to howl, he would signal Ernie Gephart to let the rounds run on, and whenever, on the contrary, a bout was tame, he would cut them short. Once I saw a set-to between two ferocious colored youths, Young Corbett, of Yarmouth, England, and the Zulu Whirlwind, of Cape Town, South Africa, in which the average length of the five rounds, by actual timing, was twelve and a half minutes, and another time I saw Ernie put through a flabby six-round bout in ten minutes flat."[17]

The newspapers circa 1900 were nearly unchallenged in the formation of public opinion. And thus one can trace the trajectory of Gans' transfor-

mation from his early per-formances, when the papers used the casual racial epi-thets of the day, "the dusky one," "the colored boy," even "the coon," to his regal performances where he drew accolades as the "Old Master." Even early on, Gans became recognized more for his brains than his brawn.

Boxing is a demon-stration of physical and mental excellence and box-ing matches are a determi-nation of superiority. With the coming of marquis heavyweights John L. Sulli-van and "Gentleman Jim"

This is perhaps the earliest boxing photograph of young Joe Gans (right) and his sparring partner, "Young" Peter Jackson in Baltimore prior to the 1900s. Gans demon-strates a right hook. Jackson fought lightweights, middleweights, and heavyweights. During his illustrious career he fought Joe Walcott, Sam Langford, Philadelphia Jack O'Brien, Jack Johnson, and Gunboat Smith. Jackson remained Gans' loyal chief sec-ond in many fights throughout his career.

Corbett, pugilism became a chance for ambitious young men to choose a life other than crime or menial labor. But in Jim Crow America, Gans would struggle to get to the top of his profession, so fearful was the country of naming a black champion. It is a testament to his greatness that Gans could rise from the chaos of the ring of battle royals and overcome the racist obstacles set before him to garner a shot at one of the most famous world titles of his time. It is also an unfortunate testament to Ralph Ellison's theme of invisibility that today Gans languishes as an invisible man in the memory of popular sport, his accomplishments forgotten. But during his era, the boxer from Baltimore would succeed in becoming the most visible man of his time. With Joe Gans, the African American people would see the rise of a superstar.

3

Boxing in 1900 Baltimore

By 1850, Baltimore was the second-largest city in the United States behind New York, second only to Ellis Island as an immigration site.[1] A center of culture, finance, and industry, Baltimore straddled the political line between the North and the South. While Maryland was considered a "slave state," Baltimore had in its numbers as many "free" working African Americans as it had slaves in servitude. It had the financial strength of a northern industrial city forged from its marine economy. By the turn of the century it would be known in fistiana as the home of Joe Gans.

That the harbor was at one time the venerated domicile of pirates and privateers gave its citizenry an indomitable spirit of *defi*. Fells Point, the rowdy seaport town which met the harbor on the east, dated back to 1730. Along with nearby Jonestown, Fells Point was incorporated into Baltimore City in 1773. The famous Fells shipyard at the end of Washington and Aliceanna streets gave birth to the Baltimore clipper ships, notoriously agile and swift. Whereas merchant ships typically averaged 5 knots, the clippers could reach up to 20 or 22 knots. They were the fastest sailing ships on water; their remarkable speed was often posted in the news. Flying like the wind over foreign seas, the sleek, narrow-bodied, top-sailed schooners transported valuable commodities of trade: tea, coffee, silk and people. They earned an unmatched reputation during the Revolutionary War, with sporty names such as the *Wasp*, the *Scorpion*, and the *Hornet*, helping to win the young country's independence. Ships such as these, with their stalwart sailors, captured over 500 British ships during the war.

During the second war with Britain, the War of 1812, Baltimore with its commanding production of ships fell once again into the crosshairs of the British Navy. In 1814, the American captain of the *Chasseur* sailed alone to England planning to blockade the British Isles, an implausible threat but one taken seriously by the British. The infamous vessel was hunted by warships without success, and was one of the reasons Britain wanted to take Baltimore by land and by sea, to stamp out the pesky clippers which guarded Washington from a home port in the largest, deep-water American harbor south of New York. The heroic schooner returned home undefeated and was dubbed in the news as "The Pride of Baltimore."

In that same Chesapeake harbor after the British had taken Washington, D.C., in 1814, a young lawyer and poet came aboard a prison ship to negotiate the release of his friend, an elderly physician. There, lawyer Francis Scott Key penned the "Star Spangled Banner" during the decisive naval battle that would keep the American republic free of the British yoke. As he looked to Fort McHenry through the cannons' red glare, Key captured the spirit of American freedom. Unfortunately, this freedom was still denied to many people of color in Baltimore.

After America's wars with England, the clipper ships were no longer needed as sentinels and they were converted for use in the slave trade. By 1835 there were at least a dozen recorded slave markets, or "slave pens" as they were called, within Baltimore City. Stanton Tierman of *The Baltimore Sun* reports that during 1838 one of the larger traders, Hope Slatter, of Clinton, Georgia, ran as many as 27 ads in *The Sun*.[2] One of these read, "Having a wish to accommodate my Southern friends and others in the trade, I am determined to pay the highest prices with good and sufficient titles. Persons having such property to dispose of would do well to see me before they sell, as I am always purchasing for the New Orleans market." Another announced his new building for the auction and keeping of slaves (he would charge 25 cents a day for the temporary housing of others' slaves). "The subscriber has built a large and extensive establishment and private jail for the keeping of slaves. This new building located on Pratt Street ... is not surpassed by any establishment of the kind in the United States. All rooms above ground. Office in basement story." An office in the basement would prevent a person from digging a tunnel to freedom. Baltimore was the last major stop for many attempting to slip through the clutches of bondage, and the most famous person to do so in 1838 was Frederick Douglass.

Douglass had dreamed of freedom, and Baltimore was his hope for escape. There it would be difficult to distinguish between slave and free man. Few questioned the workers on the waterfront, since indentured immigrants of many races and nationalities worked to repay their passage to America. Young Douglass was given on loan from one slave master in southern Maryland to another residing at Aliceanna Street at Fells Point first at the age of 9, and a second time when he was 16. After experiencing the rural plantation life, Baltimore City was "like living in Paradise."[3] Daily he was sent to assist shipbuilders, learning a trade that would earn income for the master who housed him. Douglass eventually became a ship caulker, and in 1838 while dressed as a working sailor, he was able to escape north to freedom.

The slave pens of Baltimore operated as part of the status quo for the next twenty-five years. On July 24, 1863, Colonel Birney, along with Sergeant Southworth, upon military orders, released the women and children held in these Baltimore jails and conscripted the men into the Union forces to fight in the Civil War.

As fate would have it, the southern plantation owners of America would be responsible for re-invigorating boxing when it was in decline in Victorian England. Boxing matches were popular activities among plantation owners who were accustomed to the idea of strong, black fighting champions; they had staged contests for years with their slaves, pitting them against slaves from other plantations. As Armond Fields states in his biography of James Corbett, "What better way to promote friendly rivalries and wagering between plantation owners than to have the strongest of their slaves battle for supremacy."[4]

The first recorded account of American pugilism dates back to Philadelphia in 1788. "Zachary Thomas Molineaux, who fought for the colonists in the recent strife with England, was hauled before our Magistrate last Friday to answer a charge of assault, brought against him by Silas Freeman. Molineaux, whose record of loyalty served him well at the hearing, was admonished and dismissed after an apology. He is known in Virginia as a Negro whose maulings have downed many opponents. The warlike hero, the conquering pugilist of America and who retired undefeated, was a member of a family that was distinguished for pugilistic excellence. He promised never again to commit an assault. He has four sons."[5]

One of these sons would be responsible for bringing boxing as a popular sport to America. Boxing came to the attention of Americans in the young country when "the Virginia Slave" Tom Molineaux issued a stout challenge to the British heavyweight champion Tom Crib. In 1810, Maryland born Molineaux was freed by his master after winning a boxing match upon which his master won a large sum of money. Molineaux set his sights on England and the heavyweight championship of the world, professing himself the American champion. But as early boxing historian Nat Fleischer notes, "How to get abroad was the problem. He hired out on a vessel that sailed the Chesapeake Bay. When he got to Baltimore, he skipped and started to trek the roads in the hopes of reaching a place where he could embark for England. He didn't get very far. He found tramping too difficult and hired himself out as a stevedore on the Baltimore docks where he kept a close watch on the outgoing vessels."[6] By way of the Monumental City, Molineaux finally made it to England, where his fast-growing fame was soon heralded all the way back to America. Molineaux fought twice for the world title in Britain but was defeated. It remained for another black fighter to earn championship laurels.

In the decade following the Civil War, the decade when Gans was born, the steamship replaced clipper ships such as the "Pride of Baltimore." The two wharfs at Fells Point, Brown's Warf at the end of Broadway and Bell's Warf at the end of Fells Street, were too small to accommodate the larger vessels. The steamships moved to Locust Point nearby and Fells Point was left to accommodate local watermen supplying the fish markets and the remaining clipper ships that now transported mainly coffee. How befitting it is that an African American hero for the ages would grow up in that same Baltimore town where Francis Scott Key put the fire of freedom into the hearts of generations of Americans to come. And, from a fight quite different from a naval battle, Joe Gans would emerge as the new "Pride of Baltimore."

Born November 25, 1874, in Baltimore, Joe Gans was named after his father, baseball player Joseph Saifuss Butts.[7] At the age of four, his father gave him to a foster mother to raise, Maria (Jackson) Gant, a laundress living in the gritty section of Baltimore. Young Gans witnessed the hard work of his caring foster mother. Washing the household linens and clothes was so stressful in that era (where a batch could take up to two days to clean) that sending laundry out to a washerwoman was one of the few luxuries even the working poor afforded themselves. Laundry had to soak, usually overnight, before it was boiled and rinsed, all of which could use "about 50 gallons of water, which weighed 400 pounds, and had to be lugged from somewhere," usually a city hydrant.[8] After the washing came the starch dips and the laborious, heavy ironing.

While African Americans were free to earn their own living during the years after Reconstruction, they were relegated to low-paying jobs in the service sector, whether as "washerwomen," "watermen" or as laborers in the tobacco, sanitation, domestic, or transportation industries. But what the young Gans experienced in Jonestown next door to the Fells Point harbor was the lively interaction of races and nationalities, the seeds of enterprise from a working class, the convivial brawls among the waterfront workers, and the brewing winds of political and social progress about to sweep the country from the pulpits of Baltimore. He could attend a church where the pastor was no longer required to be white. And, for the first time, black Americans could be buried with dignity in a city cemetery instead of under the streets and alleyways.

The historic area later incorporated by Baltimore City where Gans spent his early life was named after the Quaker William Fells of Lancaster, England, who gave the streets English names such as Thames and Shakespeare. Many of the privateers who sailed from Fells Point during the heyday of the clipper ships came back to the waterfront neighborhood to live. Wealthy sea captains and industrial merchants built magnificent multi-storied, brick homes. Clerks rented the brick row-houses with courtyards in the back, and laborers rented smaller homes and residencies in the unpaved alleyways. When mosquitoes plagued the city with malaria and yellow fever in the early eighteen hundreds, wealthy residents abandoned Fells Point for higher ground, leaving a community of working middle class and poor with the unsavory reputation as the Baltimore toughs of "Mobtown."[9]

By the late eighteen hundreds houses in the district could be purchased for a few hundred dollars. Attics atop the row houses were converted into upstairs living quarters and embellished to look more Victorian than Federal. Then, as now, the area was a mix of commercial and residential buildings. At night, the "novalux," or hydrogen gaslight, illuminated the many taverns and their keepers' residences on the upper levels. Much of this district would be saved from the destruction of the Great Fire of 1904 in Baltimore and also from an ill-advised network of freeways in the 1970s.[10] And so, visitors to the historic district today can see the glory of its past much as Gans did. In such a city, Gans, like Muhammad Ali several generations later, was born with a better chance to assimilate into mainstream American culture than other blacks, thanks to the popularity of his chosen sport. This would prove vital as Gans navigated the treacherous waters of professional boxing.

Living in a racially mixed community with a tradition of self-sufficiency, Gans absorbed a culture that valued grit, determination, and hard work. The Douglass Institute, established for the purpose of promoting African-American causes in 1865, located at 11 (today 210) East Lexington Street, remained until 1890. Baltimore's city fathers established a "colored occupational school" in 1868 near Orleans Street to instill the value of work in children of the new freed-men. Gans must have been keenly aware of his own fortunate adoption as he passed the "colored" orphans' asylum on West Biddle Street. Gans' father had given him to a caring woman in the late 1870s, whereas only a few years earlier, had his case come before the "orphans court," he would have been indentured to a white tradesman in a new form of Reconstruction-era bondage.

As a young black male with minimal education, Gans worked near the historic harbor at the Broadway Market in a fish stall as an oyster shucker. Census reports at the time show that male African Americans recorded their occupations as laborers, shuckers, waiters, porters, and plasterers. A working black woman listed her occupation primarily as laundress, cook, or seamstress. The toil these jobs required and the health risks they posed at the turn of the century are almost inconceivable to Westerners today. Occupations which might sound a bit exotic to the modern ear remind us upon closer examination that the townspeople earned their living through backbreaking jobs as stevedores, grain-runners, hod-carriers, scrapers, draymen, and scow-men.

The great American melting pot was at high boil in the late nineteenth century, and Baltimore was one of the great entry ports, taking its place along-side New York, Philadelphia, and Boston. Boats with names such as *Hohen-zollern*, *Narnberg*, and *Salier* docked the first two weeks of November, 1890, telegraphing to newspapers back home their passenger lists to signal a safe arrival. These new, mostly Germanic, immigrants competed for the service jobs with the sons of the Monumental City.

Living among the grandeur of Baltimore, Gans was on the lookout for an opportunity to partake of the riches. Along Lexington were grand hotels and a plethora of shops. In the middle of the great boulevard was the Lex-ington Market, chartered in 1782 under private ownership, today rebuilt into one of the world's largest markets. Visitors to Baltimore can see several of the historic supermarkets where some of the family-owned businesses go back four and five generations. Gans was lucky to have a stable job on the water-front in a public market, an institution as old as the country.

Gans worked in what is now the oldest surviving of the public markets—The Broadway Market at 1640 Aliceanna Street. Located across from the Masonic Lodge in the center of Fells Point, it was known as the "fish mar-ket." Chartered in 1784, the building Gans knew was re-built in 1864. The market, now without its second floor, has otherwise changed little in style or accommodations since the Civil War. The market served a seasoned crowd of sailors and immigrants who inhabited the area. The oyster business was one of the largest industries in the country, and Baltimore's canned oysters were considered luxuries at America's early tables.[11] The year 1885 set a record for production, helping to lift African Americans out of poverty. Wagons from the harbor docks brought barrels full of oysters to the market and the nearby canneries, where able-bodied immigrant laborers worked elbow to elbow packing the cans. Streets absorbed the oyster shells, toughening the feet of shoeless children who walked to work. So abundant was the refuse over time that yards of new land crept into the bay.

The Broadway Market in 1890 sitting in the middle of the street resem-bled a church with a cupola overlooking the bay. Open-air stalls packed with fish, local vegetables, tobacco, and coffee faced the street. The second floor, the size of a barn, above the market stalls was used as a meeting hall for civic

The Broadway Market, where Joe Gans worked as an oyster shucker, faces the water-front on the Chesapeake Bay and occupies the center of historic Fells Point, Balti-more. The ground floor market stalls opened out to the streets with canvas awnings covering the fish and produce during the warmer seasons. The second floor was used for civic events, dances, and boxing matches. The Broadway is the oldest public market remaining in the city, dating back to its charter in 1784. Many stall numbers can still be seen along the curb (courtesy David W. Wallace, 2007).

dealings and social affairs like boxing matches. Standing on a wooden ship-ping crate, Gans worked next to other men at a table in the fish stall. As a shucker, Gans worked with his face to the frigid winds blowing off the Chesa-peake Bay with his shoulders hunched over the table. At a time when boxers routinely soaked their hands in brine to toughen their skin, Gans' young hands were being fortified in the icy, dark, watery secretions from the oys-ters. Knifing open the mollusks without stabbing a numbed finger was harsh work during any season, but particularly cruel in the dead of Baltimore's win-ters. Work was measured by how fast a person could shuck, and Gans was known to be a hard worker with strong, fast hands. Serious injuries occurred with great frequency. But from these harsh circumstances would be formed the pearl that was the boxing career of Joe Gans.

Baltimore had achieved a name as a boxing center dating back to the mid-dle of the nineteenth century. Yankee Sullivan was perhaps the best known early nineteenth-century boxer who walked the streets of Baltimore. He fought Tom Hyer, son of boxer Jacob Hyer. (Jacob Hyer fought in the "first organized fight" in the United States in 1816.)[12] The contest between Yankee

Sullivan and Tom Hyer at Rock Point, Maryland, on February 7, 1849, is considered the first recognized American championship fight.

By 1867, the Queensberry Code for boxing had been penned in England and adopted in America. Prior to these rules, fighters worked bare-fisted and resorted to whatever ring tricks could be imagined for downing an opponent. Vaudevillians and self-made "professors" of the sport toured various opera houses giving boxing demonstrations with great fanfare. The "Irish Strong Boy" from Boston, named John L. Sullivan, got his lucky break at one such performance. In Boston's Dudley Street Opera House in 1877, heavyweight boxer Tom Scannel "skipped rope, shadowboxed, and sparred with partners chosen from the audience."[13] Urged on as town favorite, Sullivan was selected for a go with the performer. His reputation was sealed when he knocked the vaudevillian into the orchestra pit. Soon Sullivan was fighting professionally. In February 1882 Sullivan met popular champion Paddy Ryan for the bare-knuckle heavyweight championship and ascended the pugilistic throne in their famed Mississippi title fight. Sullivan became an American celebrity, a name recalled by most Americans, boxing fans and others, to this day.

The greatest battle of Sullivan's reign was against the Baltimore heavyweight John "Jake" Kilrain in what was to be the last bare-knuckle championship fight. Kilrain was the most famous boxer from Baltimore before the 1890s.[14] The gyms where he trained sported their own notoriety. His national appeal would soar when Richard Kyle Fox, editor of the *National Police Gazette,* a New York sporting tabloid recognized as an authority on train wrecks, crime, and boxing events, picked Kilrain in the Sullivan contest. As Robert Lipsyte and Peter Levine state in their discussion of John L. Sullivan and the *Gazette's* coverage of the match, "America's icon of masculinity, like so many sports heroes to follow had begun to believe his own press clippings: that he was invincible, a raging beast beyond everyday morality."[15] In actuality, he had become an alcoholic, accused of drunken rages and spousal abuse. According to the *Gazette,* Kilrain was more worthy of the title because he was "respectable," a sober, true "family man." Nellie Bly, on the other hand, reporting for the *New York World,* was transfixed by Sullivan's newly found goodness and decency before the fight.

In Kilrain's corner at the famous battle in Richburg, Mississippi, on July 8, 1889, was none other than Bat Masterson, the famed deputy from Dodge City, who would later be third man in the ring with Joe Gans. Kilrain's loss to Sullivan did not dampen the spirits of the Baltimore boxing fans. Details of Kilrain's 75-round struggle took on heroic proportions in the Monumental City, where every schoolboy tried to emulate the bravery of the hometown idol on the streets. Only two years from the last, great bare-knuckle bout, Baltimore would premier its new boxing sensation, Joe Gans.

While the Broadway Market was the hub of economic activity, it was Fleet Street that was known for boxing, gambling and promoting. Kilrain trained at the corner of Fleet and Dallas streets. Gambler and boxing promoter Al Herford, credited with discovering Joe Gans, also had his establishment, restaurant, saloon, and gambling parlor on Fleet Street.

The accounts of Gans' early fights after 1891, as recorded in the *Baltimore Sun*, show his rising star while at the same time allowing the reader to see, through the looking glass of history, what an incredible phenomenon boxing was in Baltimore at the turn of the century. In the newspaper, reports of the boxing matches are given multiple columns, and after popular matches, sometimes entire pages of coverage. Compare this with today, when most people do not even know the name of the heavyweight champion, much less the names of rising stars of the lighter weight classes.

Depictions of Baltimore today focus on the squalor and high crime rates to such an extent that it is difficult to imagine a magnificent metropolis, poised at the beginning of the twentieth century to join Paris and London among the well-springs of the arts and sciences. Recent television depictions overshadow the important cultural institutions that can still be experienced today. The Enoch-Pratt Free Library — the first free public library with branches, the Peale Museum — the first public museum in America, Johns Hopkins Medical Institute, the Catholic Cathedral, historic African-American churches, and Druid Park, built two years after Central Park, all contributed to Baltimore's image at the turn of the century as a socially progressive and intellectual wonder of the New World. It was second president John Quincy Adams who, in 1827 after visiting the city's memorials, bestowed the moniker "the Monumental City."[16] Baltimore erected the first monument to Columbus in 1792 and the first monument to George Washington (designed by Robert Mills with 228 steps to the top) in 1815. The statue of Scotland's freedom-fighter William Wallace stands 40 feet tall on a rise in Druid Park. Not far from the boxing gyms, the park was a favorite outdoor destination. So with visions of grandeur around him, Gans began a true up-from-the-bootstrap voyage to stardom. From oyster shucker and the frenzied, barbaric battles royal to world-renowned athlete of gentlemanly status, the journey was achieved by Gans in a few short years.

The 1890s, and the time of Joe Gans' ascension in the world of boxing, bridged the gap between bare-knuckle battlers and the first generation of gloved professionals. His rise also witnessed the shift from the Victorian Age to the ragtime era. Two sensational murder cases, one in 1896 and the other in 1906, served as bookends of sort for the two epochs. In 1892, according to lore, "Lizzie Borden took an axe, gave her mother forty whacks...." Despite overwhelming evidence against her, the jury found her not guilty, in part because the jurors could not conceive of patricide in an upper-class family like that of Lizzie. How different it was from the 1906 saga of the "girl in the red swing," where a murderer was shown leniency, as the public seemed almost to wink and nod at the shenanigans. Into this strange and sometimes macabre setting, where freak shows, cockfighting, and peep shows vied only with boxing for the attention of the newly invented moving pictures, entered Joe Gans and his larger-than-life, impresario manager Al Herford.

4

Ghosts in the House

In New York's Madison Square Garden, tour guides tell of a ghost that reputedly haunts the most famous boxing venue in America.[1] Is it there to redress some long forgotten injustice or just curious and benevolent, there to bid good luck to those who pass? The spirit who reportedly haunts the Garden is that of Joe Gans. Whether or not his ghost actually resides at Madison Square Garden, his life-sized likeness does appear there, in the form of a bronze statue, posed for all time.[2] And boxers to this day, before entering the ring at the Garden, pay a respectful visit to Gans' effigy as though they were in the presence of a boxing saint.

It is no wonder that superstition and religion are so much a part of boxing. In no other sport is a person so exposed in facing the danger and hostility of his opponent, and often the crowd as well. Waiting for the opening bell can seem like facing the gallows. Fighters often have to tap a deep well of courage and strength to emerge victorious. How else can one explain the endurance shown by a half-starved Joe Gans during 42 rounds under the blistering Nevada sun in 1906, or the incredible courage shown by Muhammad Ali in weathering the blows of two of history's most murderous punchers, George Foreman and Joe Frazier, in Kinshasa and Manila?

Through the better part of Ali's career, Drew "Bundini" Brown, a one-time shaman-at-large turned corner-man, was creating a new art that would put the modern-day motivational speaker to shame. Part preacher, part rap-star, Bundini presented himself to Ali in the early sixties and the two formed a life-long bond, as Bundini would verbally lift Ali time and again from such depressions as would accompany fighters in the ring. "Ghost in the house," he would exhort Ali. "The ghost of Jack Johnson is watching."[3]

Bundini, the one and only, was a true original. But he was not the first to speak of ghosts of the ring, and certainly not the first superstitious man in the world of fisticuffs. The great Benny Leonard, in a 1926 interview with *Boxing Illustrated* magazine, claimed that the ghost of Joe Gans had come to him in a dream in which the two master boxers sparred several rounds.[4] If the ghost of Jack Johnson represented racial pride, the ghost of Joe Gans represented artistry and mastery of the ring. Anyone who has ever been in a boxing match knows how alone a person can feel when climbing up through the ropes and into the ring, awaiting the opening bell. Old time trainers would tell their charges, "Once you're in that ring, your conditioning is the only thing you have."

Whether or not one believes in ghosts, old fight trainers tell the story of Benny Leonard's obsession with Joe Gans. Leonard claimed this experience gave him the mental confidence to believe he could beat any opponent. In the 1920s, Leonard was asked so often about whether he could have bested Gans that he snapped, "If you need to dig up a corpse to beat me, I must be pretty good." It is quite believable that Leonard's subconscious brought forth the ghost of the Old Master, real or imagined, in response to the constant questions from ring aficionados of his day.

Before his fights in the seventies, Ali would turn symbolically toward Mecca to pray. Latin fighters will cross their chests in a prayer to the Virgin Mary, all in the hope of assistance from the other world. From all accounts, Gans was a religious and spiritual man, and he also had a manager with a rather macabre good-luck charm.

A reporter for the *Baltimore Sun* noted that "Fighters and fighters' managers are strongly superstitious."[5] In the pre-fight press to Gans' first title fight with Erne in 1900, he noted that Gans took a "number of gewgaws along" that included a large American flag to be used in case he won. He also took his black silk belt, embroidered with small American flags and the initials "J.G." But because he lost the bout in question, Gans never again took those items to any match away from home — he left them on the desk designated for his use at the athletic club. In 1906 when he fought Nelson in Goldfield, Gans brought along his tattered leather boxing shoes. Without a penny to his name to even get to the match in the first place, all he had was the five-year-old shoes. Yet when a wealthy gambler offered to replace them, Gans promptly refused. He felt he couldn't afford *not* to wear his winning shoes into the match where his very life would be on the line.

While asserting that he didn't believe in superstitions, Gans' manager Al Herford felt compelled to acknowledge a strange coincidence before Gans' winning bouts, one involving a corpse. Herford noticed that every time he took Gans away to a fight where they emerged victorious, the train they rode to the fight had a corpse in the baggage car. So when they boarded the train for the most important fight of Gans' career, the championship bout with Frank Erne in Fort Erie, Canada, Herford looked for the corpse. Herford reported, "We did not have one when we started on this trip to Canada and I made remarks about it. Well, it was our lucky ride anyhow, for we ran over a man on the way up and killed him. Now, wasn't that enough to make a gambler bet all he had?"[6] The newspaper headline, "Train Killed Man and Herford Took it for Good Luck Charm," helps to explain Herford the promoter and eerily foreshadows Gans' final days. A trip west to Arizona years later in a desperate attempt to overcome his tuberculosis would fail, and Gans would spend his last days on a train trying to get home to Baltimore before he died. Part of boxing's fascination has always been the proximity of death. All one need do is read the papers or watch the news to confirm the lurid human fascination with the Grim Reaper.

The subject of boxing and its association with the fringe elements of society in the Gay Nineties was a topic of hot political debate. The "manly sport" was so dangerous, causing frequent injuries and an occasional death in the ring, that it was eventually banned in most states and countries during Gans' lifetime. Gans' own fight in Chicago would be the death knell of boxing in that state for several decades. All that, plus the public perception of a "low life" pastime that included gambling, eventually caused politicians to submit to pressures by religious leaders to "protect the populace" by legislating the sport out of public life.

John L. Sullivan spoke to the issue of public opinion and civic choice: "People have got a bad view of boxing. If a horse gets killed or a jockey, the race goes on just the same, but if two men box and one gets killed, a lot of ministers get up and call it an outrage. They ain't fair. Boxing ain't brutal, and we are going to try to show that it is just as legitimate as any other sporting proclivity. If a man wants to go to church, let him; if he wants to go to a fight, he's got a right to."[7]

In the 1890s, many newspapers reported boxing stories near sensationalized crime reports. On the page below a rather uneventful report of a YMCA bicycle show, one paper reports star boxer Bob Fitzsimmons' trouble with a conductor. It seemed that the boxer "made at" the conductor after claiming that he insulted the women in Fitzsimmons' crowd. A policeman called to the scene warned the boxer to remain quiet. The placement of the news event above a more threatening headline implied just how endangering a boxer could potentially be on public streets. Below the Fitzsimmons was an article titled "Pugilist Convicted of Manslaughter," referring to the death of Louis Schmidt by a blow from boxer Frank Klein. Below another sports report of a bout was an account of a police raid of a proposed boxing match. Both boxing stories appeared next to the doleful account of the life sentence in Paris of American Bunco O'Brien, who had shot and killed an "American crook."[8]

That the sport of boxing was frequently associated with unseemly behavior, something other than the YMCA's wholesomeness, is evident in the vivid reportage of the boxing world's undesirables, death, and public threats.

In Baltimore the specter of death was not limited to the ring. Anyone familiar with the gritty harbor life in old east Baltimore was intimate with the Grim Reaper. There, the frequent brawls and disagreements cut life expectancy short. Sailors came and went, and some sort of commerce to accommodate them existed in most every three-story row house in the old

section, renowned for its bars, boarding houses, and brothels. Fleet Street, the location of Al Herford's restaurant, was particularly notorious for gambling.

Boxing and betting were tandem public entertainment. When laws were enacted to ban the sport, athletic clubs were privately chartered to circumvent them. Cincinnati had the Olympic Club, New York, the New Manhattan Athletic Club, and Long Island City, the Eureka Athletic Club. The great American painter George Bellows, who enjoyed the sport of boxing but was critical of its elitist establishments, depicted the action at one of these "private" clubs in 1909.[9] Ironically, in George Bellows'

The statue of Joe Gans was sculpted in the 1930s by Mahonri Mackintosh Young, grandson of Mormon leader Brigham Young. Located in Madison Square Garden, New York, the statue draws fighters going into the famed ring who rub the Old Master's bronzed mitts for good luck. Some say the ghost of Gans haunts the Garden to this day (courtesy Madison Square Garden, L.P. All rights reserved. Used with permission.).

painting *Both Members of This Club*, neither fighter in the depicted match would have been a member of the club, the white fighter being socially unacceptable and the black fighter being of color. In Baltimore, Al Herford would adopt the name of the New York establishment for his club. On March 6, 1895, Abraham L. Herford incorporated the Eureka Athletic Club and leased the Front Street Theater from J. L. Kernan in Baltimore for his boxing events. Kernan owned the Monumental Theater and the Front Street Theater. Management included his brother, Maurice.[10] For years such clubs were the "speakeasies" of fistiana.

On that same day, March 6, 1895, luck was a lady for Gans when his bout with Soloman English drew the largest fight crowd of the season and *The Baltimore Sun* gave him his first great press coverage. He was finally visible to the world. And so, indebted to Al Herford for his interest, enthusiasm, and patronage, as well as his luck, Gans' career was launched. Early accounts from New York refer to Gans as "The Baltimore Wizard." The images of wizardry and magic would attach to Gans throughout his illustrious career. If boxing and death are soul-mates, the occult is a not-too-distant cousin.

Boxing as practiced by men such as the Old Master is both science and art. It is also, to a larger extent than most endeavors, a pursuit in the realm of the spirit. Fear of attack is a basic instinct, and it is human nature to turn to mantras, prayers, talismans, or whatever will inspire strength to face such a threat. Perhaps this is boxing's great allure — to witness mortals combating life-threatening attacks. Joe Gans, the father of modern, scientific boxing technique, although not immune to the need of spiritual uplift, would be the first prize fighter to prove throughout his career that ring-science is the antidote to superstition, and whatever malevolence awaited a fighter inside the four ropes. Be that as it may, boxers at Madison Square Garden still rub the bronzed left glove of Joe Gans for good luck as they pass by his statue on their way to the arena before they climb through the ropes.

5

⚭

Straight Hitting

Wait for your opportunity, and when it comes, avail yourself of it.
— Joe Gans

Gans attributed his success to what he termed "straight hitting." He said, "The idea of boring in and sending smashes helter skelter without reason doesn't amount to a row of pins. In the long run, save if you are a man of abnormal strength, nine times out of ten it will beat you. Every time you miss a swing it is worse than being hit. I could be the champion of the world until I was as old as Methuselah if I could have for opponents fellows who just rushed at me with swinging blows. All I would have to do would be to let them waste their energy and when they were weakened just land one blow, a straight one, to be sure, and it would be all over in a jiffy."[1]

The importance of straight hitting is, to this day, well known in boxing circles. "Straighten up that right cross," a trainer will tell his fighter. "I gave him the round because his punches were straighter," a fight judge at a Golden Gloves tournament will remark. Straight hitting is one of the gifts that Joe Gans gave to the world of pugilism. It would also come to represent the integrity he brought to the sport. As the first black American world sports champion, Gans would endure outrageous criticism aimed at his character before gaining acceptance during his lifetime as an all-time great sportsman. Before becoming known as the "Old Master," even the "Grand Old Master," he gained attention in his earliest fights as a clever boxer and as an astute general of the ring.

Gans Won 60 Bouts Before National Newspapers Took Note

Because the newspapers didn't take note of Gans until he became a star, we know very little about his professional fights between 1891 and 1895, the year that catapulted him into the public's eye. During these early years, Gans won decisive battles against renowned hitters such as Johnny Van Heest, Dave Horne, and Dave Armstrong, where the winner's portion of the purse ranged from $1.40 to $15.00.[2]

By the time the national papers began to follow Gans' career, he was noted for a remarkable string of wins, at least 60 wins by 1896. Whatever the actual number, ring historians have always noted that Gans had more fights than what were actually recorded. Bill Gray, in his book *Boxing's Top 100*, says that Gans' early recorded bouts may only represent half of his actual ring activity.[3] To put Gans' record in perspective, in the first five years of his professional life, he had already won more fights than Joe Louis or Muhammad Ali would win in their entire careers. While Gans had fought a solid career's worth of fights by the time he achieved notoriety, when he was discovered by the rest of the world he was hailed as a wonder boy, seeming to appear out of nowhere. It was as if the public had uncovered a long hidden treasure, and yet he was only beginning.

Gans brought a disciplined, professional style to his work that earned him the admiration of white as well as black Americans of his day. His was a new, scientific approach to what would become a mainstay of American culture, the professional prize ring. How sadly ironic it is that for much of the 20th century his name would be muddied in gossip, scandals, and speculation about shenanigans determined, even during Gans' own lifetime, to be the sole fault of his management. While many have said that Gans never needed an Al Herford and would have risen to the top with any wise management, Gans was steadfastly loyal to the man who had discovered him and set him on a professional path, showing Herford the same gratitude and respect he showed the woman who had taken the orphan Gans to rear as a son. And regardless of what would happen later with Herford's schemes gone awry, it was the smooth handling of the Baltimore boxer by Herford that originally brought press attention to the prodigy.

The year 1895 gave Gans his lucky break. While his fights were all staged in Baltimore, he was moving up the professional ladder and onto the national scene thanks to Al Herford's plotting. Before the end of the year's 18 fights, Gans reigned as both Maryland's champion and "the colored featherweight champion of the South." He would also benefit from the genius, or as some said, "craftiness," of his manager.

The first press article of any length describing a Gans battle appeared when his March 6 bout with Soloman English drew the largest crowd of the season.[4] Fight fans were not particularly interested in seeing their hometown boy, nor excited by the main event's meager purse of $100. To debut his new

Eureka Athletic Club and put Baltimore back on the fighting map in the company with clubs such as those of New York, Herford brought one of the most famed fighters of the time to the Monumental City. The great Australian Bob Fitzsimmons was the first triple titleholder in history.[5] Herford put Gans on the same fight card at the Monumental Theater with the great "Fitz," also known as "Ruby Robert." Four years earlier in 1891, Fitzsimmons had traveled to America to beat world middleweight champion Jack Dempsey (the original), aka "The Nonpareil," from New York in a 13-round battle in New Orleans. (In 1896 Fitzsimmons' colorful destiny would bring him to one of the most remote spots "west of the Pecos" "inhabited by rattlesnakes and scorpions but spurned by buzzards and coyotes" where he would KO Peter Maher in one round in Langtry, Texas, under the infamous jaundiced eye of Judge Roy Bean.[6] That same year he would KO heavyweight Tom "Sailor" Sharkey, but referee Wyatt Earp would call the fight in Sharkey's favor. The following year, 1897, he would win the world heavyweight title from James J. Corbett.)

In Baltimore on the same evening as Fitzsimmons' appearance, Gans was to fight Solomon English in the preliminary fight. The main event was to be a four-rounder between Bob Fitzsimmons and Fred Fredericks of Norfolk, Virginia. That night, Gans soundly beat English, but no verdict was rendered because the police stopped the bout in the ninth round. Gans would have many fights like this, where he was clearly the winner, but the police intervened before he was officially declared the victor, resulting in many "No Decisions" on the early records.

Herford Pulls a Rabbit from His Hat, Puts Gans in the Limelight

With excitement building for the main event, Fitzsimmons in his fighting togs, and the police ever attentive, the crowd and the news reporters were greatly disappointed when Fredericks failed to show. The crowd suspected they had been deceived. (Herford later explained that Fredericks backed out of the fight. But with the wisdom of hindsight, it might be assumed that Herford fabricated the whole charade to draw the spotlight to his new club with the appearance of Fitzsimmons and shift the attention to Gans.) With his showman's hubris, Herford appeared on stage and, with a puff of cigar smoke, transformed the convulsive jeers of the crowd's near riot into bantering jibes when he invited anyone who would like to stand in for Fredericks to do so. After appeasing the crowd, the evening ended such that the last fight anyone had seen was Gans' remarkable performance. The fact that the newsmen had nothing to write about the great Fitzsimmons' appearance in Baltimore was a stroke of luck for Gans, whose boxing career received its first significant notice from the press. The world got a great description of the punching power of Joe Gans when the following day's sports report was devoted to a mere preliminary bout rather than the main event. The great Fitzsimmons garnered only brief mention and Gans an entire column.

Fitzsimmons spent the next few months giving exhibitions on the East Coast. To Herford's credit, he supported Gans and encouraged him to attend Fitzsimmons' exhibitions to study his boxing style. This early experience was perhaps the most formative in Gans' professional career. From these ring bouts, Gans studied, analyzed, adopted and modified the moves and techniques of this early master of boxing. Fitzsimmons can be credited for giving Gans his short straight-arm jolts. Years later Gans remarked, "I regard Bob Fitzsimmons as one of the greatest exponents of straight hitting that the prize ring has ever known. Fitz was a wonderful fighter and all of his straight punches were very effective. Until age set in, and his hands went back on him, there were few fighters able to withstand that famous shift of his. When Fitz delivered this blow he carried the whole weight of his body with it."[7]

While Herford may have had his hands tied to a certain extent by public prejudice when promoting fights for his young charge, by March 18, 1895, the promoter was overtly and successfully playing the race card in the press with Gans' career, arranging a series of bouts with the "best colored fighters" north and south of Maryland. Gans' work at the Monumental Theater in Baltimore against Howard Wilson, a 125-pounder from Washington, D.C., was described in the *Baltimore Sun* with admiration, noting Gans' "clever, strong left."[8] The two "colored boxers," as the paper noted, "put on a fine exhibition."

Herford and his sporting buddies had been fighting the heat of public backlash against the rising tide of the sport's popularity. That its welfare depended upon political support is evident by the formation of an early lobbying group. The day after the Gans-Wilson fight, notables from nearby Ellicott City in Howard County, Maryland, held a meeting at the courthouse to form a committee called the Maryland Game Protection Association.[9]

In April, Gans' notoriety skyrocketed when he beat Walter Edgerton, "The Kentucky Rosebud," at the Eureka Club at its new Front Street Theater location on two different occasions, the 1st and the 25th. His first fight with Edgerton, of Philadelphia, was billed as the main event following three preliminary fights. The Rosebud was famed for beating featherweight champion George Dixon in three rounds. Gans and Dixon were already good friends, and as historian Nat Fleischer noted, Gans may have been highly motivated to beat the Rosebud to make up for Dixon's loss.

Gans beat Edgerton in six rounds on April 1 and again in the rematch in eight rounds on April 25. The press thought that Gans would be forced to fight on the defensive in this last fight, but "he proved himself the more clever man, and the bout showed that Edgerton was only a right-arm fighter who is not dangerous to a fearless man who goes at him."[10] The *Baltimore Sun* noted, "Gans had the Rosebud groggy in the last, the eighth, he had him at his mercy and the gong had to be rung in the middle of the round to save the Bud, who was nearly knocked out."

By October of 1895, Joe Gans was called the "colored lightweight champion of Maryland." Spectators called him a ring genius when he knocked out the previously undefeated Joseph Elliott. Gans was able to land punches with extraordinary power because of the leverage and precision of his straight-hitting style. To this day he represents the gold standard when it comes to pugilistic form. In the 9th round he delivered what the *Sun* called "a most unusual knock-out combination." Gans threw a right hand to the body. When Elliot tried to block it, Gans ducked and let his left hand go. It struck Elliott so powerfully on his right shoulder that it grazed his jaw and landed firmly on his forehead. Elliott stepped back and dropped to the floor.[11]

By the end of the year, Herford was anxious to promote his new athletic club and to garner national attention for his star boxer. In November Herford arranged a boxing tour de force between Gans and former featherweight champion Albert Griffiths, aka "Young Griffo," a world class champion from Australia who had contended in the previous year with American icons George Dixon, Jack McAuliffe and Kid Lavigne. The bout with Gans was scheduled for a day when Baltimore would be packed with sporting men for the horse races at Pimlico. This was also the first fight in which Gans' management was publicly accused of having "rigged" the deal, and the only fight to have favored Gans in the deal making, if the rumors of the fix were true.

Undefeated as a featherweight, Young Griffo had left Sydney for America in 1893 when boxing was banned "down under" due to deaths resulting from ring contests. Griffo was as much a character as he was a boxer, equally at home in the bar as he was in the ring. Stories were numerous, but the favorite among journalists was his handkerchief bet to get free drinks. He would walk into a bar, spread out his white hankie, and announce he would buy the drink if anyone could knock him off the linen. "Befuddled strong men" would advance, he would duck, pick up the hankie and order his drink.[12] Griffo was known to enter the ring inebriated. Nevertheless, he was a formidable fighter and fifteen years later Gans said of him, "He was a straight hitter from the word 'go.' Had he possessed the punch and taken care of himself he would have been in harness today."[13] Instead of billing Gans as the Maryland champion, Herford dubbed him the "colored Southern lightweight champion" to bring his protégé up to the level of his world-famous white adversary and to take promotional advantage of the residual political divisions and apartheid-like social tensions of the time. (The fact that Herford claimed the title seemed of little concern to anyone.) The place was packed and no one expected Gans to last the scheduled ten rounds against the Australian champion. The majority white crowd did little wagering because the betting scales were so tilted in favor of Griffo. Before the fight, Herford announced that if both of the contenders were still standing on their feet after the tenth round it would be called a draw. Herford's strategy backfired when both fighters fought defensively and Griffo failed to put Gans out. Gans was unable to knock out the Australian wonder, and the crowd grew indignant. Gans landed more punches than Griffo: and while the paper reported that Griffo "let go several vicious blows ... they all fell short." If left to the press, the decision that night would have gone to Gans.[14]

Whether or not the favored Griffo was embarrassed by his poor showing against Gans or was simply frustrated from coming off three draws with George Dixon that could have gone his way, or the controversial decision that favored Jack McAuliffe the previous August, Griffo left the ring stating that the bout with Gans was a "fake." He said "management" (Al Herford) had told him that Gans would not go on unless Griffo promised to let Gans stay the ten rounds.[15] Such was the recorded beginning of Gans' career of fighting to Herford's direction. Before leaving Baltimore, Griffo challenged Gans to a fight to a finish. Regardless of Griffo's claim of a prearranged fight, the resulting draw looked good on Gans' record, precisely what Herford was crafting. Even decades later, boxing expert Nat Fleischer noted that Gans drew national attention by drawing with "the superbly clever 'Young' Griffo in ten rounds."[16]

The final fight of 1895 earned Gans the imprimatur of "colored featherweight champion of the South" when he beat nationally acclaimed George Siddons, who was brought to Baltimore from New Orleans by a Philadelphia backer to meet Gans, the black kid with the soaring reputation. The bout was set for 25 rounds with the men weighing in at 125 pounds. Gans beat Siddons with the repeated use of his straight left jabs and feints. Then, when there was an opening, Gans landed his right squarely on Siddon's jaw. With his keen observation, Gans used the early rounds to study his opponent's reach, nuances, favored punch, and to measure how best to get at his opponent's head. By the third round, Gans had sized up Siddons and throughout the fourth to the sixth rounds, nothing seemed to block Gans' left lead. When Siddons went for a body punch in the seventh, Gans knocked him to the floor with his right to the jaw. The press noted that by the timer's watch Siddons was out for fourteen seconds, but the referee counted slowly and Siddons was up at nine. "Gans was at him in a flash," and with his left and right "put him to sleep."[17]

The exchange was billed as a "scientific exhibition" without the benefit of coaching from either side, and was the first time the *Baltimore Sun* covered a Gans event round by round. On November 29, 1895, the paper reported, "His victory last night gives him a just claim to the title." "Joe Gans, colored, knocked out George Siddons in seven rounds at the Eureka Athletic Club last night. Gans' victory was a most decisive one.... Gans is a natural fighter, never having had an instructor, and only lately has had the use of training apparatus."[18] This was a masterpiece of understatement, Gans having taught himself in a true up-from-the-bootstrap effort.

Although he had been called a champion lightweight, Gans had been fighting at 125 pounds, generally considered a featherweight limit. Gans never tried for the world featherweight title, held at that time by his good friend George Dixon, although Gans was considered the best fighter at that weight. More money was to be made in the lightweight division, where the best warriors of the day plied their trade.

The toughest, most athletic men in Gans' day could be found boxing professionally in the lightweight division. Stripped of excess weight, the men of that era averaged in weight from 125 to 155 pounds, so the talent pool was full in the lower weight classes. Lightweight fights were action-packed and provided real entertainment.

In these early years of his fighting life, Gans was already so good that it was reported he could signal his black friends the round of his bout-ending blow. From this, they could exit the hall early to avoid being victimized by white spectators desiring a different outcome. (Many of the club fights denied attendance or membership to blacks. When they were allowed to attend public events, they were segregated into sections of back rows.) Gans was laying a foundation for athletes that would provide income, opportunity, and a source of hope for black Americans in the twentieth century. His grit, determination and professionalism are evident even in the 1890s newspapers, where denigration of African Americans was commonplace. All this time, Gans was creating a new art form, now taken for granted.

By January of 1896 Gans reached another milestone in his early boxing career: he became a traveling man. Gans was at the top of the ladder Herford had constructed, and he and his promoter anticipated spending the year fighting as the "colored featherweight champion of the South," traveling away from Baltimore, meeting the challenges that his reputation had earned. Herford would spend the year 1896 protecting the Eureka Club from local legislative threats to boxing, growing his professional team, and trying to win big-name matches for Gans. But the steady progress upward was marked by events outside of their control, and before the year was out Gans would be forced to work his way back up the ladder.

The year started positively, with Herford reporting that his fighters were in great demand.[19] James Wescott, manager of the Suffolk Athletic Club of Boston, wanted Gans to meet "Spike" Sullivan in Boston on February 10. Samuel Austin of the Lenox Club wanted Gans and Jack Ward, both managed by Herford, to meet challengers in their weight divisions for opening night on Long Island. Herford had matched William McMillan, of Washington, to meet the famous Kid McCoy at the Eureka Club on March 12. But Herford also faced the challenge of a political faction that wanted boxing matches halted in Baltimore. The ensuing controversy gave Herford as much publicity at the time as his boxers.

Political Threats to Boxing

Fight promoters in Baltimore were required to obtain a permit for their boxing matches; however, during the year, the mayor decided to stop issuing them. Many promoters moved outside the city limits, where politics forced the county commissioners to take a stand. By January 28, the president of the county commissioners issued an order to halt boxing matches. The state attorney, the marshal, and the county sheriff weighed in on the matter. The attorney said the law stipulated that if the matches became brutal or the crowd boisterous they were to be stopped. The sheriff reported that he was doing his job because he had stopped one match in the second round because he thought "the crowd would get to fighting."[20] The marshal doubted that the commissioners had ever been witness to a fight. In essence he said, "Let them come see one and judge for themselves."

Sensing sporting opinion on his side, Herford stated in one interview, "I do not intend to break any law of the State, and boxing contests are not unlawful so long as they are conducted in conformity to the legal restrictions that exist; that is, so long as the gloves are of the prescribed size and the spectators are orderly."[21] He proudly announced to the news media that the crowds were not a problem at the Eureka Club. Herford's financial success depended on his ability to promote fights. He preached his case, "Now, it is far better to have the matches under the management of a responsible, incorporated club, whose events are announced and can be supervised by the police, than to forbid boxing altogether and thus encourage fights to a finish in private, where no representative of the law can see them." He ended his verbal sparring match with the commissioners in his typical, playful way, with a final joust, "Boxing is not half so brutal as football, and I may add that the long period in which boxing was publicly permitted in and around Baltimore has not been so productive of misfortune as has the short skating season of this winter."

With a reputation for knockouts and having been undefeated for five years, Gans made his first appearance outside of Baltimore on January 11, 1896, meeting Benny Peterson in Philadelphia. It was the first time the *Baltimore Sun* devoted a column announcing the fight of the "undefeated featherweight of the South" and full coverage of his fight.[22] Gans knocked his man down in the first, third, and (final) fourth rounds. When he returned to Baltimore, his last two fights in January were billed as "Scientific Glove Contests" and part of a "Boxing carnival." He knocked out Joe Elliott January 17 in the seventh and beat Howard Wilson in the eighth with Samuel C. Austin of the New York *Police Gazette* refereeing the match.

Gans Attempts to Get Bouts with Top-Rated White Fighters

Gans was now fighting world-class opposition, having beaten the best black fighters in his weight category, but some of the best white fighters were still drawing the color line. His next two significant opponents scheduled at the 125-pound weight limit bowed out. "Spike" Sullivan of Boston, February 22, and Frank Erne of Buffalo, March 12, both failed to show up to fight, and Gans would not get the chance to fight Erne until 1900, four years later. When Sullivan failed to show, Gans fought 129-pound James Kinnard, the "St. Paul Kid," to a Boston crowd of 4,000. The fight was stopped in the 6th round, with Kinnard considered out.[23] The March 12 bout with Frank Erne was to be Gans' first fight scheduled in New York at the new Manhattan Athletic Club. Tragically, Gans' wife died four days before that scheduled bout.[24] His weight shot up to 137 pounds. However, by the time he left for New York, his weight was down to 127, with Gans stating that he could be below the 125 pound limit by 3:00 P.M. the day of the fight. The publicity for this fight was so great that, for the first time, Gans' fight history was listed in the papers. Frank Erne had beaten John L. Sullivan of Buffalo and George Siddons. He had fought draws with George Dixon and, like Gans, drawn with Griffo. Erne was climbing the lightweight ladder and considered a possible championship contender, and he saw Gans as a definite threat to this upward mobility.

The match between Erne and Gans was not to go forward, but the cause was not as subsequent histories have suggested, i.e. that Gans failed to make the weight. The *Baltimore Sun* reported that Erne was anxious to avoid Gans.[25] By the 3:00 P.M. weight deadline, Erne weighed 128 and Gans 130—both fighters were clearly above the agreed upon 125-pound weight limit. Erne refused the match, and history has blamed only Gans' weight for the cancellation, even though neither fighter made the original weight limit. Before leaving New York, Herford challenged Erne to a fight at $1000 per side, one more of Herford's dogged attempts to get Gans in the ring with Erne.

Although Gans had trouble getting the big match, this period did witness a spike in popularity of the sweet science (one that Gans was at the forefront of creating). The *Baltimore Sun* now had a regular column titled "The Boxers." So close to having a shot with a major title contender and losing it, Gans was forced to work his way back up the ladder. On June 8, he fought James Watson, champion of New Jersey, and beat him so thoroughly that by the 10th round, Watson had to be carried to his corner.[26] On June 29, Gans got another opportunity to fight in New York, but it would be in a preliminary to Erne's main event. Before Erne would fight with Jack Downey of Brooklyn at 135 pounds, Gans would fight Tommy Butler of Brooklyn at 130, and Jack Ward, another of Herford's charges, would fight Jack McKeck, at 110. Gans' win in a 12-round "hard fight" made news on the same page as Robert Fitzsimmons' challenge to Tom Sharkey. Fitz was in London when he issued the challenge, and speculation was that the battle might be held in Mexico.[27] Both Gans and Erne were now fighting as lightweights, Gans at 130 and Erne at 135. These two up and comers were headed for an eventual showdown.

While in preparation for another marquis preliminary fight, this time in Baltimore with New Yorker Danny McBride in late August, Gans fought "Professor" Jack Williams of Pensacola, Florida. This match was really a favor of Gans to the professor in that Herford had previously refused to match him with Gans, infuriating the "Professor," who wanted a chance to "stop the colored man." On August 20, 1896, Williams showed up at Gans' training quarters with the press requesting a match. Gans was playfully called "Pocahontas" for the bout and displayed his clever footwork in the first round. When the gong rang to open the second round, Gans sent a direct right to the professor's jaw and knocked him so hard against the ropes that he refused to continue.[28] The match with McBride was considered one of the best and most clever boxing matches Baltimore had witnessed. "Fifteen hundred lovers of fistic work" attended the 20-round official draw, the *Baltimore Sun* announced. The paper noted that McBride was the best fighter Gans had met to date. Gans out-pointed his opponent that night, according to the newspapers.[29]

By the end of September 1896, Herford was again drawing offers for Gans, one from Tom O'Rourke of the Broadway Athletic Club in New York. But Gans' remaining bouts for the year had already been scheduled. Gans fought Jack Ball of Newark in Philadelphia on September 28 and knocked him out in the 3rd round. (Ball would die a few years later in an opium den.) Gans had been scheduled to fight two men that night, but the unnamed second contender failed to show.

One of the greatest left-hookers of all time was Gans' next opponent. In New York on October 6 Gans fought a main event at the 130-pound weight limit with Dal Hawkins of San Francisco, who was originally slated to fight Frank Erne. When Erne dropped out, Gans was recruited to fill in. Gans had severely weakened Hawkins by the end of the sixth. While Hawkins delivered more punches to the body than Gans, Hawkins could not reach Gans' face. When he did connect, the press called them "taps." Gans landed repeated hard lefts and rights to Hawkins' jaw. After fifteen rounds, the referee gave the decision to Hawkins, a decision which "drew hisses from the audience that thought the match should have been called a draw."[30] On the spot Tom O'Rourke offered a rematch to the men, to take place at the Broadway Athletic Club; however, it would be several years before this would happen. When it did, Gans would avenge the decision by knocking Hawkins out in the 2nd round.

Toward the end of 1896 boxing purses were increasing. By December 1, Martin Julian had negotiated a $10,000 purse for Bob Fitzsimmons for a 10-round match in San Francisco with Tom Sharkey. Fitzsimmons was able to get $500 for training expenses. At this time Gans was only able to negotiate a $500 side for a 20-round battle with Jerry Marshall, the "colored featherweight champion of Australia." The bout was scheduled during the week of the Preakness at Pimlico to attract the horsemen. It was noted that Gans was on the heavy side, even appearing "flabby." The sportswriter assumed that had Gans been in better shape he could have won the battle before twenty rounds. By the end of the 19th round the Australian was clearly fatigued and Gans made a frustrated statement to Herford when he went to his corner. "I can't put him out. I can't get at him." When they met at the center of the ring for the final round, Marshall pleaded, "Don't do it," asking Gans not to knock him out.[31]

For the last fight of the year, Herford and Joe Gans went to San Francisco to scout out possibilities in the Wild West. Fighting on the same card as Jim Jeffries on December 14 at 132 pounds, Gans knocked out Charles Rochette in the fourth round. Again it was Gans' powerful straight left that staggered the opposing fighter. Before he could recover Gans had hit him squarely in the jaw with a right.

1897 — Rumors of a Fixed Fight

The next year Gans crossed the country fighting in New York, San Francisco, Baltimore, and Philadelphia. On April 13, Gans fought Howard Wilson at the Polo Athletic Club and knocked him out in the ninth by a left uppercut that "nearly took him off his feet," followed by two straight rights to the face and jaw.[32] In August, Gans faced Isadore Strauss of Philadelphia, who seemed invincible in his recent wins. Both fought at 133 pounds. Gans was called both the "Southern champion" or the "colored lightweight champion of Baltimore." The match drew a crowd of 400 to Baltimore, along with strong wagering. As in most of his fights, Gans used the initial rounds to study his opponent and was clever at avoiding Strauss' leads. Through round 4, Gans had avoided Strauss' reach. Strauss grew weary by the 5th round and Gans landed 3 quick blows to his face, and his opponent went down after a feint and final blow to the chin.[33]

Although Griffo had previously stated that he wanted to fight Gans to a finish, in September Young Griffo and Gans met again, this time at the Olympic Club in Athens, Pennsylvania, for another 15-round bout to be called a draw if both were left standing. Gans appeared to instigate most of the fighting and the 7th round was vicious. The fight was otherwise considered relatively tame until some brisk action in the 12th, and again rather tame until the 15th, when it was declared a draw. This time Griffo did not call the fight a fake.[34]

Gans' second career loss came on September 27, 1897, to Bobby Dobbs at Greenpoint Sporting Club of Long Island, New York, when Gans confidently out-boxed his opponent causing him to fall into repeated clinches. The match was initially called a draw by the referee and after some local pressure, the referee changed the decision to a win for Dobbs.[35] Bobby Dobbs would go on to found several boxing schools and become known as the father of boxing in both Germany and France. The great heavyweight champion Max Schmeling and the great French middleweight titlist Marcel Cerdan can trace their roots to Dobbs' work. Schmeling's life was a whirlwind of controversy as he went from champion to Nazi poster-boy and finally to a hero who saved holocaust victims and became a wealthy philanthropist. Cerdan's boxing

The *San Francisco Examiner* shows boxers in action in one of the first newspaper representations of Joe Gans. Such primitive drawings gave image hungry readers graphics to look at when photographs were not readily available. Depicted as the black boxer, Gans was featured in the lightweight bout with Mike Leonard of New York (the "Beau Brummel of Fistdom") on May 19, 1897, in the "Olympic Boxing Carnival" showcasing rising stars of the ring at Woodward's Pavilion. An audience of 2500 paid $2, $3, or $5 seats to view contestants, which included Jim Jeffries in a heavyweight battle with Harry Baker of Chicago. The caption under Gans reads, "Gans Lands His Left." Leonard and Gans split the $1750 purse although Gans soundly defeated his opponent.

prowess (he was a top fighter during World War II), along with the music of his chanteuse girlfriend Edith Piaf, helped to buoy the spirits of Nazi occupied Europe and keep the resistance alive. Strange as it may seem, later historians accuse Gans of throwing this fight against Dobbs, which most observers thought he won.

The last battle of the year, on November 29, was also the last boxing exhibition to be given at the concert hall of the Academy of Music in Baltimore. The evening was filled with unusual entertainment.[36] There were 3 preliminary bouts followed by Gans and Englishman Staunton Abbott. No decisions were given by the referees; the crowds determined the contest winners. Herford also introduced a bag-punching contest between the boxers. Frank Farley, known as the "Adonis" of Maryland for his good looks and physique, won a large gold medal for the championship for skillful display on the bag. Gans, who came in second, won a bag, and William Anty won third in the 3-minute contest. After the bag contest Gans left such red marks on Staunton's face and body from his "terrible straight left jab" followed by right hooks that sent Staunton to the floor that the Englishman's seconds threw up the sponge after 2 minutes of the 5th round. Gans ended the year in print as the "colored lightweight champion." At the close of 1897, Gans could already boast of an accomplished career, even though he wouldn't make his mark in most history books until 1900. And, he had done so as a black man in a white man's sport. But he was only beginning. The only thing left for him to win was the world's title. Gans would have to win another year's worth of fights before New York's boxing fraternity would bless him as a contender to the throne. But 1898 would see him in a different league. His first fight of the year would take him to Cleveland, Ohio, drawing the largest crowd in the city's history, in his 20-round bout against Frank Garrard. Police stopped the fight in the 15th round as George Siler (the same referee for the Corbett-Fitzsimmons fight at Carson City) was about to "give the decision to Gans."[37] By the end of the year and after beating "Kid" McPartland in November 1898, *The New York Times* declared, "He is now in line for a fight with Lavigne and others of the first class."[38]

And so Gans proceeded in a straight line to boxing immortality. Traces of the mystique of fighters in Gans' day can be found in the expressions used, such as for Kid McCoy's "cork-screw punch" and Robert Fitzsimmons' "solar plexus punch," which became household terms. Barbados Joe Walcott coined the expression "the bigger they are, the harder they fall." Gans would also be immortalized for coining the phrase "bringing home the bacon" in reference to another battle. And the style and skill that Gans developed, simply called "straight hitting," would be passed down through the ages.

In boxing parlance, Gans was known as a "true boxer," which meant that he put science and craft at the forefront on all occasions. Throughout his boxing career he would be known for his brainy ability to size up and attack his opponent and defend himself with great economy. Boxing authority Tad Dorgan of the *New York Evening Journal* would summarize his style, "It certainly must be said that Gans, when fully extended is a boxer of rare merit. He never seems to become ruffled when in action. There is no wasted motion about his system of attack. He stands straight, and makes use mainly of short–arm blows. His best punch, probably, is a kind of down chop with the right, and he knows how to send it through the smallest of openings."[39]

Gans' ring craft laid the foundation for the moves that are taught to this day by boxing trainers throughout the world. Gans was the first to fully realize how much leverage and power could be achieved with a minimum

of physical effort. The foundation of Gans' style was his stance and the balance it provided. Simple in concept, difficult to execute, the Gans stance maintained feet always at 45-degree angles, weight centered so that it could be easily shifted by moving left to right or backward and forward.

Jack Johnson, who copied his own stance from Gans, said it was "the key to all scientific boxing." Gans even predicted Johnson's rise to the heavyweight throne. "Jack Johnson is also in this class [of straight hit-

Gans' ring craft laid the foundation for boxing moves that are taught today. The Old Master demonstrates in Chicago how to pull back from a punch while maintaining perfect balance (Chicago History Museum, Photographer: *Chicago Daily News,* 1907).

Gans' uppercut, ideal for fending off a low charging opponent (Chicago History Museum, Photographer: *Chicago Daily News,* **1907).**

ters], and to my mind Johnson will soon be the superior of all the big men."[40] Years later Johnson would predict Joe Louis' loss to Max Schmeling. "His stance is all wrong. He is open to right hands." Louis' was a puncher's stance, both feet and weight going forward. Gans' stance, by contrast, was more akin to a fencer's stance, allowing for mobility and quick escape.

Today, not only boxing coaches but karate instructors as well are apt to teach the punching techniques and clever defense perfected by the Old Master, Joe Gans. With feet at 45-degree angles, elbows in, a quick twisting motion of body and left hand can shoot a straight jab at an opponent, providing openings for other punches. It is also a defensive move, used to block a right-handed punch. Gans' quick guard and powerful punch were immortalized in the painting by American artist George Bellows. In *Both Members of This Club*, the viewer gets a vivid look at the overpowering strength of Joe Gans and his famous "right punch after blocking a lead."[41]

With weight on his back foot, a boxer can cross his right fist through an opponent's guard or over his left, achieving tremendous force. A quick shift of weight from left to right, hooking the left arm, and POW, a left hook crashes against the opponent's jaw, or to his mid-section. All of these punches were perfected by Gans. Perhaps the punch Gans developed best was his uppercut, a quick shift right, followed by an upward swing, up and through the opponent's guard.

A modern how-to book on boxing reads like a dissertation of the techniques and moves perfected by Joe Gans. Joe may have learned a thing or two from Bob Fitzsimmons and other contemporaries, but in each case he raised what he learned to a higher level. Gans was at ringside when Fitzsimmons first came to Baltimore in 1895. He spent several weeks following the famous future heavyweight champion, studying his moves. The Fitzsimmons uppercut, a brutal blow indeed, was raised to an art form as sophisticated as ballet by Gans. Fitz, standing straight with his head exposed, would trade punches and bull his way until he maneuvered his opponent's elbow high enough so he could dig a shot under the ribs. Gans, with feet always at perfect 45-degree angles, would time his opponent's rushes, slip neatly to his right, then drive the uppercut through his opponent's guard.

Joe Louis was a disciple of Gans. In the mid 1930s, with Nazi Germany and the "master race" on the upsurge, Louis arose as a black hero who would provide a powerful symbolic victory over Aryan supremacy. When Joe Louis knocked out Max Schmeling in 1938, America rejoiced. The extent to which Joe learned his awesome repertoire of punches from Joe Gans' "straight-hitting" is commemorated in the Hollywood rendition of *The Joe Louis Story*. Jack Blackburn, a three-time ring opponent of Joe Gans, is portrayed in the movie as a father figure for Louis. Several times in the movie, in teaching Louis to box, the Blackburn character invokes the name of Joe Gans.

The accounts of Gans' ring triumphs in the first decade of his career indicate that for the most part he dominated his opposition, scoring knockouts at will, sometimes carrying an opponent just to provide a longer show for the paying public. Early on, the papers started a steady stream of references to Gans' "cleverness." The newspapers wrote of Gans as if he were some ring magician. He handled his opponents as easily as the Harlem Globetrotters handle their basketball opponents. As one reporter summarized his ability as a prize-fighter, "Gans had it all his own way, he could have dropped his man at any stage of the game."[42]

In addition to his boxing science, Gans was known for his iron-man endurance. Today, a professional boxer's training regimen includes running three to five miles in the morning, skipping rope, hitting a variety of bags, and sparring. Running develops endurance and "wind," rope skipping develops balance and timing for footwork, and bag-work develops punching ability and hand-eye coordination. Boxers today may also utilize weight training to build strength. Training has gone high-tech in the 21st century. Yet the maximum number of rounds in the present day is twelve, which in Gans' day was considered a short fight.

In the day of "finish fights" and 45-round bouts, boxers would regularly do ten to twenty miles of road work per day. Fighters from the Gans era expressed criticism of the "sissified" depression-era fighters who trained with headgear and 16-ounce gloves. Boxers transitioning from the bare-knuckle era typically wore 5-ounce gloves, like ski gloves today. Boxers in the thirties didn't learn how to block or slip punches, according the old-timers, because in training they would let punches graze their heads, not worried about cuts because of the security provided by the extra padding. It is amusing to think of depression-era fighters as "pampered," as they were described by men from Gans' era.

Gans had the ability to fight 40 rounds and more against top opposition and emerge without a mark on his face. Today there is hardly a brisk fight without cuts or bloodshed. It is more due to the deterioration of defense than to the improvement in hitting ability. Gans' career provided one of the best proofs that necessity is the mother of invention. He fought the toughest, hardest hitting men of his day, and usually fought an average of two fights a month. He needed to replenish his funds constantly because of his greedy manager and the fact that he usually got the short end of the stick because he was black.

And so it went for Gans, who won almost 100 recorded fights before he was ever allowed a title match, a majority by knockout. Some ring historians credit him with a higher total. Before the turn of the century, he had lost two disputed decisions and one brawl against George "Elbows" McFadden, one of the dirtiest fighters in the history of the ring. He later beat McFadden and also avenged his two disputed losses. By the dawn of the 20th century, Gans was the top lightweight contender, poised for the rocky ride that would be the strange year 1900.

6

Saving an Eye, Losing a Title

Broadway turns into Highway 130 leaving New York City. The famed street has been called the "graveyard of hopes" and the "front porch of opportunity." As it rolls westward, the road leads to Buffalo, which in 1900 was the home of 25-year-old Frank Erne, the Swiss-born world lightweight champion of the day. Erne was a fistic luminary in the Northeast, having gone undefeated in the prize ring from 1891 until 1897. In '94 he battled to draws against famed boxers George Siddons and Solly Smith. In '95 he battled to a standstill both George Dixon and Young Griffo. Down in Baltimore the black phenom Joe Gans also fought both George Siddons and Young Griffo to draws. In a rematch with Siddons, November 28, 1896, Gans knocked him out in the 7th round. Gans won his next four matches before March of 1896, but was still awaiting the chance to fight the now-famous Erne.

Heading for a Show-Down

These two rising stars both began prizefighting in 1891 and were of similar ages, Gans only a year older. They had been scheduled to meet at the Manhattan Athletic Club on March 12, 1896, the Marylander's first opportunity to fight in New York. Dal Hawkins was originally scheduled to fight Erne that day, but when Hawkins dropped out, Herford grabbed the date for Gans. However, the 1896 Gans-Erne bout would not take place. Gans wife died suddenly, leaving behind two small children. Herford wired Erne's manager saying that Gans would not be able to make the weight agreed upon due to the pressure of his personal affairs. Gans could not go into training to reduce an extra pound and a half. Erne answered through his manager that he would fight Gans at "any weight."[1] Herford took the offer at its face value, but when Gans and his manager arrived at the clubhouse for the fight, Erne was not there. Gans would have to wait four more years before getting another opportunity to fight Erne, when it would then be for the lightweight title.

After skipping out on the '96 match with Gans, Frank Erne beat George Dixon on November 26, 1897, to claim the featherweight championship.[2] He earned a chance at the lightweight title but it slipped through his gloves in a draw with champion George "Kid" Lavigne on September 29, 1898. Lavigne had won the world title in London, in June 1896, in an elimination bout against Dick Burge. (The initial title holder under the Marquis of Queensberry rules, Jack McAuliffe, had retired undefeated.) Lavigne, aka the "Saginaw Kid," was a formidable title-holder (and also a newsmaker when Andy Bowen died after their bout at the Auditorium Athletic Club in New Orleans in 1894). Lavigne successfully defended his title 11 times over three years against such tough opponents as Jack Everhardt, Kid McPartland, Eddie Connolly, Joe Walcott, and Jack Daly. Gans tried unsuccessfully to get a match with Lavigne during his title reign.[3] Erne fought a rematch with "The Kid" and won the title on July 3, 1899, in a battle that saw Erne decisively beat Lavigne over twenty rounds. For Gans to have an opportunity at the title after Erne's win was no small feat. It was more like a miracle, one that Gans owed to the magic of his manager. Unlike Lavigne, who entertained numerous title contenders, Erne allowed only two challenges to his hard-won championship during his reign, one given to "New York" Jack O'Brien, on December 4, 1899, and the other to Joe Gans.

It was indeed a great time to be a champion. In the age of ragtime and syncopated rhythms, New York's Broadway stages were graced by actresses of overpowering sensuality, such as Evelyn Nesbit, who inspired both the images of the Gibson Girl and the girl in the red velvet swing.[4] Their raw sexuality was matched in the realm of male sex symbols only by professional boxers. Gentleman Jim Corbett (frequently described as a tall, broad-shouldered statue of ivory), Frank Erne, John L. Sullivan, and other white pugilistic champions were the rock stars of the era.[5] Their fame drew box-office dollars to theaters where their lectures, exhibitions, or mere appearance (half-naked in their boxing attire) were sensational attractions for society crowds stepping out of the Victorian era. The handsome Erne was considered not only one of the greatest fighters in the world, but also an up-and-coming stage superstar. And, during his world title reign, he was determined to keep both his good looks and his crown.

In 1900 so much attention and talent was concentrated on the lightweight battlers of the ring that the world lightweight championship was as coveted as the heavyweight title. As one Baltimore writer put it, when interest shifted from the heavyweights to the lights, the lightweight limit provided the perfect specimen for the sport in that it "precludes the idea of lumbering heft or insignificant smallness."[6] During the last two decades of the nineteenth century, boxing was dominated by a quartet of great heavyweights: John L. Sullivan, Jim Corbett, Bob Fitzsimmons, and James J. Jeffries. By 1900, when Joe Gans received his first title shot, Jeffries' reign was dull from lack of competition, and the heavyweight division boasted no new blood to speak of other than in the up-and-comer named Jack Johnson who would one day set the world on fire with his cool and deadly boxing skills and his fast life. Johnson would not win the world heavyweight title until 1908 in Australia and would not fight Jim Jeffries in America until 1910.

In 1900, fistic enthusiasts recognized the little giants more so than at any time before or since. Frank Erne was one of the titans among the lightweights, regarded by many as the best fighter, pound-for-pound, plying his trade at that time. And of course there was Joe Gans, who had fought a long and hard road for a decade in search of his place in the sun in American life and boxing history.

In that day, the weight categories in which professional pugilists sought championships were quite fewer than the plethora of weight classes and associations of today. By 2007 *Ring* magazine listed some 60 so-called world champions. In 1900 there were only six world boxing titles.[7] Furthermore, the best fighters were in the lower-weight classes. Jack Johnson, the greatest heavyweight of the early century, has stated that the smaller battlers—Gans, Walcott, and Dixon—were the greatest fighters ever.

Overcoming the Color Barrier

Before Gans won his title shot, a type of apartheid ruled boxing, wherein white champions "drew the color line." After 1892, black fighters were for the most part simply not given the chance to insult the white race by being a champion in the manly art of self-defense. After Canadian-born George "Little Chocolate" Dixon defeated the white boxer Jack Skelly in the same New Orleans tournament where John L. Sullivan lost his heavyweight crown to Gentleman Jim Corbett, the *New York Herald* wrote, "The colored people on the (New Orleans) levees are so triumphant over the victory of the negro last night that they are loudly proclaiming the superiority of their race, to the great scandal of the whites, who declare that they should not be encouraged to entertain even feelings of equality, much less of superiority."[8] So when Gans earned his title shot against Erne, widely regarded at the time as perhaps the world's best fighter, it was nothing less than remarkable. As several proponents of keeping the "color line" distinct stated, they did not approve of "mixing the coffee with the cream in the boxing ring." But Herford was making friends with the match-makers.

Because Herford had previously arranged a match with Erne before he became a titleholder, Herford had his foot already in the door and he wasn't going to let Erne's manager forget that. Gans had defeated all of the top challengers. And so Herford, through perseverance, and Gans, with his gentlemanly conduct, had finally won a chance to take the title from Frank Erne. Erne was a fast-handed boxer-puncher and when the match was arranged, it was eagerly anticipated. On the day of the bout, the *Baltimore Sun* reported, "Those familiar with the game say that, barring a fight between Corbett and McCoy, no other such scientific event could be arranged as the one tonight."[9] Gans and Erne were in great company with Gentleman Jim Corbett, John L. Sullivan, and Kid McCoy, the man for whom the expression was coined "The Real McCoy."[10]

On the night of March 23, 1900, the two masters of the ring, one from Buffalo and the other from Baltimore, met under the hot lights of New York's Broadway Athletic Club to contest the world's lightweight championship. It would be a fight of 25 rounds at the 133-pound limit, winner-take-all.

The method by which the fighters earned their purses is noteworthy. In Gans' day, a boxer's financial prospects rose and fell in direct proportion to his ability to draw crowds. That is, the live gate was the only source of revenue other than gambling. This contest was expected to draw a large crowd. Five hundred were expected from Buffalo, and at least two hundred and fifty from Philadelphia would join the throng of hometown spectators. The gate receipts were expected to draw $30,000, illustrating the popularity of the fighters. The match would be "winner take-all," which actually meant that the winner would get 50 percent of the gate, the loser would get nothing. Betting, pari-mutuel or otherwise, was another way to make money. Since Gans was black, he was accustomed to receiving the short end of the purse or a lower percentage, although he was the better fighter in virtually all cases. Since he was the better fighter and everyone knew it, he would often have to risk several dollars of his own money to match the other fellow's fifty cents in the betting.

The title match between Gans and Erne promised to be a pugilistic and aesthetic gem of a bout. Both boxers were known as "scientific" boxers, that is, they came up through the ranks, studied the game, and fought thoughtfully, relying more on their brains than their brawn. The day of the fight the papers strangely foreshadowed an "accident."

The *Baltimore Sun*, "Any two men can fight, but not every pair of men can contest for mastery in a game of blows where the brain is the most potent factor that leads to a decision. Of course, accidents can happen with anybody, and they are barred from the present consideration. Both Gans and Erne are strong, healthy fellows, but neither approaches in brute strength the power that exists in many men of their weight, and yet either could go through the world mowing down men of nearly double his weight and strength, because he knows by practice, instinct, and inborn pugnacity how to move, watch, wait, attack, defend, reserve, expend, escape and strike. Both are trained to the minute and both will be in the fullest flush of health, again barring accident."[11]

A Horribly Cut Eye

The match was recorded as one of the most furiously fought bouts through eleven rounds, with the most disputed of conclusions in the twelfth. There is no disagreement that Gans had a wicked cut to an eye in round twelve. But the severity of the wound was variously reported in different parts of the country as anything from superficial to so bad that Gans' eye had literally fallen out of the socket, requiring a doctor to jump into the ring to put it back in place. They went at each other furiously, exchanging brutal blows to the head, but in the twelfth round Gans dropped his hands. The bout was stopped and Erne declared the winner.

As boxing's premier historian, Nat Fleischer's opinion has always been recognized as the final word on turn-of-the-century boxers. His interpretation of the bout, written in the late thirties, was simply that the Gans fight with Erne "was an unsatisfactory one."[12] His conclusion about Gans would negatively affect Gans' reputation to the present time. He says, "Erne won, but the measure of glory which victory brought to him was not so broad or so deep as the measure, pugilistically speaking, of disgust which defeat brought to Gans." For Fleischer, there was simply no excuse for Gans' quitting the fight. Fleischer compared Gans' fight with Erne to the Baer-Barlund fight when Buddy Baer quit. Fleischer summarily declared that Gans was still able to fight Erne, but "decided he had had enough" and, like Baer, turned to the referee and said "I quit," words considered to exhibit cowardice when spoken by a fighter. Unfortunately, readers of boxing history have read no other conclusion to this fight.

Fleischer did great damage to Gans' reputation by his account of the fight. His description is inconsistent with Gans' behavior and gives the impression that Gans lacked courage, "didn't like the gaff," as Fleischer states.[13]

A common prejudice of the time was that black fighters lacked courage or "gameness." For example, Jim Corbett would say of Jack Johnson, "Trust me, the colored boy has a yellow streak."[14]

As Gans would prove time and again, he was certainly not lacking in courage. But Fleischer's words left an impression on generations of boxing fans. Some prejudices, much as the evils that men do, live on well past the men who generate them. Amateur boxers today weighing in for fights and around the gym will often hear old-timers opine, "The black boys can't take it to the body, and they get scared when they see their own blood."[15] In fact, black fighters are just as courageous as any others. Although it is not clear where this example of character assassination of black fighters originated, Nat Fleischer's description of the Gans-Erne fight certainly contributed to it and marred the legacy of Joe Gans.

In fact Gans had been temporarily blinded in the ring by the injury to the eye. Blindness was a realistic fear for Gans to have. Many prize-fighters of the age went blind. One of his most famous contemporaries, Sam Langford, went blind, one eye at a time. In Ellison's *Invisible Man* the narrator is taken by "The Brotherhood" to a former boxing arena where he noticed a picture of a former prizefighter who had gone blind in the ring. "It must have been right here in this arena, I thought. That had been years ago. The photograph was that of a man so dark and battered that he might have been of any nationality. Big and loose-muscled, he looked like a good man. I remembered my father's story of how he had been beaten blind in a crooked fight, of the scandal that had been suppressed, and how the fighter had died in a home for the blind."[16]

Ellison's frequent allusions to boxing certainly paint an ugly picture of the sport. But on the other side of the coin, the ring was one of the few places where a poor-born child like Gans or Langford could aspire to be a king. Ellison, like the existentialists of his day, offered dead-on descriptions of society's ills, but gave little in the way of suggestions for improvements.

As evident from reports by newsmen and spectators from Baltimore who saw the fight, Gans' injury was severe. The Baltimore and New York press accounts printed after the fight, however, differ as to the cause of the injury. The Baltimore papers say a foul head-butt produced it, whereas the New York columns, following the round-by-round reports telegraphed from ringside, indicate that Erne's clean punches caused it.

The following ringside account was sent out over the wires, printed on billboards at newspaper offices or read to fight fans who showed up to hear the results live printed seconds after each round at local railroad stations:

ERNE'S FIRST BLOW.

Round 1— Both were careful: Erne forced Gans into his corner and tried left and right, but Gans blocked. Erne forced again and landed a straight left on the abdomen and got away cleverly. Then he tried left and right for the head, but failed to land. At the close of the round Gans landed a straight left on the face.

Round 2 — Erne opened with a rush and forced Gans into his corner again. The Buffalo lad was very quick and sent right and left to the head, cleverly blocking a left hook which Gans tried. Erne then forced Gans across the ring and landed three straight swift left jabs on the face, and uppercut Gans under the chin with his right. Gans tried a left for the head, but Erne blocked it and sent his own left to the wind, forcing Gans to the corner once more, where Erne planted another left on the face.

KEEPS GANS IN HIS CORNER.

Round 3 — Erne kept Gans in his corner and landed a light left on the wind. Gans shot a straight left as he jumped to the center of the ring, but Erne dodged it. Gans sent his right to the body. An exchange of lefts on the face followed, Erne leading and Gans countering. Both blocked cleverly until Gans landed a straight left on the jaw. Erne tried to send his left to the wind, but Gans stepped out of reach. At the bell the men were in a mixup in Gans' corner.

Round 4 — Erne led his left for the head, but was blocked. Gans sent a well-directed left swing to the jaw, but Erne stepped in quickly and planted his right on the wind at close quarters. Erne swung a light right to the wind and Gans hooked a very light left to the face. Erne led his left to the face at close quarters. Gans sent his right three times rapidly over the kidneys. Gans sent right and left to the wind just before the bell.

COLORED MAN LANDING HARD.

Round 5 — Gans landed left to face and Erne returned a straight left, which was the hardest blow landed up to the time. Erne tried a left for the abdomen and failing to land stood in an awkward position, that got well settled before Gans could take any advantage of it. Gans sent his left to the head and followed with right hard on the body and again on the head. Erne sent back left swing on the jaw to which Gans replied with a short left to face and right cross to the head.

Round 6 — There was a lot of fiddling, Gans breaking ground. The colored man stopped suddenly and swung his left to Erne's right eye and cut it. Gans then went in, sending right and left swings to the head, and Erne surprised everybody by applying with similar blows. Erne continued to slam both hands on the colored man, reaching Gans' head a half dozen times. He stopped Gans' rushing and forced him to back away. Erne was bleeding from mouth and nose at bell.

TWO STAGGERING BLOWS

Round 7 — Erne rushed and staggered Gans with a right swing on the head. He tried a left but fell short, and stepped in and shot his right up to Gans' chin. Erne sent a hard left to the body and Gans planted a good right on the head. Gans swung his left to the jaw and Erne staggered, but quickly recovered and rushed back with left and right to the body. The bell found them sparring, with Gans on the defensive.

Round 8 — Erne jumped right to his man. He tried a left swing for the head, but Gans got inside of it. Erne then put straight left to face and hooked it again to the ear. Gans failed to counter and Erne reached the body and head with his left, forcing Gans to break ground. Gans stepped in after falling short with the left and uppercut Erne on the face with his right. He tried a left for the head, but Erne blocked it at the close of the round.

HAMMER AND TONGS NOW.

Round 9 — Erne rushed, sending his right over to the head. Then the Buffalo champion jumped right at his man, but Gans landed right and left on the head. This started Erne and both let their arms go like windmills, Erne having the better of the mix-up. Erne hooked three lefts to the ear and Gans reached the body with left lightly. Erne had all the better of this round, keeping up his attack until the gong rang.

Round 10 — Erne resumed the attack, landing left on the wind. He tried for the head and Gans slipped and almost went through the ropes. Erne stepped in, sending a hard left to the abdomen and Gans failed to reply. Gans then swung his left to the head and Erne countered. Erne rushed his man around the ring and planted a heavy left to the wind. Then he sent a straight left to the face and swung his right to the face, but too high for a knockout at close quarters. Gans planted a left on Erne's body.

THE CHAMPION WHIRLWIND.

Round 11— Erne opened with a right hook on the head, Gans countering on the ribs. Gans swung his right for the jaw, but Frank stepped back and going in quickly sent his left to the ribs. Gans landed a light right on the ear. Erne attempted right and left swings for the head, but missed, and Gans sent right and left to the body. Erne jumped in with left to body and right to jaw. Erne then came like a whirlwind, starting Gans with a left swing to the jaw, and both went at it hammer and tongs until the bell separated them, Erne having the call by long odds.[17]

Here the description of the final rounds, from over the wire, differs from what was reported after the fact. Fleischer writes, years after the fight, that for the first 21 seconds of the 11th round Gans had a safe lead, but that Erne landed several punches to the abdomen that "winded him." He says that Gans went to his corner a "disturbed gladiator," and that he came out for the 12th round "down-hearted." Fleischer elaborates, "It appeared that he was ready to throw up the sponge despite victory staring him in the face. He apparently didn't like the 'gaff' and when, to the punches that Erne had delivered in the last round, was added Frank's prestige as champion, Gans seemed to lose all heart."[18]

Fleischer says of the final round that it began with a lightning-quick sparring exchange. He explains the gash to the eye as a head-butt. Erne landed a body punch followed by a right uppercut to the jaw, and when "the Negro rushed to a clinch, head down, Erne's head caught him just over the left eye and opened a gash about two inches long. The blood flowed freely filling the left eye." Fleischer explains that Gans didn't wait for the referee to decide, but that Gans said 'I quit' and walked to his corner. He reports that the referee couldn't believe what he was hearing, that the "wound was not sufficiently dangerous to warrant the action Gans took and that the referee ordered Gans to fight." Only in one sentence does Fleischer acknowledge out of "partisanship" that "perhaps Gans was correct in saving his eyesight at the expense of victory."[19] Fleischer's account of the final two rounds is decidedly biased against Gans and his character.

Below is how the final round came into Baltimore via telegraph:

Knocked Gans' Eye Out.

Round 12 — Erne opened with a left to the eye and followed with one on the right eye. Then he smashed his right to the abdomen and Gans started toward him staggering blindly. He dropped his hands to his sides and Referee White, seeing that the negro was in distress, caught hold of Gans, who said: "I'm blind; I can't see any more."

White threw up both hands and told Erne to go to his corner. He then led the colored man to his corner and for the first time saw that Gans' left eye was out of its socket. "Erne wins!" shouted White, as Dr. Creamer jumped into the ring and replaced the injured eyeball. "My right did the trick," said Erne as he left the ring, and the Buffalo crowd carried him to his dressing room.

The large crowd assembled at Baltimore's Eutaw Athletic Club at Germania Maennerchor Hall had attended the fight between Patsy Corrigan of San Francisco and Tommy West of Brooklyn that night primarily to hear the early reports of the Gans-Erne fight. Between the rounds "a dapper young man read dispatches from the Broadway Athletic Club."[20] Reactions did not appear to support the hometown athlete. "Once when the announcer stated 'Gans staggers,' the crowd yelled so that the finish of the sentence could not be heard." When it was announced that Erne had beaten Gans, "the applause was deafening." But a clue to the reaction comes in a tag that was added: "An old stager remarked: 'There is hardly a man in that howling crowd who wanted Gans to lose. There must be some other reason.'" Certainly there were those in the crowd who had bet on Erne. As we shall see there was plenty of money to be made betting against favorites.

Although he wisely saved his eyesight, Gans was roundly denounced for "quitting," by displaying "the yellowstreak." When those who were at ringside and saw what Fleischer called a "gaff" returned to Baltimore, they thought that Gans should have been declared the winner as a result of a foul, an intentional head butt by Erne. Gans had unquestionably led the rounds prior.

Two years later in a chat among friends at the Germania Maennerchor Hall in Baltimore, Harry Lyons, one of Herford's boxers who attended the fight, would capture Gans' fighting style, astutely describing Gans' behavior that night: "On the occasion when Erne got the decision over Gans it was because of Gans' over-cautiousness. Gans knew he could hit Erne whenever he tried. He proved it in the fight of 1900, but fought the 12 rounds like a fellow writing a letter to his best girl and afraid he would get a blot on the paper."[21]

Most observers thought that Gans was comfortably ahead when the wound to his left eye occurred. The cause of the cut, punch or head-butt, is in dispute, but the preponderance of the evidence is that the gash was caused when Erne crashed his noggin against Gans' brow. It would be a cut he would wear the rest of his life, with a scar covering a swath of skin from his eyelashes to his eyebrow.

The wound was still palpable when two weeks after his loss he married Madge M. Wadkins in a ceremony at the home of her uncle in New York City.[22] Her background was as colorful as the times. She had been raised in Cincinnati, where her father owned a Turkish bath. At the time she met Gans, she was an actress touring with the famous vaudeville theatrical troupe of Walker and Williams. For years, white minstrels had painted their faces black to stage comedy routines. The team of George Walker and Bert Williams had met in the 1890s in San Francisco and had been the first among African Americans to play the roles in Broadway-styled plays. They were tremendously successful, popularizing the music and dance of the Cakewalk, a promenade of a high-stepping, back-bending dance where couples clasp hands and step-dance across a stage.[23] (A remnant of this dance is the drum major's strut leading a marching band.) Having its origin in the antebellum South, the Cakewalk had migrated to trendy Paris cafes by the time of the scandalous trial of Evelyn Nesbit's husband Harry Thaw.[24] The music to this dance would evolve into ragtime, the first to cross over racial lines from black to white, largely the result of the "black and tan" clubs. The Cakewalk would be a dance endearing to Gans and his close friends, and we can only surmise that it was a part of the happy nuptials, one of the few high points for Gans during the year.

The ring loss in March was a hugely disappointing blow to Gans, but his troubles during the year 1900 were only beginning.

7

❧❧

Fixed Fight in Chicago

The year 1900, which started with such promise for Joe Gans, would by its end see him as a scapegoat for the chicanery ingrained in pugilism and gambling. Few today remember or have even heard of the biggest boxing scandal in history, the 1900 "fixed fight" between Joe Gans and Terry McGovern that took place one cold December night in Chicago.

Sports betting and doping in recent years have resulted in a variety of scandals from point shaving in basketball to congressional inquiries in baseball. The "Black Sox scandal of 1919" lives in infamy for its cast of characters and the audacity and the manner in which the American public was scammed. Boxing has a rich tradition of controversy, but perhaps no single event caused as much furor and misunderstanding as the "Chicago fight fix of 1900," which caused boxing to be outlawed in the state of Illinois for a quarter century, and nearly spelled *finis* to the manly art in the United States.

Chicago: Turn-of-the-Century Paradox

Rivaling Baltimore in the number of ways it epitomized Americana at the beginning of the twentieth century, the great city of Chicago, known variously as the Windy City, an epithet coined in the 1890s referring to its politicians, and the City of Big Shoulders, Carl Sandburg's description evoking the city's machismo, was bursting at its seams with immigrants. With three quarters of the metropolitan area's population of "foreign stock" living in densely packed areas, what limited public services existed at the time were strained. Transportation for the masses generally meant two legs and a place to walk. City fathers promoted parks, open-air spaces, and recreation yards at schools for the otherwise cramped citizenry. Alleyways and streets in packed areas challenged any notion of sanitation. Brothels were permitted and about 8,000 saloons and inns provided drink and entertainment. The homeless slept and ate at police stations, which logged in 126,000 lodgers in 1900.[1]

The city was run by an elected mayor, Carter Henry Harrison, Jr., a democrat whose father was murdered while holding the same office in 1893, and a city council of republican majority composed of aldermen from 70 city wards. Mayor Harrison had no ax to grind against boxing if matches didn't turn into brawls that threatened the peace, making his opinion clear when he spoke to representatives of the clergy that he personally "would have a boy brought up to play football and to box."[2] When ministers of a reformers group wanted to have the highly publicized Gans-McGovern fight cancelled, the clergy protested to the mayor by pointing to a law already on the books that prevented boxing in the city. The mayor responded simply "that the law had been enacted nearly forty years ago and always had been a dead letter."[3]

As in other large cities at the time, crime was semi-officially tolerated. Drugs were not illegal, considering all the concoctions advertised in newspapers promising to remedy aches, agues, and infirmities of all types. The largest drug addiction at the time was to opium, and Chinese opium dens were plentiful and considered legal pleasure-doms. Police raids were formalities, and arrests were meant only to harass disorderly troublemakers and quell disturbances. For the most part, if people behaved themselves and didn't cause problems, they were usually left alone. Boxing was considered a great entertainment and gambling was not frowned upon, unless a fight had been fixed by racketeers. But by the end of the year 1900, after the Gans-McGovern fight of December 13 and the public clamor that it drew — first from clergy and their "Reformers" and then from newspaper editors when they reported the bout as a fake — the mayor and city aldermen announced that boxing would be banished from Chicago.

For a city with a reputation as a historical Mecca for the mob and gangsters — Al Capone, the Saint Valentine's day massacre, the bootleggers and others chased by Elliot Ness and the Untouchables — how ironic it is today that for the first part of the 20th century, leaders of the Windy City made ordinary public boxing matches quite illegal, in their efforts to protect the "moral fiber." Grass-root associations developed to ensure the moral rectitude of the city. Chicago, although a future haven for gangsters, would also give birth in 1905 to the Rotary Club, which sought to encourage an ethical climate for Chicago business.[4]

Also known as "the Second City" for a time, Chicago vied with New York for attention in the latter part of the 19th century. In 1890, Chicago received worldwide publicity for beating out New York as host for the great Columbian Exposition, honoring the 400th anniversary of the European discovery of America. Attendance at the show in 1893 set a record for visitors at an exposition. Twenty-seven million people rolled into Chicago by train to see various new inventions and wonders of the world displayed in astounding architectural settings. This was an amazing number considering the population of the United States in 1890 was 63 million.[5]

At night, the great exhibition became a new wonder of the world, a "White City" where 93,000 incandescent lights illuminated the Neo-classical buildings covered in white stucco. The city was so white that Frederick Douglass protested: the exhibition did nothing to reflect the culture of the 8-million American blacks. (The only vestige of black culture was the Dahomey village depicting half-naked Africans.) Douglass was not the only protestor. Ida Wells brought her campaign against lynchings.

After paying a fifty-cent fee, visitors could enter the Court of Honor, where they would be entertained by "uplifting" classical music. But Americans, it seemed, didn't want to be entertained by the conventional; they wanted to be thrilled. When most people raced past the Court of Honor to get to the Midway Plaisance, exhibition directors brought in John Philip Sousa to enliven the musical fare. Nothing, however, could compete with the Midway attractions (an idiom remaining today from the exhibition). (The Chicago Bears are sometimes known as the "Monsters of the Midway.") There visitors could take a ride on George Washington Gale Ferris' giant wheel, see performances by Little Eva, the "hoochie-coochie" girl, Harry Houdini, Buffalo Bill and his Wild West Show, and boxing celebrity Gentleman Jim Corbett.

The exhibition featured entrepreneurs to entertainers, from inventors like Thomas Edison to architects like Frank Lloyd Wright, who became celebrities overnight. They inspired writers like Edgar Rice Burroughs, who gave some thought to becoming a professional boxer after seeing Jim Corbett demonstrate his skills. So fascinated was he with the sport that the main character of his most ambitious novel, *The Mucker*, was a boxer. The Great Sandow, dressed as he was at the fair in his leopard costume, inspired Burroughs' character Tarzan. And Chicagoan L. Frank Baum would transform, in 1900, the magnificent "white city" into the "emerald city," creating the classic American fairy tale.

The year 1900 had been an incredibly busy one for Gans and a year of tumultuous activity in the sport of boxing. The amazing lightweight "Kid" McCoy was flattening the likes of Joe Choynski, who had knocked out Jack Johnson. McCoy did this with his famous "corkscrew punch," a punch inspired by watching a cat snatch the life from a mouse. That feline predator would spin his paw in a corkscrew manner, which did not fail to KO the hapless rodent. (A derivative of McCoy's corkscrew punch would later be called by Muhammad Ali "the anchor punch," which he used to put Sonny

Liston's lights out in their second fight.) Bob Fitzsimmons had perfected his "tremendous belly clout" and "six-inch wallop" which had killed one man and left several others prostrate on ring aprons across the country.

Boxing an International Craze, but Reformers Wanted It Banned

Boxing was making news locally, nationally, and internationally. Church leaders and other social reformers ran boxing out of town in St. Louis. The papers reported that the game was almost dead there anyway since Al Neist, the Big Butcher, had died after a bout at the Fourteenth Street Theater the previous year. One of the local ring managers said he wasn't worried because the in-coming administration looked favorably on the art of self-defense.[6] The year 1900 also saw the heyday of the tabloid murder, starting with the tale of the star-crossed lovers Frankie and Johnnie. Frankie and Johnnie, written (or adapted from an earlier ballad) about the murder of Al Britt, also known as Johnny by his jealous wife Frances, known as Frankie.

Prizefighting was so popular that gates brought in vats of money to local athletic clubs, club managers and fight promoters. Gamblers also had high stakes in the fights—in the Gans-McGovern fight, $75,000 was expected to change hands. Whenever an upset went against the betting majority, gamers screamed foul. Kid McCoy and Corbett were accused of "jobbing" their Madison Square Garden fight. The fight was actually a brutal brawl with Corbett hammering the smaller McCoy, and rumor of the fix came from the wives of Gentleman Jim and the Kid. As Armond Fields states in his biography of Corbett, "Immediately following the contest, McCoy's wife blew the entire issue beyond control. She publicly stated that she was filing for divorce and, while alleging extreme cruelty by her husband, also declared that the McCoy-Corbett bout had been fixed. That was all the tabloids needed to brandish headlines of 'fix,' 'deception,' and 'greed' for the next several days."[7] Mrs. Corbett also weighed in on the matter, "fully aware of Mrs. McCoy's sensational declaration that the fight had been fixed, Vera had now captured headlines by denouncing Jim, confirming Mrs. McCoy's accusation and adding a few spicy anecdotes of her own to the bubbling stew."[8]

"Barbados" Joe Walcott, a dominant black welterweight of the time, had been forced to throw a fight for fear of his life. Nat Fleischer recalls that Walcott's manager, Tom O'Rourke, personally told him that "Walcott didn't dare to win that night. I got the tip ... he must lose ... if West had been stopped in the 12th round ... I'd probably been laying nice, peaceful and natural on the next slab."[9] Heavyweight contender Jack Root was accused of faking, and the Erne-McGovern fight was also considered a job. By year's end, no one knew who was on the level. As the *Chicago Tribune* reported, "Jeffries, Corbett, McCoy, Maher, Walcott, Creedon, Lightweight Jack O'Brien, McFadden, West, Ryan, Root, Zeigler, Burns, Gans, Erne, and McGovern have all been accused of being mixed up in shady transactions."[10] But of all of the fighters accused of trickery, Gans bore the brunt of the scapegoating and would end the year as an outcast in boxing. These were the headlines in 1900, right up there with murder and political corruption.

Boxing was such a powerful and controversial phenomenon at the turn of the century that it was identified with a political movement on the other side of the globe. In 1900 a grassroots insurgency, which sought to maintain traditional Chinese values against the rising tide of Western influence and missionary zeal, spread through the northern provinces of China and threatened U.S. and other Western trade (including the lucrative opium trade) in Peking. Notorious for a rigorous martial arts training that to Westerners looked like something akin to boxing, the Chinese soldiers became known as the "Boxers" and their final siege of the foreign political legations in the Chinese capital was called the "Boxer Rebellion."[11] American servicemen, not to be out-trained by militias elsewhere in the world in the art of self-defense, were required to take classes in the "manly" sport.[12]

In America, another Gans fight, between Gans and McGovern, held center stage. According to author J. J. Johnston, "At the time, the two best boxers in America — unquestionably — were Joe Gans and featherweight champion Terry McGovern."[13] So popular were these two fighters that Herford had a choice of two venues for the fight. J.J. Groom, of the National Athletic Club of San Francisco, had offered either a purse of $5000 or 65 percent of the gross receipts. Perhaps Herford and Samuel Harris, McGovern's manager, didn't realize what they were getting themselves into when they selected the offer from the Tattersall's Athletic Association in Chicago, which included both a purse of $7500 and 50 percent of the gross receipts.

A crowd of ten thousand — some estimates put the number as high as fifteen thousand — people entered the famed Chicago hippodrome to see featherweight champion Terry McGovern go at the famous lightweight wonder. McGovern was a great fighter. Nat Fleischer rated McGovern the greatest fighter ever to campaign at 126 pounds. In the two years prior to his fight with Gans, "Terrible" Terry McGovern had fought an amazing total of 32 bouts. To put that in perspective, Sugar Ray Leonard had 40 fights in his twenty-year career. Of McGovern's 32 bouts, he won 25 by knockout, without losing any. He had knocked out such great fighters as George Dixon,

Tony White, and Frank Erne, whom Gans had been chasing for a match. An even more impressive fact was that in just two years, he had knocked out 15 top professionals in three rounds or less. His image was heroic, of David and Goliath proportions. His fans believed he could take on the heavyweight champion and knock him out.

The Chicago contest was pegged as little man against big man, knockout artist vs. the expert, and, of course, white man vs. black. According to the Articles of Agreement for the fight, the men were to weigh 133 pounds or below at 7 P.M. on fight night, and Gans had to knock out McGovern within six rounds if he wanted to earn the winner's purse, set at 65 percent of half of the gate receipts. If McGovern could last the six rounds, he would be declared the winner. (Six rounds was a perfect length for the new movie invention, and the fight would be filmed.)

It was the first time Gans fought in Chicago, and it was a fight like no other. Events surrounding the fight included a war of words between the reformers who wanted boxing abolished and the athletic exhibition, an unsettling mix of threats, arrest warrants, and counter threats. As a result, elaborate preparations were made by police and the fight crowd to properly choreograph the arrests of the pugilists. The original plan was for the fighters to be arrested and jailed, if necessary, after the fight for "disturbing the peace" if the boxing abolitionists successfully convinced the mayor to punish the offenders.

Threats of interference pitted a group of "crusading reformers," led by Frank Hall, against the fight club's boxing promoters. Hall wanted to have arrest warrants served days before the fight against the boxers and other principals to prevent the fight from going forward. In order to head off any actions from the reformer's group, Lou Houseman, the fight manager for the club, had his own arrest warrants issued first. Houseman's pre-emptive, more "friendly," warrants were supposed to "protect them" by invalidating any warrants that could be served later by Hall or members of his group. (Houseman had a $3,000 investment in film equipment, and he wasn't going to let a group of crusaders ruin his movie venture.) Management had McGovern placed under arrest on Tuesday prior to the fight while he was still in Milwaukee. Gans was staying in New York with his wife and friends and could not be reached or arrested. Both Gans and his manager would be served arrest warrants upon arriving in Chicago. The timekeeper Frank Kennedy was also notified of his forthcoming arrest by Hall's people.[14]

It was a three-ring circus of arrest warrants and no one had yet entered the prize ring. The president of Tattersall's Athletic Association attempted to serve arrest warrants on Hall's primary Reformers to discover what they were actually after. By noon the day of the fight a committee of ministers, which included Frank Talmadge, an iconic evangelist whose popular Sunday lectures were serialized in newspapers across the country, appeared before the mayor to induce him to cancel his fight permit. The mayor refused. In the meantime, each fighter was kept under cover and placed, at least technically for the record, in the custody of a constable who remained with each of them at all times.

In a tragi-comedy of errors, the arrest warrants were served before the weigh-in — and the affair continued to go straight downhill for Gans. Later in the afternoon a bailiff appeared and all of the parties to the boxing match were required to post bail. At 7:00 P.M. Gans failed to meet the Articles of Agreement regarding the weight requirement. The weight forfeiture clause would not cancel the event, but it would affect the earnings. If the boxer weighed in above the 133-pound limit, then he could receive only half of his share of the purse at the end of the contest. Gans and McGovern weighed in at Malachy Hogan's gym on Clark Street and greeted each other amicably. The scale was set to 133. McGovern, the featherweight, weighing closer to 124, stepped on the scale first and the bar never moved. It was Gans' turn.

When Gans stepped on the platform the bar slapped the top of the scale and never moved, indicating that he was over the weight limit. When the scale was tipped to 134, the bar never inched down. Again the weight was shifted to 135 and the bar moved only slightly, hovering close to the top. Reporters jotted notes at the scene. Gans was "crestfallen" by the outcome and said that when he left Harry Forbes' gym just prior to the weigh in, he was at 133. McGovern's manager Sam Harris was quick to waive the weight forfeit question if McGovern were to win. If McGovern lost, however, the clause would be in full effect. Gans' camp happily accepted the offer and the fighters sealed the deal with a cordial handshake.

"Well, goodbye Joe, I'll see you later,"

"Goodbye Terry."[15]

That night in Chicago the Gans-McGovern fight didn't begin until 11:00 P.M. After four six-round preliminary bouts, new canvas was laid, and the movie-making device set in place. Thomas Edison's new invention of moving pictures allowed promoters to replay the event at other venues and garner additional revenues. Boxing matches were the first live events to be captured in the "flickers," as they were called. Six lights were turned on and four giant reflectors set around the ring. Because of the scorching heat generated by the light of equal to 200,000 candle power, the doors to the giant hall were thrown open and the cold December winds kept the spectators shivering the remainder of the night.

The announcer moved to the center of the stage to the great anticipation of a crowd waiting to hear if the bout would go forward. "Patrons of the Tattersall's Athletic Association will be pleased to know," he bellowed, "That despite the efforts of certain fakers and blackmailers, which resulted in failure, the program of the association will be carried out as announced, with the sanction of his Honor, Carter H. Harrison, Mayor of Chicago."[16] The term "faker" caught on and can be seen in use during more contemporary events, such as the 1968 Democratic Convention in Chicago where Mayor Daley shouted at the protesters in the crowd, "You're a faker." Ill-informed of the long history of the term in Chicago, the press confused it with another "f" word.

One sportswriter described the colorful pageantry of boxing retinues that followed, "The arena looked like the stage of a Bowery museum with a picnic scene in progress."[17] (It was a reference to the stage play "The Bowery after Dark" which starred Terry McGovern.) Danny Dougherty, one of McGovern's seconds, walked up and placed in his man's corner McGovern's good luck chair, the one he always sat in for his bouts in Chicago. Gans entered the arena to a respectable greeting from the crowd. It was noted that he was wearing a "mixed striped affair of gray and red." Al Herford, Harry Forbes, Henry Lyons and Samuel Bolen entered his corner. Hearty cheers went up from the crowd as soon as the fans caught sight of McGovern, "togged out in a sweater of crimson color, with an olive green collar." His entourage also included Jack Donahue, Charles Mayhood, and his manager, Samuel Harris (flamboyantly dressed in "a salmon pink creation, having a green collar, with three black buttons along his left shoulder").

Almost as soon as the bout began that night, it was over and the controversy began to rage. Sportswriters dictated and telegraphers tapped out headlines and stories that would appear in papers the following day. Baltimoreans would be shocked at the news from Chicago "Gans Knocked Out," "All Over Within Two Rounds."[18] Headlines in Chicago denounced the bout as a bald fake, in a bout "heavily scented with crookedness."[19] The unlucky thirteenth of December was also the night the lights went out in public boxing halls in Chicago, shutting down the sport for more than twenty years.

Each time participants engaged in an illegal boxing match, they risked going to jail. Gans especially had a lot to worry about with respect to criminal charges, afraid as he was of being incarcerated in the atmosphere of the times. Newspapers in the cities where he fought reported lynchings in the United States with mobs storming jails and yanking their victims from the legal process to exact immediate revenge. Reports of lynchings in American papers offer a chilling reminder of the era and what it must have been like to be a black gladiator facing a white audience.

For Gans his ring opponents were the least of his objects of fear. Chilling accounts of blacks being lynched appeared alongside coverage of Gans' fights. On the day after the first Erne fight, the *Atlanta Constitution* reported, "this morning in the heart of town the body of a negro, Louis Rice, was found dangling from the limb of a tree. The lynching is said to have been the result of a trial in the circuit court of Lauderdale County, during which Rice testified in favor of one of his color who was charged with the murder of a white man named Goodrich."[20]

In his book *One Hundred Years of Lynchings*, Ralph Ginzburg cites other headlines from 1900 and 1901, the time when Gans made his ascent to the title. Some of those headlines read:

"An Innocent Man Lynched" (*New York Times*, June 11, 1900)

"Two Blacks Strung Up, Grave Doubt of their Guilt" (*Houston Post*, June 11, 1900)

"Negro Freed, then Lynched" (*Chicago Record*, Jan. 4, 1901)

"Negro Suspect Eludes Mob, Sister Lynched instead" (*N. Y. Tribune*, March 17, 1901)

"Negro Burned at Stake" (*Chicago Record Herald*, Aug. 8, 1901)

"Lynch Mob May Have Erred" (*Chicago Record Herald*, March 31, 1902)

"Negro Tortured to Death by Mob of 4000" (*Chicago Record Herald*, May 23, 1902)[21]

Details from the crimes reported are either shockingly grotesque: "His head was mashed almost to a pulp before he was dragged out of his cell" (*New York Herald*, June 8, 1903); or morbidly matter of fact: "William Carr, Negro, was lynched without ceremony here today by an orderly party of thirty masked men who carried him to a railroad trestle and hanged him. He had been accused of killing a white man's cow" (*New York Tribune*, March 18, 1906).[22]

Lynchings in America were commonly understood at the beginning of the twentieth century to mean the torture of a black man by either hanging him from a stake (tree, pole, etc.) or burning him at the stake, a torture usually associated with medieval times rather than the Progressive Era in America. These horrific acts were not specific to the South. Before the Gans-McGovern fight, the Chicago paper, *The Broadax*, ran this front page article, December 1, 1900, with the title "Words of Warning to the Negro." "It is from the northern state of Colorado and not from the South, that news of the latest horrible torture of a Negro comes. This Negro was a mere boy of 16." He was "tortured at the stake."[23] Only a few days earlier in Phoenix, Arizona, *The Anaconda Standard* reported an attempted suicide of Ernest Scott, a youth charged with attempted assault of two white girls. He had swallowed broken glass from a medicine bottle for fear of "being burned or hanged." The paper reported that he would probably die the next day.[24]

Details of the human burnings at the stake continued for decades and could fill ghastly volumes. "Burning pieces of pine were thrust into his eyes, the burning timbers were held to his neck, and after his clothes were burned off to other parts of his body. He was tortured in a horrible manner." "His flesh began to drop away from his legs and they were reduced to bones, once or twice he attempted to pick up hot coals and swallow them in order to hasten death. Each time the coals were kicked from his grasp by members of the mob" (*Memphis Press*, January 27, 1921).[25]

Newspapers of the day offered grim reminders of what happened to black men who did not follow white men's orders. Muhammad Ali said of the pioneers of the prize-ring who had to fight during this era, "I was inspired by the courage and confidence they must have had during the days when blacks were being lynched and jailed in the South for just bumping into a white man on the streets or talking back to a white policeman."[26]

Because of the prefight legal shenanigans, Gans' life was at risk in front of the hostile Chicago crowd whether he won or lost. If he had to "fight to orders," and his orders were to lose, he risked being charged with fraud and jailed. Immediately after the fight, Gans and his manager Al Herford defended themselves against accusations of fraud by stating that Gans had been hit by hard body blows, much like the "solar plexus" punch that Bob Fitzsimmons had used to wrest the heavyweight crown from Gentleman Jim Corbett. The explanations fell on deaf ears.

In viewing the fight film it is clear that Gans looked out of sorts from the get-go. Terry McGovern was a fearsome puncher. But Gans was very experienced and, in addition to the weight advantage, he had a distinct height and reach advantage that he certainly knew how to use. However, he did not use it against McGovern. He also did not use his piston-like left jab to keep McGovern at bay. Gans allowed his foe to wade in unmolested whatsoever by Gans' own punches. Even so, his defensive mastery is evident on film in the way he ducks and parries McGovern's "knockout blows," as if his body is too well-trained in avoiding punches for him to credibly fake being knocked out. As Joyce Carol Oates explains, "A boxer-turned-actor might be expected to perform, with no excess of zeal or talent." But "boxing is so refined, yet so raw a sport that no match can be successfully thrown; the senses simply pick up on what is not happening, what is being held back, as a sort of ironic subtext to what is actually taking place."[27]

McGovern, a powerful spark plug of a man, threw every punch "with bad intentions," as Mike Tyson used to say. And while some, including the referee, claimed that he never hit Gans with a blow hard enough to rock a baby much less knock him out, there is credible evidence from the film that Gans was hit with a solid body blow in the first round, the one that he later said incapacitated him for the remainder of the bout. But he does not double up or even show any sign of being hurt. If Gans was earnestly trying to win, he could have easily kept the shorter McGovern at the end of his marvelous left jab, which even Joe Louis acknowledged as the best ever in boxing. Gans made no attempt to clinch after the knockdowns, which from his other fights he obviously knew how to do, and his corner men never objected to the foul reported at the end of the first round.

Here is the round-by-round report that came into Baltimore from Chicago:

Round 1— McGovern led with his left. He rushed Gans to the ropes, pounding him very hard on the ribs with his left glove. McGovern missed right and left and then sent the colored man back with a left to the jaw. Gans was acting on the defensive. McGovern rushed, landing right and left on the ribs, and Gans uppercut under the heart.

Gans next put right and left to face and McGovern sent left and right to the jaw. He sent Gans staggering with right and left, and following him up closely, put right and left on him again. Terry next sent Gans to the ropes with right and left to the face; then he landed a stiff right upon the jaw, staggering his man. A left on the face nearly floored the colored man, and another left smash on the jaw knocked Gans down.

Gans arose at the count of seven. He was knocked down again one second after the bell rang. He was assisted to his corner in a groggy condition. No claim of foul was made by Gans for the blow after the bell.

Round 2 — As soon as the men came from their corners McGovern made a rush and put two lefts and a right to the jaw. Gans went down flat, arose slowly to one knee and took the count of seven. As he rose McGovern came in again with a fierce rush, sending his left to the body and whipping his right across to the jaw on the break away.

Gans kept backing, but twice swung feebly at McGovern's jaw. The blow would not have injured a baby, and McGovern paying no attention to them came in with a hard right on the ear and a left to the mouth. He kept right after Gans, who kept backing around the ring. When the colored boy stood his ground McGovern was at him like a flash, landing two lefts on the jaw and a right on the jaw immediately after it, sending Gans flat on his back. He took the full count of nine, but was very unsteady when he arose.

McGovern caught him flush on the jaw and down he went once more. Up he came again and down he went faster than he got up. A left and right to the jaw did the business this time. It was all over and McGovern was a sure winner. He sent a right to the jaw as Gans wobbled to his feet again and the colored boy went down again. He came up, almost gone, without a chance in the world to win, and as he lifted his knees from the floor McGovern settled him. It was left and right to the jaw, then a right again and Gans lay on his back, the blood oozing from his mouth, the beaten man in a fight which had no share of credit or glory for him. He rolled over on his face, got up on one knee and remained in that position while Siler called off the 10 seconds. He was able to walk to his corner with the aid of his seconds and with the exception of a bleeding mouth showed no sign of hard punishment.[28]

After falling down five times without being hit cleanly, Gans casually rose and shook McGovern's hand. Terry McGovern turned and waved to the crowd acknowledging the deafening cheers. Before he could reach his corner, his manager and corner men lofted him into the air and carried him to his chair. Those nearest the ring poured onto the canvas, swarming his corner. "He only hit me once and that was in the first minute of the first round," McGovern said jubilantly, still panting from the fight, "He poked his left into my mouth good and hard, but I knew I had him on the next exchange."[29]

The loss was shocking to a country of fight followers. In Milwaukee a Frenchman by the name of George Rondeau had bet all of his money on Gans. He was so distraught at the loss that his friend, Charles Ryan, recommended the "liquor cure." When they were both totally soused inside the Bintz Hotel bar, Ryan pulled a gun and created quite a stir among the patrons. Rondeau grabbed the gun from his friend and went out into the alley, where he tried to commit suicide. Luckily his hand was so unsteady that when he fired, the bullet "missed its mark." The man lived, but the episode illustrates the high profile of the fight and its betting stakes.[30]

What had happened to Gans? His seconds offered only one excuse for their man, that his stomach had been a problem for him all day.

The exhilaration of the McGovern win had hardly set in when spectators began calling the match a fraud. Al Herford telegraphed a statement to the *Baltimore Sun* on the night of the loss:

No doubt you have got reports of the Gans-McGovern bout not being a genuine contest and on its merits. Now I want to say this for Joe Gans and myself that Joe got a left hand, body punch in the stomach the first crack out of the box in the first round which completely upset him. It was the same blow that Fitzsimmons whipped Corbett with in Carson City — a solar plexus one. There is no one in the sporting world who has ever found me to be mixed up in a transaction of that kind, as I brought Gans up from the bottom of the ladder when he was fighting for a $100 purse and got him as near to the championship class as any other lightweight has ever been. So how could I afford at this stage of the game to be mixed up in that way? The cause of all the rumors is that there are some people in Chicago who believe Terry McGovern can whip Jeffries in a six round bout and this class is mostly a pot of sure thing gamblers, so when Terry went out of his class to meet Joe they said from the beginning he would knock Gans out. Why the betting here in Chicago three weeks ago was 1 to 2, Terry would stop Joe. You can't stop people from betting their money. Now, If any one paper will show one proof that Joe Gans laid down to Terry McGovern, I will say they are right, but I don't believe in people accusing one of being implicated in a thing of this kind unless they can prove the same. Now another thing. It is taking credit from Terry McGovern to use those 'fake' remarks. He won from Gans and he won fairly. Now, if McGovern will give us a return battle of 20 rounds at 133 pounds at 7 o'clock I will bet any part of $3,000, let the winner take all."

— Joe Gans

— Al Herford[31]

Each of the fighters made statements to the press. Gans issued a signed statement to the *Chicago Times-Herald* that was reprinted in the *Baltimore Sun*: "The better man won. That is all I can give in explanation of the result. I did not 'lay down.' I was hit hard early in the fight and that seemed to take the wind out of me. I don't think there is anyone who can stand up before McGovern at the lightweight limit."[32] McGovern issued this signed statement to the *Times-Herald*: "I did not fake, that is a certainty. I tried to finish the fight as soon as I possibly could, but I must confess the result was somewhat of a surprise to me."[33]

The next morning, promptly at 9:00, Gans, Herford, McGovern, Harris, Siler, and Houseman found themselves in court. Because Prosecutor Frank Hall was not able to produce witnesses and because the charges were brought and the arrest warrants issued before the bout actually took place, the charges were dismissed. The judge told the fighters, promoters, and managers to go home.

George Siler, referee for the fight and sportswriter for the *Chicago Tribune*, wrote the next day "I do not wish to accuse any fighter of faking but if Gans was trying to win last night I do not know much about the game. Gans, of course, is entitled to the benefit of the doubt as to whether or not numerous body blows which Terry pumped into him in close quarters during the early part of the fight weakened him. But the fact remains that the few blows he delivered were the weakest ever seen from a man of his known hitting ability."[34]

The *Times Herald* concluded that the match was "heavily scented with crookedness."[35] The conclusion was based upon two things: a betting pattern observed when men at ringside passed through the aisles offering even money that Gans would be knocked out, and Siler's report that the "fight had a bad look," in that he didn't see any blow that could have caused Gans' grogginess in the first round. The *Tribune* reported that the betting had turned from Gans to McGovern on the day before the fight, that Gans had been up nearly all night the evening before the fight, and that "colored" sports all over the city were betting for McGovern.

When Herford returned to Baltimore, he said that the newspapers had called the fight a fake, but he insisted again that Gans had been dealt a hard hit to the ribs. He said, "When [Gans] went to his corner he told me that he felt as if the flesh had been torn from his ribs. That punch weakened him so much that he was an easy proposition after that."[36] Herford went on to say that to this point Gans had made for him a total in purses and bets a sum of $87,000 and that he would not be a party to a fake. He said that Gans typically fights 6, 8, even 14 rounds defensively before he knocks his opponent out.

Gans and his manager professed to have lost a good bit of money on the fight. Herford and Harris had bet each other $2500 on their men the night before the fight and Herford bet additional money with spectators. Back in Baltimore at the Germania Maennerchor Hall during a fight that night set up by the Eureka Athletic Club, Herford's brother Maurice placed a bet that Gans would win. George Mantz, referee of the Broad-Whistler fight that night, bet money on Gans. There were few people betting for McGovern, so when money was shown for McGovern, bets were quickly taken up on Gans. It was noted that these few betters on McGovern won big. When the returns were announced in the ring that night that Gans had lost, a shout went up.[37] The shout may have come from the money-winning crowd that had bet on McGovern. One simple explanation for the rejoicing was that Gans was not fighting in Baltimore; he had been scheduled for fights in venues other than Baltimore, perhaps making for anti–Gans sentiment in the Monumental City.

Among those in attendance in Baltimore the night of the fight was Joseph Marias, manager of "Kid" Broad and secretary of the New York Broadway and Lenox Athletic Clubs. Marias stated that he felt sorry for Herford. "Al is one of the greatest directors in pugilistic battles who have ever visited New York," and, he added, "one of the best losers."[38] He wagered a guess as to how much money Herford lost on the event and suggested that $5,000 would not cover it.

By losing the fight if the fight were "faked," what had Gans stood to gain? Gans had more to lose than just the winner's purse for this match. A dispatch immediately sent out from Denver cancelled Gans' next bout, scheduled for January with "Kid" Parker at the Denver Athletic Club.[39] Gans had defeated Parker in the previous match less than a month earlier, but sentiment was so high against Gans and Herford that the rematch with Parker was cancelled. Sentiment would be similar in other parts of the country.

Much has been made of the big shift in odds. Before the day of the fight the odds were even that Gans would be knocked out within the six rounds. There were numerous stories going around 24 hours before the fight that it had been fixed. This report caused the odds to shift, for example, 2 to 1 that

McGovern would be on his feet at the end of 6 rounds. Betting was heavy and in favor of McGovern on the day of the fight. There was plenty of money to be bet against the Gans backers, but as soon as some of "the colored sporting men" began to bet similarly against Gans, the manager of Tattersall's in Chicago smelled a rat. He brought Herford in and said that if there was any sign of a fake, the bout would be ruled no contest, all bets would be called off and McGovern would win Gans' portion of the purse.

But the most damning story was launched when William Arthur, assistant attorney for Chicago, said that "a colored gambler" came into his office offering to bet $8,000 at 8 to 5 on McGovern. Upon questioning, the gambler said that he had seen a written agreement whereby Gans would quit before the 5th round.[40]

Another story circulated that the Baltimore crowd knew Gans had partied the nights away in New York instead of working in the gym during his training period. Perhaps the fear apparent on Gans' face before the fight came in part from the realization that he had entered the ring without the fighter's most reliable friends, training and conditioning. Nobody will ever know for sure exactly what happened in Chicago that night. That's a secret Gans, McGovern, and their managers took to their graves. But we do know that the repercussions of the evening made the aftermath a desperate time in the life of the Old Master.

To review events leading up to the fight: Gans had a nervous stomach, an arrest warrant, and a problem at weigh in. Had he been in hiding in New York to avoid the arrest warrant? Did he go into the ring as a result without proper training? Was he afraid of McGovern? Was the injury to the ribs excruciatingly painful, as anyone who has ever had a rib injury can attest to? Or was he afraid of the mob?

Herford's Quid Pro Quo: What Really Happened

It should not be ruled out that McGovern hurt a weakened Gans with body blows. Eight years after the fight Gans recalled the power punches of Terry McGovern, "When he connected with one of those swings, his rival was certain to collide with the floor."[41] Perhaps Gans was so weak or afraid of being shot or lynched that he was truly dazed by one or several of McGovern's grazing blows and although not truly knocked out, he was indeed hurt. However, our research indicates the following logical explanation for what happened, an explanation that has not been suggested in previous discussions of the fight. Although historians have said that McGovern was not in on the fix, he and his manager were often seen publicly chumming around with Herford. McGovern and his manager would be seen a year and a half later celebrating Gans' victory over Frank Erne, riding in a car, sitting next to Gans in a parade through Buffalo when Gans won the lightweight crown.

In October, two months before the Chicago fight, when Herford was still chasing Frank Erne for a match with Gans, newspaper accounts showed that Herford traveled to St. Louis to see Samuel Harris and Terry McGovern to enlist their help in obtaining a rematch for Gans against Erne.[42] By October of 1900 the fixing of fights may have seemed the logical order of events to Herford. In Herford's desperation to secure a rematch with Erne and enlist Harris' aid in this endeavor, it would not have been above Herford to offer to throw a match to McGovern. Six to eight weeks after enlisting their help, Herford and Harris had arranged for Gans to meet McGovern on December 13, 1900. We can only speculate how Sam Harris could help Herford. Since McGovern had beaten Erne in a non-title fight, he may have agreed to forego a title bout, letting Gans have it instead in return for losing in Chicago. Shortly after the Chicago fight, Gans met Erne for the lightweight title.

It is possible that the fear on Gans' face in the Chicago ring reflected the realization of one of Herford's shenanigans gone wrong. The arrest warrants, the climate of lynchings in America, and Gans' knowing that he would probably be made a scapegoat all contributed to the psychological pressure on him that night. Gans knew that, in going forward with the bout, he would be served papers, and that he risked being put in jail. If he won the match and was subsequently incarcerated, his freedom, possibly his life, could be threatened.

Four days after the battle, the Chicago City Council passed an ordinance that codified the match as a "fake": "Be it resolved that the City Council of the city of Chicago hereby expresses its disapprobation of ... the fraudulent affair which took place at the Tattersalls Building December 13, 1900."[43] The ordinance would ban boxing contests in the Windy City, except at private clubs where no admission could be charged. This put an end to the large gate receipts and rich purses that could be made in a prizefight in Chicago.

Boxing was on its way to becoming a major industry when Chicago outlawed it at the end of 1900. The Windy City's actions were the equivalent of putting the skids on HBO or MTV in the 1980s' environment, in terms of economic impact. Imagine canceling baseball today because of the betting or steroid scandals. It is simply inconceivable. And yet, with a black boxer as a convenient sacrificial lamb, the biggest sport in America was nearly forced out of existence because of a match that lasted less than five minutes. What would have been lost in terms of American culture if the country had paid heed to the strident demands for the abolition of boxing in the wake of the Chicago fix?

Why did Chicagoans react so vehemently? The city had paid a hefty price tag to get the fight, having out-bid San Francisco and having paid nearly $100 million in today's dollars to bring the fight to Chicago. Part of the outrage was likely caused by the feeling of those in the Chicago area that they had been duped in a big way by small-time crooks. Faked boxing matches were certainly common and the outrage could not be credibly attributed to surprise.

And what of Herford's and Gans' claims that the fight was for real? Even today, some who watch the film are not convinced that Gans was faking. A recent on-line discussion on the internet site East Side Boxing showed more than one commenter who thought the fight was genuine, and that Gans had been hit cleanly. To this the authors would say that it is not only the lack of punches taken by Gans, but even more to the point the complete lack of punches thrown by Gans, which marks the fight as fake. The best combination puncher in history to that point, Gans makes only feeble pawing motions at his attacker.

Gans' and Herford's statements the night of the bout are unconvincing, and Herford's comments seem like a well-planned attempt to avoid fraud charges and obtain a lucrative rematch for this fighter. How quick and eloquent was the

A poster for a burlesque show starring Terry McGovern. In addition to boxing exhibitions and fight films, McGovern headlined in the Broadway plays *Gay Morning Glory, Bowery After Dark,* and *Road to Ruin.* He made $20,000 in the movies and spent $15,000 on racehorses. His manager estimated he made and lost over $203,200 during his fistic career. When McGovern's family was penniless, Manager Sam Harris and boxing friends gave him a benefit at Madison Square Garden on January 23, 1907 (image from the H. C. Miner Lithograph Co., 1899).

written statement of a man who should be expected to be somewhat shell-shocked if his greatest "pro-teege" had just been mowed down so easily by the much smaller McGovern. Surely he would have appeared to be more distressed. To his credit, Gans said very little, and what he did say has the look of having been contrived by others.

L'audace, toujours l'audace! Napoleon had said. Audacity always—that was his motto. And so it was also with Herford. How brazen and bold to stage a fake before the nation's press and the movie camera to boot! But one must consider the stakes. For example, what would have been the odds of Gans losing in the way he did? At 10-to-1, Herford could have bet $5,000, won $50,000, and had quite a fortune. And if in addition Gans would get a future shot at the title, the whole shenanigans would have been worth the risk to a gambling man like Herford. The subsequent chumminess of the Gans and McGovern managers seems to contradict the idea that McGovern's side was completely innocent on the fix. And yet Gans ended up taking all the blame.

A report on Terry McGovern from the *New York World* indicated that the Brooklyn Whirlwind had earned for the year 1900 a total of $70,000 in prize winnings and another $13,000 in earnings from exhibitions and acting in the play *The Bowery After Dark*.[44] This amount was twice what President McKinley made that year. Only a mention at the end of the article reminded readers that the Gans match should not have been called a fake considering the fact that no boxer against McGovern that year had gone longer than 8 rounds, and that included George Dixon. The Chicago fight had not harmed McGovern's reputation. On the contrary, it appeared to have enhanced it.

The Fate of Gans' Predecessor, Peter Jackson

In evaluating the fight, which resulted in the biggest scandal in boxing history, and whether or not Gans "strayed from the straight and narrow path," consider the fate of an all time great black fighter who did play by the rules just prior to Gans' day.

The most celebrated black fighter in the years prior to Joe Gans was the great heavyweight Peter Jackson. In *Black Dynamite* Nat Fleischer describes Jackson as the model of how a black fighter should behave: "His record as a square battler was as clean as the proverbial hound's tooth. Although little more than a light-heavyweight when in his prime, he defeated star heavyweights all through his spectacular career."[45]

If we assume for a moment this behavior was to serve as a model for what was expected of Gans, let us take a look at what it did for Jackson. Did it lead him to wealth and glory? It did not. At the zenith of his career he was living hand to mouth. After Jackson had climbed to the top of the heavyweight ladder, he was ready to take on California super-star Joe McAuliffe. When the match was made, Jackson asked that a portion of the purse be set aside for the loser. "I suppose there'll be no harm in letting the loser get $500 out of the $3,000 purse," he remarked, "but of course I don't intend to be the loser. Then, you see, I have no money and couldn't get any more fights, so I'd like to be protected in having at least enough to take me home."[46]

Fighters at that time had to put up a forfeit to secure the upcoming fight. A prizefighter without a stake was out of luck. In his last years as a fighter, Jackson wrote to heavyweight champion Gentleman Jim Corbett, "I ask in all fairness, what earthly chance have I of meeting the champion next December?... Age is now coming on me.... I am thirty-two.... Boxing, I think, is a manly sport.... If a man is fainthearted he should never step over the ropes. The man whose heart fails him suffers ... like the poor wretch on the way to the gallows."[47] Fleischer describes the last days of Peter Jackson's life. "His fortune dwindled, his fame gone, drink having shattered his health, Peter was in a sad plight. He gave himself up to the Demon of drink and it wasn't long before he was a physical wreck. He slept in the back room of saloons and ate only when friends came to his rescue. He was a pitiful figure. Already in an advanced stage of tuberculosis, Peter didn't live long."[48] And yet Fleischer holds up Peter Jackson as a role model.

Was Joe Gans forced to accept "deals" to achieve a chance at the world title? The evidence shows that he was. Boxing was known for shady deals and flimflam at the turn of the century, and the Chicago fix would be neither the first nor the last. So the sanctimony and outrage to come against Gans seems in part an opportunistic backlash against his inexorable rise through the ranks of great fighters that had taken him from oyster shucker to the brink of world title glory. Gans' path may have strayed from the straight-and-narrow, but he found his way back in due time.

Gans had fought the last match under the Horton law in New York in 1900 when he beat Dal Hawkins and the last fight in Chicago on that cold December night. The year 1900 came to a close with much moralizing, grandstanding, and humiliation on the part of the politicians. Alderman Patterson said that Gans' "fake" fight made Chicago the laughingstock of the United States, at which the Chicago City Council quickly passed an ordinance to ban boxing. Editorials in the *Chicago Tribune* proclaimed the end of Gans' career, while the *New York World* still proclaimed Terry McGovern "that wonderful little fighter."[49] Meanwhile, Gans went back to work to become a champion, do or die.

8

Long Road Back

While the pundits in Chicago were hypocritically patting each other on the back for their courageous stands against the scourges of pugilism and gambling, in the wake of the *fin de siècle* corporate scandals, flimflam, and a presidential race that featured bombastic warnings of a nation "crucified on a cross of gold," Gans went quietly back to the daily grind in his quest for a world boxing title.

More so than in other professions or callings, morning comes early for a prizefighter. The bruised and battered body screams for rest, but there is none. Only a powerful, driving force can propel the fighter outside, day after day, for his crushing routine of roadwork, to be followed by long days of hard training and sparring.

Boxing comebacks were legend worthy in twentieth-century America. Gans' plight rivaled that of Ali in the late sixties when he was stripped of his title and livelihood for refusing induction into the army to fight in the Vietnam War. The second-coming of Muhammad Ali has been raised to the level of American myth in such movies as *When We Were Kings*.

Songs of redemption resonate in African-American art perhaps more than any other psychic arena, for reasons that are the subject of many other great books, which the authors could not possibly do justice to in this story of Joe Gans. Suffice it to say that the quest to overcome past adversity is seen throughout African American and Caribbean art and literature. From slave-era spirituals to Bob Marley, redemption songs allow one to feel the pain through a triumphant spirit of hope.

At the end of 1900, no one was more in need of redemption than Joe Gans. He had been used by the boxing establishment as a scapegoat, scandalously criticized in the papers for quitting in his title bid against Frank Erne, and he seemed destined to fade into obscurity after the Chicago fiasco. The loss of the title fight, after he had spent his mature life working up the professional ladder to attain it, meant that there would be no quick ride to a second chance, only a steep, uphill march. Gans' future would tax both manager and fighter. Who would take him on now? He was 26 years old (although newspapers said he was 24). Could he maintain his stamina and winning record, or was he on the backside of his career? And most importantly, could his manager ever entice Erne to grant him another shot at the title?

Amid the uncertainties, Gans was back in the prize ring. Anticipating a more successful year for 1901, Gans and his wife Madge moved to Druid Hill Avenue in Baltimore. It would be years later when the civic health authorities determined the Druid Hill area to have been a concentrated incubator for tuberculosis.

In the interval between Gans' two fights with Frank Erne, manager Al Herford proved himself a bulldog in his quest to get Joe a second chance at the title. And Gans proved conclusively that he could take his lumps, learn from a loss, and come back to defeat fighters who had beaten him. His first defeat had been a disputed 15-round decision loss against Dal Hawkins of San Francisco in 1896. Gans had been substituted for Erne when Erne bowed out of the fight, and a famed referee, ironically known as "Honest" John Kelly, had given the decision to Hawkins against the view of the crowd and the New York sportswriters who saw Gans winning every round after the fifth. Over a fight that should have been to his credit, Gans appears to have suffered twice from the loss, first in the record book and second in the rumor mill.

Nat Fleischer notes that there was talk of scandal surrounding this fight, implying that Gans had perhaps been instructed by his manager to fight so that the decision would go to Hawkins. In fact, it was popular referee Kelly who suffered the greater consequence from the bout. Kelly was conspicuously absent from the ring in his hometown afterward, refereeing only rarely during the next four years.[1] Fleischer said of this fight, "At times it seems that Gans was purposely refraining from doing his best, and judging by the speed with which he ended the return encounter, there may have been ample reason for such conjecture, but there was no proof that he was not trying."[2]

Gans Wins Two Brutal Bouts with Old Nemesis Dal Hawkins

The indisputable fact is that Gans used the time between the Erne fights to avenge losses on his record with definitive wins in return bouts. In his second meeting with Dal Hawkins, Gans was felled by Hawkins' potent left hook in the first round. Gans barely made the count, and as Fleischer writes, "Never before or since, with the exception of the wild first round of the Dempsey-

Firpo fight, has a scene such as this been duplicated with two great fighters taking and giving with no quarters taken and given without a letup."[3]

It was on May 25, 1900, in a torrid two rounds at the Broadway Athletic Club in New York that Gans starched Hawkins, considered at the time the hardest hitter in the lightweight division. New York reporters called it "two rounds of the fastest fighting ever seen in the clubhouse."[4] Immediately after the fighters touched gloves to begin the match, Hawkins landed a powerful left hook on Gans' chin, sending him to the floor. But Gans came to his feet at the count of nine, and was able to block Hawkins' punches. While against the ropes, Gans landed a right to Hawkins' jaw that knocked him down. Hawkins rose on the count of nine and the two fought furiously until the bell. One minute and fifteen seconds into the furious second round, Gans landed the punch that knocked his opponent out.

Their third match, at the same club on August 31, was the last boxing match fought under the Horton Law in New York. The Horton Law had legalized boxing there since 1896, under the Marquis of Queensberry rules. In their third match, Gans again knocked Hawkins "senseless" in what the papers called "three rounds of the fastest fighting ever seen in New York," the most "vicious ever fought."[5] Gans' right hook fell so hard on Hawkins' jaw that the pug was still unconscious several minutes after he was counted out and carried to his corner. The contest impressed the New York fighting crowd, and Al Herford jumped on the event and tried to strip Frank Erne of his title by boldly claiming the lightweight championship for Gans. Since Erne had "flatly refused" to meet Gans' title challenges, Herford took the initiative to claim the crown for his fighter. Herford not only claimed the title, he announced he would post $1000 forfeit money to defend the title against all comers.[6] Of course, no one in the boxing establishment took Herford's title transfer seriously.

On the same day that Gans beat Hawkins, Jim Jeffries was halfheartedly seeking to defend the heavyweight crown, complaining that he needed 30 days to prepare for a fight, but he would be willing to meet either Corbett or Fitzsimmons, only if the winner could take all, announcing that would be the only way he would do business. "As for Corbett's present standing in pugilism, I believe he can give any man a good fight.... But I do not believe it is in him to get back to the top of the ladder. Last night's was the first fight he has won in five years. When he fought Sullivan he fought an old man with a big abdomen. The men who forced Sullivan to meet him should have had their own teeth pulled out for it."[7]

In the meantime, Gans remained the top aspirant for the lightweight laurels. While waiting for another battle with Erne, Gans would have only three options for fights. He would have to fight with local boys in new territory, all of them eager to knock off a top star; boxers he had fought previously who wanted a rematch; or ring notables who, once they lost to Gans, became fighters "past their prime." One of the latter was Australian Albert Griffiths, known as Young Griffo, a man thought to be unbeatable just a few fights earlier. His rematch with Gans went only eight rounds before the referee ended the bout. Blood was streaming from Griffo's mouth from the punishment he had taken, with the press noting that Griffo was not quite in the same fighting form as before. Unlike the fight earlier Griffo praised Gans' abilities. There was no talk of a "fix." Gans had taken his new wife to this fight in New York and was trying to juggle his ring responsibilities with a new marriage. He had rented a cottage at Atlantic City for the summer.

Two days after the fight with Griffo, Whitey Lester, who had studied Gans' bout in New York, lost his bid against Gans in Baltimore on a knockout in the fourth. Gans had lost previously to New York's George "Elbows" McFadden in April of 1899, in a 23-round bout. McFadden was one of the toughest and most aggressive boxers of the time, and Gans happened to be sick during the match. Gans would go on to beat him decisively six times in other tussles, even though two of the bouts would be called draws.

Gans had opened the year 1901 by winning a $1000 purse against Cornelieus T. Moriarity, aka "Wilmington Jack Daly." Daly wanted to beat Gans to clear his own record since Gans had one decision over him and they had fought two draws. The 25-round match ended in the fifth stanza when Referee Charles White of New York disqualified Daly for dirty tactics. Gans explained that it was easier for Daly to disqualify himself than take a knockout since he did not appear to be adequately trained for the event.

Fighters were caught in a trap whenever they landed a bout-ending punch early in a fight. Spectators wanted their money's worth, which usually meant a long and bloody fight. Such was the case when Gans knocked out Martin Flaherty April 1 before a crowd of 2000 at Ford's Theater in Baltimore. The crowd yelled "April Fool!" and called the fight a fake.[8] Actually, Gans had absorbed many fouls, as he did often in his career. Flaherty started fouling in the second round when the referee, after only two minutes of fighting, sent the men to their corners and announced that "if Flaherty continued to fight foully he would be disqualified."[9] After Gans won by knockout, Herford asked if anyone wanted to come back stage and see the bleary-eyed Flaherty, who said Gans had blinded him with a punch between the eyes in the first round, and that he never fully recovered from it when Gans hit him in the jaw in the fourth. Reports filled the news space with the discovery of a woman spectator disguised as a man. She was arrested as she attempted to flee the event.

This created quite a scandal, that a woman had illegally attended an "illegal" boxing match. One of the participants in the 3-round preliminary bouts was a "colored fighter by the name of Buck Washington," the same fighter who had participated in the barrel fights in 1895. Apparently, he was still trying to make a name for himself in the fight game.[10]

At the end of May 1901, Gans had the opportunity to clear his record of the loss to Bobby Dobbs. The bout promised to be interesting. Dobbs had toured Europe and beaten some of the best men overseas, and Gans had a formidable record. Gans won by a knockout in the 7th round. But this fight was considered by many to be a fake, with Dobbs laying down to Gans. The papers noted that both Gans' wife and her sister attended the Dobbs fight. Unlike at the Flaherty fight, no one in New York seemed to object to women being in attendance.

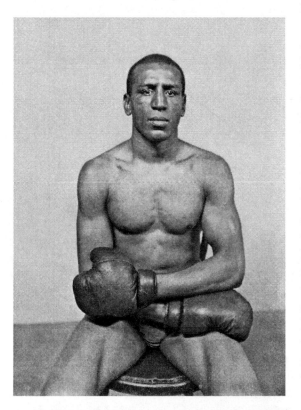

In July, Gans staked his claim to his top marquis lightweight ranking by calling on any man to beat him in a go at six rounds. In a single evening, July 15, 1901, three men took up the call: Harry Berger of Philadelphia, Jack Donahue of Philadelphia and "Kid" Thomas of New York. Each was paid a $50 appearance fee and a chance to appear at the top of the lightweight division by beating Joe Gans. None were able to do so. Gans "outclassed each of his opponents and had the better of each battle."[11] The second fight was so rough that it was halted by the police after Gans knocked

In Gans' day, prior to the modern era's readily available nutrition from cradle to grave, men were generally much smaller. Gans was called "the closest thing to a superman that the lightweight division ever produced." His magnificent body, husky in scanty briefs, made his 5'6" lightweight frame look larger. In this picture (assumed to be 1907 but probably taken in late 1900) his body still looks healthy (Chicago History Museum, Photographer: *Chicago Daily News*, 1907).

Donahue out of the ropes in the second round. Two days before these fights, the *Washington Post* printed the following account of a lynching. Such was the psychological landscape in the period when Gans fought. The account read,

> Negro Rapist Hanged: Ed Payne, the negro who attempted to rape Miss Duncan, at Dublin last June, was hanged here to-day. Payne was led on the scaffold by the Rev. Leroy Diggs, who offered prayer for the condemned man. Payne and the preacher sang a hymn. After singing, Payne talked for eight minutes, the substance of his discourse being that he had been pardoned of his sins, and was on his way to glory. Just as the black cap was being put over his head he asked to be allowed to sing one hymn, which request was granted, at the conclusion of which his hands and feet were tied, the cap put on, the noose adjusted, and, exactly at 10:30, the trap was sprung. In fifteen minutes he was pronounced dead. When the body was taken down it was placed in the coffin, and set just inside the crowd on the outside, there being several hundred present.[12]

As Frederick Douglass noted in his autobiography, "to strike a white man is death by lynch law."[13] Such was the atmosphere, where black men were hanging from ropes, in which Joe Gans would climb through the ropes for the express purpose of beating up white men in front of a white audience.

In August Gans continued his uphill battle. He fought Steve Crosby in Kentucky for the "Colored Lightweight Championship," and at the end of 20 rounds the referee declared it a draw. They met again the next month to decide the championship, but Baltimore's Deputy Marshal Farnan pulled the boxers apart from a clinch in the twelfth round and disqualified Crosby.

On September 30 when "Joe" Handler challenged the "colored champion," Gans knocked him down four times before knocking him out 2 minutes and 24 seconds into the first round. In October, Gans toyed with Dan McConnell of Philadelphia until he struck him with a stiff left jab on the forehead in the fourth round and Referee Mantz stopped the bout. Gans concluded the year in Philadelphia with a 6-round bout against Joe Youngs of Buffalo. Youngs quit after 4 rounds. Nat Fleischer writes about this time as "a veritable whirlwind of brilliant feats, tending to show with lucid clearness just what Gans could really do when he was out to win, and had the handcuffs off."[14]

It is a sad fact for posterity that the Gans-McGovern fight of December 1900, featured on many compilations of history's most controversial boxing matches, is how most people see and remember Gans. Virtually all of his other bouts are described as masterful performances or epic battles. There has been speculation that Gans not only threw the fight against McGovern, but maybe even the first Erne fight, based on promises for an "on the level" future title-shot opportunity. This speculation is consistent with what is known about the boxing world when it was run by gangsters in the middle of the twentieth century. In the movie *Raging Bull*, this is the same deal presented to Jake Lamotta. To get along, he had to go along.

A closer look at Gans' record, however, reveals that despite possible deal making he received both his title shots the old-fashioned way: he earned them. The number of bouts Gans had, against top notch fighters, during the interval between the two attempts at the title is extraordinary. Thirty-four fights, with no losses except against McGovern. Compare this with the formidable comeback of Muhammad Ali, who fought a total of seventeen bouts in the entire ten years between his title-winning efforts.

Between the years 1900 and 1902, before his second title shot, Gans fought some of the best fighters of the era. He knocked out Joe Youngs, who had only recently lost the welterweight crown, in four rounds. Dal Hawkins, Young Griffo, and Bobby Dobbs, all vicious punchers, were each put to sleep by Gans' fast mitts within the two-year period.

In his 34 fights between the two bouts with Frank Erne, Gans fought some of the roughest, best boxers the lightweight division has ever hosted. And the bouts were no mere exhibitions, but rather death struggles for an eventual chance at the ultimate prize, the lightweight title. As Nat Fleischer said, "No fighter had ever faced a tougher field in the journey to the title."[15] At the end of this journey awaited Frank Erne, considered one of the best fighters alive at the time.

9

Bringing Home the Bacon

Having fought longer and harder than any man in history to earn a professional boxing championship, Gans won his title match on May 12, 1902, quicker than anyone in the history of pugilism. By virtue of a 100-second, flash knockout of his 1900 nemesis, Frank Erne, Joe Gans ascended to the lightweight throne. Although it was a quick win, Gans had been on Erne's trail for over six years.

Erne Evades Herford

Gans was able to get a second shot at the Buffalo boy through the persistence of his manager, Al Herford, who went after Erne like a hound chasing a fox. Before the 1900 bout, Herford had waged a long battle that had become all too personal to land his charge a fight with Erne. During that time, Frank Erne was busy making a name for himself and going after the reigning title-holder Kid Lavigne. The last thing Erne had wanted was a tough opponent like Joe Gans ruining his career.

After Gans' controversial 1900 match against Erne, Gans felt entitled to a quick rematch. At a time when honoring challenges and re-matches was part of the ethical code of pugilistic conduct, Herford publicly faulted Erne for failing to live up to his word for a re-match. The betrayal had started even earlier, in Herford's eyes, back in 1896 when Erne bowed out of the fight in New York even though Gans had made the trip despite his wife's death. Instead of Gans getting a shot at Kid Lavigne, the lightweight champion, it was Erne who would go on to secure a fight and defeat the "Kid" for the lightweight title in Buffalo on July 3, 1899, a title that Herford desperately wanted for Gans.

After Erne won the title, he was reluctant to defend it. The only fighter other than Gans whose challenge he accepted was that of "New York" Jack O'Brien. The fight with O'Brien ended in a 25-round draw. With Herford's stubborn tenacity and a little help from Penn Art Athletic Club manager (a Herford associate in the venture) Walter Schlichter, the two were able to go to Buffalo and secure in December of 1899 an agreement with Erne for a title contest to be held February 10, 1900, in Philadelphia. Herford posted money for an appearance forfeiture for Gans, while Erne posted none. When the Gans contingent arrived in Philadelphia they learned that Erne had come to Philadelphia and then left without notifying the club manager. Erne had heard through the grapevine that Gans had figured out how to beat him, and he suspected trickery. With money on the table as proof of a valid challenge, Herford managed to get another shot at Erne on March 23, but Gans lost the bout because of the eye injury.

Herford pursued Erne from city to city. While Gans was fighting in Denver, he and Herford took two weeks off to travel to Buffalo to try to convince Erne to grant another match. As noted in the discussion of the Gans-McGovern fight, Herford traveled to St. Louis to see Samuel Harris and Terry McGovern to enlist their help in obtaining a rematch. It appeared that Herford and Gans returned empty handed to Denver, where in November Gans knocked out Kid Parker. An entire year went by with Herford offering enormous sums of guarantee to Erne, before Herford secured an agreement for a title fight in Buffalo. When Erne finally granted it, Herford was forced to make major financial concessions, concessions he would not soon forget.[1]

For the 1902 bout, Herford gave up much of his fighter's interest in the Articles of Agreement. When a 65/35 split of the purse was considered common practice, Erne's arrangement demanded 75 percent for the winner and 25 percent for the loser (so certain he was that Gans would lose). The guaranteed total fighter's purse was $4000. If the gate receipts exceeded $12,000 then the total purse would increase to $5000. The weight clause stipulated that the fighters would weigh in at 9:00 P.M., and their weight could not exceed 136 pounds, with the forfeiture clause for exceeding the weight limit set at 25 percent of the forfeiting party's share of the purse.

Gans' Scientific Approach for the Rematch

The press promised "one of the most stubborn and greatest boxing bouts ever witnessed in this country."[2] Because the white boxing establishment in the United States frowned upon matches between the two races, and sentiment still ran high against Gans as a result of the Chicago fiasco, the bout was held across the Niagara River from Buffalo in Fort Erie, Ontario. The threat to white superiority was too great a risk to take stateside after the immense publicity drawn when a Canadian black featherweight, George

Dixon, soundly thrashed a white opponent on the under-card of the famous Sullivan-Corbett fight in New Orleans in 1892. Sportswriters had watched and given menacing notice as a group of brilliant boxers appeared to be conquering the white field in the gay nineties, paving the way for the inflamed calls for "Great White Hopes" in the years to follow.

Statements about the fighters were in demand from both camps. Each lightweight reported having trained hard for the match. They were in exceptionally good condition and each promised not to blame any defeat on a lack of preparation. Gans was training in Leiperville, Pennsylvania, and all accounts said that he was in the best shape of his career.

Typical of Gans' method of preparation, he analyzed with precise measurement his opponent's weapons, especially those that had been successfully used against him in prior bouts. Nat Fleischer reports on Gans' strategic study of Erne in *Black Dynamite*, "Gans had noticed that Erne had a trick of feinting and drawing quickly back about twelve inches, when he would stop short and come in again with a blow. Working out with Harry Lenny in the gymnasium one day, Gans said: 'Mr. Lenny, you have a left hand like Mr. Erne. Will you keep on trying it with me? I want to sort of study out something.' The two sparred together for about a week working various left-hand leads. Then Gans said, 'I think I've got the idea now. Let a left come in for all you're worth.'

"Lenny obeyed, and quick as a flash Gans nailed him with a counter right cross to the chin. 'That's good enough,' commented Joe, as he pulled off his gloves. 'I've got Mr. Erne's number now. That lead will beat him.'"[3]

And it would, when Gans threw a perfectly timed right cross to the point of Erne's chin.

Fight Night in Fort Erie and Baltimore

Joe Gans arrived on Saturday, May 10, 1902, in Buffalo, New York, with his manager and corner men, Young Peter Jackson and Herman Miller. The group stayed in Buffalo until fight time.

Erne worked out with his close friend Frank Zimpfer. Also in attendance at his training quarters on Rose Street was the middleweight wrestling champion of Buffalo, Jack Kreiger, and George Halce, boxer and trainer. Erne had won his title from Lavigne in the city of Buffalo, but the bout with the black fighter Gans had to be held in nearby Fort Erie, Canada. Erne spoke to reporters: "You can see the condition I am in. I expect to win and I will win." Erne announced his strategy, "I will not say I will throw science to the winds that night, but I will go after Mr. Gans from the ringing of the gong. I am going to get to his stomach and will win by whipping him there. I don't care to say anything further regarding my plans."[4] During the interview, Erne was handed a telegram from Charles "Kid" McCoy stating that he would be "in his corner" at ringside.

On Saturday the odds were 10 to 9 in favor of Gans.

On Sunday trains from every destination began bringing "sporting men" to Buffalo from New York, Chicago, Boston, Philadelphia, Baltimore, and Detroit. Erne emerged from his residence at the Cottage Hotel with his handlers that evening after eating a big supper and greeted well-wishers.

The International Athletic Club's new venue accommodated 5,000 and nearly all the seats were taken by noon, Monday, the day of the fight.

Back in Baltimore the stage was set at the Germania Maennerchor Hall, where Al Herford had arranged to have a direct wire of the 20-round championship bout sent from ringside to the club. He had also arranged two bouts in Baltimore for May 12. The first was between Jimmy Farren and Johnny Leckner, the winner to fight top contender Tommy Feltz. The second was between Kid Monahan and Johnnie Smith for the chance to box Dan Dougherty, Terry McGovern's sparring partner.

Local chit-chat in Baltimore that evening centered around a more local fight that had taken place in Cumberland, Maryland, the previous night between Jack Bolan and Denver's George Strong. Jack Bolan was a hearty character. Although Bolan had recently been beaten by Kid Sullivan of Washington, he managed to win a blood-bath with Strong in the fifth round. However, the punishment he meted out was not the talk of the evening. What was remarkable was that Bolan had won the match after being stabbed in the back in a brawl earlier in the week. Few in the smoky entertainment hall, however, came for the on-site fights or the local boxing news. The fans were there for one primary reason: to hear the round by round telegraph report of the world's championship bout from Canada. Back in Fort Erie at 8:30, Ed MacBride was introduced as referee for the 8-round preliminary. The fight between Joe McMahon and Eddie Kelley, 118-pounders, was ordered halted in the 4th round by Fort Erie Police Chief Griffin. As a result, referee MacBride called the bout a draw. Guests and boxing luminaries at ringside were then introduced. Terry McGovern, who held wins over both of the warriors slated for the title event, was there with his manager Sammy Harris. McGovern's money was known to be on Gans.

At 9:35 Gans entered the ring, followed by Erne. When Gans walked to ring center to shake Erne's hand, an immense cheer erupted from the crowd, so highly anticipated was the moment.

At 9:45 referee Charley White of New York was introduced. The Athletic Club had originally offered him only $100 to referee the marquis event.

For the "Fight of the Century" against Battling Nelson in Goldfield, Nevada, Gans' mother sent a telegram to ringside telling her son to "bring back the bacon." The phrase took on its own celebrity with spectators expecting the famous telegram prior to subsequent Gans events. This grotesque caricature of Gans and his mother mocking the famous telegrams that coined the phrase was printed in the *San Francisco Examiner* in September 1907 as part of the racially charged, pre-fight publicity for the Gans-Britt match.

What he actually re-ceived was something between that figure and the $250 he had requested. White called the boxers to the center of the ring to explain the Canadian interpretation of the rules of the famed Marquis of Queensberry. "No holding and hitting, nor hitting while in clinches...."[5]

One-Punch Knockout

Back in Baltimore, Gans' wife tried to enter the Maennerchor Hall to hear the telegraphed report, but she was denied entrance. She waited for news by the door. Inside sporting fans faced an empty ring on stage and listened intently when the report began:

> Round 1— They came out and sparred away briskly. Gans led his left for the face twice, but missed. Then he led with both hands for the face. Erne ducked and they clinched. Then Erne tried his left, but it was too high. He next tried a straight left but the shifty Gans side-stepped.
>
> There was a slight mix-up and Gans had the better of it. When they got out of the mix Gans sent his right to the ear hard. There was a quick exchange, when the Baltimore boy sent both hands to head, and Erne looked dazed.
>
> Gans now felt out his opponent with a left punch to the face, drawing blood from Erne's nose. Erne seemed fully dazed now and Gans rushed in and banged his right plump on Erne's jaw.
>
> Frank fell slowly to the floor with mouth and nose bleeding. He rolled over on his abdomen and was counted out before he could attempt to regain his feet. The time of the round: 1 minute and 40 seconds.[6]

The crowd back at Maennerchor Hall cheered wildly, many in disbelief that the match could be over in such short order. While there were a few hisses, the cheers overwhelmed the room for over a minute. A black spectator rushed out to give Mrs. Gans the good news. She left overjoyed.

After fighting longer and harder than any man in history to earn a chance at the title, Gans won it swiftly. Having studied Erne's habit of feinting with his left jab and pulling back his head to avoid a counter, Gans had practiced the timing of his own power shots. When Erne started this move early in the first round, Gans fired a crushing right to where he knew Erne's chin would be. The fight was over with one perfect punch!

The fight was short. Erne's defense was described the next day in the papers as "pitiably weak."[7] Gans' left punch through Erne's guard allowed him to land his right on the jaw and Erne sank to the floor. After this fight it was Gans who was pleasantly surprised: "Of course, I did not expect to win so quickly," Gans said, "But I believe the end would have been the same had the fight gone much further."[8] At ringside the Herford party was inundated by excited fans.

After being led to his corner the former title-holder was still in a daze. When Erne came out of his stupor, he cried, shocked by the sudden defeat. The comments collected by the press that evening sounded very much like those heard in the previous Erne-Gans bout, only this time the tables were turned.

Unlike the first fight with Erne when Gans left in disgrace the next morning, or the McGovern fight where he had to appear in court the morning after the fight, on the day following this victory, Gans was given a hero's welcome:

an automobile ride through Buffalo. Joining him in the victory drive were Terry McGovern, Sam Harris, and referee Charley White. (No one has commented on the strange friendship struck between Gans and McGovern. Obviously they seem to have become good friends after Chicago, despite the hysteria of the "fixed fight." Whatever deal had been struck was one Gans took to his grave.)

Al Herford was not in the celebration party. He was busy entertaining bids from potential contenders to the newly won title, making statements to the sportswriters, and self-righteously listing demands to Erne's management. Herford told reporters, "Erne is very anxious for a return match now. I will give him a dose of his own medicine, as he dictated the terms when he held the title." Wanting to make sure everyone knew who was in command of any possible Erne re-match, he added, "Now as Gans is the champion he must do as we say. The purse must be divided on the 75 per cent and 25 per cent basis." Like a barker at the biggest fair in the country, Herford had a captive audience and was back to his cigar-chomping sales pitch, "First come, first served. So all you lightweights who have aspirations to become champions here is your chance."[9] Gans' victory and Herford's invitation would be printed in papers across the country.

At Last a Champion

Finally, Gans had his title and with his share of the purse could afford to buy a piece of property. Gans' share, after expenses, was split 50/50 with his manager, an arrangement made between the two from the beginning of their relationship. They had also agreed to split Herford's bets, both wins and losses. It was estimated at the time that from this fight the two split a little over $9,000, a total from the purse and the bets. And the title was a valuable commodity in itself, enabling future exhibitions and higher guaranteed purses.

Newspaper reporters were quick to point out that in less than two minutes, Gans had made more than the annual salary of the president of the United States, more per minute even than John D. Rockefeller. The press had so much fun with the elaborate financial evaluations that they occupied several column inches in the *Baltimore Sun*. Included at the end of the article was a chart comparing John to Joe, the first "badly dyspeptic," the other "can digest broken bottles." Unlike Rockefeller, Gans was "not too proud to speak to anyone."[10] While tongue in cheek, the lengthy comparison was an illustration of how the color barrier could be broken. For the first time in the history of Gans' news coverage, the Baltimore fighter was seen outside a racial context. The color of money had put the champion on a pedestal, in the same hallowed realm as the president of the United States and alongside one of the wealthiest men in the world.

When Gans' mother told him to "bring home the bacon," it stood for more than just providing for his loved ones. By ushering in a future filled with opportunity for black athletes of generations to come, Gans would be, as he stated in his famous telegraph to his mother in 1906, "bringing home the bacon with lots of gravy on it."[11]

There are expressions that bespeak the heart of a generation. America circa 1900 was not yet a preeminent power and was still in search in many ways of a national identity. So when a celebrity boxer would say something that captured the mood at the time in a catchphrase, it would become exceedingly popular. When the newspapers said that the fans had seen the "Real McCoy" after one of Kid McCoy's great bouts, the phrase caught on in no small part because of the trickery that was so ingrained in the American experience during the Gilded Age, and a longing among the people for something earnest. The Vietnam era echoed a similar sentiment when a soft drink called itself "the real thing." While few today are aware of the origin of the phrase "bring home the bacon," it goes to the core of what it means to be a provider in America, where the stakes are so high and the world so uncertain.

When Gans returned to Baltimore and the Eureka Athletic Club, a large photograph of Frank Erne had been draped in black "crepe." Gans' canvas belt, embroidered with small American flags and the letters "J.G.," lay prominently across the desk. It was left behind for fear that it might be a bad luck charm, associated as it was with the first Erne fight. But in the final determination Gans' boxing skills were what mattered. Science had beaten superstition.

Joe Gans had made history, becoming the first African-American–born world titleholder. He had legitimately earned the praises of the world, but what he wanted to regain most was the love and respect of his fellow Baltimoreans. And to show his devotion to his birthplace, he would bring the lightweight belt home. When hometown reporters asked him how it felt to be the world's greatest lightweight fighter, he said, "I hope the Baltimore public will take kindly to me now. I am anxious to fight Erne or the best man the club can get to meet me in this city."[12]

But Frank Erne would not fight Gans again or anyone else in America. Instead, Erne went to London for one last fight and then on to Paris, where he helped to train the first generation of French boxers.

Joe Gans had finally crossed the color barrier. He stood atop the fistic world. He had won well over 100 bouts, most by knockout. Even before he won the championship, sportswriters had called him the "Old Master." But his greatest deeds were still ahead.

10

Defending the Championship: A Gentleman and a Gladiator

Socrates: "And do you suppose, Adeimantus, that a single boxer who was perfect in his art would easily be a match for two stout and well-to-do gentlemen who were not boxers?"
— *Ancient Greece, 5th Century B.C.*

As historian Nat Fleischer wrote, "No man ever conquered a tougher field than did Gans in winning his title." He could have added that no man ever conquered a tougher field than Joe Gans when defending his title.[1]

Gans Wins Acceptance in Jim Crow America

Gans defended his championship title against the world's best, usually in their hometowns. He never put his crown on the shelf as was customary in his time, and indeed during much of the twentieth century. Muhammad Ali, the most popular of recent champions, traveled the world defending his championship against the best heavyweights of every country. While Ali was a true "world champion," Gans was the original traveling champion who took on all comers.

By 1902 Joe Gans was the headline attraction throughout America — the man to beat. In a few years Jack Johnson would draw the spotlight to the heavyweight division, but for now the so-called "questions" about ability and character surrounded Joe Gans. "The quick defeat of Erne astounded the boxing world for Erne was rated among the truly greats of fistiana."[2] Would the American public accept the fact that Gans was really that good?

From Reconstruction to World War II, newspapers consistently illustrated America's conflicting attitudes toward blacks. Reportorial admiration for the skills developed by the black fighter appeared next to denigrating cartoon figures, perhaps masking an underlying fear that exceptional physical abilities might be racially inherent. Darwin's theory of evolution and natural selection upset Victorian thinking but took scientific, literary, and popular thinking by storm. Wild imaginings and frail logic helped to fan flames of fear between the races, especially the notion that one race could, over time, develop superiority to another. Black champions like Gans, Dixon, Langford, and Jack Johnson to come, were super men — physically superior to their white competition, and this challenged prevailing attitudes of the establishment and its hope for white supremacy in the new century.

Cartoons about Gans appeared in newspapers around the country from the 1890s through 1942. Ty Cobb, sports editor of *The Nevada State Journal* in Reno, titled his lead story of September 27, 1942, "The Greatest Fighter Who Ever Lived? This Writer Lauds Joe Gans, Old Master." While the story proclaims Gans as the greatest, a pen-and-ink sketch under the headline reminds the modern reader of popular thinking at the time. The cartoon-like sketch tells a different story of the black athlete, one that illustrates that the black super-athlete evolved from some monkey-like form. Pictured are two figures: one strolls inside a Greco-Roman–styled Hall of Fame. The champion is depicted with a jaw larger than his skull, arms stretched below his knees, awkward and inhuman. Next to this picture is a more realistic sketch of Gans. His face is serious, his chin and jaw smaller than the crown of his head, with his shoulders and muscles befitting those of a boxer. The drawing is captioned with: "We is all jus' natchally inclined champions!" The implication is that Gans would say something like this.

Although Gans had little formal education, quotes from newspaper interviews indicate that he was highly articulate, especially when compared to many of the fighters of his day. Newspapers did try to capture the voice of the fighter, but no paper ever quoted Gans using such vaudeville-styled diction as that above. Gans spoke in lucid, complete sentences. The same newspaper that had called him a "coon" quotes Gans responding to the outcome of the Walcott fight: "What's the use of complaining? Mr. Welch says it was a draw. I refuse to express my opinion concerning the decision. I think it ... well, I won't say what. I wasn't hurt at all and could have gone on for another twenty rounds. The only punches that hurt me were those that Mr. Walcott drove into my ribs."[3]

Sportswriter Bill Moran says of the group of black boxers, "In proportion to their numbers, the Negroes have produced a larger percentage of great fighters than any other race. Today, the greatest box office attraction is Joe

Louis. And it has always been that way: when a Negro was good he was really good."[4] He goes on to point to Tom Molineaux, a bare-knuckle fighter, born a slave in Virginia but considered by many an English boxer, followed by George Dixon, Joe Walcott, and Jack Johnson, as being great boxers. But the "daddy of them all," Moran writes, is Joe Gans.

Gans Scores Knockout Per Month — and Four Title Defenses in 1902

In addition to the pride that comes with owning a title at the top of a professional rung is the ability to "cash in" on being the champion. The book about former heavyweight champion James J. Braddock, "Cinderella Man," explains matter-of-factly how Braddock's income soared into the stratosphere during his brief rein as champion, as he fought exhibitions and made appearances without risking his hard-won title. Defending a world boxing title is a notoriously risky proposition. A champion faces his stiffest competition when a title is on the line. After training long, hard days for the occasion, the challenger comes full of fight and determination to take the meat from the lion's jaws. As a result, many title-holders are reluctant to accept title challenges. Gans was lucky to get a chance at Erne. In 1903 heavyweight champion Jim Jeffries defended his title only once, and middleweight champion Tommy Ryan avoided his rivals for the crown all year. Championships came at such a price and were such a valued commodity that title challenges were difficult and costly to arrange. But unlike many, Gans didn't rest on his laurels. He was a fighting champion from the get-go, not only defending his lightweight crown several times per year, but also during this time taking on and defeating bigger, heavier men in non-title fights on a routine basis.

Before he could defend his title, he had to defend the integrity of his title win. It was not easy for the sporting public to accept Gans as champion or to let go of Erne's glory. Some San Franciscans considered his championship win a "fake," in line with the many other "fakes" they accused him of perpetrating, which they claimed invalidated the title. All the talk about Gans during his career as a faker would help to stigmatize him throughout history.

It was as if reporters were trying to rewrite history by casting aspersions on this and previous fights, and in doing so bring the championship title back to its rightful, white owner by nullifying Gans' achievements. Using a backhanded logic to attack Gans' integrity and skill, sportswriters said that the title fight with Erne was supposed to have been a fake and that Gans didn't play fairly by not faking! They said the fight with Erne had proven that Gans couldn't keep his word, and that by tricking Erne he had gained claim to the crown crookedly. "It was a breech of faith on the part of Gans that he turned what was scheduled to have been a defeat into a victory."[5] The paper said that it "was vouched" (source unnamed, of course) that Gans had agreed to go out and by his *not* doing so, Erne was caught off guard in the first round and was "given the double cross." It appeared Gans couldn't win public opinion even when he won the match.

After winning the title from Erne, Gans would go from coast to coast, and up to Canada to take on four of the toughest fighters in the division: George "Elbows" McFadden, Rufe Turner, Gus Gardner and William "Kid" McPartland. The June 27, 1902, bout with New Yorker "Elbows" McFadden at Woodward's Pavilion in San Francisco would cement public opinion if Elbows won. The fight was Gans' seventh with McFadden, but McFadden was always remembered as the only lightweight to have knocked out the great "Kid" Lavigne. The odds in favor of Gans, called the "subtle negro" in the local paper, were 10 to 7.[6] The initial question looming over the fight was whether or not Gans could make the weight and how much strength he would have if he did make it. After his morning training run the day before the fight, Gans weighed 136½ pounds. McFadden was already under the 133-pound weight limit at 131.

When the betting odds fell from the opening 10 to 4 in the pool halls the afternoon of the McFadden fight, people argued that something no good was afoot. Apparently, no one at the time saw the irony of the comments that appeared side by side with the description of the rough and tumble fight. It made no difference that the round-by-round coverage of the fight in the city's own paper indicated that Gans carried the day with a flurry of pin-point blows. In the first round after a few moments of sparring, Gans landed a strong right on McFadden's jaw. And in swift succession, a series of lefts and rights to the challenger's head left him wobbling until he slipped to the floor. Gans then unleashed his rapid-fire short arm punches to the head that caused McFadden's eyes to roll, leaving him in a state that made him look either drunk or doped. In the second round when a groggy McFadden was unable to land a punch, and Gans had made "a succession of lefts and rights on the head," the crowd yelled "fake."[7] In the third round Gans landed a "hard right" to the side of McFadden's head that sent him to the floor. And when he rose, Gans hit him again with a "hard right cross" to the jaw that caused Mac's seconds to throw in the sponge.

Which interpretation of the fight stands up to reason? Round-by-round reports of the fight shown in San Francisco papers are not significantly different from those in Baltimore. The papers indicate that Gans' blows landed solidly. There would have been also no financial incentive for a contract between the two fighters to stage a fake. Little money was bet on the fight by anyone. Gans would have no financial incentive to risk his title if he didn't intend to win. And McFadden had every financial incentive to win the title and all the benefits that went with it.

Efforts in the Press to Discredit Gans

In a concerted effort to discredit Gans, reporters cried "Sold again!" when Gans won the bout.[8] The moral attitude taken by the papers was that the fight had robbed statesmen, politicians, and athletic supervisors of the $5 ringside ticket price, and the poor sporting public who paid $1.50 to sit at the back could little afford to throw their money away. In the afternoon before the fight, rumor had it that McFadden was planning to "go out." But rumors of a fake surrounded nearly every fight then. Jimmy and his brother-manager Billy Britt were at ringside and Jimmy said he would like to take on Gans, "if he were only white."[9] His brother commented that Jimmy could take on both simultaneously and win.

Even the preliminary bout involving Gans' sparring partner and chief second, Herman Miller, was called into question by the press. Apparently it was like a bar-room brawl, quite pleasing to the crowd, until the fourth round when Miller wrestled the local San Franciscan to the ground and the referee gave the fight to Miller. The paper noted that Baltimore Police Captain Anderson quickly jumped into the ring, somehow causing referee "Handsome" McDevitt to change his decision and give the fight to Lewis. What seemed like pre-arranged wins for the Baltimore contingent that day caused the sportswriters to say that actions like these proved Gans' "shady" past.[10]

This was the era of the big con, which included the "rag," the "wire," and the "pay-off," all scams involving sports betting.[11] Boxing had no corporate sponsors or cable television financiers— it was fueled by gambling, to a large extent. In this context, the public often viewed prize fighting as a con game, a view especially convenient when the champion was a black man. Although confidence games are as American as apple pie, Joe Gans was the real deal, as proven by the frequent defenses of his title. Ironically, his image was continually besmirched and he became known as a consummate "faker."

Gans won his next three bouts decisively. In Oakland, he beat Rufe Turner of Stockton in 15 rounds and afterwards remained on the West Coast to see the Fitzsimmons-Jeffries battle. In September Gans made his first appearance in Baltimore as the world champion, against Gus Gardner. It was a cause for celebration for the spectators and concern for Gans. He had left his trusted friend and sparring partner Herman Miller in San Francisco, where Miller was fighting. Gans was not familiar with Gardner and was very worried about his ability to get adequate training for this fight. He had tried local sparring partners, but after a few rounds with Gans, they both quit. Some said that this would be an easy fight for Gans, but all of Philadelphia believed that their man could beat him.

The contender for the eight-round contest proved no match for Gans, although the champion certainly didn't know that beforehand. Fans came from all walks of life to watch Gans "bring the title home to Baltimore." With over 4,000 fans, the Baltimore Music Hall was stuffed to capacity with politicians, merchants, professionals, and the Maryland horseracing crowd. When Gardner failed to make the weight requirement before the match, manager Al Herford came into the ring and announced that the bout would not be considered a title fight. The crowd showed their displeasure, but was, never-

theless, anxious to see the champion fight. Reporters at the match said Gans could have put Gardner out in the first round if he had wanted to, but he let it go to the fifth. "Gans played with his man for three rounds, touched him up a bit in the fourth and then went in and knocked him out, an act that he could have done in any one of the rounds."[12] It was said that this was some of the easiest money that New York referee Charley White ever earned on a fight.

On October 12, 1902, in Fort Erie, Ontario, with odds on Gans 2 to 1, Gans knocked out William Lawrence "Kid" McPartland in the fifth round

Gans appears in his evening attire. As H.L. Mencken stated, "His manners were those of a lieutenant of the guards in old Vienna" (Chicago History Museum, Photographer: *Chicago Daily News*, 1907).

in what was to have been a twenty-rounder. Gans did the trick with opponent McPartland's signature punch, a left hook to the stomach. Gans let McPartland, who was two inches taller, do most of the fighting, picking off his punches with lightning speed and scientific precision. It was said that in the entire battle McPartland was able to land only eight solid blows. Gans dropped him in the third round with a straight right to the jaw. Gans' sparring partner Herman Miller lost his preliminary battle to Warren Zurbrick in seven rounds. What ties this match to the next one is their close proximity in time. The morning after this bout, Gans got on the train and headed for Lancaster, Pennsylvania, for a fight that night with Dave Holly of Woodbury, New Jersey. This would be unheard of today. For one thing, the ring physicians would not permit it. The Holly bout was a ten-round fight called a "no-decision." Pennsylvania law held that anything other than a knockout was ruled "no-decision." The newspapers, however, called it a win for Gans.

Gans opened the New Year by giving Gus Gardner, his 1902 rival, another shot at the title, again fighting only one day after a previous bout. On December 31, 1902, Gans had fought Charley Seiger in Boston and then gone on to New Britain for the title match. Gans won the Boston match against Seiger in ten rounds and said he would have won sooner if it were not for the fact that he had to wear 8 oz. gloves. In most of his title fights he used 5 oz. gloves. Gans soundly defeated Gardner in the New Year's Day fight in New Britain, Connecticut. Gans struck no blows in the first two rounds. As in many of his fights, he simply used the first rounds to size up his opponent, parrying his victim's jabs and smothering his punches. Gans began attacking the body in the third round, and while Gardner looked for openings for his punches, they landed only occasionally. By the seventh round Gardner was fading. In the eighth he went down on his knee. In the eleventh round, when he realized he was about to be knocked out, he intentionally fouled Gans by tripping him with his knee. Because the referee had given Gardner two prior warnings about this behavior, he awarded the match to Gans. Some of the gamblers were pleased in that Gardner was able to stay ten rounds with the champion — allowing them to win some of the side bets.

Gans' next title defense was scheduled to be with Steve Crosby of Louisville, Kentucky, on September 27 at a private club, the Chicago Athletic Association. Because "protests came in a storm when the booking was known," public opinion being against Gans since the McGovern bout two years earlier, the match in Chicago was cancelled and Gans was banned from ever boxing there again.[13] Gans, however, would return to Chicago in 1910, where his appearance would attract a large and devoted following, but it would on his deathbed, where he would be carried like royalty on his stretcher.

Al Herford rescheduled the Crosby fight to March 11 at Hot Springs, Arkansas. The fans got a good show for their money, seeing two champions in the ring: Gans, the lightweight champion, and Tommy Ryan, the middleweight champion, serving as referee. Gans came out fighting, and Crosby's form was admirable but no match for the champion's, who in the eighth round knocked the contender through the ropes. Crosby repeatedly fell in the ring, and in the eleventh round, his seconds threw in the sponge.

America during Gans' Championship Reign

What did America look like when Gans reigned as champion? Teddy Roosevelt, nicknamed the "Trust Buster" for his actions against the abuses committed by corporate conglomerates, was president during what would later be called the Progressive Era. And yet a casual perusal of the periodicals of the time indicates that Jim Crow laws dominated the lives of black Americans. Lynchings of African Americans were reported in the papers as casually as the weather. Booker T. Washington had founded Tuskegee Institute. The school taught that blacks should "cast down their buckets" in society as it existed, emphasizing industrial education over political empowerment. In 1903, W.E.B. Du Bois wrote *The Souls of Black Folk*, which made a bold case that economic gains were ephemeral without access to political rights. And all through the strife and rhetoric, Joe Gans was showing the world what a man could accomplish with determination, hard work, and courage. Having mowed down the field of seasoned lightweight challengers, Gans took on the younger fighters of his day.

By May of 1903 Gans was on the West Coast again, fighting Tom Tracey in Portland, Oregon, before going down to San Francisco to fight Willie Fitzgerald on May 29. Once again, sportswriters discounted the champion. W. W. Naughton of the *San Francisco Examiner* claimed that Brooklyn fighter Willie Fitzgerald would have a "royal chance" with Gans, in that he was younger, gamer, could endure punishment, and had great punching ability.[14] He said he was simply pointing out the fact that Gans had both won and lost against Erne and McFadden and that Gans had only beaten them when they were in their decline. Further proof of this point was that they had been beaten before and after Gans had gained his victories over them. Despite the implications in the news that Gans was shot, the betting odds were still 2 to 1 with few takers on Fitzgerald's side.

On the day of the Gans-Fitzgerald fight, Al Herford issued a novel challenge that caused quite a start in the papers. He challenged Jimmy Britt. The idea of a world champion's manager issuing a challenge to another fighter was a complete novelty. But then, no one ever accused Al Herford of being a man to follow protocol. Actually, Herford had something up his sleeve for later in October. Herford was looking for big money for the fight he was about to arrange.

The morning of the Fitzgerald fight the odds had risen to 10 to 4 on Gans, and Naughton's pen was no longer flaming. The veteran editor of Hearst's San Francisco newspaper was supportive of Gans in his report, almost extolling his career: "The sporting public evidently regards Gans as a sure winner. He is the lightweight champion of the world and the hero of hundreds of battlers. Despite all that has been said about his drawn face and his "ribby" appearance, he is in tip-top shape.... Gans is known to be one of the headiest fighters in the ring. He is particularly clever at blocking blows and never overlooks a chance for a telling smash. He can hurt a man from short range and always takes things easily and bides his time. He is one of the greatest artists in the world at handling headstrong or impetuous opponents. Joe's record is little short of voluminous. Every year since 1894 a sufficient number of battles are jammed into the story of his life to warrant the suspicion that training with him has been a continuous performance."[15] With Pinkerton men guarding the ring, Gans entered Mechanic's Pavilion with his face drawn and his ribs visibly showing. So it came as a total surprise when Gans was overweight at the agreed upon weight limit of 135 pounds. No one knew if the fight would go forward. Manager Weedon for Fitzgerald and Herford for Gans haggled over the situation until almost eleven P.M., when Herford finally agreed to let Gans go into the ring and split the purse 50/50. They would each make $3000 regardless of who won.

Fitzgerald began in fine form but was soon outclassed by Gans' expertise. The sixth round saw frenzied activity, but Fitzgerald took a wicked blow to his left eyebrow that caused the blood to flow. He tried to punch inside the clinches, but in the tenth round he was socked on the jaw and fell to the mat. The next day, Willie Fitzgerald issued this statement: "Gans got me before I got him. That is the luck of the game. He won a clean, honest victory and deserves all the credit he can get."[16]

The fourth of July in America was one of the most decorated and celebrated holidays of the year. Independence Day, Labor Day, Christmas and New Year's were among the few days that workers were allowed off. These days were highly anticipated and, except for Christmas, usually filled with parades, civic fanfare, and to cap it off, a round of boxing. With the popularity of the sport increasing, athletic clubs competed for the services of the coveted boxers during these major holidays.

Gans' last lightweight title fight of 1903 would be on the Fourth of July in Butte, Montana. The city was celebrating the patriotic holiday with a week's worth of festivities that included parades, troubadours, a terpsichorean artist, and the finest lady singers that could be found to entertain in Montana (which included the "Voluptuous Queen" Nellie McPherson). But the granddaddy of events was three days of boxing, ending on the 4th with a world title contest: champion Joe Gans against Denver's Buddy King. The inclusion of the boxing event was hyped even more because it was expected to put an end to the sport in Butte due to all the bickering among the various clubs. Even though the *Butte Miner* predicted a "fast" fight between the two boxers, at the end of the three-day-boxing festival, the fact that the dominant fighters so outclassed their opponents (Joe Walcott had fought the day before Gans) caused the celebration to be called a "triple farce comedy" and "unequal and uninteresting."[17]

The day before Gans' fight, his customary training bout, a 10-rounder (always described as "rough") with his cornerman Young Peter Jackson was well attended by the fight fans. The day of the fight at Reilly and Mackey's Liquor store, King failed to meet the 136-pound weight limit and forfeited his $250. The bell rang for the first round at 3:20 in the afternoon. The fighters came together and began sizing each other up, which was not uncommon in the championship ring, with the fighters sparring with steamless light blows. Suddenly, the referee stopped the fight and warned the participants that the crowd had come to see a fight, and that they had better "go in and fight."[18] By the end of the first round, Gans had drawn the first blood. In the second and subsequent rounds Gans used his strong right to the body and short left hook to the jaw to knock King to the floor. Gans played it cool in the third, while King, encouraged by the crowd, attempted to mix it up at close range.

That afternoon Gans' ring deportment, which had always been considered calm, would be tested. In the fourth round someone in the crowd, more than likely inebriated, and certainly without good judgment (considering the town had assembled one of the mightiest contingents of the world's best boxers) yelled, "Fake!" Gans had been forced over the course of his career to answer to this cry, and the constant reminder of his reputation for fakery had begun to wear on him. Gans paused, and "invited the man who made the remark to step in the ring with him and he would show him a thing or two about faking." In the crowd was Joe Walcott, and accusations against Walcott for "fakery" had been even more stinging than those assigned to Gans. Lou Houseman of Chicago had written that "Walcott is one of the worst fakers in the business."[19] Walcott, who had fought the previous evening, Friday, July 3, had been accompanied to Butte by his chief second—future heavyweight Jack Johnson. Walcott wasn't going to sit there and see his fellow fighter heckled. So as the *Miner* reported, Walcott "then 'butted in' and offered to lick any man in the crowd."[20] The spectator was silenced, sitting amid three of the men whom Nat Fleischer considered the greatest fighters of all time.[21] As the newspaper noted, by the fourth round Gans had decided "that the crowd had its money's worth ... and started in to do his man up."[22] Gans proceeded to plant lightning fast jolts on King's face, although several vicious swings missed. It was over for King by the fifth round when the referee counted ten.

Thirteen Wins in 1904

Gans fought Fitzgerald again in January of 1904, and by then sportswriters began to feel that Gans could be beaten. Of the six titleholders in the various weight divisions, Gans was the one the sportswriters predicted would lose his title in the year to come. In early January, a headline read, "Is Joe Gans in Danger? Experts Beginning to Figure that He Can Be Beaten in His Class."[23] And the *New York Morning Telegraph* noted that Gans was near "All-in": "Gans has shown that he is on the wane. A great lightweight, this coffee-colored fellow — the greatest that ever shoved his hand into a glove."[24]

The fight was held in Detroit, and high hopes rested on Fitzgerald's ability to bring the title back to Brooklyn. It had previously been held by Jack McAuliffe of Brooklyn. While Fitzgerald landed a vicious blow to Gans' stomach that slowed his momentum in the fifth round and landed a punch to his jaw in the ninth, it was Gans' short right to the jaw that brought Fitzgerald down in the first, and hammered his ribs over the course of the fight to give him control.

Gans went on to make a total of 17 title defenses in the lightweight division, while also gaining weight and fighting heavier men. At this point in his career, sportswriters and other boxing experts were still assessing Gans' place in history, calling him the greatest lightweight fighter of all time. In 1904 he fought and won "newspaper decisions" against all-time greats Jack Blackburn and Joe Walcott.

Before Gans' reign as lightweight champion, successful title defenses were rare occurrences in the boxing world. Since a champion, especially a white one, could earn a living making appearances and exhibitions, he had no incentive to risk his valuable title. But Gans defended his title regularly, and in the process brought a renewed interest and respectability to the sport.

Most contemporary historians of boxing's lightweight division indicate that Gans relinquished the title in 1904 to pursue welterweight laurels in California. In fact, Gans never relinquished his lightweight title. However, it is true that he continued to take on heavier fighters, winning, in the opinions of many, the welterweight crown. One month before he battled Jimmy Britt on October 1904, he had traveled to San Francisco, where boxers were re-creating the lore of the Wild West for the new century.

11

Stolen Title

Attempts to discredit Gans and deprive him of his rightful place in fistiana accelerated after he had eliminated all of the lightweight contenders and even outfought the reigning welterweight champ, "Barbados" Joe Walcott. Fleischer writes of the late-round action, "Walcott was almost finished when a powerful smash to the jaw put him into distress. Gans battered him about the ring. The Baltimore Wonder outfought his opponent landing blow after blow with telling effect. The decision of the referee was hissed and hooted when he called the bout a draw."[1]

From 1902 to 1904 Gans fought three all-time greats of higher poundage than that carried by the Old Master: Walcott, Langford, and Jack Blackburn. His three-bout series provided some of the cleverest exhibitions of gloved fighting ever seen. In their title match Gans won a fifteen-round decision over the taller and heavier Blackburn. "In the last two sessions Gans was lightning fast of hand and feet. Cunningly, he took advantage of every opportunity offered him. He showed the material of which champions are made. At the final gong the crowd favored Gans, but no decision was rendered."[2] Blackburn, who gained later fame as the teacher of Joe Louis, spent long hours complaining to the press that Gans was avoiding him, even though they had fought three times.

Gans' performances against these all-time greats not only failed to gain for him laurels at welterweight, they started a controversy over the Old Master's claim to the lightweight throne. One of the many instances in which history has mistreated Gans is that the record books show someone else holding the lightweight championship from 1904 to 1906. Nat Fleischer, in particular, said that Gans "forfeited" his title to Jimmy Britt.[3] Unfortunately, a reissue of the *Ring Record Book*, compiled by others after Nat Fleischer died, perpetuates the notion that Gans relinquished his crown in 1904 after the Britt fight. Record books and other brief biographies that indicate Gans did not hold the lightweight title between 1904 and 1906 usually explain that he regained the title when he beat Battling Nelson in September of 1906. As of this printing, the official record book for the International Boxing Hall of Fame indicates a skip in Gans' lightweight title reign between 1904 and 1906, explaining that Gans "relinquished the lightweight title to fight Walcott, though in some quarters he still was considered the titleholder."[4] The Walcott fight was a month prior to the Britt fight in 1904 and Gans was, by all newspaper accounts, still called the lightweight champion going into the lightweight fight with Britt; clearly this is an unfortunate error. However, the word "relinquished" in the hall-of-fame record book, and in other accounts by writers who quote the error, whitewashes the fact that the title was virtually stolen from him.

In the summer of 2004, boxing historian Monte Cox proved beyond a doubt in his meticulously researched ring results for the years in question (1904–1906) that Gans never lost a title defense, and as a result, historical records should reflect his lineal championship from 1902 through 1908. Furthermore, his comprehensive research points to the fact that newspaper accounts (with the opinion of the press holding court) going into and including the Gans-Nelson fight (Cox quotes the *Police Gazette*, the *Boston Globe*, the *Chicago Record–Herald*, the *New York Times*, and the *Washington Post*) considered Gans the champion going into the fight and Nelson the "challenger" to the lightweight title.[5] So what happened that caused record books to veer from standard historical practice and press reportage to crown as Gans' "successor" the loser of his 1904 match with Jimmy Britt?

Many record books simply assert without explanation that James Britt became the world lightweight champion. Others attempt to support Britt's erroneous claim to the title by stating incorrectly that:

- Gans gave up the title to fight in the welterweight division,
- Gans couldn't make, in the lightweight division, 133 pounds,
- Gans refused to fight Britt in a return challenge, or that
- Britt made a better showing in his bout against Gans, "proving that he was Gans' master."

Of course, none of these explanations ring true. One newspaper, however, is key to understanding what really happened between 1904 and 1906 — the *San Francisco Examiner*, owned by one of the most effective power-brokers in the country whose papers were read by one in four American readers at the turn of the century. With the help of the San Francisco newspaper, Britt simply misappropriated the championship title in one of boxing history's biggest lies, starting a new lineal lightweight title succession, and most historians since have agreed with him. Britt later lost by seventeen-round knockout to Bat Nelson, the Battling Dane, who, in turn, claimed to be prince of the lightweights.

The adage that the "best lie is the big lie" has been attributed to various individuals ranging from Augustus Caesar to Richard Nixon. Tricky Dick's "I am not a crook" speech, delivered solemnly to the world, had even the most skeptical viewers grudgingly admitting that he was either telling the truth or demonstrating unprecedented gall.

Credit for theorizing the big lie, in fact, rests with Joseph Goebbels, Adolf Hitler's liar-in-chief, the Nazi reich minister of propaganda. Before Goebbels, in Gans' day some of the biggest liars were often ring managers, those gamblers and con-men profiting from the popularity of fistiana. In his book *Boxing's Greatest Champions*, Bert Randolph Sugar writes of Gans, "The only qualification he lacked was a sense of discrimination, associating with confidence men who would exploit their own mothers if the price was right."[6]

Starting with the Britt brothers' statements to the *San Francisco Examiner* in 1904, a big lie was concocted to deny Gans of the respect he deserved. Willus Britt, brother and consigliore to James Britt, pretender-to-the-throne, was either a prescient master of the big lie or a blowhard whose complete disregard for reality was so vast, that he could convince himself and others that any idea he found advantageous for his family was, *ipso facto*, the truth. There were many stories. One was that refusing to see himself among the victims of an act of God after the great San Francisco earthquake, Willie Britt sued the city for negligence. As evidence he cited that God owned many churches in the area and so it could not have been His act, because He would not have destroyed His own property.[7]

When Al Herford, no small liar himself, made his odd challenge to Britt earlier in 1904, there was clearly something rotten in Denmark, because the custom was not for a master champion's manager to challenge a relative novice like Britt. If boxers had to be tough during this age, boxing managers were ruthless, and Herford was no exception to the rule. Because Gans was so good, Herford was having difficulty making money from bets, and he saw in the rising popularity of the San Francisco pug James Britt an opportunity to reinvigorate the waning gambling interests in his prized talent. Getting Britt in the ring with Gans would not be easy because Britt had told reporters he would never fight a black man.

As Gans would painfully learn after he exposed Herford's machinations at the height of his career and the two parted ways, Gans was at his manager's mercy and would go penniless, unable to secure fights. The truth of the matter was that the pool of contenders willing to fight the champion was drying up. Gans had simply become too good and Herford was unable to match fighters with him. With odds always favoring Gans, Herford was unable to garner the big gambling bucks that he had made earlier in Gans' career with the fighter coming up through the ranks, unless he was willing to make deals.

The Gans-Britt fight of 1904 was one of those deals that would ruin the year 1905 for Gans. Herford told Gans to allow James Britt to "make a good showing," and in return, Britt would agree to "foul out."[8] There had been many occasions where Gans had been ordered to extend a fight so the fans could get their money's worth, but the set-up for the Britt fight seemed foul to Gans from the outset.

One-Thirty-Three Ringside

When he fought the great Joe Walcott at the higher welterweight limit to a 20-round draw a month earlier, Gans had weighed 141 pounds. For his lightweight title defense with Jimmy Britt, Herford had negotiated in the Articles of Agreement that Gans would drop to 133 pounds at ringside. This precipitous weight-loss prescription is but one of many instances of Herford's disregard for Gans' health. The notion of "133 ringside" was not a standard in the lightweight division under the Marquis of Queensberry Rules, as weigh-in any time of the day was acceptable. (The actual 135 weight limit was not established until later. Gans and others fought at a variety of weights in this division.) In retrospect, it seems that Gans was probably "set up" by his own manager and Willus Britt. In purse winnings, the match was a no-lose proposition for the Britts. According to the Articles, if James Britt won the match, he would collect 75 percent of the purse; if he lost, he would still get 50 percent. Such an agreement, so heavily weighted in favor of the challenger, was quite unusual; but for many reasons, and his race was certainly one of them, Gans had to take what he could get.

San Francisco's native son, white fighter extraordinaire Jimmy Edward Britt, was already being promoted as the master of the lightweights. The pride of the bay area, Britt had defeated only a handful of stout opponents, but the papers proclaimed him as a boy wonder. No fans could be more eager to see their hometown hero beat the black champion. Four days before the fight Herford told Gans that he had arranged with Willus Britt to let James Britt make "a good showing" against Gans. In exchange for the good showing, Britt would foul out by the 5th round. Publicly, Herford put up a $5000 bet that Gans would win, against Willie Britt's $4000. Gans was furious about the arrangement, there being no love lost between him and the Britt camp. Gans' strategy was to have been to put the young San Franciscan in his place early in the fight. He argued with Herford about the new arrangements, but his manager held the upper hand: if Gans refused to play by the rules the two managers dictated, Herford would drop Gans and see that he would never get any other promoter or future fight as punishment for "double-crossing his own manager."[9] Furthermore, if Gans revealed the arrangement, he would likewise suffer a fate of destitution, which in fact happened.

The day before the Frisco fight, betting was light and favored Gans. Final odds were expected to be 10 to 8 in favor of the champion. Comparisons between the fighters made the news. For speed the fighters seemed on equal footing. Britt had the longer reach by three and a quarter inches. But as expert boxing analyst Charley White said about the fight, "Gans is the cleverest man and the greatest ring general we've had in the lightweight class since McAuliffe. He can punch hard, too."[10]

On Sunday Gans did roadwork in the morning and the afternoon. Reports about Gans' weight varied and created an additional "buzz" for the fight. Some said he had reduced below 133 and remained strong. Others said that he was still several pounds overweight and would not be able to make the mandatory limit and maintain his strength. Britt was at his top weight of 133 and strong. He sparred with Frank Rafael but did no other training the weekend before the fight. The rumor that Gans couldn't make the weight may have come from Britt when he announced to reporters that if Gans didn't make the weight, he would forfeit and the fight wouldn't go forward.

Back in Baltimore, the upcoming fight filled twice as much news space in the sporting section of the *Sun* as the opening week at Pimlico, even though the turnout at the old track had surpassed the expectations of the gentlemen from the prestigious hunt clubs. Additional stalls were still being built to stable over 200 thoroughbreds, which were exercised on Monday morning for the handicap events.[11]

In San Francisco, James Britt had been hailed as a renaissance-man dandy of the progressive era. Behind the scenes, plans were even being laid for his vaudeville tour after he took Gans' title. Gans knew that the fight was cooked that night, he just did not know he was on the menu as the entrée.

Rather than "putting up a good showing" as he had agreed to do, Britt charged the unsuspecting Gans like a bull that sees red, throwing low blows and debilitating, energy-sapping fouls early in the contest. Referee Ed Graney would in the coming year engage in a bitter war of words about this fight with the Britt brothers. Graney and Willus Britt became two of the partners

GANS - WON - 5 ROUNDS - OCT· 31 - 1904

Gans squares off with James Britt before their controversial title fight, October 31, 1904 (photograph by the Dana Brothers Studio, San Francisco, courtesy F. Daniel Somrack, boxing historian).

in a boxing trust of four athletic clubs (the other two partners were Jim Coffroth and Moris Levy) that, for all intents and purposes, controlled boxing in San Francisco. From the evidence, it appears that young Britt was to be given more than the chance "to make a good showing," and thereby gain lucrative boxing engagements for himself and the club. Not content with a showing, he double-crossed Gans (and possibly Graney) by going for the kill from the opening bell. Gans was caught off guard and struggled through the fight.

Crowds Desire to See Local Boy Dethrone the Black Prince of the Lightweights

On that October All Hallows Night, the house was packed with spectators wild with pride. News had reached them from the St. Louis World's Fair of the daring feat of the captain of an Oakland-built airship. The dirigible had failed earlier in the day after its inventor, Captain Thomas Baldwin, and the navigator, A. Roy Knabenshue, of Toledo, had worked feverishly for 26 hours straight. It was airborne for only a few moments before it fell to the ground, breaking a propeller blade. But by the afternoon, the *California Arrow* ascended into the Missouri sky, floated down, and made a pass at about a thousand feet over the heads of a cheering crowd, completing a successful trip of approximately three and a half miles on its own power and proving that it could make "headway against a modest breeze."[12] Now another Bay Area son, Britt, was ready to add to the honors of Northern California. Beating the greatest black fighter alive would make the native son a home-grown hero indeed.

The up-and-coming heavyweight Jack Johnson was at ringside to support his friend and mentor Gans. For two years, Joe Gans had reigned supreme in the boxing limelight. Now Johnson, the black dynamo heavyweight, appeared to be climbing the ladder threatening the heavyweight crown. Johnson had handily defeated Denver's Ed Martin in Los Angeles. Johnson's supporters circulated the idea of a fight with retired hero Jim Jeffries. But Jeffries was quoted as saying that he would never fight a Negro, although he had previously defeated black fighters Hank Griffin, Peter Jackson, and Bob Armstrong. It would be six more years before Californians would see "great white hope" Jeffries come out of retirement to fight Johnson, in the second great fight promoted by Tex Rickard. In 1904 the man who would be Rickard's first attraction, Gans, was already the Old Master of the ring, and Tex Rickard hadn't even seen a professional fight.

At 9:00 P.M. boxing officials opened the main-event ceremonies, and Jack Johnson was the first celebrity introduced. Rather than issuing the customary challenge to a specific individual, Johnson challenged anyone in the world to fight him. The air was thick with the desire of the crowd to see a black fighter beaten. Gans came into the ring during the introductions and leaned against the ropes. What may have been viewed as unconcern about the upcoming match was actually a cover for his impatience. Britt, having raised a ruckus about timing of ring entry, was late.

Referee Ed Graney was introduced, and he went straight to his job of adjusting the scales that had been brought into the arena for the official ringside weigh-in. Introductions continued. Mike Sullivan, Jimmy Gardner and Young Corbett each issued challenges to the winner of the match. Officials announced that the betting had closed 10 to 6½ in favor of Gans. In Baltimore, Gans was a two-to-one favorite and the *Baltimore Sun* reported that "no fight in recent years has engaged as much betting as the Gans-Britt battle."[13] Reports surfaced that Baltimoreans originally thought the fight was to be a "fake" and that Gans was to "lay down" to Britt, causing many to bet on Britt. But by the afternoon of the fight large sums of money were bet on Gans.

Al Herford's brother Maurice "had his agents out looking for Britt admirers' money."[14] Maurice was earning commissions on bets made until he could no longer find men willing to gamble on Britt.

By 9:24 Gans' impatience was noticeable. According to the Articles, the fighters were to weigh in at 9:10, but Britt was nowhere to be seen. Insisting that the weigh-in begin, Referee Graney and Club Manager Harry Corbett conferred and then Graney motioned Gans over to the scale. Corbett set the machine at the 133-pound notch. Gans dropped his plaid bathrobe, and completely nude, stepped upon the scale. The bar never moved. From its steadiness it was assumed that he was at least a half-pound under the weight limit.

Gans returned to his dressing room. It was at least five more minutes before Britt walked into the ring and over to the scale. With fans cheering, he stepped up, wearing his black boxing socks. The bar quivered, but it did not rise. He went to his corner where his seconds, Tiv Kreling and Spider Kelly, began wrapping both hands in bandages. From elbow to wrist, they rolled the boxer's forearms with the customary tire tape. From outside the ring, an unidentified spectator tugged at manager Billy Britt to get his attention. Britt looked at his watch and became agitated. It appeared that Gans had taken more than the ten minutes of rest, between the weigh-in and the fight, which was stipulated in the Articles. Britt did not want Gans to have the chance to re-nourish himself after the weigh-in. Britt was ready to take his complaint to Referee Graney when Gans climbed through the ropes. Gans went directly to Britt's corner and shook hands with his opponent before taking his seat on the opposite side.

In Gans' corner stood Sol English, Kid Sullivan, and Frank McDonald. The referee announced the fighters and called them to the middle of the ring to receive the instructions. Britt wore white trunks with the Olympic Athletic Club's emblem on the side. Gans wore white elastic briefs and no bandages on his hands. The fighters touched gloves and waited for the bell.

The *San Francisco Examiner* reported the scene as "Worse Than a Spanish Bull Fight," that at the sound of the gong, Britt exploded at Gans, "fighting fiercely" and throwing full-steam barrages at his body. Ramon Corral, vice-president of the Mexican Republic, was at ringside and said that he had never seen such a group of spectators at any bull fight in Madrid as the "maniacs I see gathered around me here."[15] According to the round-by-round returns that came into Baltimore, Britt missed his mark with the punches. Nevertheless, the first round seemed fairly even as Gans permitted Britt to do most of the work. Britt sent out numerous punches while Gans appeared to be sizing up Britt's reach. Britt tried to attack Gans' body, but the blows were not forcible, according to the Baltimore papers. Britt missed with a left hook to the body and a right to the face. Then Gans missed a straight right to the head. Just before the bell rang to end the round, Britt missed two attempts with lefts to the body.

In the second round, according to telegraph returns, Britt rushed in and missed a left and then a right hand punch to the body before connecting with a left to Gans' head and then a left to his body. Gans forced Britt around the ring and they fell into a clinch. Then a heated exchange ensued. Britt missed a left hook to the body but hit Gans in the nose with a straight left. Each returned lefts to the body. They exchanged a mix of rights and lefts to the face, and then Britt "missed a vicious left for the body," which landed below the belt. The *Examiner* claimed the next day that "after (Britt) had sampled some of the colored fighter's punches and found there was little sting to them, he increased his pace until he fought at whirlwind speed. That he was in the humor to commit infractions of the Queensberry code was evident in the second round, when he struck Gans a palpably foul body punch with his left hand."[16] Graney warned Britt, but the early foul came as a surprise to Gans and took its toll on his energy. The *Examiner* reported that "Gans was wide-eyed and open-mouthed," while Britt "was as full of vim and venom as an enraged tiger," and "just warming up to his work."[17] Britt missed another right to the body before he connected with a left and right on the face when the bell rang to end round two.

All that was said of the third round in San Francisco was that "Gans was holding on like grim death in the clinches."[18] In this round Gans fought back and both fighters connected with several punches in close quarters. Britt sent Gans a hard right-cross on the jaw and it appeared that Britt's punches were more powerful than Gans.' The fighters were clinched when the gong sounded.

In the fourth round, the fighters continued to clash, block and clinch. Gans appeared tired but continued to rally. The Baltimore paper reported that "it was apparent that Gans was scared."[19] More likely, he was extremely confused about Britt's agreement to perform well and then foul out, as well as the referee's failure to call the fouls. After one of Britt's body blows followed by a right to the neck, Gans fell to one knee in a half clinch. He rose and continued fighting and then fell to the other knee. When he fell a third time, Britt hammered him in the jaw. Gans' seconds jumped to the side of the ring and cried "foul," but Graney ordered the fight to continue.

In the fifth and final round, Britt rushed at Gans at the bell, punching fiercely at close range. The *Examiner* noted that Gans "stood his ground, but he was in bad shape. His eyes had a glittery look and he seemed to be choking in his efforts to suck air into his lungs. He stopped some of Britt's body smashes with his elbows, but he could not cope with them all and he cringed visibly when Britt rammed his fists into the midriff.... In the long run he was almost 'dead on his feet,' while his blows had no more force than baby taps."[20] Britt hit Gans with a succession of rights and lefts to the jaw that sent him to the floor. With Graney refusing to call the fight on fouls, Britt's victory appeared imminent. But as Gans attempted to rise, Britt could not contain his excitement and "pummeled him," according to the *Examiner*, "on the side of the head with left and right punches."[21] With Gans down again, Britt expected Graney to call the fight in his favor. But when the referee jumped between the two fighters, pushed Britt out of the way, and slapped Gans on the shoulders to give him the win by disqualifying Britt on the foul, the challenger pulled back and in full attack mode socked Ed Graney, a former fighter himself, with a right squarely in the face.

Pandemonium ensued.

The San Francisco paper said,

> Then there was trouble of various kinds. Graney smashed back and the referee and the native son pugilist went to the floor together, pummeling each other. They were dragged apart by big policemen and rushed into different angles of the ring. Britt wept in his chagrin at the way things had gone and Graney's fighting blood was aroused.
> "He struck me; he struck me," Graney cried, and he wrenched off his Tuxedo and tried to get at Britt again. They were kept apart and Britt's friends reasoned with him.
> "Graney is technically right," is a remark that was tossed around among the Brittites.[22]

The San Francisco paper summed up the fight in a self-serving, "Britt-serving" way, "It may be said that disinterested onlookers also felt that it was a pity circumstances should have arisen to deprive the local lad of a full measure of credit when he had shown himself to be the master of a pugilist who has always been hailed as the greatest lightweight the world has produced."[23]

Because of his manager's strange arrangement with the Britt clan, Gans' showing that evening was poor. Spectators never saw his clever offense, his stinging jabs, his invincible guard, or the clever techniques he had learned from spending half of his life in the boxing ring. Britt said when he issued Gans a challenge to a return fight: "I will fight him again for a side bet of $5000 or any other sum of money. He did not hit me a jarring punch at any stage of the game, and he did not seem able to stand the body punishment I gave him."[24] It took a seasoned boxer who had been in the ring with the master to comment on how unusual it was that Gans did not land his own jarring punch. Terry McGovern, listening to the telegraph reports with Tom Sharkey in New York, noted that Britt "did what few fighters have ever done to Gans in getting through his guard as he did."[25] Throughout his career Gans' reflexes were as quick as a cat's; he could virtually catch any punch with his mitts. He was too professional, too experienced in his art, to make such elementary blunders as were seen that night. There was an earlier time in Chicago when Gans put up an equally poor showing, but the papers at the end of 1904 never made the comparison with the McGovern fight. Britt had given his hometown what they wanted to see — their favorite son beating the black champion.

Gans' Words Distorted and Used Against Him

The next day, Gans issued a statement loaded with subtext, one that would be misquoted to the present time. Gans said that he was willing to fight Britt "at any time he wants." Gans' next words appear hauntingly lucid a hundred years later: "I am sorry that the fight had to be decided on a foul, as I am confident that I can whip Britt any day in the week in fair fighting."[26] While the public was too intoxicated by Britt's showing to take note of the words "fair fighting," the statement was not lost on Al Herford and Willie Britt. It would cause manager and Gans to part ways.

Gans went on to say, "I am willing to fight Britt any time he wants to, but not at 133 pounds ringside."[27] The San Francisco paper's headline read, "Sorry He Won on a Foul, but Says He Will Never Train Down Again to 133 Pounds Ring-side, as He is Too Old." These words have been used to support the idea that after the Britt fight Gans left the lightweight division. But this is false. First, there was no stringent regulation weight for a specific title at that time. Clearly Gans fought Erne for the championship at a weight above 133. Fight managers negotiated weight and rules for a title challenge in the Articles of Agreement for the fight. And second, even more germane to the dispute over Gans' title is the fact that only part of his statement is ever reprinted. Within the same breath he went on to say, "If we ever meet again I will insist on 133 at 3 o'clock, as it is asking too much to have me make that weight at ringside."[28] Gans was not refusing to fight at 133 pounds, he simply wanted to have the official weigh-in earlier in the afternoon, a demand not unreasonable and in perfect accordance with the Marquis of Queensberry Rules.

As early as the week after the fight, on November 8, a sum of $1,000 was deposited with the sports editor of *The Chicago American* to bind a return match between Joe Gans and Jimmy Britt at 134 pounds ringside. When asked by a reporter about this, Britt responded in what has become his self-proclaimed crowning as the lightweight champion, "I'm strickly a lightweight and I regard 133 in the ring as the lightweight limit. In short, I want the *Examiner* and the country to understand that Jimmy Britt is the best lightweight on earth. I want the nation to realize that Gans isn't ready to meet me at the lightweight limit. He asks for 134 pounds. I feel sure I can beat Gans if he weighs 180 pounds, but for the present I am going to make matches only with pugilists who have an idea they can beat me at 133. In other words, I figure I have shown there isn't a 133-pound man who stands a 500 to 1 chance with James Edward. After I have had all the ease and theatrical money I want I may think of beating Gans at catch weights and of taking on all the other 140-pounders on the horizon."[29]

By the end of 1904 Gans had headed back to the East Coast. His wife was suing him for divorce and he and his manager would soon part professional company. For Gans, the outlook for 1905 looked bleak.

In January 1905, Jimmy Britt won the audience over with his humorous monologues and his brilliant boxing display at the "best Ladies night the Olympic Club has had for some time."[30] But it was a series of headlines in the *San Francisco Examiner* by sporting editor W.W. Naughton that put the nail in Gans' championship coffin: "Lightweight Laurels Belong to Boxer James Edward Britt," "Britt's Punches Mayn't Act 'Mediately but They've Made Him Lightweight Champ," and "Gans Admits That He Cannot Make the Weight," with subtitle: "Though the Native Son Lost on Foul, in Sporting Minds He Won the Battle."[31]

Newspaper opinion was so weighty that what was written in the paper could become fact. The famous sports editor was no novice to the number one sport. And while he was in a league of racist newsmen (consider the condescending language he used to describe "Mistah" Gans in one headline), he knew talent and he knew about ring titles. Lagging in time as his article did, over a month after the fight, his lead editorial with its bold headline seemed out of place and time, but it nevertheless declared Britt the lightweight champion for several reasons: because he outfought Gans, and with a subtitle that indicated Gans refused to fight Britt again (i.e. relinquished the title) because he couldn't make the weight. With its strange logic, the article was written as though Naughton's boss had given him a directive to make Britt the world lightweight champion. Here is the first half of the editorial (the second half is titled "Britt Fills the Bill") and the elaborate conceit that has influenced public opinion over the decades, leaving trails of misinformation that continue to haunt the Old Master's legacy to this day:

> If claims to pugilistic titles were aired in courts of law, the same as titles to real estate and other things, Joe Gans of Baltimore would have little difficulty in establishing his right to be called lightweight champion of the world.
>
> In the first place he could produce ample testimony to show that it has been the custom from time immemorial for men contesting the lightweight championship to box at 133-pounds, ringside weight. Having thus laid a foundation, as the lawyers say, for the introduction of further evidence, Gans could proceed to make clear that he recently entered into contract with one Jimmy Britt to box for the aforesaid championship at 133 pounds ringside; that said Joe Gans and said Jimmy Britt did box for the lightweight championship; that Referee Edmund M. Graney declared Gans the winner, and that the title, purse and bets followed the decision.
>
> On the face of it, it looks as if a judge and jury would be bound to regard these things as uncontrovertible facts, yet every fair-minded sporting man knows that Gans is champion only by virtue of a technicality and that the youngster who has proved himself the king pin of the 133-pound class in the year that is past is James Edward Britt.
>
> In support of this contention it may be instanced that something tantamount to an admission that Britt is Gans' master at the lightweight limit has come — and is still coming — from Gans stronghold. Manager Herford, according to report, wishes to arrange another match between Gans and Britt. Herford claims that illness and suffering prevented Gans from showing up in his usual form in the contest held in October, and from the fact that he asks for an afternoon weighing in case another match is arranged it is to be inferred that he considers it unwise to have Gans attempt the task of making 133 ringside a second time.
>
> Incidentally Herford claims that of late years pugilists boxing for the lightweight championship have been permitted to weigh in hours before the gong summoned them to midring. Such may have been the case on sundry occasions when Gans was supposed to be boxing for the title, but it did not establish a new custom by any means.[32]

As history would prove, Gans could beat Britt in fair fighting. (Britt would quit after five rounds with Gans three years later, when Gans should have been even more "ringworn.") It would be more than a year before the public would hear another side to this story, but by then Britt had taken the limelight with the help of a powerful newspaper, and effectively had stolen the title. Gans, although still champion, could barely make a living in 1905.

In Britt's subsequent fights, many newspapers of the day, as Monte Cox has shown, referred to him only as the "white lightweight champion of the world." But this distinction seemed enough to establish a new title line. Bat Nelson fought Britt and won. On March 14, 1906, Nelson fought Terry McGovern and the *New York Times* carried the headline "Crowd Hisses Fighters Clinched for 6 Rounds: Champion is the Stronger."[33] Nelson is called "the lightweight champion" in the Philadelphia bout, with the *New York Times* continuing to promote the erroneous lineal championship title. Six months later in Goldfield, these two "lines" would meet back up, and in pre-fight press every paper in the country would call Gans the champion and Nelson the contender.

For later record books to identify Britt in 1904 as Gans' title successor to the lightweight championship is to whitewash history, mistaking the "white" lightweight champions during the years 1904 through 1906 for the "world" lightweight continuous champion, Joe Gans.

Gans did everything in his power following the fight with Britt to set the record straight. He left word with Ben Selig, a manager on the West Coast, to accept a rematch on his behalf at any time with Britt, but, drawing the color line, Britt refused to fight him during these years. By 1906 Gans had seen his title absconded and a new succession of lightweight title holders crowned. Because the white lightweights refused to fight him, he was forced to fight heavier men, men who would grant him fights. The consequence of the San Francisco coverage of the Britt fight was his absence in the ring during 1905. The *Baltimore Sun* reported on his September 15 fight with Mike "Twin" Sullivan that "Gans has not been seen in the ring in public since he met Britt, and many are anxious to see his form."[34] Even in his own hometown paper, Gans' title was reduced to the "colored champion."

In an editorial turn-about, W. W. Naughton would call Gans the "Idol of Boxing" after Gans beat Mike "Twin" Sullivan for the welterweight title on January 15, 1906, and say there was no better man living to be found fighting at equal weights. Still frustrated by the situation with the lightweight fighters, in February of 1906 Gans decided to expose the truth of the details concerning the 1904 bout and his manager's arrangements with Britt and his brother. Gans mistakenly believed that public reaction would be sympathetic, but the Britt establishment proceeded to tarnish Gans' reputation further. Discussing the history of the 1904 fight and its consequence Gans explained, "Britt calls me a faker, but if I had the money and friends he had at our last meeting, I would never have faked as he did…. Britt was boosted as the real lightweight champion and I was called a 'dub.' Britt took my reputation into the ring with Nelson and Nelson took my reputation away from Britt, and now I can't get a match with either of them, though the public now feels that I can lick them both."[35]

No one believed that Gans was innocent or that Britt was guilty, but history shows that manager Willus Britt five years later arranged the same type of "good showing" for his man Stanley Ketchel before he would let him go into the ring with the formidable Jack Johnson. As Gans said to the media, "It is a strange thing, but a fact, that a colored boxer and a white boy engaged in battling for money are two different mortals. A white boy is looked upon as an idol and is never under suspicion until he actually commits a mistake in the ring, whereas, a colored boy is not only under suspicion, but because he is a colored man is given the worst of it and must fight 'to orders.' If I hadn't fought 'to orders' in the past I would not have been matched, and therefore could not have earned a livelihood with my fists. I merely make this statement, not as an excuse for what I have done in the past, because I have blotted that all out by my last victory, and from now on will always strive to win, not only for myself, but for my many friends and admirers."[36] Jimmy Britt continued to boycott Gans until the Old Master had beaten Nelson, and when they did meet, the pre-fight publicity would be vicious.

Although California in the early twentieth century was progressive in many respects, equality among the races was not one of them. Gunboat Smith, during his interview for "*In This Corner...*," had this to say about the famous Johnson-Jeffries fight that took place in Reno, Nevada, six years later: "If that fight would have come off in San Francisco, it was in the bag for Jeffries to win. I'm telling you this because I got that from good authority in San Francisco. Jeffries would have won. It was common gossip. They wouldn't stand for a nigger to beat a white man in California."[37] There had been a concerted effort to make Gans risk his title in the Golden State. While the city of Fort Erie petitioned for the fight with a guaranteed purse of $6000, the managers did not accept the Canadian bid. Gans' title defense would be in Britt's home-town.

Willie Ritchie, the lightweight champion from 1912 to 1914, said in his interview for "In This Corner...," "Poor Gans had to do as he was told by the white managers. They were crooks, they framed fights, and being a negro the poor guy had to follow orders otherwise he would have starved to death. They wouldn't give him any work."[38]

No doubt, the Britt fiasco of 1904 has contributed to the diminution of the Gans legacy. But once more the Old Master would rise from the ashes of a ruined reputation and career. The second rebirth of Gans' career would come in the welterweight division in early 1906. From reading boxing history, one must keep in mind that the sport was for the most part illegal at the turn of the century. In an attempt to keep the popular and lucrative big fights in New York, boxing had been made legal there with the Horton Law beginning in 1896. Otherwise it was illegal in the United States until the Golden State welcomed it out West, where pugilism was relatively tame compared to the gunfights they were used to.

The year 1905 would be a disaster for Gans. His split with Herford and the San Francisco boxing trust left him unable to make a living. His personal life was in a shambles, his wife having left him, seeming one step behind his earnings prospects.

After his problems with "133 ringside," it would be at the higher welterweight division where he would re-establish himself. In that weight category, some of the greatest fighters were plying their trades in the twentieth-century's first decade.

12

Boxing Moves West

At the great Columbian Exposition in Chicago in 1893, the young historian Frederick Jackson Turner, in his lecture "The Significance of the Frontier in American History," advanced a homespun, less traditional explanation of American history and American character. He said that the "free" land of the American West drew Europeans back in time to a more primitive life, where they could throw off the shackles of tradition and, through freedom and self-reliance, experience the principles that forged the new democratic nation. The rugged life, in Turner's opinion, encouraged individuality and developed intellectual characteristics of tough-minded strength, curiosity, and practicality. But with the encroachment of civilization and the Old West vanishing in the latter decades of the nineteenth century, how would Americans be able to return to a raw, primitive experience necessary to continue the shaping of their strong character and their egalitarian beliefs? Sports would, in part, answer this philosophical question.

The Census Bureau had officially noted the end of the frontier wilderness by 1890. Only a few years earlier, the cowboys had driven herds of wild Spanish longhorns from South Texas through the Indian territories on the great cattle trails, first on the Chisholm and then on the Western Trail. By the nineties, the wranglers would meet up with the trains and ship their cattle by rail. Western outlaws such as Billy the Kid would be dead by 1881. The dime novel would recreate his story and others for nineteenth-century readers, and film would recreate the "Westerns" for the twentieth-century.

The doorway to the American West was aptly portrayed in Clint Eastwood's movies, in which he frequently filmed himself in doorways in Old West montages. In movies such as *The Outlaw Josie Wales* and *Unforgiven*, Eastwood is filmed at the doorway of shanty houses and saloons. To his back, glimpses of the untamed wilderness let the world know that he has recently returned from the great unknown. In front of him is civilization, with all of its glory and corruption.

The gunslingers of the western movie genre were mostly myth built around a few hard-case men whose lives were nasty, brutish, short, and devoid of heroism. Billy the Kid and Jesse James were cold-blooded murderers who did not deserve the hero worship that they received. But their Robin Hood–like stories made sensational reads for the penny press. In his popular New York tabloid, *The National Police Gazette*, publisher Richard K. Fox reported the story of Billy the Kid's exploits over several months in 1881, creating a folk legend for his readership which numbered in the hundreds of thousands. (Fox wrote proudly and perhaps erroneously in August of 1881 that the "Kid" was originally a New York "tough" from the Fourth Ward.) He published a fictional account of a "Billy LeRoy," "King of American Highwaymen," with an alias of "The Kid."[1] Many boxers in subsequent years would incorporate this moniker, giving rise to a plethora of "Kid" this-and-that.

Publisher Fox would be equally smitten by the exploits of the prizefighters, as the popularity of stories about gunslingers, gamblers, and saloons of the eighties gave way to the legendary warriors of the ring, and protectors of the law like Wyatt Earp who became pit bosses in gambling houses and referees in a profession on the cusp of illegality. Plying their trade with their fists under the Marquis of Queensberry rules, the early prizefighters were hard men who used their talents to test their "gameness" in the ultimate (and symbolically primitive) confrontation between men. With boxing legal only in a few western states after the turn of the century, San Francisco became a center for pugilism. Adventure called and Gans took his chances out West.

Claustrophobia on the eastern American seaboard and a flood of immigration from Europe circa 1900 added to the ever-increasing lure of the New West. While the Old West became a modern metaphor for self-reliance and integrity in Turner's famous essay, it was still looked upon by the eastern establishment circa 1900 as a Mecca for ruffians and ill breeding. Enormously popular entertainments for the middle class such as vaudeville and boxing were looked down upon by the upper crust of society. As the city politicians of the Midwest buckled under the moral crusade to shut down public boxing events, the sport became a forbidden fruit to be enjoyed in San Francisco. Gans made over a dozen long trips west. Aboard the great railways, he must have had feelings of infinite possibility in a future still wide open.

Before the great railroads stretched across the continent, a trip to San Francisco took two months over land and one month by sea because the voyage meant a trip around South America. During the 1830s in Gans' hometown of Baltimore was founded the first of the great passenger railroads, the Baltimore and Ohio. Eventually railroad tracks would carry Americans across the continent. Gans made many trips out of Baltimore by train to Philadelphia, New York, and Chicago.

The rails also made it possible for the frontier spirit to be shipped east. By 1887 Buffalo Bill Cody brought over 100 Indians and trick riders and a bevy of bear, buffalo, elk and moose to his Wild West Shows. His four-part dramatic rendering of the great Western epochs of Turner's famous thesis met rave reviews in New York. Act I set wild game and Indians in a primeval forest. Act II brought prairie schooners to the buffalo. Act III depicted the cattle ranch with real cowboys and cowgirls, and Act IV, the grand finale, had a mining camp blown to bits and pieces by a cyclone. Wild west shows continued to be popular for the next three decades. Madison Square Garden, magnificently redesigned by architect Stanford White in 1890, hosted the Miller Brothers' 101 Ranch Show in 1909. Its show illustrated the racial mix of the working western ranches with stars Bill Pickett, the black cowboy bulldogger, Tom Mix, the cow-runner from Mexico, and Will Rogers, the Cherokee lasso artist.

Vaudeville actors, theater troupes, circus performers and others in the entertainment trade spent a good deal of time in railroad cars. On a trip across country, Union Pacific's Overland Limited made it from Omaha to San Francisco in just under 72 hours. This was considered a very fast train. For Baltimore to Chicago, add two days, probably another day more for Chicago to Omaha, to account for any layover. It took Gans at least a week to get to 'Frisco. Gans' cross-country fight schedule caused him to spend a good deal of time in railroad cars.

The story of the American railroads took its place alongside boxing as an essential piece of Americana. The Pullman porters, who succeeded in obtaining the first collective-bargaining agreement for African American workers, started the first black union. Pullman porter jobs were considered high status positions in the early to mid 1900s. The porters took care of the important travelers of the day, such as Joe Gans.

As he rode out from the East towards San Francisco for the first time in December of 1896, he must have grasped his own special rendezvous with destiny. Equally anxious to travel and take his fighters to other, bigger (and "greener") venues was Al Herford. The West was brewing boxers. Jim Jeffries, Jim Corbett's sparring partner, would have his first professional bout in 1896. The cost of the cross-country trips for fighters coming from the East was borne by the fighters and deducted from their purses, usually before the 50/50 split with their managers.[2]

Gans had already made a name for himself, having won sixty bouts before his first trip west, where he followed Bob Fitzsimmons for his bout with Tom

Sharkey in California. With the help of introductions by Fitzsimmons, Herford hoped to convince promoters to secure a rematch with San Franciscan Dal Hawkins (Hawkins fought from featherweight to welterweight) to avenge Gans' first loss in the ring, which had occurred two months earlier.[3] While the rematch with Hawkins in California failed to materialize, Gans was able to display his skills to the western sporting crowd when he took on local boxer Charles Rochette. The *San Francisco Examiner* reported that the Easterners in the crowd had often seen Gans perform, and they were responsible for making Gans the two to one favorite of the betting crowd. He was so dominant and in control of the fight that the sports editor said the next day tongue-in-cheek, "A few more tame boxing contests such as were given at Woodward's Pavilion last night will put an end to boxing in this city."[4] Gans spent the first two rounds fighting as usual, studying his opponent. The two mixed it up in the third round with spectators awed by how Gans could "dance" around the ring and corner the local boy to the ropes. Rochette had no hope but to fall into clinches. By the fourth, the dance was ended when Gans sent Rochette to the floor.

San Francisco, like Goldfield, Nevada, was a child of the gold rush. It grew from a tiny hamlet of tents on the bay in 1848 to a boomtown in a few short years. A neighborhood in old San Francisco called "the Barbary Coast" began as a hangout for the rich during the Gold Rush of 1848 to 1859. The town would come to be known as a place of gambling, prostitution, and riotous nightlife. "The Barbary Coast is the haunt of the low and the vile of every kind.... The petty thief, the house burglar, the tramp, the whoremonger, lewd women, cutthroats, murderers, all are found here."[5] Dance-halls, concert-saloons, and low gambling houses ruled the city. "Opium dens, where heathen Chinese and God-forsaken men and women are sprawled in miscellaneous confusion, disgustingly drowsy or completely overcome, are there. Licentiousness, debauchery, pollution, loathsome disease, insanity from dissipation, misery, poverty, wealth, profanity, blasphemy, and death, are there. And Hell, yawning to receive the putrid mass, is there also."[6]

The 1870s and the Nevada Comstock Lode created a wild speculation in mining stocks and soon San Francisco would have the largest stock exchange in the West. San Francisco had another boom in the 1890s when it was virtually the only major city in the country where prizefighting was entirely legal. California and Nevada were familiar with public gunfights, and welcomed boxing as a relatively tame amusement. San Francisco's Woodward Pavilion and Mechanics Pavilion hosted some of the best fighting the world has ever seen, especially in the lower weight classes. By 1900 there were four major athletic clubs vying as hosts for boxing events in San Francisco. From

1900 until the outbreak of World War I in 1914 occurred a golden age of boxing in California.

In the West young Gans would have met many adventurous souls. The line between community leader and flim-flam artist was not well drawn in the West that Gans would come to know. In fact, Gans' San Francisco debut fight with Charles Rochette was overshadowed by the heavyweight bout, straight out of Wild-West lore, between Bob Fitzsimmons and Tom Sharkey. Wyatt Earp, legendary gunslinger and "upstanding" lawman that he was, appears time after time in the sports sections of the 1890s. He was famous for refereeing and betting on fights, at times in suspicious combination. For the Sharkey-Fitzsimmons fight, he managed to have himself appointed as referee of the contest, reputed though he was of having a financial stake in Sharkey's campaign for the heavyweight crown. The aftermath of the fight proved far more interesting than what occurred in the ring. Earp placed a stout wager on Sharkey, but much to Earp's dismay, Fitz knocked him out. Undaunted, Earp declared Sharkey the winner by foul, and collected on his bet. Fitz publicly accused Earp of corruptly and feloniously awarding the verdict to Sharkey. After several heated exchanges in the *San Francisco Gazette*, Fitz dropped the matter, and proceeded to take the crown from Gentleman Jim in 1897 in the first fight ever to be filmed.[7]

Joe Gans would have his own battle with a Western lawman turned referee when Bat Masterson became third man in the ring with Gans and George McFadden in Denver, October 2, 1900. The fight was wild — something quite expected in Colorado. Gans, by all accounts, out-punched (by some estimates 5 to 1), out-rushed, out-blocked, and otherwise out-pointed the man known as Elbows. To the outrage of 2,000 spectators who thought Gans the victor, Masterson called the fight a draw. So upset with the call, a man by the name of Red Gallagher jumped into the ring to challenge Masterson. The papers noted that "no blood was spilled" in the ensuing fracas, although the crowd screamed "robber" at Masterson.[8]

Charismatic brawlers like Kid McCoy, Bob Fitzsimmons, and Gentleman Jim Corbett were covered in great detail in the *San Francisco Examiner*. Corbett had been a banker in San Francisco and for years the fight everybody wanted to see was Gentleman Jim versus Kid McCoy. In the buildup to Gans' first fight with Frank Erne in 1900 one reporter mused that no other conceivable match-up could be its equal, with the exception of a Corbett-McCoy fight. Kid McCoy was showbiz, manifest destiny, and the American dream all rolled into one slick hustler and helluva fighter. McCoy and Corbett finally fought in 1904. McCoy was easily battered by the much bigger Corbett. The fact that the middleweight McCoy was even considered a match with the heavyweight is due mainly to the Kid's chutzpah and flair for self-promotion.

Boxers: The First Movie Stars

Top boxers were the first rock stars of popular entertainment from the very beginning of the sport in America. The 1890s saw a gilded age in America that was unprecedented. The rise of the leisure class in the wake of America's industrial expansion, the proliferation of transportation and communication technology, and the nation's growing swagger and self-awareness as a world power can be seen in the newspaper accounts of the day. Such a nation created a fertile ground for the rise of vice and entertainment. Even the working middle class now had money to spend on things other than essentials, and they were eager to spend it enjoying the theaters and entertainment pavilions that catered to their desires and pocketbooks.

Vaudeville acts toured the country. A sampling of the burlesque can be seen November 1, 1899, when the *Baltimore Sun* reported on the comedy called *Signal Lights* staged the previous night at Kernan's Monumental Theater where Herford held many of his fights. Admiral George Dewey at the time was one of the most eligible bachelors in the government, and the minstrel that evening declared he had seen seven young ladies kissing the grass in Druid Park in Baltimore. When asked why they did that, he responded, "Because they thought it was Dewey!" The audience roared with laughter. Music houses and theaters offered classical opera and theater, along with newer stage plays, comedy, and vaudeville acts. The public also went to the theaters to see prizefighting and boxing exhibitions. While women were excluded from an actual fight, they were permitted to see boxing demonstrations with men disrobing to scant pugilistic attire. The draw for these exhibitions was so great that theater owners vied for top prizefighters, and they, in turn, cashed in on their ring fame both during and after their careers. Newspapers reported that star pugilists could draw $1000 a week or more from stage performances.

After John L. Sullivan successfully defended his heavyweight title by defeating Jake Kilrain in 1889, Sullivan spent the next three years touring on stage in *Honest Hearts and Willing Hands*. (Kilrain and Sullivan would spend time in their fifties touring together, both overweight, but still giving boxing expositions.) In 1892 Sullivan lost his title to Jim Corbett. *Gentleman Jack*, a play written for Corbett by Charles T. Vincent, opened at the Temple Opera House, Elizabeth, New Jersey, in 1892.[9] The great adventure writer and boxing journalist Jack London first met Bob Fitzsimmons on a theatrical tour in

San Francisco in October of 1894. The two became close friends and London wrote a vaudeville piece for Fitzsimmons and his wife in 1910 called *The Intruder*. The piece also appeared in San Francisco as *Her Brother's Clothes*.[10] By 1900 New York theaters would draw popular black vaudeville entertainment with such troupes as Williams and Walker in *Papa's Wife* or Cole and Johnson in *A Trip to Coontown*. Fighters were immensely popular on the New York stage when the doors to public fights closed at the turn of the century. Bob Fitzsimmons headlined *The Honest Blacksmith*, Terry McGovern was featured in the immensely popular *Bowery After Dark*, and Jim Jeffries in *A Man from the West*.[11] Before Fess Parker, John Wayne, Johnny Cash or Billy Bob Thornton played Davy Crockett, king of the wild frontier or hero at the Alamo, heavyweight champion Jim Jeffries played the character on stage in 1905.

Because the theater already had successful box office stars and could draw large numbers from boxing exhibitions, it was not a leap to use those same stars in the new medium of film when it was invented. In the first half of the 20th century, California would become the world center of a new entertainment industry. Boxing events were among the very first to be commemorated by the use of Edison's new invention, the kinetoscope, the precursor of the motion picture. San Francisco's golden boys of boxing would be featured, and promoters such as Jim Coffroth could make as much money promoting boxing films as actual fights. He would be among the first to take the new boxing films outside the United States to Europe.

Thomas Edison had launched on the East Coast one of his many inventions, a device that was really just a rapid-fire series of still photos viewed in succession. His kinetoscope was a subject of much fascination, but at first the commercial applications for it were not abundant. "Peep shows" were among the most popular early uses for the machine, along with cock fighting and boxing. The investors of the day were shrewd enough to know the new visual medium needed something illicit and extraordinary to interest the paying public. While peep shows and circus freaks were illicit enough, they would not be approved by enough of the public to create a sustained market. But boxing was a heroic and manly art and also had the necessary appeal of the illicit — and it was already wildly popular.

In the early days of "the flickers," Edison's kinetoscope could take 40 pictures per second, and the making of the first boxing films produced miles of footage. The first film produced was shot in May 1891 and was titled *Men Boxing*, directed by W.K.L. Dickson and William Heise. During the summer of 1894, *Boxing Cats*, previously a touring vaudeville act of two cats trained to box, became one of the most popular flickers playing in New York's opera houses.

The first celebrity "movie star" was the heavyweight champion Jim Corbett, the man who beat the first gloved champion, John L. Sullivan. In 1892 Gentleman Jim, of San Francisco, dodged and danced his way to victory by avoiding Sullivan's clumsy rushes until the latter was exhausted and presented an easy mark for Corbett. (Fighting on the under-card that night in New Orleans was a clever black boxer from Nova Scotia, George Dixon, who would later become one of Joe Gans' best friends.)

The first fight film in existence shows Corbett and Bob Fitzsimmons standing flat-footed under the afternoon sun, swatting rather clumsy punches at each other. In one frame Corbett flails with an overhand right at the dome of Fitz's bald head. Fitz counters with a short jolt under Jim's rib that would gain fame as the "solar-plexus punch," the punch that won the heavyweight crown for Fitz. As Fitzsimmons basked in the glory of his championship, he took time out of his busy schedule to chat and even spar with a persistent visitor to his fights and training camp, none other than the future lightweight master Joe Gans.

By far the most profitable film subject of the kinetoscope era was the Corbett-Courtney fight, a six-round fight with one-minute rounds released by the Thomas Edison Company on November 17, 1894. Corbett made over $15,000 from the movie, a small fortune in 1894. Corbett's manager, Diamond Jim Brady, first suggested the idea of a fight to Edison. Fighting was illegal in New Jersey, where Edison had his base of operation. As Armond Fields writes in his biography on Corbett, "Jim acknowledged that his agreement with the Edison people stipulated he 'put the guy out in six rounds' since the machine was so arranged that 'a longer fight was undesirable.' The entire trip was conducted in complete secrecy since New Jersey laws prohibited the aiding and abetting of a prizefight."[12] Corbett's unlucky contender was Peter Courtney, a fighter from Trenton. Because Corbett was famous and Courtney was unknown, inexperienced, and not expected to win, Edison offered a purse of $5,000 to the winner and $250 to the loser. Edison's Kinetoscope Exhibiting Company was in fact formed for the express purpose of handling boxing "exhibit" films (since only boxing "exhibits" were legal).

The Raff and Martin Company also produced the highly popular comedy *The Comic View of Boxing, the Tramp and the Athlete*. The viewing public's obsession with violence and sex had been well established by the end of 1895. In addition to boxing films, the most popular flickers included *Cockfight #2* about chickens fighting to the death, *Princess Ali Egyptian Dance, Annabelle Serpentine Dance, The Execution of Mary, Queen of Scots*, and *Interrupted Lovers*.

By 1900, the moving pictures evolved to a point where they featured places of interest and real life dramas. One film to take on a more serious note was *Searching Ruins on Broadway for Dead Bodies*, about the devastation from the hurricane that destroyed Galveston, Texas, the hometown of future black heavyweight champion Jack Johnson. The first romantic comedies were *The Kiss*, and *The New Kiss*, filmed in February 1900. Along with *The Great Train Robbery* and *Uncle Tom's Cabin*, theater audiences saw *A Scrap in Black and White*, where two young boxers, one black and one white, fought to a finish with a twist at the end in that both were counted out.

Gans fights were popular. And while we have not turned up any Vaudeville play written directly for him, in 1906 a documentary-style attempt was made to capture on film the actual Fight of the Century between Joe Gans and Battling Nelson at Goldfield. It has been a little over one hundred years since that sweltering day in Nevada when Gans and Battling Nelson brawled for the packed crowds at the Goldfield stadium. The moving picture machine produced a ghostly primitive movie of the greatest fight of Gans' career. Knowing that they were making movie history, thousands of men, and even women, dressed in formal "theater" attire replete with summer straw hats and handlebar mustaches, came to sit in polite awe as Gans threw combination upon combination at the iron man from Denmark. The poor quality of the film and its uneven speed (because the film had to be hand-cranked before the lens) cannot obscure the mastery of his footwork or the relentless rat-a-tat rhythm of his punches in what remains the longest title fight ever to be filmed. Gans is listed today in the international movie database (IMDB) as the "star" of the 1906 silent movie *The Goldfield Fight with Joe Gans and Battling Nelson.*

After the silent era, Gans is portrayed in the 1929 film *The Seven Faces* starring Paul Muni, based on the short story "A Friend of Napoleon" by Robert Connell. Paul Muni earned an Oscar nomination for *The Valiant* in 1929 and played the original *Scarface* in 1932. That Joe Gans, one of the faces Muni portrayed, was given movie significance among the likes of Franz Schubert, Don Juan, and Napoleon suggests that at least in the popular imagination Gans' historical significance on the stage of sport put him in good company and had been well established two decades after his death. Connell's story, the basis for Muni's film, won the O. Henry Prize for short fiction, and dealt with the subject of respect for tradition and old masters such as Joe Gans. Connell also wrote *The Most Dangerous Game*, which was a forerunner of such movies as *Fantasy Island* and the James Bond movies.

The drama of the boxing ring and its stars also influenced the literature that was eventually brought to stage and screen. One of the earliest and perhaps most famous of American fairy tales influenced by boxing's popularity at the turn of the century was the story of the Wizard of Oz created by L. Frank Baum and immortalized in the 1939 Victor Fleming film. The first book by the Chicago author, *Wonderful Wizard of Oz*, was an instant success when it began rolling off the press in September of 1900, and the book and its subsequent series remained such for the next decade.

The book's illustrator, William Wallace Denslow, was an editorial cartoonist, and from this background biographers and scholars have theorized that the images in the story are drawn from politicians of the day. They say that the metaphors point to the economics of the 1890s, when silver replaced the gold standard (in the book Dorothy's shoes were silver instead of ruby as seen in the later film version). However, the fourteen books in the series reveal as much about the popular culture at the turn of the century as they do about political events. Both writer and illustrator, and later stage and film directors, were certainly aware of the high-profile figures involved in the phenomenon of boxing, as well as the culture of boxing with the same stereotypes of black fighters as of black actors in the early years of the entertainment industry. As a Chicagoan, Baum was aware of the imbroglio that occurred there in 1900 when Gans was said to have faked the fight and quit. When Gans attempted to fight in a private exhibition there in 1902, public opinion was so against him his match was cancelled. Black fighters could not escape being objects of debasing cartoon stereotypes from the white press. Gans and Walcott, and later Johnson, were seen as fakers, quitters, guilty of the yellowstreak, and they were consistently labeled as such to make them seem inferior to white fighters. Cartoons of various black fighters were similarly illustrated to show a shiftless, spineless, half-wit, watermelon-eating character.

Denslow's representation of the ragtag scarecrow in the Wizard series is reminiscent of the language used and the racist cartoon figures drawn in the newspapers during the Jim Crow era. "Jim Crow," or more simply, "crow," became a term of mockery of American blacks. And while there is no vaudevillian-like black-faced paint on Denslow's cartoon crow face, readers of the Oz books clearly recognized the implications in the caricature. The scarecrow, low on Darwin's evolutionary ladder, needed a brain. The scarecrow is certainly more frightened than frightening. And while he is found initially hanging from a pole, he is also deathly afraid of fire, reminding the reader from that era (with a perverse sense of comedy) of those who had the most to fear from lynchings, either by hanging from a pole or from burning at the stake. Dorothy, a concerned white woman, must extricate or liberate the helpless scarecrow.

The cowardly lion is also a figure drawn from the times. He is a fighter,

Boxing was the richest and most popular sport at the turn of the century. In 1900, Chicagoan J. Frank Baum published *The Wonderful Wizard of Oz*, a children's story, brought to life with images from the boxing ring (and symbols of the racial tensions of the time) that resonated with his adult readers. Here Dorothy must rescue a helpless, witless scarecrow from a pole. The scarecrow is deathly afraid of the flame. In 1925, the first full-length silent film of the story would paint the comic scarecrow black. The artist for the Oz book, William Denslow, was a newspaper cartoonist, and his lithographs seen here are similar in style to newspaper depictions of boxing in the prize ring.

The Oz characters meet for the first time. The "cowardly" lion on the "yellow-brick" road, actually a boxer who shows the "yellowstreak," has punched the hapless scarecrow off the page and threatened Dorothy's beloved dog.

Modern readers are unfamiliar with these original characters because they did not appear in the 1939 film *The Wizard of Oz.* The hammerheads were head-butters, like famed Battling Nelson. Head-butting was an acceptable tactic for bare-knuckle brawls, but considered a foul under the gloved rules of the Marquis of Queensberry. The blow from the long-necked head-butter knocks the cane and top-hat from the gentlemanly dressed scarecrow and turns the straw-stuffed character into a punching bag. The hammerheads are garbed for the spotlight as ring seconds, in suspenders and colorful sweaters, typically worn by the boxers.

a pugilist who throws blows with his paws, strikes at the woodman, and knocks the helpless scarecrow off the page. He bounds out of a forest thicket where trees shadow box. The problem with this brash talking, rough and bruising character is that he is a coward. This is the same accusation of the "yellowstreak" made against the black boxers at the time. News stories of Gans' first title fight with Erne in March of 1900, accused Gans of cowardice. And while the McGovern fiasco in Chicago was in December of 1900 and the book was already rolling off the press, the theme of cowardice resonated with author Baum and his Chicago readers. The "yellowstreak" had become a part of a racist mythology that would plague pugilism for years to come. Gans' life story was a total repudiation of that mythology. The values of courage, heart and home seen in the Wizard of Oz stories are those same values embodied in the best fighters of Gans' age, and are epitomized during Gans' courageous trip home to be with his family at the end of his life.

Baum adapted the Wizard of Oz for the stage in a musical that opened in Chicago in 1902 and played in New York with a successful run on Broadway beginning in 1903. It was the longest running Broadway musical of the first decade. Actress Indiola Arnold, whom Baum directed in the original play, became none other than the boxer's wife, Mrs. Kid McCoy, in January of 1904.[13] (It is said that the Kid was married ten times, four to the same woman, and he would have re-married her had he not shot her when she left him.)

The first Oz film was produced by Baum in 1908. Radio versions of the stories aired during that same year. The first full-length silent movie *Wizard of Oz* was made for Vitagraph in 1925 by director Larry Semon, a contemporary of Charlie Chaplin.[14] Semon made as much money on this film as Chaplin made on *The Little Tramp*. This silent movie included the actor Oliver Hardy who, along with his comic partner Laurel, appeared in other Semon directed films. Recognizing the ethnic implication in the original cowardly lion, Semon takes the character in this film to the most racist extreme. African-American actor Spencer Bell is given the screen pseudonym "G. Howe Black," and his character is a brainless, watermelon eating, lazy bum in coveralls, extremely superstitious, named Rastus. Director Semon, like so many others of this era, ended up in a sanitarium and died from TB at the early age of 39.

Unlike the slapstick, vaudevillian comedy of the earlier racist version, the 1939 film version of Oz minimizes this caricature. The modern viewer sees, certainly through a different cultural filter, a story of humorous characters set upon a more virtuous quest. Nevertheless, vestiges still exist of the Jim Crow age and the popular culture of the ring from which the characters are drawn. The lion is a fighter who issues a comical challenge, but a formal challenge by a contender nevertheless, in a growling bravado: "I'll fight 'em till...." The dialogue comes straight from the pugilistic challenges printed in the newspapers of the day by editors entrusted to hold match forfeiture deposits. To the sporting editor of the *Baltimore Sun*, for example, George McFadden insists that he be allowed to fight Gans: "I am willing to make all the concessions.... I'll box Gans at his own style.... I will box Gans in his own town."[15] The language of these challenges by up-and-coming contenders was familiar copy to newspaper readers of the day, as they looked to the sports reports to see which matches had been secured. Those same readers certainly recognized in the language of Baum's lion the boastful talk of the boxers.

Other characters in the book that did not make it into the 1939 movie with Judy Garland are drawn from the dirty antics of some of the prize-fighters when boxing was moving out of the bare-knuckle era and into the gloved era when the rules were more or less determined by each referee. Head-butting, for example, was considered acceptable behavior in the bare-knuckle brawls. It was quite disallowed in the gloved-rings under the Marquis of Queensberry rules. That was not to say that a head-butt was always considered a foul at the turn of the century. It was a vicious antic to be sure, and the cause of Joe Gans' terrible eye injury in the ring with Frank Erne in March of 1900. Many referees turned a blind eye to these and other fouls, but Gans' eye injury was the kind of gory image that made ring news countrywide.

Like many brutal gladiators in the ring, such as Battling Nelson, the hammerheads of the Oz books are experts in head-butting. Their powerful long necks, exaggerated for effect, are hidden behind their proper bow ties, but their head butts pack a wallop, as Denslow illustrates. The artist gives the hammerheads a fine set of clothes, and many historians have suggested that these clothes point to the rich and powerful businessmen of the day. However, readers of that period recognized a rising social class that could afford $5 suits, such as the flashy men of the ring. The hammerheads are illustrated wearing the colorful clothing worn by boxers and their seconds. Their shirts are far too bright and interesting — with polka dots — to have been worn by white-collar, suited businessmen. But ring men, on the other hand, enjoyed dressing up for the occasions when they would be in the spotlight. Like the hammerheads, ring seconds seldom wore coats and were invariably seen wearing suspenders in their active attendance.

The scarecrow dressed as a gentleman suffers a dirty assault when the hammerhead butts him and sends his top hat and cane flying. Adult readers of the early Oz children's books certainly recognized the familiar and scandalous characters of the ring and the social humor of the day portrayed by writer Baum and artist Denslow.

Some scholars of American society suggest that by the end of the nineteen hundreds the movies had replaced religion in forming the country's identity, mythologies, and cultural touchstones. Boxing movies such as *On the Waterfront*, *Rocky*, *Raging Bull*, and *Cinderella Man* explore the heroism as well as the dark underbelly of American life. Boxing as metaphor has outstripped boxing as sport in its importance to Americans today. Although moviemaking would find its primary home in Southern California, it would become a central part of all American and world culture, and its ties with pugilism would draw ever tighter.

From 1902 through 1909, Joe Gans made nine pilgrimages to California. His biggest bouts would be staged in the West, still very wild. Each event was covered with keen interest by the local newspapers. The *San Francisco Examiner* and the *Los Angeles Times* reported on the training camps of Gans and his opponents, the weigh-in, the fights and their aftermath. The chronicles of Gans' triumphs and tragedies as told in the newspapers of the Golden State provided entertainment and inspiration, as part of the real-life action drama of the boxing ring.

Gans had become the Old Master of fistiana. In addition to dominating the lightweights of the era, Gans squared off against some of the greatest welterweights in history, who were at that time plying their trades in the rings of California.

13

Forays at Welterweight

If Gans were fighting in the early 21st century with its proliferation of world boxing titles, he could easily win five or six titles from featherweight to welterweight if he so desired. The prestige of winning titles in several weight divisions is a relatively new concept in boxing. Gans, as the record will show, could have been recognized as featherweight and welterweight champion in his own day. In fact, it is one of the curiosities of boxing history that he is not considered to be a lineal welterweight champion.

Joe Gans never failed to take on the best men, large or small. From 1891 to 1897, records show Gans as the featherweight champion of Maryland, the Southern featherweight champion, and otherwise indicate that Gans was the premier boxer at the 126-pound limit. Of course history knows him as a light-weight champion.

Gans fought more-or-less comfortably at lightweight from 1897 to 1903. After that time it was difficult for him to make the lightweight limit of 133 pounds ringside. His natural weight was somewhere between 136 and 140 pounds. Today, he would probably fight at junior welterweight and have easy pickings there. Instead, Gans was fighting men of sizes up to light-heavy-weight.

Gans Boxes Future Heavyweight Legend Sam Langford

In 1903 at the welterweight limit, Gans fought a 15-round bout to a standstill with the "Boston Tar Baby," Sam Langford. The immortal Langford is more known for his efforts against the great middleweight champion Stanley Ketchel, the "Michigan Assassin," and his ability to fight great heavyweights like Jack Johnson on even terms. Langford would go on to greater fame as a top heavyweight.

Gans fought Langford in Boston on the day after he met the tough Dave Holly in Philadelphia. Gans was always in need of money and fought Langford after his Holly bout and a train ride from Philly. A dispatch from Boston reported, "From a technical point the bout was a first-class one. Both men led well, blocked well and ducked well. The first three rounds were easily Gans.' Gans was out-pointed and did not appear at all up to his usual form. It was said after the bout that he had been severely attacked with stomach trouble this afternoon, hence his poor condition."[1]

A recent survey of boxing experts rated Langford in the top 10 of all-time fighters. According to the ESPN poll:

> "The Boston Tar Baby" was an exceedingly strong, stout fighter of overwhelming ability and punching power. He had a great chin and heart. Although a natural middleweight he was at his peak as a light heavyweight in the 1910s. Sam scored knockouts over nearly all of the top heavyweights of his time. Langford is either first or second for scoring the most knockouts in boxing history depending on whose research one accepts. Sam defeated 6 Hall of Famers: Joe Gans, Dixie Kid, Sam McVey, Joe Jeannette, Harry Wills and Philadelphia Jack O'Brien. Langford received the second most first place votes, but was a distant second to Robinson. More than half the voters had Sam in the top 10. In the poll of experts, 25 of 30 voters had him inside the top 20.[2]

Yet Gans would have likely beaten the future terror of the heavyweights if he had not been sick with a stomach ailment and exhausted from the overnight train ride from his fight with top welterweight Dave Holly the day prior. Although Gans' recurring illness during the month of December 1903 was never fully described in the news, his poor condition caused him to miss a rematch that had been scheduled with Jack Blackburn in Baltimore for December 21.[3]

Gans Wins Newspaper Decision over Barbados Joe Walcott

In 1895, *New York Sun* writer Charles A. Dana stated, "There are two negroes in the ring today who can thrash any white man breathing in their respective classes ... George Dixon ... and Joe Walcott."[4]

"Welter" means flurry, and it was an apt depiction of the century's first champion of the welters, "The Barbados Demon," whom Gans bested in 1904. In *The Legendary Champions*, Rex Lardner writes about how Walcott was Jack Johnson's mentor. "Walcott, 'the Barbados Demon,' who was to become the world's welterweight champion in 1901 (and beat quite a few heavyweights before reaching that pinnacle), was a short, thick-necked, strong-chested man with a formidable reach and a tremendous punch. Like Johnson, he had run away from home at an early age and had taken to boxing as his best way to earn a living, fighting for purses that at times were as little as $2.50. Walcott took a liking to Johnson, although this did not prevent him from handing the thin lad a walloping in their sparring sessions. The punishment meted out by Walcott, however, was a minor annoyance compared to the rods and racing on top of freight cars to avoid the cruel bludgeons of railroad guards. In the meantime, Johnson was absorbing a great deal of fighting knowledge, particularly learning how to defend himself."[5] Walcott easily battered the great future heavyweight champion, and yet Walcott was a man whom Gans defeated rather easily.

Barbados Joe Walcott talked the talk and walked the walk of the rough-and-tumble Caribbean shanty towns from whence he hailed. Nat Fleischer and other ring authorities have rated him the greatest welterweight ever. Although he weighed only 145 pounds, he knocked out heavyweights and handled the men in his own weight class with ease. In 1900, Walcott knocked out the fearsome heavyweight Joe Choynski, the same heavyweight who went on to vanquish Jack Johnson the next year in a three-round knockout. It was Joe Walcott, the 5' 2" Barbados Demon, welterweight champion of the world from 1901 to 1904, who actually coined the phrase "the bigger they are the harder they fall." In 1904, Joe Gans challenged for Walcott's title in San Francisco.

Walcott had fought the great Sam Langford to a draw. His 20-round fight with Gans was also ruled a draw, although everyone thought Gans had won handily. The decision of referee Jack Welch was hissed when he announced his verdict. Welch told the press, "I feel my decision was the only one possible. Gans was the cleverer, but Walcott forced the fighting. Gans had the shade, but not strong enough to earn him the heavy end of the fighter's share. Walcott landed frequently and I concluded that his aggressiveness offset Gans' masterly boxing."[6]

After his fight with Joe Gans, Walcott made this statement to the press: "My left arm went back on me in the third round and I fought seventeen rounds with my right. If I wasn't crippled Gans would have dropped for the count. The trouble wouldn't have lasted more than ten or twelve rounds. I was always after him and kept him dancing around all the time. I think I was entitled to the victory, and I also think that the majority of the spectators will say that I showed that I am a better man than that nigger from Baltimore."[7]

Gans responded, "What's the use of complaining? Mr. Welch says it was a draw. I refuse to express my opinion concerning the decision. I think it.... Well, I won't say what. I wasn't hurt at all and could have gone on for another twenty rounds. The only punches that hurt me were those that Mr. Walcott drove into my ribs. I stalled around near the end, figuring I had earned the decision. So far as I'm concerned I'll fight him at any time and bet every cent I can get on myself. I'm Mr. Walcott's master."[8]

The statements made by the referee and the boxers appeared the next day under the headline "Gans Outpoints Walcott, But Referee Calls It Draw: Ruling Makes Crowd Frown."[9]

Gans Defeats Jack Blackburn, Future Teacher of Joe Louis

Gans fought Jack Blackburn three times. Gans won once, a decision on points in a 15-round bout, and he fought two no-decision bouts with the man who would one day make a great fighter of Joe Louis. Blackburn,

One of the greats defeated by Gans. Here is Jack Blackburn (right) with his charge, heavyweight great Joe Louis. Blackburn is as tall as Louis, and yet Gans showed his mastery in their three fights (courtesy Tracy Callis, boxing historian).

described as a racehorse, was taller and bigger than Gans, weighing ten to fifteen pounds heavier than the lightweight. Blackburn could beat most middleweights and even heavyweights of his day. He respected Gans as a fighting master, but when his career was at its end, he became a bitter man. He would tell a young Joe Louis, "Every time you get in that ring, you got to let your right hand be your referee."[10] In other words, don't trust the judging system that had deprived Blackburn of his due because of his color.

Gans Beats the English Champ

On May 27, 1904, in his hometown of Baltimore before the Eureka Athletic and Social Club, Gans went up against the English lightweight champion "Jewey" Cook. Gans had studied his fighting record and assumed the champion to be a tough competitor. It was said that because Gans trained for the match, he "showed like the Gans of old. He fought more like himself than he has done in several months."[11] In addition to being the British champion, Cook was also the welterweight champion of South Africa. The two were to fight fifteen rounds. No punches were landed in the first round. There was swift sparring in the second and Gans knocked his man to the ground in the third. Gans took an uppercut to the jaw in the sixth, but in the seventh, Gans knocked his opponent down to a count of 9, and in the eighth, knocked him down again to a count of five, after which he got up, told the referee he was hurt, and quit.

Gans Knocks Out Twin Sullivan, Twice

Before his 1906 fight with Mike "Twin" Sullivan, the *San Francisco Examiner* reported on January 16, 1906, "If Gans Wins He'll Hold Two Championships." That he easily whipped Sullivan is clear. The day after the fight, the papers featured a splendid photo of a gladiatorial conqueror, in the person of Gans, standing over Sullivan. What is unclear is why Gans was never given proper credit for becoming a titlist at welterweight.

Twin Sullivan was clearly a lineal welterweight champion after beating Jimmy Gardner, the Lowell man who was considered practically unbeatable. Gans, in turn, beat Sullivan not once, but three times, knocking him out twice. For some reason Sullivan continued to be recognized as the welterweight champion until 1908. Sullivan was so good that he was matched with Stanley Ketchel, whom Nat Fleischer rates as the greatest middleweight ever.

Sullivan, although closer in poundage to middleweight than lightweight,

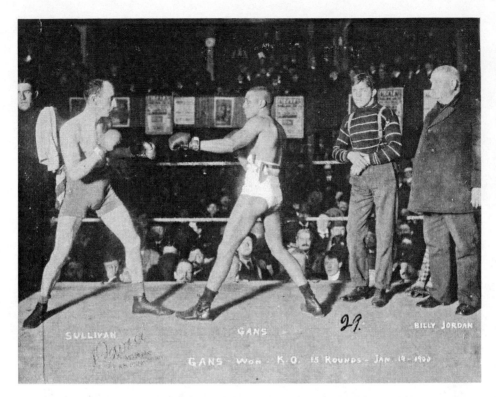

Joe Gans and Mike "Twin" Sullivan pose for the camera before their January 19, 1906, welterweight title fight at Woodward's Pavilion in San Francisco. Gans won by KO in 15 rounds. Sullivan claimed the welterweight title after facing Gans. (The Old Master knocked Twin out twice.) Also pictured are Gans' "second," fighter Willie Fitzgerald and Civil War veteran and famed ring announcer Billy Jordan at age 74. Jordan is later portrayed as the chief angel in the play "Heaven Can Wait." Photograph from the Dana Studios, San Francisco, 1906 (courtesy Tracy Callis, boxing historian).

was actually another pretender to the lucrative lightweight title that Gans had never abdicated. In the terms for his fight with Gans in January 1906, it was agreed that both fighters could weigh ten pounds over the lightweight limit. The odds before the fight were fairly even and Gans surprised the San Francisco crowd by thrashing his opponent in a one-sided fight, knocking him to the ground in the eighth and out in the tenth round.

The fight also put Gans back into the good graces of the San Francisco boxing public by defeating the rugged welterweight champion Mike "Twin" Sullivan. After the fight, famed sportswriter Naughton wrote: "Now Gans is the Idol of Boxing Patrons:" "Gans and his marvelously well balanced fighting talents being the one and only subject of discussion.... The sports of this city want to see more of him." The pen that had poisoned his reputation earlier and made life so difficult for him now added: "There was none willing to advance the argument that a better man than Gans, at equal weights, is to be found boxing for a living to day."[12] But nothing was ever mentioned again about transferring the welterweight title to the ebony champion.

Gans Shares Headlines with Kid McCoy

One of the welterweights that Gans did not meet (because he was fighting heavier men), but who is worth noting as emblematic of the era, was the famous Kid McCoy, whose real name was Norman Selby. McCoy, a slick hustler of the day, was also one of the all-time great fighters, and the first of many to use the "Kid" moniker. The Kid knocked out all comers, from welterweights to heavyweights, with his famous twist of the wrist "corkscrew punch." McCoy fought at weights from 140 to 180 pounds in the gay '90s. He defeated welterweight champs Mysterious Billy Smith and Jack Ryan. For years, fight fans eagerly anticipated a match between McCoy and Gentleman Jim Corbett.

Alexander Johnson, in his boxing history *Ten-And Out*, describes how McCoy won the welterweight title. "McCoy was always a sly bird, and he managed to have Tommy Ryan misinformed to the effect that McCoy was not in good training.... In the fifteenth, just after the bell rang starting the round, McCoy caught Ryan in the wind with his left, then crossed his right like a shot, and there was a new welterweight champion. This bout was hailed all over the country as a magnificent example of the doublecross. McCoy held the welter crown until the end of 1897."[13]

In an era fraught with dishonesty and fraud, McCoy's heroic and earnest battles with the heavyweights drew the attention of sportswriters. McCoy had been off and on as a fighter, and in and out of an institution for a complete mental breakdown, but when he was on his game, he was a terror. After his knock-down, drag-out with Joe Choynski in 1900, one of the sportswriters exclaimed, "Last night we saw the 'Real McCoy.'"[14] Like Gans, both Walcott and McCoy gave the English language a trademark phrase that would become part of the national lexicon. But unlike Gans, the Kid squandered his talent through drinking and chasing women. He frequently got drunk, engaged in saloon brawls, and was prone to street fights. In a separate article in the same paper where sportswriter and referee George Siler summarized the notable pugilistic year of 1900 and his accomplishments, the *Chicago Tribune* reported that McCoy was nursing an injured hand, with possible blood poisoning, from a street brawl.[15] On his tenth wife, the Kid was found with another man's wife. It was not his corkscrew punch but a handgun the Kid used to show the irate husband who was boss. For the man whose party never ended, the road ended in San Quentin. Kid McCoy was accused of everything from being a flimflam artist to committing murder. He spent seven years in prison for manslaughter. One thing nobody ever accused him of was cowardice.

Here is an account of his fight with Joe Choynski in San Francisco: Choynski went down once in the first round. In the second, McCoy went down four times, but the timekeeper's gong ended the round 42 seconds too early. With a one minute, forty second rest between rounds, McCoy was fairly clearheaded coming out for the third. The newspapers called that round a "melee of two madmen."[16] When it ended, each was covered with blood and so was the canvas. As the gong sounded to end the third round — or just after, according to Choynski supporters — McCoy landed a vicious blow. Choynski dropped like a pole-axed steer.

McCoy staggered out for the fourth round and could not see Choynski lying at his feet. The referee gave McCoy the fight. Enraged fans screamed "foul." Most never noticed that one of their number had died in the excitement. This type of knockdown, drag-out brawl was typical circa 1900.

Gans Paves the Way for Hammerin' Hank Armstrong

There is ample evidence that Gans legitimately deserves to be credited as a champion in three of the original six weight classes: featherweight, lightweight, and welterweight. This is significant in assessing his historical importance when comparing him to other greats. Holding three titles in the 1930s when there were only eight is the primary reason that Henry Armstrong usually finishes in the top three when discussing all-time great fighters. Like Armstrong, Gans held three titles, but Gans held them over a much longer period. Armstrong earned the nickname "perpetual motion" for his non-stop style, and it was a very appropriate nickname for the scrappy welterweight battler. In 1937 Henry Armstrong would make a splash by winning the featherweight, lightweight, and welterweight championship, 3 of the 8 recognized world titles. Armstrong is usually rated as the second or third greatest fighter to ever live, based in large part on his holding the 3 titles.

Armstrong campaigned at the same time Joe Louis was occupying the attention of the American public. He was really a natural welterweight for most of his career. The goal of going after three titles was mainly to gain publicity, and it worked famously.

Armstrong was indeed a great fighter but it should be emphasized in assessing historical greatness that Gans could have easily held three titles. He was for many years recognized as the world's best welterweight. He beat the incumbent welterweight champ in title matches twice in San Francisco. The first time was against Barbados Joe Walcott, whom Nat Fleischer, the premier boxing historian, rated the greatest welterweight ever to live. Although Gans clearly won the fight, he accepted the draw verdict in stride. "What's the use of complaining?" he said.[17] In fact he probably had no real interest in holding the welterweight crown, since all the money at that time was in the lightweight ranks.

For most of the 20th century the welterweight division was mainly a rest stop for great lightweight and middleweight fighters. The name "welter" brings to mind an image of chaos but in fact some of the smoothest, most disciplined fighters in history did their best work at welterweight.

Henry Armstrong defended his welterweight title 18 times in a two-year span. He never successfully defended either his lightweight or featherweight titles. Sugar Ray Robinson was known more for winning and losing championships than for defending them, but he did manage several defenses of his welterweight laurels in the late '40s. Even Roberto Duran, the legendary lightweight champ with *manos de piedra*, hands of stone, had his most glorious moment when he dethroned Sugar Ray Leonard for the welterweight title.

The lack of notoriety for the 147-pounders may have been nothing more than a matter of packaging and name recognition. Lightweight, middleweight, and heavyweight are all self explanatory. But few outside of boxing circles really know anything about welterweights.

Despite the lack of recognition of welterweights, Gans also had some of his best fights in that category. Many boxing historians have perpetuated the erroneous notion that Gans gave up his lightweight crown when he fought welterweights in 1903 and '04. The fact that he had been fighting against welterweights added grist to the mill.

Gans even toyed with the idea of fighting a great light-heavyweight champion. Philadelphia Jack O'Brien had defeated one of Gans' good friends, Bob Fitzsimmons. One of "the most novel challenges in the history of the prize ring" wrote the sports editor for the *Philadelphia Enquirer* on January 31, 1903, was offered by Gans to "Philadelphia" Jack O'Brien.[18] With a 27-pound difference in weight, Gans challenged the world light-heavyweight title holder to a knock-out "handicap" in 6 rounds: O'Brien would win the entire purse if he could knock out Gans in 6-rounds; however if Gans remained conscious after 6 rounds, he would win the purse. It is said that O'Brien wanted to take on the challenge but he could not fight Gans at the time because he was nursing a broken right knuckle from his previous fight with Joe Grim.

Beginning in the forties, with the Schick Friday Night Fights, the welterweights became a marquis division. Sugar Ray Robinson, Kid Gavilan, Carmen Basilio, and other greats painted masterpieces on the ring canvas at 147 pounds. In the early eighties, Sugar Ray Leonard, Thomas Hearns, and Roberto Duran fought masterfully at welterweight. Today the welterweights share the limelight, but in Gans' day it was a road-to-nowhere division.

As he would prove in each of his outings at welterweight, Joe made the grade, an A-plus at this weight. In retrospect, had the money been in the welterweight division rather than in the lightweight, Joe's rendezvous with the Grim Reaper may have been delayed until he reached old age. His forays at welterweight represent the good years athletically for Joe. Unfortunately, when he came back down to "make the weight" at 133 pounds in the 1906 Goldfield fight, his doom was sealed under the blistering Nevada sun.

Although Gans never lost his lightweight title in the ring, his ventures in welterweight contributed to the situation in which it was taken from him in the public's mind. Soon after his fight with Walcott (an all-time classic) the lightweight pretenders to the throne were claiming that Gans could no longer make the lightweight limit. The record books do not reflect just how financially bleak was the year 1905 for Joe Gans. A reader gets the impression that he was "coasting" as the lightweight champ or had moved up to welterweight, as is the common practice today.

Gans' travails are aptly mirrored in Charles E. Van Loan's famous 1913 short story "One-Thirty-Three Ringside."

> "...and there isn't a welter in the country today that would draw a two-thousand-dollar house. I suppose we'll have to go back to the six- and ten-round no-decision things, splitting the money even, and agreeing to box easy! Yah! A fine game, that is."
> "I suppose you think you ought to grab this fight with Cline?"
> "Well," said the business manager, "There's more money losing to Cline — don't get excited, kid: let me talk — than we could get by winning from a flock of pork-and-bean welters."[19]

The fact is that Gans, whom even the racist editors of his day were calling "the greatest to ever don the mitts," was down-and-out financially in 1905, without a manager, barely able to support himself and his family. The exiled king of the lightweights finally found sanctuary in southern California, regaining the spotlight by defeating the taller and heavier Mike "Twin" Sullivan in a bout billed as a welterweight championship match.

Gans' forays at welterweight did not bring him the big purses. These would come against a great lightweight, the "Battling Dane," beginning in the year 1906. Today a remnant surviving the Ragtime era, drawn from the year 1906, is the image of the "girl in the red velvet swing." Evelyn Nesbitt, the famous New York stage actress, shocked and seduced the nation at the trial of her husband, who had killed Standford White, the great architect, in the rooftop theater at Madison Square Garden. Today, the Nesbitt affair stands out as a famous news event of that year, in part as the result of the popularity of the movie *Ragtime*. However, at the time, a lightweight boxing match to be held in Goldfield, Nevada, is what most captivated the American imagination. Before Gans could "bring home the bacon" to open the Goldfield Hotel in Baltimore, he would have to fight in Goldfield, Nevada, against one of the toughest men to ever walk the earth. Gans would have to fight the "Durable Dane."

14

ᕯᘐᕯ

Epic Battle in
the Nevada Desert

The city of Goldfield, Nevada, haunts a stretch of high desert halfway between Reno and Las Vegas on Highway 95. Before its population climbed to its present number of 300, it was a ghost town, the kind that Ronald Reagan spun tales about on the television show *Death Valley Days*. In January of 1904 when prospectors discovered a belt of gold there, word of the "January Claim" spread, drawing speculators like a magnet. But it was a boxing match in 1906 that put the desert mining camp on the map and started the amazing fight-promoting career of George Lewis "Tex" Rickard, the Don King and Bob Arum of the early 20th century.

Tex Rickard: Joe Gans Was His First
Boxing Gold Mine

In a swashbuckling feat of entrepreneurial initiative, Rickard, the larger-than-life Goldfield saloonkeeper, inadvertently launched his brilliant career in the fight business by arranging the first and grandest "Fight of the Century," long before his promotion of the Dempsey-Tunney or Johnson-Jeffries fights. Speaking nostalgically about the event fifty years later, "Kid" Highley, one of Rickard's early partners and wealthy townsmen, remarked, "There has never been anything like it."[1]

Rickard couldn't have done better if he had resurrected Abe Lincoln and Jefferson Davis or Ulysses S. Grant and Robert E. Lee and put them in a ring together in some place like Tijuana. It was a match of epic proportion, triggering the largest gold speculation since the Comstock Lode of 1871. The entire English-speaking world would wait anxiously to hear the live reports of the fight telegraphed from Goldfield, beginning at 3:00 P.M., Nevada time,

Monday, September 3, 1906, Labor Day in America. The lightweight championship of the world would be determined in a gladiatorial fight to the finish between two of the world's best: Oscar Mathew Nielson, known as "Battling" Nelson, of Hegewisch, Illinois, and Joe Gans of Baltimore. As the newspapers were clear to add, Gans was "colored," making the colossal event more than a world title fight.

Tex Rickard would go on to re-invent Madison Square Garden, turning it into the world's boxing Mecca, and he would become the greatest impresario of the massively lucrative big-fight business before he died in 1929. Born in 1871 in Kansas City, Missouri, Rickard drifted to Texas as a youth, where he spent time running longhorns on the great cattle drives to Montana, earning an earthy reputation as a cowboy. At twenty-three, he became sheriff of Henrietta, Texas, and then moved on to Alaska, where he was given the nickname "Tex." There in the Klondike, he discovered a business that would make him his first fortune when he set up a "gambling tent" near the strike at Nome and began serving the miners who trusted him more than they did the local bank with their gold. Later, Rickard's hotel and saloon, The Northern, brought in a half-million dollar bonanza when he sold his partnership interest after four years.[2]

Running through his money, Rickard traveled down to Nevada with the first "rush" to Goldfield. The mines around Goldfield produced $2,300,000 that first year, 1904. With his flair for harnessing grandness, Rickard set up the biggest saloon business in the history of the Old West to garner part of the astounding wealth by quenching the thirsts and the compulsive gambling appetites of the miners who became rich overnight. His gambling hall, with fourteen game tables to accommodate roulette, faro, blackjack and craps, was serviced by eighty bartenders. The doors never closed, and two or more floor bosses, one of whom was Virgil Earp (prior to his taking the job of deputy sheriff) and the other was sometimes Rickard himself, ran an orderly operation. In short time Rickard became one of the leading financiers in the state. Considered a "settler" of the area, he put down roots by building a respectable brick Victorian home, the first building of its kind in Goldfield.

Like other Nevada mining camps where hopefuls flocked when silver or gold was discovered (e.g. 6,000 people came to Rhyolite in 1905), Goldfield grew up quickly, to a population of 8000 by 1906. But on April 18, 1906, five months before the Goldfield fight, an earthquake rocked San Francisco, the largest town and the banking center of the West. The resulting fire destroyed the city, burned bank records, and displaced over 250,000 people, immediately halting all types of service. The San Francisco Stock Exchange, the principal market for the Goldfield mining stocks, closed for over two months, creating a financial panic in the silver state. According to one memoir, "Every bank in Nevada closed down, just as every California bank did.... Nevada banks, as a rule, had cleared through San Francisco banks, and practically all of Nevada's cash was tied up by the catastrophe."[3] Goldfield merchants and bankers were left with only the cash in their vaults. Desperate for new funds, mining brokers began selling stocks directly to eastern markets to avoid the disaster suffered by other ore-made cities in the fickle boom-and-bust mining economy.

Owners of Goldfield's financial establishments felt that a public attraction of some kind on a grand scale was needed to generate infusions of cash in Goldfield mining stocks. In addition to the fifty saloons, the town had four banks, a stock exchange of its own (the Goldfield Stock Exchange, including one established by a group of women when the men tried to exclude them from financial dealings), and more rascals selling worthless mining paper than any other western town. It was said that before the second rush ended, "the American public sank $150,000,000 into worthless mining properties in that state."[4]

When a committee of distinguished citizens was formed to brainstorm proposals, one gentleman suggested that a giant hole be dug along the main street and filled with free beer. Others thought a camel race would attract attention. The notion was actually practical because dromedaries were accessible from the prospectors who were using them at the time. The miners had captured the feral animals roaming the arid western deserts long after they were abandoned by the United States government. The beasts had been used to deliver mail from Texas to California when the southwestern territories were acquired after the War with Mexico.

Rickard's notion of a prizefight would have sounded implausible were it not for his infinite luck, not to mention his deep pockets. He was a trusted, jovial fellow with a powerful personality and wealth of "worldly" experience. But Rickard's sole experience with the sport had been in meeting boxing aficionado Jack Kearns in Alaska (Kearns would later manage Jack Dempsey), overseeing a few miners' brawls in his saloons, and attending a professional boxing match that same year, on May 26 in New York between Jimmy Britt and Terry McGovern. This fight made such an impression that the innovative Texan saw in a top-notched fight an opportunity to fuse the excitement of selling shares in gold-prospecting claims with the mystique and glory of the professional prize ring.

An even more convincing argument for the entertainment was that Rickard was willing to back his idea with a personal investment of $30,000. Pooling their resources to a cool $50,000, a committee chartered the Goldfield

Athletic Club and elected another well-known community member as its first president. In his biography of Tex Rickard, Charles Samuels describes the new club official. "Though head of the Sullivan Trust Company, whose bustling office was next door to The Northern, L.M. Sullivan was an almost illiterate lout, but apt at conniving and scheming."[5] Prior to coming to Goldfield, Sullivan ran a rooming house for sailors in Seattle. He became so noted for selling off his ragtag "guests" to boats headed for the Orient that he was known as "Shanghai Larry." But in Goldfield, Larry's newfound wealth in the trust business bought him a place of respect at the civic table. As president of the new Goldfield Athletic Club, Sullivan wanted no part of the hard work necessary to pull off an elaborate boxing event. He simply wanted to be in position to name himself as announcer and master of ceremonies at the big event.

And so it was left to Rickard to organize the complex event and begin negotiations for the boxers and construction of an arena that would accommodate the thousands of fans the town anticipated. Without knowing anything about the fight business, not even the going rate for big-purse events, Rickard's instincts again proved correct. Gambling that high-priced tickets would offset the large purse and the costly initial investment, Rickard's successful event ended up paying for itself several times over, creating a stampede to buy local mining stocks, and bringing a great deal of notoriety to the state.

With ready cash to offer as a purse, and a stout reserve if need be, Rickard hoped to replicate the fight he had seen in New York. He first telegraphed an invitation to McGovern's manager, Joe Humphreys. In the summer of 1906, both fighter and manager were out of work and penniless; but Humphreys, who never in his managerial days had ever heard of a $15,000 purse, read the offer by the unknown promoter as a hoax and disposed of the telegram — never mentioning it to McGovern. Undaunted by the lack of response, Rickard's second choice for fighters turned out to be his lucky charm.

Rickard Capitalizes on Lightweight Title Controversy

The entrepreneur had stumbled into and was able to capitalize on the fact that in 1906 the lightweight title happened to be in dispute in San Francisco. Although Gans had won the title in 1902 when he knocked out Frank Erne in the first round and held better claim to the lightweight championship, by 1906 Battling Nelson was also claiming the title. During his reign, Gans had successfully defended his title against all challengers including Jimmy

Britt in October of 1904. But in the fracas that ensued after that fight in 1904, Britt argued that he had won the title by claiming a better "showing." By virtue of the fact that Gans had gone on to fight welterweights, Britt's backers argued that Gans had abandoned the lightweight division. It should be noted here that Gans would fight and win handily against Britt during 1907 in San Francisco, but Britt's phony title succession began in 1904 when he claimed the lightweight crown. By 1906, Nelson considered himself the champion by virtue of having knocked out Britt in the 18th round in September 1905 in Colma, California. With Gans unable to get fights because he "had long been rated as invincible against anyone, including heavyweights" and without a manager to speak for his interests, Nelson had become a very popular fighter in the lightweight division.[6]

Rickard, however, didn't care about reputations for fakes or quibbles in the past. Despite his inexperience with the professional sport, with unwavering nerve to handle any man, Rickard was eager to make a match with Gans. The public re-match between Nelson and Gans at Goldfield would settle the claim to the world title once and for all. The new promoter was determined to make it the grandest event the world had ever seen.

With Gans lacking a manager, Rickard had difficulty at first getting the offer into his hands. Rickard had heard that Gans was in San Francisco and requested help from W. W. Naughton, sports editor of Hearst's paper in San Francisco. With his contacts, Naughton located Gans and relayed the offer. In wiring Rickard that he would take the fight, Gans agreed to any terms Nelson demanded, so desperate was he for a fight.

Once Rickard had his contestants, he turned on the publicity spigot and it ran until the day of the fight. He knew how it felt to see gold stacked on the gambling table, and he created quite a stir when he displayed the entire $30,000 purse in twenty-dollar gold pieces in full view through a window of the John S. Cook Bank of Goldfield.

Matching Gans with Nelson created its own publicity. The two fighters' styles couldn't be any different. Nelson was the younger and a dirty fighter. Gans was a veteran technician and gentleman. Battling Nelson was born in Copenhagen in 1882. His nickname, the "Durable Dane," captured his superhuman ability to withstand pugilistic punishment. As Tracy Callis summarized, "Nelson was one of the roughest, toughest men to ever enter the ring, no doubt about it. He could box a little but rarely did. He preferred to brawl."[7] His offense was punishing. Nelson was known for his "scissors hook," a "short left hook aimed at the liver or kidneys with his thumb and forefinger extended to give a painful pinch or stab" through the thinly-padded gloves.[8]

Once when Columbia rowing coach Dr. Walter B. Peet examined the

Dane for his endurance, he found the boxer's heartbeat to be an incredible 47 beats per minute compared to the norm of 72, a heartbeat he said that was only found in the "colder-blooded animals which survived the days of antiquity and the cold of the Ice Age."[9] Consulting with surgeons and the curator of the American Museum of Natural History, Peet and his experts agreed that calculations of Nelson's head revealed the "thickest skull bones of any human being since Neanderthal man."[10] And yet for all his brute strength, amazing endurance, and age advantage (Nelson was in his prime at 24 and Gans at 32 was considered old), Billy Nolan, Nelson's manager, worried about a loss to the sterling technical skills of the master boxer. But he knew Gans was dead broke and could be forced into concessions.

Nolan ruthlessly sought to preserve his man's title. With the pounds Gans had added fighting in the welterweight division, Nolan threw his force into the weight issue. He knew that shedding the pounds to make 133 would be such a terrible strain on Gans' body that it would tax his stamina and give an advantage to Nelson, who would have no trouble making the weight. Because Gans was financially desperate and without a persuasive negotiator, Nolan was able to call the shots in the Articles of Agreement and claim an unequal percentage of the purse. Gans would get $10,000 — Nelson $20,000 of the $30,000 total fighters' purse. In addition, Gans had to succumb to the unheard of triple weigh-ins before the match. Gans argued for a single weigh-in at noon, but Nolan stipulated that there must be three: noon, 2:30 and 3:00 — when the match was set to begin. Nolan was skeptical that Gans could make the initial weight restriction, but if he did, Nolan didn't want him to try to re-nourish himself before the fight and take on any weight after reducing to the initial limit. He wanted him worn out at the start of the fight.

Gans' New Manager: Out of the Frying Pan into the Fire

Getting to Nevada proved stressful enough for Gans. In his biography of Tex Rickard, Charles Samuels states that Gans "was so broke that he had to borrow train fare to get to Goldfield with his white trainer, Frank Mac-Donald."[11] The arrival of his train at the newly constructed Goldfield station brought out the crowds. The miners were especially taken by the humble man and throughout Gans' stay in Goldfield they were decidedly in the champion's corner. He was a man of the people. Everyone said Gans had the kind of true magnetism that drew you to him. As acting president of the club, Larry M. Sullivan was at Gans' arrival to "officially" greet the fighter and chauffeur his small entourage of two through the throng of 1500 cheering miners.

During the short drive to Tex's saloon, The Northern, Sullivan learned that Gans had no manager and in fact had no money to pay for his appearance and the weight forfeiture amount necessary for the fight to go forward. Nelson's manager demanded $5000, a sum which Sullivan graciously offered to pay, with only one string attached: that Gans allow him to be his new manager.

Gans had been shanghaied again. Sullivan dropped MacDonald at The Northern and told him to "drink up" at the new manager's expense. He then showed Gans through the Sullivan Trust Company where dozens of bookkeepers sat at desks working on stock orders that had come in that day through the mail as a result of the tremendous publicity. He ushered Gans into a private office where he introduced the boxer to his partner and general manager, George Graham Rice. In that back room outfitted as luxuriously as any

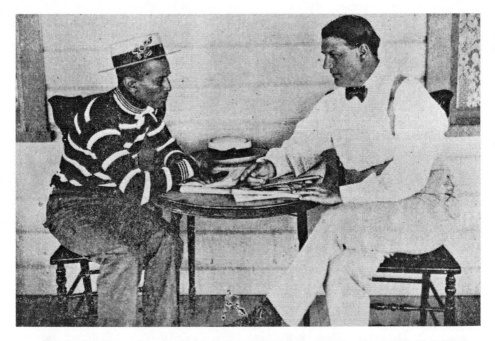

Joe Gans (left) could not afford the $5000 forfeit deposit for the Goldfield fight. A generous donation for the fee and expenses was made by "Shanghai" Larry Sullivan (right) in return for allowing him to manage the Old Master. Sullivan's celebrity never matched that of the fight's promoter, Tex Rickard. While the publicity from the "Fight of the Century" helped to create the last gold rush on the western frontier, by early 1907 the L.M. Sullivan Trust Company was bankrupt (courtesy the Central Nevada Historical Society, Tonopah, Nevada).

Eastern bank, Gans was told about "the deal" they were going to make with him in exchange for paying his forfeiture fee and training expenses during his stay in Goldfield.

It is attributed to Rice that "the Negro champion did a little dance of joy and thanksgiving on learning that all his new and generous manager required was a promise that he would defeat Nelson. 'If you lose,' Shanghai Larry explained in the kindliest tone of which he was capable, 'you'll never get out of Goldfield alive. My friends are gonna bet a ton of money on you. They will kill you if you don't beat Nelson by a mile.'"[12]

Gans explained "he could beat Nelson with one hand, if necessary, and that he was eager to win as decisively as possible to redeem himself in the eyes of the sports world."[13] According to Rice, Gans simply promised "he would do his best."[14]

Gans' comment about beating Nelson "with one hand" would prove prophetic in the 33rd round when his hand would break, and the stakes of this fight would be for more than a pot of money. Gans would be fighting for his life.

After a private conversation between Rice and Sullivan, Gans' new manager came back to tell him that he would have to prove his good intentions by turning over his end of the purse to the Sullivan team so that they could bet whatever they could get at the best odds. Gans had come into town with nothing hoping that he could win a little over $10,000. Now, the only thing he knew was that if he lost, he would lose his life.

Saturday, two days before the fight, Billy Nolan took issue in what Rickard saw as another scheme to stall the fight to worsen Gans' perilously unstable physical condition. Nolan argued about the color of the canvas, and Rickard called his bluff by saying that he planned to give the canvas a light coat of dust and that what was good for one boxer would be good enough for the other. Rickard knew that Gans had gotten the short end of the deal and openly admitted that Gans had "exhibited the patience of an Arizona monk throughout these squabbles."[15]

Sunday, September 2. The town was crowded and the stakes were high. Rooms had been sold out the week before. Miners poured in on burros and ponies and they slept on the ground, wrapped in blankets. Two hundred Pullman cars had been chartered to transport fight fans, one hundred of them on the Southern Pacific coming in from California, many of the cars serving as hotel rooms, limited as they were in the mining town. Dining cars well-stocked in libations substituted as saloons for the visiting sports.

Betting increased on the day of the fight. Rickard bet on Nelson. The Sullivan Trust had "wagered $45,000 on Gans against a total of $32,500 put up by the followers of Nelson."[16] It should be noted that this amount was considered peanuts to the Sullivan Trust. The company had within thirty days bought an interest in a mine, signed up the governor of the state to become president of the company in name, capitalized the mining company for 1,000,000 shares, sold them directly to the public, and used the profits to pay off the property and net $150,000. In the words of Rice, it "put the company on Easy Street again."[17]

Expert opinion from fighters such as John L. Sullivan, Bob Fitzsimmons, Terry McGovern, Young Corbett, Tom O'Rourke, and George Considine held that Gans would win. Both fighters had legendary careers in the ring. Gans had already won over 100 fights, Nelson close to 50. In the days of no decision contests, Gans had won more than were recorded. The simple and most amazing fact was that Gans had won more battles than any boxer in the history of the world.[18] The betting started at 10 to 8 and then moved to 10 to 7 in favor of Gans. Telegraph keys flew bets all over the country. Confidence ran high on both sides of the bets, but Gans was clearly the people's prince and favorite. Miners bet heavily on Gans. New York actor Nat Goodwin, coming in from Ocean City, California, commented that he was willing to take two cases of wine against an automobile on Nelson. The largest individual bets laid down on the contest were denominated in mine stocks. Jim Riley, owner of the largest gambling casino of Tonopah, wagered 250,000 shares of a mining company, valued at $25,000, against 400 shares of a local Goldfield mine, with controlling interests in the companies resting on the outcome of the battle.

Nelson's manager ran out of things to complain about, so he whined about suspicious betting around town. But Rickard and Esmeralda County Sheriff J.F. Bradley assured everyone that nothing was amiss. Gans' camp assured everything was on the up and up. Rickard had long ago put Gans' past reputation to bed, attributing his problems to a crooked jockey. Rickard had to quell suspicions, but his patience was running thin fearing the shenanigans that Nolan might pull. It was suspected that Nolan would try to stall the fight to further weaken Gans. According to boxing historian John McCallum, Nolan was trying to cause Gans to become so weak from the excessive weight loss that he would have to quit at the last minute.[19]

While Gans was running and sweating the weight off in a Turkish bath, Nelson was cool as a cucumber. Nolan had told him that Gans was going to quit and he told the press that his fighter didn't need to train the day before since he weighed in at 131 pounds stripped. So Nelson spent the morning sightseeing on country roads.

Fight Day, Monday, Labor Day. The newspaper accounts all reported

is BATTLING NELSON
BITING OFF MORE THAN HE CAN CHEW?

On the morning of the biggest fight in history, September 3, 1906, at Goldfield, Nevada, the *San Francisco Examiner* carried cartoonist T.A. "Tad" Dorgan's interpretation of Battling Nelson's predicament. Nelson's manager, Billy Nolan, must have perceived the same in that he tried to exact ever more concessions from Gans to force the fighter into conceding the match. Tad Dorgan became an authority on boxing. He was a prolific creator of phrases (including Joe Gans' moniker, the "Old Master") popular in the vernacular: "yes, we have no bananas," "twenty-three, skidoo," "for crying out loud," "the cat's meow," and "drug-store cowboy."

pretty much the same story. Boxing writers of that day were, if anything, meticulous to a fault. Never had they heard of three weigh-ins before a fight. First weigh in at noon: The weight limitation is 133 pounds. Gans weighs in at 133 stripped and Nolan protests. He says that Gans must weigh in with his fighting gear, shoes, gloves, and boxers. Sullivan tries to protest, but he had absolutely no experience dealing with professional managers in the fight game, and Nelson's camp refuses to concede the requirement. At 2:30 Gans must make the weight in his fighting clothes. Gans speaks to the press: "I will win just as sure as the sun shines. Nolan and Nelson have shown right along that I am the one man in the ring that they fear, and even after the match was forced on them Nolan tried to crawl out of it by asking me to make a weight he thought I could not possibly do. I have given in on every point just to secure this match. I am betting everything I can get my hands on, and I have got to win. I will have the Dane chopped to pieces and asleep inside of 15 rounds."[20]

One-Thirty-Three Ringside. "Battling" Nelson gives his comments to the press: "I am going to give Gans an awful beating, and I think he will be begging for mercy long before the twentieth round is reached. I should not be criticized for asking him to make the weight in his togs, as he is a welterweight, and if he wants to fight for the lightweight championship he must make the recognized weight — 133 at ringside — in togs. I will let Gans wear himself out, and then I'll come through and get him. Watch me. There will be crepe in Coontown on Labor Day while the Danish descendants are celebrating."[21]

At 2:30 P.M. Gans scales in at 133 pounds ringside, in full fighting togs. This was an enormous burden for Gans, who entered the ring in a weakened state. He had shaved every hair from his body and tied his shoes with thin strings to shave ounces from his total weight.

Tex Rickard announced to the officials that the sale of tickets was at $76,000, a world gate record for receipts. Moving into ringside seats were boxing celebrities and prominent socialites: Nat Goodwin, who as a result of coming to Goldfield had signed on with George Graham Rice to promote his mining stocks; Senator George Nixon of Nevada, president of the Nixon National Bank of Reno, who would partner after the fight with Wingfield to consolidate a mine merger that would capitalize $8 million of stock into $26.5 million, earning them $3.5 million of stock in fees and $1 million in direct profit; Charles Clark of Montana, lawyer to his father, Senator William Clark, the "Montana Copper King" who was involved in a million dollar bribery election scandal where he was kicked out and then reappointed to office; Boxer Jimmy Britt and Willie Britt; Harry Corbet; Jimmy Coffroth, number 1 promoter in the country before Rickard, and California boxing tycoon who would in 1916 build the Hippodrome Agua Caliente in Tijuana, where Sea Biscuit would win the Caliente Handicap in 1938; boxers Eddie Hanlon, Tim McGrath, Jack Grant and his brother Peter; referees Jack Welch and Eddie Graney; and many other political and sport luminaries.

2:40 Ringside. Battling Nelson enters the ring and Gans follows close behind, both men wearing heavy bathrobes. Point men for both camps join the group. Soon there is a flurry of action among the officials and the various law enforcement agents around the ring. Rickard is forced to tell each side that the timekeeper is nowhere to be found. Already frustrated with Nolan's game-stalling antics, Rickard tries to accommodate both parties. Nolan objects to any Californian being selected. But when Rickard chooses Goldfield resident Bert Ulmer, the Gans camp objects, Sullivan having a bone to pick with the local boy. Word around the ring was that the betting was now 100 to 60 on Gans.

Gans Pre-empts the Double-Cross

Gans' cool head at the last minute perhaps saved the bout from being fixed against him in a double-cross. He didn't want his own manager to control the fight in any way. He turned to the newspaper men at ringside and told them that he wanted to make sure for the record that "he did not want any of his men to enter the ring or throw the sponge for him ... that the end would be only if Siler asked him if he had enough or was counted out."[22] The crowd cheered at Gans' bravado and the assurance that Gans would not allow his untrustworthy manager Sullivan to double-cross him.

Realizing he was missing his cue, boxing manager Larry Sullivan, now club president, emcee and supposedly master of ceremonies, jumped into the ring to read telegrams sent to the match. From the famous John L. Sullivan: "Regret cannot see fight. It ought to be a corker. Regards to all my friends at the ringside. Please announce that I will match the winner for $10,000 aside, the men to fight in Goldfield."[23]

Then he read what has become one of the most famous telegrams in all of sports, from Gans' mother in Baltimore: "Joe, the eyes of the world are on you. Everybody says you ought to win. Peter Jackson will tell me the news, and you bring back the bacon."[24]

The fighters shed their robes. Gans wore blue trunks and Nelson wore green with red, white, and blue ribbon. Sullivan announced that the men weighed 132½ pounds each, and Nolan came out arguing that Gans should have been made to wear the bandages. When the crowd heard Gans' response that he didn't want any tape anyway, they cheered wildly. Then Gans flashed a handful of money to see if Nelson would take his bet "at any odds." Nelson refused and Nolan threw a fit of objections. The ring was cleared.

Sullivan began, "Ladies and gentlemen: The battle will be for the lightweight championship of the world. There are about 300 deputy sheriffs in this town to preserve order and to be on the outlook for trouble."[25] The posse of sheriffs had dressed notably in their slouch hats, corduroy pants, and open vests displaying a variety of .45-caliber pistol handles from their well-worn holsters. Wanting to assert his authority over the crowd, he continued, "I warn you all against jumping into the ring during or after the fight."[26] The warning seemed unnecessary for the obviously well-behaved crowd.

Announcements were made regarding honored guests, one of which was

With his face gaunt, Gans poses for a re-match, July 4, 1908, with Battling Nelson at Colma, California. Referee Jack Welch and veteran announcer Billy Jordan stand behind the two boxers. After the bout, Jack Welch announced that he had "refereed his last fight." Betting was heavy for the fight, at 10 to 4 odds for Gans. Tex Rickard, promoter for the previous fight between Gans and Nelson, bet over $25,000 on Gans (photograph by Dana Bros., San Francisco 1908).

that the Athletic Club had sent President Roosevelt a telegram, and although there was no reply, his son was thought to be at ringside. The crowd again cheered and someone yelled, "Show yourself and turn your face toward the moving picture."[27] Then Sullivan introduced Tex Rickard, "Give him three cheers!" and the spectators responded accordingly.

While Jimmy Britt was being dragged up into the ring from his front-row seat, Rickard announced that Jack Welch of San Francisco would be the official timekeeper. Britt was presented to the crowd. When the applause died, he announced that he would take on the winner of the bout. Then Eddie Hanlon and Eddie Graney were introduced and each shook hands with the contestants, wishing them the best of luck. Then bantamweight Frankie Neil was introduced. And finally, Sullivan introduced referee, George Siler. Siler had achieved a degree of fame as a referee and sports writer, most notably in Chicago before prize fighting was outlawed in the Windy City.

Before the referee could begin the coin toss, Nelson asked Sullivan to announce that he, too, didn't want his men to throw in the sponge for him. He would only be considered beaten if Siler asked him. And the crowd cheered. Then the arena was cleared and the fighters were brought to the center to pose for the moving-picture camera. The cheers for the men were evenly divided. They returned to their corner and Sullivan announced that the world lightweight championship would be a "fight to the finish," which in those days meant 45 rounds, or until a fighter could not continue. Siler called the men to the center of the ring and gave them their boxing instructions.

Nelson and Gans then left the ring for the beginning of the preliminary bout, Nelson to hisses and Gans to cheers. A purse of $1000 was offered between two lightweights, Bob Lundie of San Francisco and Jack Clifford of Montana. In the second round, the Montana fighter landed a right to Lundie's jaw and he was knocked down. The referee counted nine before he could rise, but as he did so, Clifford pounded him with another right to the jaw, knocking him out and leaving the spectators to languish in the hot sun for forty-five minutes between bouts. People continued to bet as hawkers peddled their wares through the crowd.

A round-by-round description was reported over the wires via Western Union as crowds gathered, amassed in saloons and hotel lobbies, and stood outside telegraph offices throughout the United States to hear the live reports, reports that would appear in the newspapers the next day.[28] One young boy with his father in Amarillo, Texas, went to the train station to hear the fight returns and explained, years later, how frightened he was of the results should Gans win. His heart raced with every report. He said that everyone expected all hell to let loose and riots to occur in the streets should the black man win.

Anticipation mounted as the fighters waited for the bout to begin. Heartbeats per minute are monitored by marathon runners and prize fighters as closely as blood pressure is monitored by physicians. A novice amateur may fight six minutes and feel afterward as if he just worked an eighteen-hour shift on the loading docks. The nerve-racked amateur's heart would begin racing in the dressing room, and he would already be tired when the fight begins, just from the anticipation. As they awaited the call to the ring, Gans would be calming his mind prior to walking into the valley of the shadow of death, keeping his heart rate low.

Siler called the fighters to the center. They touched gloves.

Goldfield's telephone and telegraph line arrived in January of 1904, ahead of the first train in September of 1905. After each of the 42 rounds of the "Epic Battle in the Desert," telegraph messenger boys were sent with the ringside stenographer's report to the Goldfield Telephone and Telegraph office about a mile away from the boxing stadium. Listeners waited anxiously for the results at telegraph, newspaper, or other offices that leased a line across the nation. Incoming bets kept stenographers busy in the telegraph office. In his book *Gold in Them Hills*, C.B. Glasscock reports that incoming tolls to Goldfield from Western Union during the year 1906 amounted to $240,000, which excluded those that came into banks and brokerage offices on private lines. Publicity from the world-famous fight started the Western frontier's final gold rush.

Gans Batters the Dane, Dominates Early Rounds

The wire report told the story this way.

Round 1—Gans led off with two light lefts for the face and they clinched. Nelson received a right on the body and Gans quickly shot a right and left to the face. He followed it with a right to the face and Nelson sent three left swings for the jaw.

Gans in a mix shot his right twice to the face and out-boxed his man at every point of the game. Gans jarred Nelson with two rights to the jaw and followed with a left to the face.

After breaking from a clinch Nelson walloped his right to the jaw and followed with a left to the same place. Gans then peppered Nelson's face with trip-hammer rights and lefts to the face and jaw and kept this up until the gong rang. Gans went to his corner with a big lead. Blood flowed from Nelson's ears as he went to his seat.

NELSON THE AGGRESSOR.

Round 2 — Both were up quickly; Nelson was the aggressor, Gans uppercut twice with his right and then jarred Nelson with two terrific punches to the jaw. He followed it with a straight right to jaw. Nelson seemed impervious to punishment and came in all the time.

Gans measured his distance and time and again shot his short-arm rights to the Battler's face. They went to close quarters and Gans uppercut Nelson twice to the jaw. At close quarters he chopped Nelson on the jaw again with a stiff right.

Nelson fought him to a clinch and landed a terrific right to face. In a mixup Gans rocked Nelson's head with two wicked rights to the face and followed it with a short-arm jolt to the ear. As the gong rang Gans worked a hard left to jaw. Gans had a good lead and outboxed and outgeneraled his man throughout.

A FURIOUS MIX.

Round 3 — Nelson tried to get close and Gans whipped his right to the ear. At close quarters Gans uppercut twice with his right to the chin, and as they fought at close range Gans swung right and left to the head.

Nelson got in a high right over the eyes and Gans hooked a wicked right to the abdomen and Nelson shot a straight left to the face. Several of Nelson's swings went wild. They went to a furious mix in the middle of the ring, in which Gans drew blood from Nelson's nose with a straight left.

Nelson got in a good right to the face as the bell rang. Nelson was being out-pointed, but he never gave ground and seemed to thrive on Gans' punishment. It was Gans' round.

BATTLER'S FAINT SMILE.

Round 4 — Nelson missed a left for the body. Nelson charged Gans, but his blows invariably fell into a clinch. Gans worked his right and left to the face. Nelson went after Gans' body and bored in with his head, the black man backing steadily away, but at the same time peppering his man with right and left to the face.

Nelson caught Gans a terrific swing to the jaw and then drove Gans against the ropes, landing both hands to head. Nelson was then bleeding from the nose. He kept after Gans, but this time Gans shot a straight right to the face, which he duplicated a moment later. Gans then put a right to the abdomen and the bell rang.

Nelson brought the great crowd to its feet as he went to his corner with a faint smile on his face. Nelson had a shade the better of it.

DANE'S WILD SWINGS.

Round 5 — Gans shot a left to the nose as Nelson rushed in and they went to close quarters. Nelson swung a right to the ear, forcing Gans about the ring. Nelson drove a right to the kidneys, but the black man rocked Nelson's head with a series of lefts and rights.

Nelson swung back wildly and Gans smashed Nelson's sore nose with a terrific right drive. Gans brought blood afresh from Nelson's sore nose with stinging left punches. In a mix Gans uppercut with his right to the jaw.

Not for a moment did Nelson break ground. He swung heavily to Gans' face with his left, but was rebuked by a stiff right to face. The gong clanged and Nelson went to his seat spitting blood. Nelson was badly punished in this round. The betting was now 2 to 1 in favor of Gans.

On the film spectators can be seen waving money around, placing bets. The fight odds were moving as fluidly as the prices on the New York stock exchange. In both corners, the fighters were fanned by huge towels by their seconds in an effort to stave off the heat.

BLACK BOY IS RUSHED.

Round 6 — Nelson rushed Gans, but the Negro smashed him on the face three times with his right and easily avoided Nelson's attempts to land. Nelson bored in, forcing Gans to the ropes.

The crowd objected to Nelson's boring tactics, especially with his head against Gans' chest. After breaking from a clinch Gans planted his right to the jaw and followed it with several terrific right drives to the face, sending blood from Nelson's mouth in a stream.

Gans sent Nelson's head back, hammering his man almost at will. Nelson fought back desperately, but could not locate his antagonist. Nelson was in bad shape when he took his chair. His face was cut into ribbons. Gans had a big lead and here looked a sure winner.

WORKED LIKE IRON MAN.

Round 7 — As usual, Nelson forced Gans about the ring. Gans contenting himself with watching for an opening. Gans pecked away at the face with left and right blows.

Nelson missed two right swings and Gans met him with a fusillade of right and left punches to the face that staggered the Dane. Gans received a slight punch on the body as they worked into a corner. Gans swung right twice to face and Nelson swung wildly.

Nelson neatly ducked two right swings again and Gans kept up a merciless hammering on his face. The bell rang and Nelson went to his corner with blood streaming from mouth and nose. In spite of all the punishment Nelson did not break ground at any time.

JOE LANDED AT WILL.

Round 8 — Gans had no trouble in avoiding Nelson's onslaught and met Nelson with a right swing over the kidneys. He then swung right and left to Nelson's face and found no trouble in getting away from Nelson's swings.

Gans played with the Dane, sending a raking right to jaw, and then on a shift worked a left to face. Nelson swung desperately for Gans' face, but seldom found the black man. They closed in, mixing it roughly.

Gans swung his right and left with fearful force and Nelson slipped to his knees. He got up in a jiffy and Gans went at him fiercely and landed almost at will. The gong was a great relief to Nelson, as he appeared groggy when he fell into his seat.

SHOULDER TO SHOULDER.

Round 9 — They stood should to shoulder in the center of the ring. Gans walloped the Dane with right and left to the face. Nelson tried desperately to work in two hard swings to the body and for his pains received wallops of the short-arm variety to the jaw.

At close quarters Nelson swung his left twice to Gans' jaw and a moment later swung right to same place. They mixed it—furiously, Nelson getting four punches to the other man's one.

Nelson swung right and left hard to Gans' jaw, but Gans more than evened matters by sending the Dane back with rapid-fire rights and lefts to the jaw. Gans bled slightly from the mouth after the bell rang.

A SHADE OF CHAMPION.

Round 10 — Gans met Nelson with a straight left to face. "Stay with him; don't let him get away!" was the injunction from the Battler's corner. They went in close and Gans smothered Nelson with rights and a succession of lefts to the face.

Nelson bored in with and whipped his right and left to the Negro's jaw. Nelson then brought blood from Gans' mouth in a stream with a succession of lefts and rights to that member.

A terrific mix-up resulted at close quarters. Both men fought at fearful pace. Nelson having the better of heart breaking rally. The men bled from mouth and ears. Nelson had a shade on most of this round.

At this point, had this been a modern-era fight of ten rounds, Gans would have been the decided victor by a wide margin, so badly was Nelson cut to ribbons. After ten rounds both men knew that there would be no easy victory. Nelson repeatedly head-butted Gans and hit below the belt. Siler later told the Associated Press that while he knew Nelson was head-butting whenever he saw an opportunity, he did not disqualify him because no other referee had disqualified him for the same actions and the people came to see a fight. Nelson would, two years later, tell the press that his life's only ambition had been to defeat the great Old Master, Joe Gans. For both men, it was a matter of victory or death, there would be no surrender.

LITTLE TO CHOOSE HERE.

Round 11— They closed, with Gans fighting hard and with the request of Referee Siler that Nelson stop butting with his head. Nelson apparently realized that his only chance was to fight breast to breast, and, judging from preceding rounds, he was the better man at this game.

Nelson started a stream of blood from Gans' mouth by two wicked uppercuts. They broke from a clinch and Gans immediately whipped in two rights to Nelson's jaw.

Gans was cautioned to keep away, but Nelson kept at close quarters. Nelson finally swung a light left to the mouth as bell rang. If anything, Nelson had a slight lead in this round.

BUTTED JOE ON JAW.

Round 12 — Nelson rushed on, and they fought shoulder to shoulder for an advantage. Gans, getting Nelson away from him, whipped a stiff right to face. Nelson forced Gans against the ropes and slipped to the floor. Gans held out his hand and assisted him to his feet, and they immediately renewed hostilities.

Gans rested himself and seemed content to permit Nelson to do the leading. They fought breast to breast like two bulls, and Nelson butted Gans on the jaw with his head. They bent very low, head to head, in a monotonous fashion, each seeking to fight according to the style best adapted to his peculiar style.

The bell rang. Gans had a slight lead of a tame round. Siler said he thought Gans was resting up.

MUCH WRESTLING HERE.

Round 13 — Nelson rushed in, sending Gans back with two left and two right swings to the face. At close quarters Nelson uppercut with his left and right to the mouth, and a moment later swung his left to the mouth, bringing blood again from Gans.

Both men resorted to wrestling tactics, Gans being chief offender. They exchanged right swings to face in the middle of the ring and went to a clinch. They again fought breast to breast, and at these close quarters, Gans worked his right and left several times to the jaw.

They went to close quarters again, and Nelson worked in two left uppercuts to the jaw that made the champion wince. The latter, however, had a shade the better of the round.

A KICKING MATCH.

Round 14 — Both men fought at close quarters, but very few blows were landed. In a shoulder-to-shoulder contest, Nelson sent Gans against the ropes with a right to the head. Nelson smashed Gans' body with a right. At the close of the round Nelson kicked at Gans, and the latter promptly retaliated in kind. The belligerents had to be separated by their handlers.

CROWD CHEERS BALTIMOREAN.

Round 15 — This opened with a clinch, and Nelson butted and elbowed Gans constantly. He was warned to desist by Siler, and the seconds yelled foul in unison. No attention was paid to the claim, and the men roughed it at close quarters, Nelson forcing Gans to the ropes.

The men fought at such close quarters, or, rather, wrestled, that little execution could be accomplished. Nelson, in a break-away, was sent to floor with right straight to face.

Nelson looked a bit shaky, and he got to his feet and immediately went to close quarters to protect himself from further long-distance swats. The crowd cheered Gans lustily as he went to his corner.

Gans and Nelson had already fought as long as Ali and Frazier in their first match at Madison Square Garden, which left both of the heavyweights in a debilitated state. At this point Gans was the winner by a huge margin. The entire Ali-Frazier trilogy consisted of a total of 41 rounds, one less than was fought on this day at Goldfield.

DANE KEPT ON ROUGHING.

Round 16 — Nelson missed left and right swings, Gans dancing away. Gans tried to keep Nelson at a distance, but Nelson followed about the ring, trying to land some vicious right swings.

Gans whipped his right to jaw and Nelson wrestled Gans about ring, Gans holding on. Nelson scored with stiff right to the face and once more they leaned one against the other. Gans wrestled Nelson clear through the ropes and in falling Nelson pulled the negro after him.

They were pushed back into the ring and immediately resumed their wrestling tactics. In a mix Nelson drove his right twice to the face and a right to the mouth at close quarters, sending Gans to his corner with blood streaming from his mouth.

A Twist of the Arm.

Round 17 — Nelson landed his left on mouth and they went to a clinch. Siler cautioned Nelson against hitting low. Nelson swung his right to the kidneys and they wrestled about the ring, during which Gans worked in a left uppercut to the mouth and a moment later applied a similar punch.

Gans, after Nelson had twisted his arm, sent the Battler back with two hard short-arm right jolts to the face and a moment later shot his right to the wind.

Both men rested on their oars for some time and the round ended with honors a bit in Nelson's favor.

The Eighteenth Tame.

Round 18 — Gans rushed in with straight right to face and Nelson swung two lefts to the negro's face. Siler warned Nelson about using his head. Gans blocked Nelson's lefts cleverly and the latter again bent down.

Nelson sent in two left swings to the face, but Gans retaliated with two stinging rights to the face. Wrestling continued and Gans drove Nelson against the ropes with two right smashes to the face.

Nelson nearly went to the floor, Gans backing away and at the end of the round Gans got in a good right punch to the Dane's face. The men did not hear the gong ring and were pulled to their seats by their seconds. It was a tame round.

Tactics of a Goat.

Round 19 — Siler warned Nelson once more for butting and laid his hand on Nelson's head twice as a reminder that the Dane should cut out this kind of work. Nelson continued to butt and Siler stepped in and pulled Nelson from his reclining position.

The men remained in a locked position, Gans resting and Bat wrestling. Finally Gans sent Nelson back with right and left jolts to the jaw, staggering Nelson.

Just before the gong rang Gans sent in a left and two stiff rights to the jaw and Nelson put in a right on the head. There was more wrestling than fighting in this round and derogatory comments were passed around the ringside.

Volley of Rights and Lefts.

Round 20 — The men rushed together and Siler grabbed Nelson by the head, indicating that the Dane should cease boring in with his head. Gans straightened Nelson up with two lefts to jaw and Nelson landed several lefts to the body.

An exchange followed, both landing lefts to the chin. Nelson pushed Gans almost to the ropes and then missed a left for the face.

In a clinch Nelson landed a severe left uppercut to jaw and they mixed, Gans putting right and left to the jaw. He followed his advantage and sent a volley of right and left swings to the jaw as the round closed.

In the Thrilla in Manila, the famous apocalyptic struggle between

Muhammad Ali and Joe Frazier, Ali remarked after ten rounds that it was "the closest thing to dying." At the 20-round point in Goldfield they had fought twice as long as had Ali when he made his famous backhanded compliment to Frazier and his left hook. Gasping for air, throwing up between rounds, intent on destroying each other, the lightweight giants battled on under the scalding Nevada sun. At this point, both fighters may wonder, "You are going to die anyway, why must the Grim Reaper get both of us?"

ALL RIGHT STILL.

Round 21—Nelson came up as though nothing had happened. His left eye was badly swollen and his right discolored. They fought to a clinch, and Gans poked right and left to the face.

Gans then sent in a stiff uppercut over the eye. Nelson sent in two right body punches, and at close range Gans hooked his left to the mouth. Then they stood off and Gans trimmed Nelson beautifully with straight rights to face and a left to the jaw.

Nelson missed two vicious swings and Gans shot in a straight left to the face as the gong rang. Gans had a shade the better.

ONCE MORE THEY FOUGHT.

Round 22—Gans sent a straight left to the face, and Nelson retaliated with a left hook to abdomen. Nelson drove a straight right punch against Gans' ribs, and then wrestled Gans to the ropes.

Mixing it, Gans worked in two right uppercuts to the body. They again leaped shoulder to shoulder and did little more than wrestle, Nelson pushing Gans almost through the ropes. This thing continued.

Finally Gans rushed Nelson away, and smashed him twice with his right to the jaw. He followed this with two lefts to the Dane's head simultaneously with the gong. This was the only time during the round that the men had fought, and Gans had the advantage.

NELSON'S CLEAR ADVANTAGE.

Round 23—They rushed to clinch, and Siler warned Nelson constantly about boring in with his head. Gans then crossed with his right to the jaw. Then Nelson drove his left twice to the eyes after the colored man had put two lefts to the face.

At close quarters Nelson put two good rights over the negro's heart, and then followed the usual course of wrestling. They broke away, and Nelson staggered Gans with a succession of hard left swings to the jaw and several hard rights to same place.

Gans did not respond, and Nelson sent the crowd into a frenzy by driving Gans to his corner with a right hook to the body that was a peach. The crowd rose to its feet at the end of the round and yelled "Nelson! Nelson!" It was the Dane's round.

RIGHT AFTER THE BLACK MAN.

Round 24—Nelson went right after Gans, having received instructions from his corner to go in. They roughed it, and at close quarters Nelson swung his left and right to the face.

Nelson smiled determinedly, and gave Gans no chance to rest. He swung his left hard to the jaw, but Gans retaliated with two wicked right uppercuts to the jaw. Nelson then missed two vicious left uppercuts and they worked in close.

Nelson drove Gans back to the ropes and put in two lefts to the body before Gans clinched. They both missed left swings and a rally followed, Gans landing repeatedly on Nelson's face. Nelson had a shade the better of it.

GIVE AND TAKE HERE.
Round 25 — Nelson rushed and swung his right to the ear. They fought and wrestled at close quarters, Nelson breaking away, sent his left to abdomen, and then drove his right to the jaw. He then sent two short-arm jolts to the face, and a moment later whipped a left to the face.

Nelson rocked the negro's head with right and left to the jaw. He followed this with two rights and a left to the jaw. Gans awoke from his apparent somnolence, and more than evened up matters by hammering viciously Nelson's face with right and left punches.

They went close, and just before the bell rang Gans shot his left to the face. Gans was a bit worsted earlier in the round, but had the better of the closing rally.

Marathon runners reach a point they refer to as "the wall," where the body is out of energy and must literally consume itself in order to keep moving forward. Gans, depleted already from making the weight, somehow had gone over the wall, to a place where mortals do not dare. The shadows on the old film of the match grew taller than the fighters themselves.

JOE'S MARVELOUS DEFENSE.
Round 26 — Nelson forced Gans to the ropes, but could not penetrate Gans' marvelous defense while in dangerous positions. They wrestled again about the ring, Gans resting up.

Nelson landed a hard right swing on the head, but two left swings for the same place went glimmering. Then the fighters sparred and Gans landed a left swing over the mouth and followed it with three straight lefts to the face.

Then followed the inevitable clinch emerging from which Nelson uppercut Gans on the jaw with the left. Both men appeared tired at this stage of the contest. It seemed hard to predict the winner at this time.

BOTH MEN TIRED.
Round 27 — Gans sparred, while Nelson wasted his vitality with useless swings. Nelson pushed Gans against the ropes, and the latter, working himself free, sent his left to Nelson's mouth.

Nelson missed a hard left swing and in a mix Joe put in two light rights to the face. Nelson retaliated with two straight lefts to face, the last one sending Gans' head back.

Gans then cut loose. He drove his left to the abdomen with terrific force and then drove right and left to jaw. Nelson, maddened, fought back viciously and gave the negro more than he had received as the round terminated. It was an even round, with both men tired.

HEGEWISCH BOY GROGGY.
Round 28 — Gans jabbed Nelson on the mouth with his left and Nelson butted the colored man with his head. Nelson then put left and right to the jaw and shortly afterward swung his left to the body and right and left to the jaw.

Then they closed in and Nelson drove Joe to the ropes with left hook to the face. The men wrestled to the center of the ring and Gans sent two right swings to the face.

Nelson tried to wrestle Gans to the ropes and Gans, like a rejuvenated man, drove Nelson back with several fearful clouts to the jaw, the first of which sent Nelson to the center of the ring, halfway across it. Gans kept at his man when he was groggy and the bell clanged and was welcomed as he went to his corner.

BATTLER PEPPERED AGAIN.

Round 29 — Nelson rushed to close quarters, apparently as strong as ever. He followed Gans about the ring, but failed to land. Nelson's recuperative powers seemed almost superhuman.

The men wrestled and roughed it in the middle of the ring and exchanged right swings to jaw. Gans then cut loose again and mercilessly peppered Nelson's face and jaw with right and left jolts.

Nelson merely shook his head and wrestled the black man to the ropes. Gans repeated, permitting Nelson to waste his energy trying to land. Gans was against the ropes as the bell sounded. It was Gans' round.

THREE CHEERS FOR GANS.

Round 30 — They fell against each other and Siler again warned Nelson to cease fighting with his head. They then fought at close quarters, Nelson doing all the work, but not landing.

Gans then put in two right uppercuts and then stalled and rested, apparently with a view of saving his strength. It is in this manner that Gans displayed his great generalship. Gans then put in a right uppercut to Nelson's mouth, and the Dane missed several vicious left and right swings for the jaw.

As the bell rang Nelson deliberately hit Gans, and the crowd went to its feet in a storm of protest. Someone started three cheers for the negro, which drew forth a rousing response.

After 30 rounds the two men had been throwing and catching powerful blows for almost two hours. Imagine your child is having a seizure and you pick him up, then run ten city blocks to the nearest emergency room. Your heart is racing from fear and exertion. That is roughly the equivalent of the exertion of boxers in one torrid round. It is quite possible that both Gans and Nelson are in a state of clinical delirium at this point, but their bodies are trained to fight on with or without their minds. Dehydrated, battered and bloody, the gladiators may or may not really know where they are.

SURVIVAL OF FITTEST.

Round 31 — Gans cleverly blocked Nelson's attempts to land wild swings and again tested, permitting the younger man to do all the work.

Again Siler told Nelson to quit butting, and they went to close quarters wrestling and stalling. The men wrestled for fully a minute without a blow being struck.

Gans sent Nelson's head back with a straight left to the face. The men were locked in a clinch as the bell rang. The fight apparently has settled down to a question of the survival of the fittest.

GONG SAVED NELSON.

Round 32 — Gans danced away from the Dane's leads and as usual closed in on Nelson's initiative. Siler again and again spoke to Nelson about using his head on the negro's chin. Again came the almost interminable clinching and wrestling.

Finally Nelson swung a hard right to the jaw and quickly followed it with a left swing to the same place. Nelson's left eye was badly swollen and almost closed. Gans sent Nelson back with two straight lefts and three rights to Nelson's sore eye.

Gans caught Nelson a terrific clip on the jaw with a right hook and then sent in a dazing left to the face. Again the gong brought relief to Nelson and saved him from almost sure defeat.

BAT'S FACE LIKE JELLY.

Round 33 — They closed in, Nelson butting with his head. Gans peppered Nelson's face to a jelly with terrific right swings. Nelson's left eye was entirely closed.

Nelson punched Gans to the ropes and they fought at close range, Gans resting and saving his strength. Nelson bled profusely as the men worked to the center of the ring. It was a sight to behold.

Gans sent Nelson back with a left to the jaw. Both were very weak as the gong sounded, Nelson for the first time showing great weariness. It was Gans' round. It was claimed that Gans had turned his foot in this round, which may seriously incapitate [*sic*] him for the remainder of the contest.

PURELY A WRESTLING BEE.

Round 34 — The men wrestled and stalled in the middle of the ring, both seeming content to rest up. This thing continued, neither landing a blow.

It was wrestle, stall, wrestle and stall again. Nelson forced Gans to the ropes and received right and left swing on the head.

Nelson worked in two short-arm lefts to the abdomen and both men wrestled, Gans nearly putting Nelson through the ropes. Nelson appeared very tired. Joe was the fresher of the two as the round closed the wrestling match.

In a show of sportsmanship, Gans, with a broken hand, helps Battling Nelson to his feet under the torrid Nevada sun after knocking him through the ropes. In return, Nelson kicked at Gans' shins. A copy of this photograph, which was taken during the fight by the Miles Brothers in the 34th round of their 1906 fight, later hung over the bar at Gans' Goldfield Hotel in Baltimore (courtesy Tracy Callis, boxing historian).

TIRED, TIRED, TIRED.

Round 35 — The sun was now going down. It was the same old story — wrestle, stall and rest without a blow being struck.

Gans finally ripped in a straight left to the jaw and again they rested each other's head against one another's shoulders. Gans put in a right uppercut that lacked force and they went quickly to a clinch.

Both men tottered about the ring, not landing a blow. Nelson at close quarters worked two left short-arm blows to face and the bell closed a very slow and tiresome round.

In the 33rd round, Gans had actually broken his right hand, but feigned having twisted his ankle so that the Dane wouldn't suspect the handicap and take advantage of it. The warriors at this point may be thinking of the beautiful Valkeries who take the fallen heroes off to Valhalla. How else could they still be fighting?

DUCKED AND GOT AWAY.

Round 36 — Both sparred and then Gans started something with a straight right to the face. Again the wrestling was on.

Nelson missed a forceful uppercut intended for the jaw, and for a brief moment it looked as if the men were going to fight, but such was not the case. Gans cleverly ducked a right swing and then ran into a right hook over the heart.

Nelson hooked a left to the abdomen, and at close quarters got his right lightly to the jaw. Nelson pushed Gans against the ropes, and Gans just did step out of the way of a right uppercut.

THE CHAMPION OBJECTED.

Round 37 — Nelson was again told to stop fighting with his head, Gans vigorously objecting to Siler against this style of scrapping.

The men again went to the wrestling stunts and Nelson swung his left for the jaw that missed its mark by 3 feet. They leaned up against each other and few attempts to strike a blow were made.

Then Gans whipped a powerful left to the wind and they clinched. Both men were very careful. Gans woke up the crowd by catching Nelson within long distance and putting in several straight lefts to the face. Then came the rest.

VERY RESTFUL ROUND.

Round 38 — Nelson rushed in and Gans backed up quickly, trying to keep the Dane at a distance and force him to spar at long range.

Gans complained to Siler about Nelson resting his head on Gans' chin and shoulders. Nelson swung a left to the jaw, and after a clinch Gans put in two rights to the Dane's face. Both men were leg weary and stalled and clinched as much as they could.

It was next to impossible to get the Dane to fight at long range. Gans likewise seemed perfectly content to ease up and rest.

A GOOD EYE SHUT UP.

Round 39 — Gans jabbed his left twice to the face before Nelson could get to close quarters. Then followed stalling and wrestling, which was broken up by Gans punching Nelson viciously over the heart with right.

Gans followed this with two straight rights to the face, and again it looked as if the deadlock would be broken. It was only a flash in the pan, however, and the men resumed the tiresome stalling, Nelson being the chief offender.

Nelson, by way of variety, sent in a hard left to the jaw and Gans came back with two lefts to the jaw. Nelson's left eye was here closed entirely.

THIS LOOKED LIVELY.

Round 40 — They started in at a lively pace, Gans landing his left to the ear. Then they stopped.

In a clinch Gans drove his left to the jaw. Nelson came back with a left uppercut to chin. The men did very little fighting.

Gans got Nelson at arm's length and took advantage of this concession by sending his left twice to the Dane's face. Gans complained again about Nelson's head, and sent Nelson's head back with left uppercut to the jaw.

After forty rounds the lengthening shadows of the boxers speak volumes even though the film of the fight is silent. Nelson totters like a bull the picador has stuck with forty lances. Gans the matador has been gored, fouled, and kicked, but is still waiting to deliver the *coup de grace*, a blow that will come at the beginning of the 42nd round that almosts decapitates Nelson.

WHAT TIME IS IT?

Round 41— They came up slowly and clinched. Gans asked Billy Nolan facetiously, "What time is it?" Then they resumed the clinching contest. Gans shot a straight right to mouth and Nelson rebuked him with two lefts to the stomach. Nelson whipped his left to face and the men ceased fighting entirely.

Suddenly Nelson landed a hard left hook to the jaw and Gans fought him away, landing two lefts to the face and a right on the body. Both men wrestled wearily about the ring, and it was hard to tell which was the more tired of the two as the men went to their corners.

THE FINAL FOUL.

Round 42 — Gans started the round with a straight left to the face and they clinched. As the men broke from a clinch Nelson deliberately struck Gans low and the colored man slowly sank to the floor. The blow was clearly observed by everyone in the arena and there was not a murmur of dissent from the spectators as the long-drawn-out battle was terminated.

When it was all over, Gans requested Larry Sullivan to announce that he would meet Nelson again in two weeks to prove that he could win on something other than a foul. However, a rematch would be put off until much later.

Referee Siler was cheered. Gans was carried out of the ring. Nelson was hissed at as he and his crew departed.

In *Hard Road to Glory*, Arthur Ashe writes, "Gans' victory caused the first serious outbreaks of racial violence against blacks as a result of a boxing match. Police reported incidents across the country attributed to the bout. William Conway, a black bar patron in Flushing, New York, had his skull fractured by three white customers. Anthony Roberts, a black doorman at the St. Urban Apartments on New York City's Central Park West, told police he fought off two white attackers with a razor and a small pistol."[29]

The white establishment of San Francisco was so incensed by Sullivan's management of Gans and Sullivan's own buffoonery before the fight (he mispronounced several words, "areno" for "arena," and mispronounced Tex Rickard "a man of great acclumuations") that they would pull $100,000 worth of stock from the Sullivan Trust the day after the fight.

The Old Master's epic contest with Battling Nelson, the Durable Dane, was the longest title fight ever filmed. It would surpass every title bout before or since in terms of number of rounds, pure action, brilliant boxing, and incredible courage.

Jim Riley was so smitten by the fight, and hoping that he could upstage the success at Goldfield, that he would promote Gans' next fight on New Year's Day at Tonopah. On New Year's Eve before the fight, Shanghai Larry was at Riley's saloon "roaring drunk" when he discovered Rickard at the bar. Still jealous over the recognition given to Rickard with his own managerial prowess ignored, Sullivan began barking insults at Rickard. The cool promoter was unaffected until Larry pulled out his gun. "A quick twist of the wrist and Rickard had the six-shooter out of Sullivan's hands. He tossed the gun into a far corner of the place. Then, without a word to Sullivan, he turned his back again, picked up his drink from the bar, and downed it."[30]

Sullivan's partner, George Graham Rice, was exposed as a fraud whose real name was Jacob Simon Herzig who had served two sentences in the slammer. Still sporting the name of Rice, he penned the popular exposé *My Adventures with Your Money* in 1911. Two decades later, after forty million dollars were swindled from unsuspecting investors in New York, he would be called the "Jackal of Wall Street."[31]

From the Goldfield launching pad, Tex Rickard went on to greater fame, which culminated in the million-dollar gate match between Dempsey and Tunney. When Rickard died in 1929, it was said it didn't matter if the old gambler was going to heaven or hell, for he was sure to arrange a match with the other side soon after he arrived at either place.

Goldfield mining stocks ballooned and then crashed. On May 25, 1907, Mr. George S. Nixon, the U.S. Senator from Nevada and partner in Goldfield Consolidated, gave a newspaper interview. When asked what he estimated the ultimate earnings of Goldfield Consolidated to be, he responded: "I believe I am conservative when I say that the property will be eventually earning $1,000,000 net monthly."[32] The minimum value, he estimated, would be $20 per stock. But within 18 months, Goldfield Consolidated was down to $3.50 in the markets. Wingfield and Nixon became multimillionaires as inside traders from their Goldfield operations.

Gans, perhaps the only straight shooter in the whole affair, would use the money he received from the fight to build a hotel with doors that never closed back home in Baltimore, and in namesake tie it to this legendary epic battle. But the damage to his body from the over training and the savage fight would render his immune system so feeble that tuberculosis would consume him a short time later.

Joe Gans, perfect in his art and easily the master of any other boxer, was no match for the white plague, the scourge of the first half of the twentieth century. Gans sacrificed himself in the ring on that torrid Labor Day in Nevada. Round after round, weakened by the weight loss forced upon him, he fought an indestructible character in the Durable Dane. Nelson, too, left the best part of himself in that ring. When he fought Gans two years later, he announced that he was ready to retire, that beating Gans was his life's goal. There is a battle that constantly rages between health and disease, life and death. Some time during that long afternoon Joe Gans began losing that battle, as the death germs of tuberculosis took control of the Old Master's body.

15

∽ೂ᠙ఌ∽

The White Plague

And now was acknowledged the presence of the Red Death. He came
like a thief in the night. And one by one dropped the revelers in the
blood-bedewed halls of the revel, and died each in the despairing pos-
ture of his fall. And the life of the ebony clock went out with that of the
last of the day. And the flames of the tripods expired. And Darkness
and Decay and the Red Death held illimitable dominion over all.
— *Edgar Allan Poe,* The Mask of Red Death

Joe Gans' victory over Battling Nelson marked the pinnacle of his illustrious career and also the beginning of the end for the Old Master. The long
fingers of the White Plague were wrapping around his throat even as he rapped
the steely skull of the Durable Dane. Gans, perfect in his art and easily the
master of the fistic domain, would go down to defeat at the hands of tuberculosis.

Plagues Past and Present

It is estimated that in the 14th century the black (bubonic) plague, or
"Black Death" as it was called, destroyed one quarter to two-thirds of the population of Europe. Later, the disease returned in what was called the "Great
Plagues" in various countries until the seventeen hundreds. At the turn of
each of the past three centuries in the western world, a different deadly pesti-
lence descended upon the population. During each period, public health infra-
structures were no match for the furies unleashed by disease.

In 1800, yellow fever, a disease brought by an Asian mosquito, killed
large numbers of Americans. The mosquito was imported into Baltimore by
the clipper ships in their cargoes of opium from China and India, a trade that
fed the popular opium dens, which thrived alongside taverns in American

180

cities. The disease proliferated in America when masses of Chinese laborers arrived to work the railroads. Quinine became a mainstay for a household's medicine chest. When the power of U.S. ingenuity was harnessed, swamps were drained, and yellow fever and malaria in the western world were soon largely relegated to Rudyard Kipling novels and other tales of the Far East, as far as the American public was concerned.

By 1900, the White Plague of tuberculosis, or "White Death," had spread unfettered in the Eastern United States. Baltimore reported 10,679 deaths in 1900. An air-borne bacterial infection, its transmission mechanism was so poorly understood that it was often misdiagnosed as pneumonia, syphilis or even vampirism when the victim's complexion turned an ashen white — the pallor cast by this slow, agonizing death. The high incidence of tuberculosis coincided with Bram Stoker's publication of *Dracula* and the fascination with the cult of vampirism. But when the sufferer did not develop dementia or die immediately, doctors would attribute the malady to the vaguely defined "consumption."

Wafting through humid locations such as seaports with their densely populated tenements, the seeds of consumption were easily planted. Hence, the disease took a greater toll in minority populations and large cities, like Joe Gans' hometown of Baltimore, than in rural areas. Local and state leaders began to take a concerted, "scientific" approach to public health, collecting demographic and social statistics to understand and thwart TB's spread. Records indicated that morbidity and mortality for African American citizens was two to three times greater than records indicated for Caucasian Americans. Added to the fact that the disease was associated with unsanitary conditions, the doleful numbers provided another opportunity for racial denigration and separation. With the development of bacteria-fighting drugs, particularly streptomycin, the fear of TB would be replaced by complacency in the second half of the twentieth century.

The white plague that took Gans still holds its dominion today. The best known plague of the present age, AIDS, is even today less of a killer than tuberculosis. One would suspect from the accumulation of press coverage that AIDS is the most infectious scourge in the world. But it is not. TB remains first, infecting one third of the world's population. Successful eradication of the deadly bacteria depends upon antibiotics, and as bacteria mutate they become less responsive to existing drugs. A new strain of drug resistant tuberculosis has been identified on several continents, including America; and according to many bacteriologists, this new strain threatens a pandemic health disaster like no other since the bubonic plague.

Edgar Allan Poe reminds readers what it is like to stand helplessly by as a loved one succumbs to an uncontrolled, unrelenting disease. His soul lashes out at the great unknown that takes his beautiful Annabel Lee:

> And this was the reason that, long ago,
> In this kingdom by the sea,
> A wind blew out of a cloud by night
> Chilling my Annabel Lee;
> So that her high-born kinsman came
> And bore her away from me,
> To shut her up in a sepulchre
> In this kingdom by the sea.

The "chill" of pneumonia, which was actually many times undiagnosed TB, took the lives of many famous poets and musicians. Chopin, Mozart, Keats, the Bronte sisters, Thoreau and Emerson all fell to the ravages of the disease. It was generally thought at the time that a person of an artistic nature or a "sickly" child was more susceptible to the malady. At the age of 12, the family physician thought that the frail future heavyweight Jack Johnson might be tubercular.[1]

Frailty was no prerequisite for the disease. Even the most physically fit individuals such as boxers suffered, indicating that the white plague was indiscriminate, attacking a finely-tuned body with such a wasting effect as to make a thirty year old look sixty at the time of death. The great black heavyweight boxer from Australia Peter Jackson died of tuberculosis in 1901 at the age of forty. Baltimorean Edgar Allan Poe's own early, and mysterious, death at forty, likely of consumption, would foreshadow the death of the young Joe Gans at 35 fifty years later in the same cramped neighborhood. Gans' emaciated body would lay in final repose at his mother's house only a few short blocks away from the Poe house.

The bacteria that caused TB was identified in 1882. Robert Koch of Germany, who identified the bacteria, had also identified the bacteria that caused anthrax the decade before, establishing the "germ theory" for the cause of disease. Koch received the Nobel Prize in medicine in 1905 for his work in tuberculosis. In the 1890s he experimented with dead bacteria for a possible vaccine but the disease did not respond to it. Charlatans took advantage of a lack of a cure, promoting various mysterious potions. One can only imagine what was contained in the medicine from a company in California advertising "tuberclecide!" One ad from the company read, "Even in its last stages, progress of the malady can be checked, the tubercle bacilli destroyed, and a complete cure effected. We have incontrovertible evidence of our success. Many Los Angeles and Southern California people have been rescued from an apparently hopeless stage of the dread disease.... Your Loved Ones May Be Saved From Their Impending Doom. Tuberclecide completely eliminates the

Tuberculosis Germs from the human body. No hypodermics. No nostrums. Investigate our claims and begin treatment before it is too late. Treatment at home, surrounded by home comforts. We invite correspondence and will give full particulars by mail, or to all who will call at our offices. Tuberclecide Company, Los Angeles, Ca."[2]

Baltimore, with its world-famous Johns Hopkins University and a high concentration of the disease located near the premier institution, was at the forefront of tubercular research. Dr. William Osler of the Johns Hopkins Hospital founded the Laennec Society for the study of tuberculosis. In the winter of 1901, just a few years before Gans would contract the disease, Dr. Osler summed up the tragic situation regarding consumption, "What are we doing for the 10,000 consumptives in our midst? Not one thing that a modern civilized community should do. Plans were perfected some time ago by which two students were enabled to visit each case of consumption which applied for treatment at the Johns Hopkins Hospital dispensary, and what they found is a disgrace to a city of 500,000 inhabitants. Those people have not the slightest instruction as to the proper way to care for themselves; there is no law compelling a report to the Board of Health of cases of consumption, so that the authorities can inspect those cases; there is no provision for proper disinfection of the house after a death from consumption and if there were, the Health department hasn't means to do it, and the conditions in this respect are indeed appalling."[3] Dr. Osler argued for notification, inspection, and education, but in 1902, his was a lonely voice.

Boxing Was a Fertile Ground for Infection

Widespread use of antiseptics existed in boxing training facilities, but solutions were not used primarily to clean and disinfect surfaces. Combinations of alcohol and witch hazel were used as rubbing compounds on the surfaces of the boxers' bodies after their workouts, but seldom used on the sweaty tables where they had lain. Towels and sponges washed and rewashed bodies, and spit buckets were incubators for the germs. In some fights, during the one-minute rest break, some cornermen were ready with fresh water in their mouths to spray in the face of their charge. At the end of some brutal battles where both fighters put forth equally strong effort, it was not uncommon to see them kiss. After a bruising battle, it was considered common for a fighter to suffer with coughs and hemorrhages. Many fighters didn't know or care whether they had contracted the disease, for even if diagnosed with consumption, they figured their finely tuned bodies were able to resist the disease. Fever, chills, and weight loss were the only symptoms indicating the disease had progressed. But then again these symptoms fit any number of ailments. In gambling lingo, the disease was a crap shoot.

Personal health problems were the last thing on the mind of Joe Gans at the beginning of 1902. He was in peak condition, readying himself to fight tough opponents such as "Elbows" McFadden and waiting for his title fight February 10 with Frank Erne. Erne would meet Gans later in the year. Over the next few months, Gans' body would be trained, inspected, measured, and weighed and those results would be seen by more eyes than a modern-day beauty contest. As the leading contender, his condition made good copy. On May 11, 1902, newspapers announced that Gans was in Buffalo with his manager and his two close seconds, fighters themselves—Young Peter Jackson and Herman Miller, and that he was in "fine" condition. After all, champions were paid to be in the best of condition. Little did Gans know that one day soon he would see his good friend and sparring partner Herman Miller waste away from the dreaded "pulmonary problem."

Amid all the publicity from Johns Hopkins regarding the state of TB in Baltimore in 1902, Governor John Walter Smith of Maryland was prompted to act. He appointed a Tuberculosis Commission "to investigate the prevalence, distribution and causes of human tuberculosis in the state of Maryland, to determine its relations to the public health and welfare and to devise ways and means for restricting and controlling said disease."[4] The first commission met on August 23, 1902, in Baltimore, comprised of university and state level health care specialists. Dr. Lillian Welch (Johns Hopkins Medical School was one of the first to appoint an equal number of women and men into their program) was thought extremely valuable for her ability to get at facts concerning the sociology and economics affecting the family. Every hospital, dispensary, or any institution having medical officers in the city, county, or state was required to give the commission access to documents regarding the disease. State records showed that 13 percent of the deaths that occurred in the state were related to the "White Death." Yet these numbers were tremendously underreported because most deaths from TB were concealed. It is estimated that a more realistic number was at least double that reported.

According to reports at the time, nationwide there were only 34 hospitals, homes, or camps for the care and treatment of tuberculosis patients, and these facilities had long waiting lists for their services.[5] So feared was the disease that no hospital in Baltimore would assume care of a tubercular patient for any time longer than it took to establish the diagnosis. The *Baltimore Sun* reported that fewer than 100 people in Baltimore could be afforded institutional care. The Hebrew Hospital could take 6; the Hospital for Consumptives near Towson could accommodate 30; and the consumptive ward at Bayview, 50. At the facility near Towson, 49 people were admitted in 1901 and of that number, only 14 people showed "marked improvement."[6] This record indicates that care was limited and protracted, and the outcome for the patient not very optimistic. Mortality statistics reported in the larger cities in the United States and elsewhere in 1900 bore this out.

Like mortality statistics in other cities of the United States, deaths in Baltimore attributed to pneumonia were not included in the figures of death from TB. Deaths by pneumonia in 1900 were equal to, if not slightly more than, those of consumption, indicating that confusion between the two diseases may explain the lower total numbers of TB.

Fear of the disease spread as no solutions were found. In March 1903, the Maryland Commission set out to identify the residence and the place of employment of all consumptives. Dr. John S. Fulton, secretary to the State

Board of Health, cited his experience that consumption typically followed families that resided in crowded, unsanitary conditions. Dr. Fulton told his colleagues the story of a young man and woman who married and moved into a house formerly occupied by someone who had died of the disease. Within 18 months, "the perfectly healthy" wife expired from the white death.[7] The woman

A sign in the window of the historic Goldfield telegraph office reminded citizens and visitors not to spit on the sidewalks. Goldfield, the largest city in Nevada by 1906, attempted to stem the spread of disease, fearful as the people were of germs without the benefit of modern antibiotics. Famed Goldfield resident and deputy sheriff of Esmeralda County Virgil Earp died while in office of "pneumonia" in October 1905 (courtesy David W. Wallace, 2008).

may have contracted the disease anywhere, at any time, but Dr. Fulton did not have this understanding of the disease at the turn of the century and instead blamed her new house.

For the remainder of 1903, the commission prepared elaborate maps of the state, dividing them into segments where volunteer agents could go out, visit, and report households infected with the disease. Meanwhile, 1903 was a banner year for Joe Gans, who successfully defended his title four times. During the year he was also invited to Europe, but no reports have surfaced that he actually left the United States.

By January 14, 1904, Gans, who seemed at the pinnacle of his career, was sharing headlines in the *Baltimore Sun* with the alarming subject of tuberculosis. The Tuberculosis Commission reported that the death rates for the disease per 10,000 for 1902 were "20 for whites and 40 for the colored race in Baltimore city, and in the rest of the State were 12 for whites and 29 for colored."[8] It was also noted that births for whites in Baltimore were three times that of blacks.

Expositions such as Chicago's Columbian Exposition in 1893 were popular events, highlighting the country's innovative scientific and cultural achievements. Because of its prestigious medical community, Baltimore hosted the first Tuberculosis Exposition, in 1904 at Johns Hopkins University. During the week of January 25, stellar figures in the field of tuberculosis appeared in Maryland to share their expertise.[9] Dr. Lawrence Flick, director of the Henry Phipps Institute of Philadelphia, spoke on the "House Infection of TB," Dr. Nazyck P. Raenel of the University of Pennsylvania and Dr. D. E. Salmon, chief of the Bureau of Animal Husbandry, spoke on tuberculosis in animals; Dr. S.A. Knopf of New York discussed the possibilities of eradicating pulmonary consumption. Representing Canada and also speaking was Dr. George Adami of Montreal, the Canadian authority on tuberculosis. Perhaps the most publicly well-known authority was Dr. Edward Livingston Trudeau of New York, the pioneering founder of the sanitarium movement in America. Himself a sufferer of tuberculosis, Trudeau founded in 1885 and directed the first sanitarium in the United States, the Adirondack Cottage Sanitarium in New York. The exposition brought much needed attention to the subject of tuberculosis. Shortly after the great health exposition, the National Association for the Study and Prevention of Tuberculosis was formed in the United States.

The exhaustive statistics and exhibits by the State Tuberculosis Commission and the City Health Department, with all of their maps and charts made public, also made public what had heretofore been kept private. Widespread attention to the subject had an effect just the opposite of enlightening the public, forcing mention of the disease underground. Public notices of disease and quarantine, such as the smallpox case January 9, 1904, at Mount Pleasant, Frederick County, tended to strike fear. The William Rippeon home was quarantined by the health officer for smallpox.[10] It appeared that 30 year old Rippeon, with a wife and 5 children, had contracted the disease by simply talking for half an hour on Christmas Eve with a fellow who died from the disease on Dec. 31. Rippeon, his family, and his neighbor, who made an unfortunate holiday visit to his home, were all quarantined at the Rippeon home and all their names made public. In the newspaper immediately below this public announcement appeared an article on Dr. Charles A. Grise, pastor of Ebenezer Methodist Episcopal Church in Easton, Maryland, "who sleeps outside in a tent to take in the fresh air."[11] This had caused him to regain the strength he had lost from "catarrh." The temperature was said to have been at zero degrees. Outdoor "sleeping porches" became popular home additions. People could have their own sanitarium-like accommodation at home, where their bodies could rest appropriately to prevent or fight the disease.

Even before antibiotics, not everyone diagnosed with the White Plague died from it. With rest and fresh air, some seemed to recover, which gave those health-seekers with more active stages of the disease at least some hope for recovery if they had the resources to travel to one of the new "health spas" or to a more healthful climate. This form of treatment seemed recreational, and sanitariums, catering to those who could afford the luxury, took on a resort-like flair. It meant fresh air, sunshine, good food, rest, non-strenuous exercise (such as horseback riding or golf), and positive thinking.

Some sufferers chose to visit the sea where they believed the salty air and warm breezes would speed recovery. The seacoast wasn't just for those already in ill health, it was considered a healthy location for summer vacations away from the congestion of the packed cities. Between his boxing bouts, Gans rented a cottage at Atlantic City during the summer of 1900. One might speculate that Gans suspected he had the disease by 1900. But the more likely reason for his summer retreat was that he was newly married and he certainly had the financial means to escape to the seacoast.

With the awareness that fresh air and sunshine were needed for healthy living, city officials at the turn of the century began to allocate land and funds for public parks where people of all walks of life could take in healthy outdoor activity away from the dark, polluted confines of cramped city dwellings. Gans, and other athletes who came to Baltimore to train, frequently did road work around the lake at Druid Park in Baltimore. During this time schools acquired land for playgrounds and students were encouraged to spend time outside, partaking in physical education. Rules that we take for granted today as standards of etiquette were preventive health measures for a people terrified of spreading and receiving germs. Public anti-spitting ordinances were adopted in cities. Mothers taught their children to turn their heads or to cover their mouths when sneezing. But Gans couldn't avoid close contact in dark training gyms and tough contests. Even the best-conditioned fighters, their muscles starving for oxygen, will gasp and spit on each other inadvertently over the course of a long fight.

From 1904 to 1906 the papers noted that Gans, on occasion, was not the Gans of old. His strength had noticeably diminished in several bouts even though he was fighting men at welterweight. Gans had only two fights in 1905: a no-decision with Rufe Turner earlier in the year and a disappointing draw with Mike "Twin" Sullivan in the fall. In the Turner fight it was reported that by the sixth round "Gans himself was dead tired, and the two swings that he landed ... had no steam behind them."[12] Again, the papers noted that Gans' blows in the Sullivan fight lacked steam. It was said that if Gans had landed the same blows on Sullivan that he was capable of a few years earlier, his man would have been floored. Regardless, Sullivan's left shoulder was beaten raw by Gans' many right overhand swings that failed to reach Sullivan's jaw. Gans was seen panting, and it was unusual to see the champion falling into clinches. After the fifteen-round fight, Gans immediately left the Lyric Theater in Baltimore, speaking to no one. Later it was learned that Gans had been terribly ill.[13]

The year 1905 had not been good for Gans personally. With a lack of fights and a lack of money, his wife, Madge, had left. Gans filed for divorce in July on the basis that she had been unfaithful. Gans would appear back in the Baltimore court on February 6. Sitting next to Gans was his principal witness, Al Herford. Many of the local sporting men showed up for the trial. The defendant failed to appear in court, but her correspondent, Jeremiah Hill, gave a "sweeping denial of the charges."[14] The judge ruled against Gans and denied him the divorce.

By 1906 Gans clearly needed money, and recognition in the ring would help to bring him that. In January he took on Twin Sullivan again, for the welterweight title. The title weight was set at 142 pounds, although Gans was clearly only 135 pounds. W. W. Naughton, who was now in Gans' camp, wrote (over seven months before the Gans-Nelson battle in Goldfield), "If he loses at that weight he will not forfeit the lightweight championship which has never been taken from him, and he will have a pretty strong claim to the welterweight championship if he wins. This because Sullivan defeated Jimmy Gardner who was regarded as the world's welterweight champion."[15] The match was in Gans' control from the outset, and it was all over by the fifteenth, with Sullivan lying on the floor and his head propped up against the bottom rope of the ring.

In 1906 Gans had to convince the public that he was still the rightful owner of the lightweight title, not to mention the welterweight title. He petitioned repeatedly to get a fight with Nelson in order to reclaim the lightweight title that had never been rightfully taken from him. When he would get the fight, he would have to reduce to 133 pounds, a weight that the Nelson camp thought he could never achieve. But Gans would do whatever it took to be successful in the ring, even if it meant hours of roadwork, poor nourishment, and numerous Turkish baths to sweat off the pounds, dehydrating himself to a dangerous degree. Undoubtedly, his body would be weakened by the strain of this conditioning, and Gans' draconian measures to make weight only made him more susceptible to the death germs coursing through his body.

Today, we know that TB can be transmitted through blood or wounds, and that it is most often transmitted through the air from coughs, sneezes, or sputum which can send moisture into the air containing germs that can be inhaled by others. Once in the lungs bacteria can pass through the bloodstream to various parts of the body, infecting bones or other organs. After infection from bacteria inhaled into the air sacs of the lungs, the bacteria may remain active inside the body but cause no symptoms. Whenever the body's immune system is weakened by age, disease, or some other condition, the bacteria may attack the body and move into an active stage. Medical author Diane Yancey says that about half of all active cases come from previously dormant or latent cases, the other half result from infections within the past two years, causing active disease. Scientists do not understand what causes the bacteria to reactivate.

Once active, the bacteria reproduce and spill into the bloodstream. A nodule may appear in the lungs within a week and a hole in the lungs within a month. When patients have active TB, they must be isolated to prevent the spread of the bacteria to others. Symptoms of the disease include a persistent cough, blood in the sputum, chest pain, fatigue, weight loss, fever, chills, and night sweats. Without treatment 40 to 60 percent of victims will die a slow, agonizing death. At first the lungs will produce thick mucus secretions in an attempt to purge the infection. From the lung damage, a patient may spit up blood and experience chest pain. Eventually in severe cases the lungs become so damaged and blood filled that breathing is extremely difficult and painful and the victim eventually dies from strangulation. Tuberculosis can also exist outside of the lungs. It can lodge in the intestines, in bones or joints,

even infecting the spinal cord. Drug resistant TB has been found widely
throughout the United States. According to Yancey, 50 million people are
infected with drug resistant strains of tuberculosis. She states that in countries with high rates of resistant tuberculosis about one third of all TB cases
are incurable. Ninety percent of people without a drug resistant strain of the
bacteria can be treated effectively.[16]

No Cure for the White Death in 1900

In 1906 medicine was decades away from any cure for TB. American
physicians, usually sufferers themselves, operated the sanitariums as quasi-
medical facilities. German doctors were the first to establish the health
retreats. The American West and Southwest, with its wide open spaces, low
humidity and relatively pollen-free environments, offered exotic, tourist-like
destinations for the extended trips necessary to effect a cure. Prescott, Arizona, was one such place. Located south of the mountains of Flagstaff and
north of the desert area of Phoenix, Prescott, with its dry, cool air at the mile-
high altitude, became a health resort after the state's capital moved to
Phoenix.

By the summer of 1910 Gans was fortunate that he had the means to
travel to the West, where many believed that consumption could be cured in
the dryer climate. One can be assured that he had probably exhausted whatever remedies he could get his hands on in the East. Testimonial evidence of
a cure with potions were advertised throughout the United States. One company advertised: "To neglect a cold, bronchitis, lung trouble or Consumption is dangerous. We all know how prone people are to deny they have
Consumption.... Call consumption by its own dread name — and then — take
Echman's Alternative.... Write for Evidence to the Echman Laboratory, Sixth
and Market Streets, Philadelphia."[17]

When the mining industry declined, many areas of the Southwest began
to realize the potential income of the lengthy stays of the "lungers." By 1910
sanitariums had been established across the Southwest advertising various
treatments for the diseases of the throat and lungs where physicians and grad-
uate nurses were in constant attendance. Residents could choose from tent
houses, mission-styled bungalows, cabins, or hospitals. Many had their own
clubhouses.[18] And because they catered to the middle and upper classes, the
resorts did not mix races. African Americans had to find private homes or
lodges built specifically for them. For many health-seekers, the American
Southwest was their last hope.

At the sanitarium, daily regimens were highly orchestrated by the doctor. Up at a designated hour, conversation, fresh air, lunch, bedtime at same time every night. Positive thinking was mandatory, even though many of the treatments were excruciatingly painful. When breathing became difficult and labored, some physicians attempted to collapse the lung by repeatedly poking the patient with hypodermics, injecting solutions or drawing them out. The mention of death was strictly *verboten*. Nurses and attendants told everyone they were going to get better, and they could point to patients who improved and were sent home even though patients who were not expected to live were put on the train to avoid having them expire at the sanitarium. The initial deposit for treatment included the cost of a train ticket home. Because the trains couldn't accommodate dead bodies for longer than 30 hours, conditions were scrutinized to make sure the patient could survive the time on board.

The grim reality of society stricken by plague, as described so well by Albert Camus in *La Pest*, was played out also in response to the White Death. When it became obvious that Gans would expire from his disease, he hired a doctor to travel with him from Prescott, reassuring train officials that they wouldn't have to deal with his condition. Time was critical in Gans' final days when he was attempting to return to Baltimore before he died, and this explains why he exited the train temporarily in Chicago. It was believed that he would expire on the day he arrived there and officials were reluctant to put him on a train bound for Baltimore.

Euphemisms for death became popular expressions among patients at the sanitarium when they noticed that someone was "going out soon," or "would not be here much longer," or even "passed in the night." Cemeteries as we know them today became popular during this period. The church yard fell out of favor, replaced by the more appealing spot outside of town, among rolling hills where people could find eternal "rest" in the beauty of pastoral, open spaces.

As much of life in America was segregated, so was death. The first and only cemetery for a number of years for African Americans in Baltimore was Mt. Auburn, originally named "The City of the Dead for Colored People." At the time of Gans' death in 1910, the location was known as the Sharp Street Cemetery, even though it was miles south of Sharp Street in an area called Westport. The deed to the property had been granted to the Sharp Street Methodist Episcopal Church in 1872.

By the end of 1907 Gans had opened the Goldfield Hotel and finally established himself as one of the immortals of the prize ring. And he would keep fighting with the death germs of TB in his body, well into 1909. As he engaged in the final fights of his career, did he consider his TB an inevitable death sentence, or did he think boxing would offer him a reprieve? What is clear is that he fought on, leaving his family secure and leaving rich legacies to the boxing world, and even to the worlds of ragtime and jazz music.

16

A Dream Deferred, a Dream Realized

In March of 1914, the play *Granny Maumee* by Ridgely Torrence opened at the Lyceum Theater in New York with a white cast from the Washington Square Players. It received great reviews. In 1917 it played again at Madison Square Garden Theater with a cast from the Colored Players, and the play was met with mild applause by the *New York Times* critic who preferred the original cast, commenting that it wasn't technically necessary to have black roles played by a black cast. The drama opens in an old cabin with a blind and withered black great-grandmother discussing her son's gift to her — a bed. Under her white hair, her face bears the horrible scars she received from the flames set by a brutal gang of white thugs.

> GRANNY: W'en my Sam wuz er babe we laid on cotton sack. We didn' have no baid, an' w'en he little shaveh he say, "Mammy, I goin' git you nice baid w'en I git er man." An' sho' nuff, w'en he grow up he took'n do hit, an' he mek pu'chus in de attehnoon an 'de baid come nex' day. But at midnight betwix' dee tuk'n bu'nt 'im.
>
> PEARL (her nineteen-year-old granddaughter): Now, Granny —
>
> GRANNY: In de black dahk dee come on 'im, de bloodyhanded mens, an' wheah dee cotch 'im dah dee bu'nt 'im, de right man settin' de wrong man afieh at de i'un hitchin' pos.'
>
> PEARL: [Going to her.] Granny Maumee, don't leave yo'self go that away.

This poignant scene dramatized the conflict between white Americans who feared that blacks might infringe upon their opportunities and black Americans who wanted to make something better of their lives. How could fear of a dream for a better life in a land of promise result in such brutality? Americans have lived and died with such high regard for the flame of desire for opportunity on an equal playing field that it has shaped a national character by encouraging the underdog to reach for his dream. Yet at one time in the dark recesses of history, the torch was used in a ruthless attempt to extinguish that dream. The question that remains may never be fully answered: how could this happen?

This was the historical context in which one young fighter dreamed of a better life in a land of opportunity, a man fighting his way to the top in the white rings at the turn of the century. No doubt Gans' mother shared an anguish and fear similar to that of Granny Maumee every time her son stepped over the rope line and into the prize ring. Like Sam in the play, Gans' goal, and his fear, swelled from the wellsprings of a basic need: to provide for his mother.

It would take another decade before the black singer or the poet would come with the truth, but the great contest had begun. It would continue with Jack Johnson, Joe Louis, and Muhammad Ali. One can only imagine what life would had been like if Joe Gans had lived a longer life. Jack Johnson stirred fear and prejudice in white America. But Joe Gans, through a combination of persistence and talent, overcame the racist times. Gans had a universal "every-man" appeal that eventually brought about his acceptance by white society. The *Los Angeles Times*, September 25, 1907, edition carried the headline "Study in Pathos is Face of Joe Gans." An article read, "Joe Gans, the negro prize-fight champion now training at Baldwin's Ranch, is the most genuinely interesting character in the sporting world. There is something appealing about him. To the sporting world he is merely "de champ," a God and an idol and a dog tomorrow — if he should be licked tomorrow. But to real people, there is a curious and wistful interest surrounding him."[1] The subtitle to the headline read: "Sadness and Humility Written Large in the Features of Noted Negro Fist Expert." While the white establishment at the time felt more comfortable with a 'humble' negro, it is the 'sadness' that is so telling in this article. Harry C. Carr observed something in Gans' face, unlike anything that appeared before: "He is not in the least like a prizefighter. As a general thing a prize fighter is an excessively offensive person, whether he be a Jimmy Britt and attempt an intellectual pose, or a 'rough-neck' like Tommy Burns, and affect a valet and cane. Gans is a meek, humble mulatto with the saddest face the writer has ever seen. It is a puzzling and remarkable face."[2]

While this description of the prizefighter recalls the offensive plantation stereotypes that carried over into the age after the Civil War — stereotypes which his readers characterized as a race of either merry half-wits or sad-eyed melancholics — Carr describes Gans' face as exhibiting a puzzling look of inquiry. He clarifies:

> The tragedy and pathos of his race and not its merriment are written in the deep eyes of Gans. His puzzled look is not the fretful peevishness of stupidity; it is the look of one who sees and wonders why. It is as if he were asking why it should be

his destiny to beat men's faces with padded gloves.... It is the face of a general or a war eagle; not of a brawler. Gans fights because he knows how to destroy, not because he is a fighter. Many people have seen Gans bitterly insulted, without resentment on his part. Bat Nelson fights because he is a pugnacious little boy and he would just as soon fight on a sidewalk. Gans could not easily be drawn into a quarrel. Down in the bottom of his heart Gans hates prize fighting. He may not know it, but he does. This in spite of the fact that he is, without doubt, the greatest expert the world has ever known in the use of the human fist.[3]

That Gans, a black man, could be seen or compared to a general or a war eagle, the greatest symbol of American fighting strength, is almost unbelievable reportage during the Jim Crow era. It took courage to recognize this and even more to write about it. Carr sees through the stereotypes of the age. He paints Gans not as a "colored" fighter, but as a human being, a sensitive, thinking man, and the sportswriter elevates him to the status of a great leader of men.

In practical terms, knowing as we do now that Gans was suffering from the white plague, we can only speculate what Gans had to deal with. Was he trying to reconcile his life with the grim reaper? Did he have some reason to feel that he could not sustain his championship form? That he was more than ever fighting in the shadow of death?

In the play *The Rider of Dreams* by the same author, Ridgely Torrence, Lucy Sparrow is a washerwoman, like Gans' mother; and Madison, her husband, has a dream, to make her a good living in a white man's world.

> MADISON: Las' night an' day befo' yistiddy night an' night befo' dat. I wuz layin' groanin,' "O Lawd, how long," an' I heah a voice say, "Git up an' come a-runnin.'" Looks up an' sees a fine w'ite saddle hoss. Hoss say, "Ride me right an' I'll guide you right."
> On I gits an' off he goes, slick as a rancid transom car. Comes to high hill lookin' down on de sun an' moon. Hoss stop an' say, "Brung you heah to give you noos De worl' is youahn to pick an' choose."
>
> • • •
>
> Dat what de hoss say to me in my true dream ev'y night dis week an' I'm a-goin' to bide by hit twell de las' er pea time. 'Cause I'm er true dreameh an' my mammy she wuz befo' me.
>
> LUCY: What come of de hoss in de dream, Madison?
> MADISON: Dat's all. Hoss went up in smoke an' I come down in bed.
> LUCY: Hoss went up in smoke! No, hit went down in smoke an' fiah.

This metaphor of a dream gone up in smoke is an apt portrayal of the spirit-crushing shenanigans that took place in America as blacks attempted to make the transition from bondage to meaningful citizenship. The accusations of "yellowstreak" and others against black fighters can be explained as basic reactionary backlash at someone who defies the existing power structure. But while the desire for social equality would be a dream deferred for several decades, Joe Gans achieved in his lifetime the amazing accomplishment of world recognition as a champion athlete. The quiet courage displayed by Gans in doing this cannot be overstated.

Boxing and Race in the Literary World

Charles Dana was the first to write about the negro domination of the fistic world, stirring the simmering pot of fear in a previously white dominated sport, a sport familiar to everyone where supremacy could be challenged and was unequivocally defined. In 1895, the publisher of the *New York Sun* wrote an editorial on the subject where he called public attention to the menace confronting the Caucasian race and warned the white pugilists to be on their guard or there would soon be no white man at the head of any division in boxing. "We are in the midst of a growing menace," said Mr. Dana. "The black man is rapidly forging to the front ranks in athletics, especially in the field of fisticuffs. We are in the midst of a black rise against white supremacy. Just at present we are safe from the humiliation of having a black world's champion, but we had a pretty narrow escape. What almost happened a few months ago, may happen sooner than we anticipate unless the white man perks up and follows the narrow path in his training. Less than a year ago, Peter Jackson could have whipped the world — Corbett, Fitzsimmons, Choynski, Joe Goddard, Frank P. Slavin, Peter Maher or Charley Mitchell, but today he is a human wreck and thus the white race is saved from having at the head of pugilism a Negro."[4] If black fighters could prove their supremacy in ring records, the only thing left for white writers to attack was their character or their endurance. Joe Gans would become that pugilistic lightning rod for the new century. He would refute the charge of the "yellowstreak" and prove his endurance.

In 1938 Nat Fleischer, who received his journalism training from the New York editor Charles Dana, appears at best condescending towards blacks, and it would not be a stretch to find racism in his words. In the least, Fleischer exhibits a casual acceptance and a condoning attitude with regard to racial inequality. Of the great pioneer boxer and trainer Bill Richmond, Fleischer points out how strange and bizarre it was that a white patron had decided to "educate the negro."[5] Molineaux, Peter Jackson, George Dixon, and other great black fighters are portrayed as hopelessly debauched in Fleischer's famous *Black Dynamite*.

Another famed journalist at the turn of the century was Jack London, known best for his novel *Call of the Wild*. When covering the Johnson-Jeffries match in 1910, he says of Jack Johnson, "But the question of the yellowstreak is not answered for all time. Just as Johnson has never been extended, so has he never shown the yellowstreak."[6] London was, of course, a great novelist and respected boxing scribe. But for all of his verbose prose, London would not get to first base if he were writing for a fair and discerning audience. He offers no justification for the assumptions upon which he pontificates. If Jack Johnson had never shown "the yellowstreak," then why did London devote so much ink to it, concluding his report by asking, suggestively, who will "remove that smile and silence that golden repartee?"[7]

In a fit of cleverness, London later writes, "The man of iron, grim with determination, sat down in his corner. And the carefree Negro smiled and smiled."[8] He uses this expression several times in discussing Johnson, an obvious literary allusion to the villain from Hamlet who "can smile and smile, and yet be a villain."

From 1890 through the early part of the early 20th century, the ridiculous myth of the "yellowstreak" was espoused by white fight writers, most of whom had never stepped into the ring. In fact, boxers like Joe Gans, Sam Langford, and Sugar Ray Robinson all fought well over 100 often brutal fights against the toughest opposition, while the most vocal fighters promoting the yellowstreak myth typically fought a few bouts and then rested on their laurels. Who proved their courage and durability?

The insistence by white fighters to "draw the color line" had its origins in a strange set of emotional and psychological fears. Part of the Southern code of honor was respect for the white woman, and laws were instituted to protect that respect. In many Southern states, for a black man to flirt with a white woman or touch her were grounds for assault. Miscegenation, where a black man impregnated a white woman, was abhorred more than death. The expression "to suffer a fate worse than death" probably did not arise from the mere physical act of sex, but from the fear that the victim would become pregnant with the child of the rapist. Hangings of blacks for rape were quite common in the Jim Crow south. *Mandingo* and other movies in recent history portray not a black rapist, but rather a white seductress, playing her black lover against her neglectful white husband, who of course had his own black mistress keeping him busy. The impregnation of a black woman by a white man was quite common in the time of slavery, and the offspring were often sold as slaves. But what about the offspring of the white rapist? What would become of mother and child? Consider the ending of Granny Maumee. When her sight is returned in the final scene of the play, Maumee realizes she is hold-

What Will Be the End of the Dead-Earnest, Menacing Uprising of Atlanta to Crush Out With Guns, Rope and Dogs the Fearful Epidemic of Negro Crime Against Her Women?

This drawing in the *San Francisco Examiner* accompanied the story of the Atlanta Race Riot in the wake of Gans' victory at Goldfield in September 1906. The article begins, "Periodically, the whole country is horrified by news of the lynching, by hanging, shooting or burning at the stake, of negroes found guilty of attacking white women. In spite of these examples of swift retribution, often made so terror-inspiring by torture in the flames, these crimes of degraded blacks against women of the white race seem to be increasing.... The Ku Klux Klan — that ghostly organization ... saved the whites of the South from being mongrelized."

ing in her frail arms her great grandson, who is part white. The play is a poignant reminder of race relationships in a country that proved to be unable to come to terms with its own inhumanities by 1914. Unfortunately, for the next fifty years, the situation would become worse, not better for all.

The "mixing of the races in the prize ring," at the time, as John L. Sullivan put it, was but one step away from miscegenation. Gans' win in September of 1906 against his white challenger coincided with the trumped up charges of rape of white women by black men in Atlanta. The "Fight of the Century" was only weeks before the Atlanta Riot in which 10,000 angry whites searched the city for any black faces, killing 25 people and injuring 100.

The great paradox of the color line was that boxing, the very sport where mixing was most feared, came to lead the way toward integration not only in sport but in society as well. If a black man is the best man in the one contest where physical and mental prowess and superiority can be definitively established, how could it be logical not to grant equality elsewhere? Many social commentators of Gans' day held the firm belief that he had done more for blacks than Booker T. Washington or any of the other theorizers of the turn of the century.

Boxing is the most egalitarian and individualistic of sports. No one blocks for you, you don't have to worry about your team members coming through with the big play. It is one person alone with his skills versus those of an opponent. When all the chips were counted at the end of the day a great champion could not feel as such if he had avoided the best contenders. In the third *Rocky* movie, the aging fighter is crushed to learn that his manager has skillfully protected him against the challenges of Clubber Lang, who had brutally mowed down the best heavyweight contenders, because he had no doubt that Rocky would be destroyed by the fearsome challenger.

It was as if his manhood had been compromised. Rocky, as any noble champion would, immediately demanded to fight the best contender. Thus has it often occurred with a great champion. Joe Louis demanded a rematch with Schmeling even though the German was the most dangerous contender. Boxers showed the way toward equality. It did not flow so much from the pens of academics as it was begot on the pride of the gladiators. When Joe Gans paved the way for black sports champions, he also paved the way for social equality.

The desperation of American blacks and their longing for heroes in the first half of the twentieth century is perhaps no better demonstrated than when the first victim of Georgia's gas chamber cried out plaintively, in his dying words, "Save me, Joe Louis!" No politician, but rather a boxer, was the hope for salvation.

Before Joe Gans' reign as lightweight champion, no American-born black had ever held a world boxing title. There were no rich black football, baseball, or basketball stars with million-dollar endorsement deals, no mass electronic media to spread fame over the airways. Gans made his name and fame through sheer perseverance.

Gans must have known that he had, as Nat Fleischer put it, "the death germs in him" before the year 1906 had closed. Accounts of his personal life indicate that he had already taken to sleeping more and having a doctor visit him frequently. One can only surmise what drove him to continue fighting. Unlike the vociferous Ali, who let the world know in no uncertain terms his view of his own destiny, Gans left little in the way of a verbal testament for posterity.

It was common practice for top boxers of Gans' day to write a small piece for the newspaper after a big fight. After his second fight with Jimmy Britt in 1907, Gans wrote: "There isn't much for me to say about the fight. My work in the ring is my statement. I don't think that any sane man inside the gates had any doubt that I would win from Britt without any trouble, even if the bout had gone on. He didn't put up as good a fight against me as Kid Herman did in Nevada on last New Year's Day. I've no doubt that he tried and that he did his best, but I wasn't hurt at all. I am in perfect condition and, with a little let up in my training, I will be just right for Memsic in Los Angeles later in the month. I feel sorry for Britt, but if the fight hadn't been stopped just where it was he would have been punished pretty badly and would have been beaten by the knock-out route, as sure as I am from Baltimore."[9] Gans was an articulate, accomplished black man with a ring record that left little to attack.

Carpe Diem: Gans Seized His Day

Before the swamping of American culture in mass media, certain books could send out psychic sound waves that could be heard for generations. Nat Fleischer's book discussing Gans seems to have left an indelible impression in the minds of boxing fans, that Gans was less than completely courageous and honorable as a fighter.

The Gans era was really a period of unprecedented creativity in America. Her teeming energy had not yet found an outlet in world affairs, and attentions were directed at mastering nature rather than at the Germans, Japanese, or Communists. Inventions of every sort were introduced, led by Thomas Edison's brilliant mind and ability to channel his ideas into practical uses. Vaudeville, literature, sport, and music all pitched in to expand the American mind. Foremost among the athletes, and patron of the arts when he founded the Goldfield Hotel, was Joe Gans.

Besides performing at the highest levels of creativity throughout his life, Gans suffered through the greatest calamities of the time, racism and disease. He overcame the former and succumbed to the latter, but only after a long hard road. Given his immense popularity as world title-holder and even after his death, one would expect that Baltimore, the monumental city, would honor its favorite son with a memorial befitting his greatness. But none was ever built. H. L. Mencken commented on Gans' fate, "It always amazes me how easily men of the highest talents and eminence can be forgotten in this careless world.... There is no Gans boulevard, avenue, street or even alley in the Harlem of Baltimore, and no Gans park. Some years ago I heard talk of raising a monument to Joe in Perkins Square, hard by his humble birthplace, with a marble effigy of him in ring costume on top of it, but the scheme faded out."[10] Even today, there is no statue in Baltimore to symbolize his crowning achievement or to memorialize the city that provided the bedrock for this master of the sport. There is only a cemetery stone in a forgotten graveyard.

It has become conventional wisdom that the great black boxers end up punch drunk or destitute. Gans' good friend George Dixon died young and penniless after becoming a bon vivant in the wake of his boxing success. Joe Louis ended up owing the IRS huge sums, and clearly without all of his mental faculties. Muhammad Ali's silver tongue began to fail him as a result of repeated blows to the head as he earned the adulation of the American public. In Gans' case, it can be said that he went out on his shield, fighting in the shadow of death and refusing to go softly into that good night.

17

Good Night, Sweet Prince: Fighting in the Shadow of Death

Gans had been both bribed and threatened with death in the dog days of August leading up to the Goldfield shoot-out. A posse of Tonopah gamblers had offered him $25,000 the day before to throw the fight, twice the amount he would legitimately earn. Gans made a statement to the press a few days after the fight that he had rebuffed the gun-toting rowdies.[1] One rumor spread to discredit Gans' achievement was that he had "given them the double cross" by not losing as he had been paid to do.[2]

Gans was given an ultimatum to either win or be lynched. Those who had bet on Gans threatened to kill him if he lost. Gans was literally fighting for his life, in the shadow of death, when he entered the ring that fateful September day in Nevada. He left the state carrying the death germs of tuberculosis, and thus did not escape the specter of death even by winning.

Having worked a lifetime to achieve the pinnacle he reached at his 1906 Goldfield showdown with Nelson, Joe Gans was not about to let the dirty tactics of Nelson's manager and a few pounds stand in the way of his destiny. Nelson's manager, the overbearing Billy Nolan, knew this and took every advantage of the situation. In scaling down to 133 pounds (actually 131½ when Nolan demanded at the last minute that he make weight in full fighting gear) and then enduring three blistering hours under the torrid Nevada sun, Gans allowed the tubercular germs to gain a foothold in his weakened body. On the day of the fight, the temperature hovered around the 100-degree mark. The bell for Round One clanged at just after 3:00 P.M. with the desert sun at its zenith. One of the first films in existence of over an hour in length commemorated the Goldfield showdown. As the rounds wore on toward sundown, the lengthening shadows of the gladiators on the silent film speak volumes about the longest title fight in the history of gloved boxing.

The invasion of TB can be likened to that of an invading army. Numerous assaults may be launched and repelled when the defenses are strong, as those of the Turks at Gallipoli. But once a foothold is established, as the Allies did so famously at Normandy, the doom of the defenders is sealed. In 1906, when TB was the leading cause of death in America, a very large percentage of the population carried the disease in an asymptomatic form. Soon after the apocalyptic bout with the Durable Dane the indications of Gans' illness began to surface. The strenuous training conditions and extreme fluctuations in the weather — fighting under temperature variations of over 100 degrees within a four-month period, from Goldfield's 100-plus degree day to Tonopah's 0 degree temperature — didn't help his condition.

Winning the Labor Day 1906 fight at Goldfield cemented Gans' celebrity, and on October 25, the great George "Kid" Lavigne would pass the symbolic torch to Joe Gans. The pairing of the two was a marquis coup for the city of Detroit, where the two engaged in a 3 round boxing show. The French named Detroit *Des Etroits*, meaning the narrows, after the river straights that flow between the Great Lakes. The site would connect the two boxing generations. Here were the marvels— Gans, the current master of the lightweights, and Lavigne, the former champ who was retiring into history. Lavigne had claimed the lightweight title after an exhibition fight in 1896 with the first world light-weight titleholder Jack McAuliffe, when McAuliffe decided to retire. "The Saginaw Kid" continued to hold the crown until it was taken from him by Frank Erne on July 3, 1899. Gans would be the fourth American fighter to hold the title.

Tonapah — When Nevada Turned from Furnace to Ice Bowl

Looking back at the event over a century later, and knowing how difficult it is in present times to get people together for anything despite modern transportation, the Nevada extravaganzas, Goldfield in 1906 and Tonapah in 1907, are truly amazing. On New Year's Day 1907 with the temperature sinking to zero in Tonopah, Nevada, the Pride of Baltimore met the Pride of Chicago, and the Nevada town's citizenry hoped to eclipse the success at Goldfield.

Nevada means *snow-capped* in Spanish, and that is what it was on New Year's day of 1907 when Gans successfully defended his title in a fight to the finish against "Kid" Herman Langfield, also called the "Ghetto Kid." It was a fight that pitted experience against youth; this "Kid" was nine years younger than Gans. The papers noted that Gans had no difficulty making the 133 weight. Notwithstanding the inclement weather, the bout drew so many "experts on pugilism" that the ringside seats could not hold them all — the first two rows were designated for the esteemed sportswriters. Retired heavyweight Jim Jeffries had promised the Casino Athletic Club's manager, Mike Riley, that he would referee, but at the last minute backed out, wanting no more of the fight business due to criticism he had received from his call of the Burns-O'Brien match.[3] He was replaced by veteran referee, Jack Welch.

The New Year's Day blizzard delayed the incoming Goldfield train filled with ticket holders, causing the 2 P.M. event to be postponed for several hours. Gans, having fought in 100-degree weather four months earlier, would now be fighting in frigid 0-degree weather. Upon arriving, the fight fans had to slosh a quarter mile through snowdrifts from the business district to the new 8,800 seat boxing arena, built at a cost of $40,000 (comparable to an $80 million basketball gym today without the benefit of heat). A full house was expected to bring box office receipts to almost $100,000. The purse for the event was $20,000, with sixty percent going to the winner and forty to the loser.

The sharp north winds blew through the "greatest prize-fight amphitheater ever constructed."[4] Inside, spectators huddled together in the coliseum-like enclosure, and sportswriters took notes with gloved hands. Concerned as he was about his health and about the pavilion's frigid conditions, Gans had insisted on the fight beginning no later than five minutes after the contestants disrobed. During the introductions, fight promoter Mike Riley announced that he would offer $30,000 to the winner for an upcoming match with Jimmy Britt. Not to be outdone, Tex Rickard upped the stakes. When he was introduced, Rickard offered a purse of $50,000 to the winner for a match with Battling Nelson, an offer that would be too good for Gans to pass up even though he would not be in good health. Excited by the stakes of the battle they were about to witness, the audience at Tonopah exploded with enthusiasm, when the announcer appeared on stage to read the now-famous telegram from Gans' mother, instructing him "to bring home the bacon." Instead, the announcer read a different message. Gans had sent his mother a Christmas present in the form of a check for $6000. Her telegram read: "Thanks, Keep Stepping, Joe."[5] A new phrase would become popular.

Although a top contender who could land a fair share of hard punches, Kid Herman was clearly outclassed by Gans and was forced to fall back on dirty tactics. Disregarding the rules outlined in the Articles of Agreement stating there would be no fighting in clinches, the "Kid" did just that. In the first round during a clinch he swung his right around to smack Gans' kidney. The two mixed it up, each receiving hard blows in the early rounds, with

Gans sending Herman to the floor in the third. The crowd went wild when the "Kid" pounded Gans' body and drove him to the ropes in the fifth. Gans came back in round six determined to put an end to Herman's aggressiveness. Gans landed so many short hard left and right punches to Herman's jaw, "jolting his head back a foot" that Herman's seconds screamed "Cover and fall in!" In the eighth round Gans sent powerful left and right blows to Herman's jaw that dropped him so cold it looked as if he had been "hit by a board." The fight was reported to be as "clean a knockout as ever took place in a ring."[6]

The film of the bout was one of the earliest made, yet it is a great improvement over the grainy Goldfield film from four months prior. Because it was such an exciting fight to watch, the 32 minute boxing film circulated throughout the United States for the next two years. On the film, the Old Master is lightning fast in picking off Herman's punches and landing his own counters. The quickness of both fighters is startling. Their stances differ from modern fighters in that their hands are held low. Holding the gloves up by the ears was not commonplace until the thirties. The old-timers compensated for the lower guard with quick head and hand movements. Gans cornered Herman against the ropes and drew Herman's most powerful punch, the right hook. When Herman threw his weight into the punch, Gans shifted and pulverized the challenger's head with his own right, leaving him in a heap on the canvass. Herman was counted out, during which time he seemed lifeless. His corner men rushed to his aid and Gans, ever the gentleman of the ring, was down with the group of men lifting Herman to his feet.

A point can be made here about Gans' ring genius. First, it is very hard to knock unconscious a professional fighter who is a well-conditioned athlete. Anyone who has seen bar fights or modern heavyweight boxing matches knows that a fighter is more likely to cave to exhaustion than a clean knockout. The effects of the right hook-uppercut with which Gans hit Herman can be seen in the way Herman's head seems to throw splinters all over the frame of the film where the punch lands. The speed of the film can't keep up with the concussive speed with which Herman's head is jolted back. He falls as if he is dead.

Gans and his contemporaries did not have access to films of their opponents. The viewer of this film can actually witness Gans sizing up Herman for the kill. In round three when Herman went to the ropes, he dipped his head to the left when throwing a right. Gans figured this out and used Herman's own momentum to maximize the impact of his short KO punch. A true ring scientist in action.

During the spring and summer of 1907, Gans finally took time to reap some of the rewards he deserved from his success while his new manager, Ben Selig, tried to arrange another lucrative match. In March efforts were made to stage a match between Gans and the middleweight Joe Thomas, but a disagreement on weigh-in terms shelved the bout. A planned lightweight title match between Gans and Harry Lewis also fell through. In July the *Nevada State Journal* was boasting of a Labor Day fight to be held in Reno between Gans and either Jimmy Britt or Battling Nelson, but this event also failed to materialize.

From Nevada, Gans went to New York, where he starred in theatrical engagements at one of Gotham's show houses, sparring three rounds with partner Adam Ryan. He opened on January 15 with matinee and evening performances, thrilling large audiences who favored him with rousing ovations when he appeared on stage. At one performance the crowd shouted for a speech. As professional as he was in the ring, Gans was uncomfortable in the spotlight and declined to give them a formal oration. He did, however, speak about his future boxing plans. He would take Tex Rickard's offer to meet Nelson again, but the next time would be on his own terms and conditions. "I'll fight him 65–35. That's 10 per cent better than he gave me at Goldfield."[7] He added that he would also fight him for a $10,000 bonus, winner-take-all. The papers reported that day that he looked in "splendid" physical condition. In his discussion with the crowd, he publicly stated that he was going to stay a lightweight and take on no welterweight or middleweight boxers. He also said that he had "laid the bones aside" and was no longer gambling.[8] His immediate plans were to return on February 1 to Tonopah to begin training for the Jimmy Britt return bout, originally scheduled for St. Patrick's Day in March.

Return Bout with Jimmy Britt and Easy Wins

Articles of Agreement for the second Britt fight were signed on August 9 with the Occidental Athletic Club for a guarantee of $25,000, and the fight was moved to the afternoon of September 9, 1907, to be held at the open-air San Francisco Ball Park under the management of John J. "Jack" Gleason. Since Goldfield and Gans, the purses had skyrocketed in the lightweight division, purses that would lead the way for the large ones that would come later in the heavyweight division. The signing of the articles in San Francisco created a scandal when the "fight trust" offered a "large sum of money" to the Pacific Athletic Club of Los Angeles to break up a fight scheduled in the city

of angels for August 16 between Jimmy Burns and Joe Gans.[9] The powerful
trust believed the match in Los Angeles would draw publicity away from the
Britt-Gans Occidental bout scheduled two weeks later. The Los Angeles crowd
was "agog" over the payoff.

Jack Gleason owned the Frisco Ball Club where he promoted the Gans-
Britt fight at a baseball game by tethering 100 kites to stakes around the stadium. Attached to the kites were tickets to the prestigious boxing event with
seat prices as high as $25. At the end of the game, the kite strings were cut
and the wispy bundles floated over the city to the excitement of the sports
crowd.

Before the fight, betting odds were in Gans' favor, at 10 to 7, although
not by as much as Gans had formerly known. Bookmakers explained that
Gans might have left much of his stamina in Goldfield. Gans' hometown
paper, of course, predicted that he would win. "Gans is in all respects regarded
the master of Britt. He is a more scientific boxer, he is a harder hitter and he
has more endurance. Gans' performance in battling 42 rounds with Nelson,

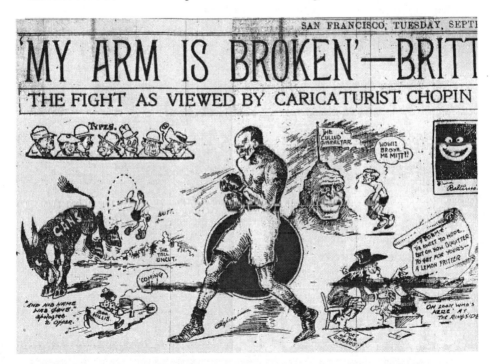

Gans seldom received major news coverage without some mention of his race. Car-
icaturist Chopin glorifies "Sir Edward" and his attempt to climb "the cullud Gibral-
tar" in the final battle between Gans and Jimmy Britt. In a racist jab, the cartoon
credit in the *San Francisco Examiner* on September 10, 1907, reads, "from Baltimo.'"

when the champion had been weakened by a compulsory reduction to 131½ pounds ringside, was a remarkable exhibition of stamina and courage."[10] One California writer said that Gans would have KO'd Nelson had he not been forced into a weakened condition before the match. California betting men, however, believed the match was leveled by age. By boxing standards Gans was considered old at 34, and Britt was a healthy seven years younger. San Francisco editor W.W. Naughton had noticed that while Gans was great at gymnasium stunts, he was unable to do roadwork or quick sprints without becoming feverish.

Anxious to take the title from Gans, Britt of San Francisco was noted to be in his best condition ever. Days before the fight, Britt was at a training weight between 135 and 136. Naughton described the unusual sparring exercise devised by Britt's trainer, Tiv Kreling, which attracted spectators to his quarters. Allowing his boxer full range of target and force during practice bouts, Kreling created a boxing mitt as "big as a sofa cushion" that he could wear on his right hand.[11] On his left hand he wore a regulation-sized glove. Britt could practice swinging with full force into the trainer's face, as the intervening pillow would soften the blow. Part of the attraction for spectators at the camp was hearing Kreling spout off Native American Indian words he had picked up as signals for various punch locations, i.e. ribs, jaw, stomach. Once when Kreling called off the Indian word for face, Britt confused it with stomach and the surprised squire stopped the assignment with a string of curse words leveled at his charge.

Naughton told his readers that Britt and Gans were, beyond argument, the two most talented of the small men in the ring, and this match promised to be the most thrilling since the battle at Goldfield. Interest was nationwide, but to Californians in particular it was the re-match of the century — a chance for the San Francisco boy to prove that he could be the real master. The pre-fight publicity in the *San Francisco Examiner* included the racist cartoon "You Joe! Bring Home Dat Bacon." The scene on Mission Street in San Francisco told the story — a throng of a thousand people gathered at fight time to read the round-by-round notices posted on the bulletin board outside the newspaper offices of *The Examiner*. The world, one more time, came to a standstill for three-minute intervals. So popular was the match that over 10,000 people assembled in front of the newspaper's branch office in San Jose.

Gans entered the ring at 3:15 with his seconds, Willie Keefe, Kid North, Alvie King and Anton La Grave. He was wearing a faded green bathrobe and a blue skullcap. With the park packed and the surrounding hills full of people looking like ants on a mound, announcer Billie Jordan introduced Gans as "the only lightweight champion of the world," a bitter reminder to Britt that Gans had never given up the lightweight title.[12] When he went to his corner, his seconds covered him in blankets as he shivered in the cool breeze. Then Jimmy Britt entered with his entourage.

It was a one-sided match. San Francisco writer C. E. Van Loan wrote that at all times Gans was the master. Britt "seemed to be losing steadily from the moment the second round started. Jimmy was game throughout and he struck back like a Trojan in the rallies, but all things considered, he was like putty in the hands of the peer of all lightweights."[13] The papers reported that Gans' wife sat in a box seat on the north side of the ring. During the second round when Gans landed a hard blow to Britt's left eye, she could be heard, "That eye is gone. Shut it!"[14]

Throughout his career, Joe Gans' would attain a skill in the ring that was almost unbelievable, controlling his opponent to a sometimes comical degree. The *San Francisco Examiner* in 1907 would report on Gans' fourth round, where he gave a great exhibition of clever defensive work.

> He had solved Britt's style of fight and lost no time in going to close quarters. Britt rapped away with lefts and rights, but Joe ducked the swings, blocked the hooks, and twisted his midsection out of the way of the left rips. He had Britt dizzy inside of a minute and then, stepping in, shot the right fist to the point of the chin. Britt's head went back and Gans prodded him with the short right uppercut, which took effect on the bridge of the nose. Britt let go a wild swing and Gans, who was in position to shoot the right to Britt's unprotected jaw, drew back with a right fist and then held it, yelling at Brit instead.
> 'Pow!' he said, and the crowd laughed. Joe was turning the contest into burlesque. Had he been willing, he could have finished Britt with that one right cross and had he known how the fight was going to end he would have done so. Toward the end of the round Gans walked Britt to the ropes and delivered two lightning rights to the point of the chin. Britt was rocking when the bell rang and there was no more fight in him. He was bleeding at the mouth as he went to the corner and he was laboring in his breathing. During the minute of intermission Gans chatted with his seconds and kept a keen eye on Britt, over whom his seconds were working frantically.[15]

In the fifth round, Britt broke a bone in his forearm and dislocated his wrist from jabbing it into Gans' forearm blocks. Referee Jack Welch stopped the match and gave the win to Gans.

Van Loan summarized the fight the next day in his editorial: "Joe Gans is still the old master of the gladiatorial college; the premier thumper of the lightweight division.... Joseph is still the past master of his bruising craft; the greatest ring general of the age and the cleanest, hardest hitter of all the lightweights now in the ring."[16] Gans' victory was thrilling proof that he was the rightful bearer of the championship laurels. Yet after this fight, to the world, Gans became an enigma. He failed to attend events given in his honor and his close friends noted that he seemed sad even when he played cards.

How some of the fans witness

Thoroughly outclassed in his second fight with Gans, "Sir Edward" quit in the fifth round, claiming he would have won but for a broken bone. Drawing in the *San Francisco Examiner*, September 10, 1907.

Gans remained on the West Coast and went down to Los Angeles toward the end of September to defend his title against George Memsic, aka "Jimmy Burns." The crowds swarmed the star's training camp at Baldwin's ranch. Heavyweight Jim Jeffries paid him a visit, but Gans was not the same man as before. Was he made aware of his own delicate condition? Did he learn something of his sparring partner Herman Miller's fragile condition, that he was suffering from the White Plague?

As with the Britt fight at the beginning of the month, experience again proved victorious, for Gans was able to remain cool against the wild swings of his younger opponent. Writing for the *Los Angeles Daily Times*, Harry C. Carr said of Gans, he "might have smoked cigarettes during most of the fight last night."[17] He compared him to an "old matador" and Burns to a clumsy bull. When Memsic's wild swings failed to connect, champion heavyweight Tommy Burns, working the contender's corner and who was responsible for giving the young fighter his name, tried to unnerve Gans through taunts. But Gans was unmoved. Carr said that Gans could have murdered the lad if he had wanted. Carr's description of the fight was almost comic: "Repeatedly, during the fiercest part of the fighting, Gans would reach out and simply hold his glove against the white boy's sore face while Burns thrashed out madly — almost insanely — into the empty air."[18]

But by the end of the fight Carr's depiction of Gans turned to a "sorrowful calm." Carr described the sweaty white boy holding his arms against his face buried in a clench as though "curled against the negro's breast for self protection, dreading the terrible fist that poised clinched to one side, waiting for [the fist to strike] like a snake."[19] He described Gans' demeanor: "His face, during the maddest of the fighting, was curiously unangered. No clenched teeth; no frenzy of battle; not much tension; merely the puzzled, wrinkled look of the expert coming to the critical part of the operation. He wasn't any more angry than a good matador should be while he waits, sword in hand, for the bull just to turn his head into the proper position."[20]

Through the looking glass of time it is often easy to see when a fighter should have hung up the gloves after a fight. Boxers who receive repeated head blows begin to slur their speech, albeit by slow degrees, after just a few years or less. The jarring of the brain must cease altogether if the man is to retain his mental faculties. But few realize when that moment to retire arrives.

Who knows what Gans was thinking at his sparring partner's retirement benefit on January 3, 1908, as he looked into the face of his long-time friend, knowing he was suffering with the same condition? Joe Gans and Al Herford gave a Boxing Carnival for middleweight Miller at Baltimore's Germania Maennerchor Hall, where they both had fought so many previous battles. Abe Ulman sold pictures of Gans and Miller to help with the proceeds that would be used to send the ailing Miller to Denver for treatment. His last fight had been in Norfolk, Virginia, only two months earlier in November. At that fight he beat Australian Jimmy Ryan in four rounds weighing 170 pounds. At the benefit, he had dropped to 130. He watched and smiled at the battle royal that had been scheduled for him. But when the strong boxers began their work, he became too depressed and was asked to be carried away. Old friend Fred Sweigert refereed the events. Joe Gans fought Bart Blackburn, slapping down his punches, and when an opening occurred, Gans would only touch his opponent's face, "showing conclusively how easy it would have been for him to have landed a probable knock-out blow." Blackburn lay down for the symbolic count.[21]

When Gans stepped upon the weight scale before his next title defense in San Francisco in May of 1908 against Rudy Unholz, reporters noticed how "drawn" his face looked in comparison to his opponent's glow of health.[22] During the match, the "Boer," as Unholz was called, was able to land a few hard punches on Gans' jaw. But once Gans figured out his style, he was able not only to hold Unholz at bay, but also to break through his guard, and with powerful punches close an eye and send him to the floor. Gans was declared the winner in the eleventh round.

As often we see in life, a person's greatest asset can create a liability in ways unforeseen. With the exception of the scar he wore over his left eye from the Erne fight, Gans' brilliant boxing defense left his face unmarked and his gentlemanly way of speaking intact. His nose was not smashed against his face and neither ear was misshapen. As the old saying goes, "If they can't hit you, they can't hurt you." A lord of the boxing ring is verily invincible if he can't be hit. But while Gans' reflexes were as sharp as they ever were, his endurance was no longer what it used to be. Perhaps his great skills caused him to overlook the weakening of his body that would lead to his early death.

Death in the Afternoon

On the fourth of July 1908 Gans met Battling Nelson in Colma, California. The afternoon Joe Gans finally lost his lightweight crown was a blistering hot Independence Day. By all accounts Gans battered his challenger throughout the early rounds, building up a big lead under the hot sun. But Gans was fighting a man known for his endurance, and who according to the leading phrenologist of the day, had the thickest skull ever recorded.

Back at the Goldfield, Joe's hotel in Baltimore, the electric piano had been turned off, and the dining room was hushed. Three thousand people had gathered in front of the hotel on Lexington and Chestnut Streets to hear the returns from the Postal Telegraph Company. Men with megaphones shouted out the round-by-round returns inside the hotel and out on the streets.

In the first five rounds Gans landed a fury of punishing blows on Nelson's face, but the enduring Dane kept coming back into the fray. In the seventh round Nelson landed a brutal blow to Gans' body which started to sap his strength. From then on it was Nelson's fight to win as he pelted Gans' body with terrible blows. In the twelfth round, Gans fell on three different occasions and took a count of nine. Gans gave it his all in the fourteenth round, slamming left and right short jabs into Nelson's face, to no avail.

As the 17th round started in the second Gans-Nelson fight, men can be seen still making side wagers, probably betting on when the end would come. Women in a variety of hats watch, as enthralled as the men in their white, round stove-tops.

On film Gans resembles an ebony skeleton. His hands are incredibly fast as he throws his textbook combinations. He moves around "like he's on wheels up there," as Jack Johnson used to say. This is especially amazing considering he has been fighting the charging bull Bat Nelson for over an hour. Nelson's charge is relentless. He is drenched in his own blood as the Old Master hits him with blow after blow, all the while perfect in his art.

But this was not a day when art would prevail. Gans wears a frustrated, almost disgusted expression, as if thinking, "Of what is this Danish head made? Granite? Marble perchance?" The bout brings to mind the breath-held excitement of the Ali-Frazier classics, where even the staunchest of Ali fans admit that, for all his ring knowledge, physical assets, and boxing skill, he never succeeded in solving the jungle beat of Frazier's Philadelphia thwack of a left hook. Ali, with his steel-belted radial abdomen, still ended up urinating blood for weeks after his Frazier fights.

Gans' internal organs were not protected in this fight by layers of muscles. His ribs were prominent and Nelson charged at them. He did not even try to hit the Old Master anywhere above the chest. Gans' head was never hittable, as his guard was never out of place. His final minute as champion is a masterpiece, despite the exhaustion, the white death, and his unrelenting foe.

Bat Nelson's hook missed its mark time and again. After the bout he would say that all he ever wanted from boxing was to defeat Gans. His final years would be spent in a home for the mentally disabled, in no small part from the beatings he took from Gans.

Every Ahab carries his spear with him out into the great blue frontier. Nelson's was his left hook. Its viciousness cannot be exaggerated. And like a mako shark rising up from the deep waters of the Atlantic, smelling blood, Nelson's hook started at ring-center, down near the floor, every ounce of weight and grim determination carried with it, to impale the emaciated champion. It literally looks on film as if Nelson's arm is buried under Gans' heart.

A powerful blow to the solar plexus can short-circuit the nervous system as surely as a hard chop on the chin. In Ali's fights against big bangers like Foreman and Frazier, he may lie on the ropes, but he always covers his chin with his gloves and the soft spot just below the sternum with his elbows. If Frazier had possessed an upper-cutting left hook, or a good straight right in addition to his short hooks, ring history may read differently.

The film footage as shot is so fast that Gans is just a frail blur of motion fighting off a steaming, pale locomotive of an attacker in Nelson. Frame-by-frame, however, it is a thing of beauty comparable to the slow fall of autumnal leaves from a mighty oak. Even the Dane is, in his own way, perfect in his art. The object of that art is to chop down Gans with his threshing-blade left hook.

The pace is frantic. Gans looks 30 pounds lighter than Bat Nelson. After an hour of fighting under the hot sun each second of the 17th round is a mini-drama in itself in a frame-by-frame analysis:

Both men come out for the final round like crouching tigers, Nelson charging with his head behind his gloves, Gans slightly more upright.

> Frame 1— Gans' left jab pierces Bat's guard, smacks him on the forehead.
> Frame 2 — Nelson absorbs the blow. Gans' back muscles thinly cover his bones.
> Frame 3 — Gans steps adroitly back, Nelson charges.
> Frames 4 thru 8 — Gans pivots around the ring, Nelson charges.
> Frame 9 — Gans is leaning back, onto his back foot.
> Frames 10 thru 13 — Gans hits onrushing Nelson with textbook left hooks, spins to his left.
> Frames 14 thru 20 — Nelson swings wildly with a left hook. Gans snaps short left hook to Nelson's mouth.
> Frames 21 thru 30 — Gans backs up as Nelson charges like a wild man.
> Frames 31 thru 34 — Gans hits Nelson on the nose with a hook, Gans is, incredibly, out-hooking a left-hooker, though this is a dangerous ploy.
> Frames 35 thru 40 — Fighters move off camera
> Frames 41 thru 43 — Gans chops a right to Nelson's chin, Nelson swings and misses, all the while Gans is moving his head so that Nelson misses

Frames 44 thru 47 — Gans ties up Nelson. Nelson hits Gans with a right below the belt

Frames 48 thru 52 — With his left shoulder in Gans' chest Nelson shoves Gans backwards

Frames 50 thru 58 — Fighters break

Frames 59 thru 60 — Gans hits Nelson with a clean jab. Nelson misses with a wild left hook; a follow-up hook grazes Gans' chin

Frames 60 thru 63 — Off-screen

Frames 64 thru 66 — Gans hits Nelson with a 1–2 punch

Frames 67 thru 70 — Off-screen

Frames 71 thru 75 — Gans hits charging Nelson with a hard right, then a left hook to the temple

Frames 76 thru 85 — Gans nails Bat with a right, then with perfect left hook. Gans' accuracy is amazing. Nelson charges kamikaze style, missing with a left swing. Gans lands left hook and chopping right. Nelson lands a hook to Gans' body; Gans winces as he lands a short left to Bat's jaw in return.

Frames 85 thru 100 — They clinch then break

Frames 101 thru 105 — Gans lands jab then right. His left hook is smothered as Bat grabs him

Frames 106 thru 110 — Nelson misses with left hook.

Frames 111 thru 115 — Gans lands left jab followed by chopping right.

Frames 116 thru 117 — Gans lands left jab; Nelson misses two left hooks.

Frames 118 thru 122 — They clinch

Frames 123 thru 126 — Gans lands left jab. Two men stand in front of the camera, exchanging cash as they make a side bet.

Frames 127 thru 130 — Nelson misses left hook to head.

Frames 131 thru 135 — They clinch.

Frames 136 thru 140 — Gans lands left and right to Nelson's head.

Frames 141 thru 145 — Nelson charges at Gans who lands a left hook to Bat's jaw.

Frames 146 thru 150 — Nelson falls to his right knee and takes a one-count.

Frames 151 thru 160 — They clinch. Gans lands jab to nose, follows with hook to same spot. Gans hits Bat with right to body. Gans blocks two left hooks with his right elbow. All the while Gans is gliding around the ring with his feet at perfect 45-degree angles. He looks as if he were on ice skates or wheels. (Young fighters are often trained to move with rope tied to feet to achieve such balance.)

Frames 161 thru 170 — Gans pushes Nelson back.

Frames 171 thru 175 — Nelson charges, Gans lands a left jab.

Frames 176 thru 180 — Nelson lands a left hook to body

Frames 181 thru 190 — They go off screen

Frames 191 thru 192 — Gans lands two left jabs

Frames 193 thru 195 — Gans misses right to head

Frames 196 thru 200 — They clinch

Frames 201 thru 203 — Gans lands left-right

Frames 204 thru 210 — They clinch

Frames 211 thru 215 — Gans backs away and lands two left jabs. Nelson grazes Gans' chin with left hook.

Frames 216 thru 220 — Gans lands two left jabs and a right uppercut.

Frames 221 thru 225 — Nelson lands left hook.

Frames 226 thru 230 — Nelson lands right as Gans lands left.

Frames 231 thru 235 — Gans lands two left jabs

Frames 236 thru 240 — Nelson in a running motion swings his left from down around his knee.

Frames 241 thru 245 — Gans' right elbow misses Nelson's swing, and all of Bat's weight goes into the left hook he delivers to Gans' stomach. Gans winces.

Frames 246 thru 250 — Gans' body jack-knifes around Nelson's arm, which impales Gans.

Frames 251 thru 255 — Nelson stares, surprised at his work, at a seemingly paralyzed Gans.

Frames 256 thru 260 — Gans doubles over and slumps to canvass.

Frames 261 thru 270 — Referee taps Gans' shoulder as if he has won on a foul. He then looks around with a confused expression. He starts to count and Gans' cornermen rush into the ring. Gans is counted out.

Frames 271 thru 280 — Great confusion as the ring fills with people.

Frames 281 thru 300 — Gans is helped from the ring.[23]

Gans' final round as champion, ironically, is quite instructive as to what a fistic genius he was. Cleverly backpeddling from the relentless Dane, the Old Master hit him with over twenty punches in the last seconds of the fight, before Nelson was able to slam a left hook under his heart, ending the bout.

To an unschooled eye, the last minute of Gans' reign as lightweight champion may bring to mind a description from *Invisible Man*. "Once I saw a prize fighter boxing a yokel. The fighter was swift and amazingly scientific.... But suddenly the yokel ... struck one blow and knocked science, speed, and footwork cold.... The yokel had simply stepped inside his opponent's sense of time."[24] But one must give the devil his due. Nelson was a dirty fighter, but no yokel. Bat Nelson was an extremely dangerous man, a small version of Joe Frazier in his prime. Charging forward, he was able to roll with the punches of Gans and still throw all of his weight into every single one of his own punches. He was drenched in his own blood, and still he charged like a rhinoceros. It is no wonder that many consider him one of the all-time greats of the lightweights. Blows from the Dane, coupled with tuberculosis, proved too much for Gans when a final hook from up and out of hell crashed under his right rib cage.

In the final act of Shakespeare's *Hamlet*, the Prince of Denmark fights a deadly duel with the brother of his doomed love interest Ophelia. Mortally wounded, Hamlet passes his ruler's mantle to Horatio, who bids the

Dane farewell, "Good night, sweet prince, And flights of angels sing thee to thy rest!"[25]

On the stage of California in 1908 a prince of a fighter took on the Durable Dane in two epic struggles for supremacy in lightweight boxing. This time around, the Old Master passed his mantle to the Durable Dane of the twentieth century. On the hundred-year-old film, Gans exits stage left, carried on his shield.

When the crowd

Two championship title bouts drew crowds to Colma, California (south San Francisco) on Labor Day 1908. Before his last fight with Battling Nelson, the Old Master sparred with all-time great featherweight Abe Attell (the "Little Champ" had fought Nelson to a draw earlier in the year). Gans spent 19 days of hard training: bag-punching, rope-skipping, "heavy bag flogging," and sparring with his friend for an unsuccessful attempt to regain his lost title. Attell successfully defended his championship against British champion Owen Moran at Coffroth's Arena on Mission Street (photograph by the Dana Brothers Studio, San Francisco, courtesy F. Daniel Somrack, boxing historian).

A very sick Gans, his body racked with tuberculosis, prepares for his final valiant attempt to recapture the lightweight championship against Battling Nelson. Both Nelson and Gans weighed 134 pounds during their training, the Battler by virtue of his natural weight. Gans had lost much of his muscle tone in his forearms and legs as a result of his illness (photograph by the Dana Brothers Studio, San Francisco, courtesy F. Daniel Somrack, boxing historian).

in Baltimore heard that Gans had been beaten, they fell silent, astounded. They had expected him once again to "bring home the bacon." Inside the Goldfield Hotel, Gans' former manager, Al Herford, sulked and rationalized, mumbling on and on to anyone who would listen, that "Joe is not the boy he used to be.... I believe Joe was not in fighting trim. It might have been a case of too much confidence. You know it requires good, faithful training to fight a battle, and Joe probably didn't work hard enough. Then again, Joe is not as young as he used to be, and that counts."[26] As Herford winded down, the player piano began to play a haunting, weary ragtime song.

Why did the Old Master continue fighting? Gans' apparent invincibility led him to fight on when his health failed him, even if his boxing skills did not. So strong was his grit and belief that he could still endure a championship bout that he fought on, challenging Nelson again on September 9 in Colma, California, even as his body carried the full viral load of the White Plague. The adulation of an adoring public is an addiction that few have been able to overcome. Indeed, after years of hearing the deafening roars of the crowds and painstakingly turning the jeers and boos into cheers, what could have possibly been the equal for Joseph Gans?

Whenever a legend arises from humble origins, it has been a matter of both historical fact and artistic license that a childhood event somehow formed a driving impulse that would carry the man to great heights. In the case of Muhammad Ali a stolen bicycle and later, a run-in with Southern rednecks, put zeal in his soul to fight for his people. In the recent hit movie about Ray Charles, few eyes remained dry in theaters when his brother drowned and thereby traumatized the young Ray. In *Braveheart*, the cruel deaths of his father and young bride at the hands of the English drove the immortal Scotsman.

We have no accounts of the childhood of Joe Gans that would pinpoint a seminal instance in the formation of his personality. But all accounts of his life reference his strong desire to provide for his loved ones. That Gans revered his foster mother is manifest in the telegraphs and other documents left to posterity. He clearly wanted to provide for her as well as his wife and children. No matter how beloved a foster parent may be, a feeling of abandonment is quite common among foster children. With the Grim Reaper approaching, Gans may have felt pangs of guilt driving him to provide further paydays for his own two children. He knew the indignities of poverty and racism as well as or better than anybody did, and the most basic feeling a father has is to save his children from the pain he has lived through.

Again turning to Ralph Ellison's mid-century classic *Invisible Man*, the author articulates a core aspect of the African American experience when he describes the eviction of an elderly black couple. After fleeing the South to the great northern land of freedom, the narrator is shocked that an old woman resembling his grandmother could be thrown out on the street. The narrator inquires as to what has happened. "'I'll tell you!' a heavyweight yelled, pushing out of the crowd, his face angry. 'Hell, they been dispossessed, you crazy sonofabitch, get out of the way!'"[27]

Gans clearly did not want his heirs to be dispossessed. His constant need for money is perhaps puzzling in that he made so much of it in the prize ring, more than almost any fighter before him. But when crooked managers, gambling, and the go-go Goldfield Club are factored, Gans' finances flowed into a sieve rather than any secure reservoir. He must have known shortly after the fight in Goldfield that he had tuberculosis, and so was determined to win as many big purses as possible. Newspaper accounts were already noting the frequent visits he received from his doctor.

After his next bout with Nelson the headline in the *Baltimore Sun* read simply, "Gans Knocked Out. Battling Nelson Finishes Him In Twenty-First Round. Never Had Chance to Win."[28] Gans went into the ring prepared. He had sparred for three weeks and had come to the weight limit early. Nelson believed that he would get a beating from Gans early on. But as his name implied, the Durable Dane's strategy was to wear down the Old Master. Gans acknowledged that he had not won the previous match with Nelson because he had become too tired and winded. At least publicly, he attributed it to a lack of training. He told everyone that if he couldn't beat Nelson this time, he would never ask for another chance.

The fight went twenty-one rounds before Gans sank to the floor and failed to rise. Realizing that his punches rarely affected Nelson, Gans seemed to lose heart. The papers reported, "Not until the count of 10 was finished did Gans, ashen pale, his face terribly cut and his eyes glassy, attempt to rise. He realized, however, that it was too late and feebly declared: 'I have positively fought my last battle.'"[29] But it wasn't his last battle. A far more brutal one with the White Plague was yet to come. And he would fight that battle with the same grit that carried him through all the other ones.

Gans' last fistic battle proved a puzzle to the members of the National Athletic Club in New York who watched it. What was he attempting by meeting Great Britain's Lightweight Champion, Jabez White, March 12, 1909? Whatever the answer, the match was described as a cat playing with a frightened mouse. No one doubted that Gans could have knocked his opponent out at any time during the one-sided match, but he didn't. He simply walked around him, ducked and parried "prettily," and exhibited his signature chivalry in the ring. He did, however, take several body punches in the fourth round that left him in agony. Some thought that he had simply gotten too old to fight. In several rounds when he sent Jabez to the floor with uppercuts to the jaw, he failed to put him out. It appeared to those in the crowd as if Gans didn't want to harm his opponent. When the crowd sensed the lagging action, the whistling commenced to "The Merry Widow Waltz."[30] Gans won his final mill on points, but the next day the papers called it one of the strangest bouts ever fought. Perhaps *The Washington Post* recognized more astutely that Gans had given them the best show he could, noting that "Gans was a shadow of his former great self. He was weak in the legs, had little strength to either take or give punishment, and would have been put to sleep if White had possessed just ordinary hitting power."[31] After the match, Gans went into retirement, and the sportswriters became more sympathetic. A reporter for *The New York Times* contacted referee Charley White in Denver, who gave the press a definitive statement regarding Gans' physical condition — the Old Master was suffering from tuberculosis.[32]

The Old Master Goes Home

With his fighting career over, Gans served as a referee in Baltimore at the Eureka Athletic Club; old wounds seemed to be healed between the fighter and his former manager Herford. It was said that at one point in a bout he stopped the fight to warn the men that they needed to step it up, that the spectators had not come to see a gentle fight.[33] Before the year was out, Jack Johnson, heavyweight title holder, engaged Gans "to act as sparring partner and chief adviser in his training" for his famous showdown in Reno with the "Great White Hope," Jim Jeffries, July 4, 1910.[34] At this point the papers began to summarize Gans' career with superlatives, praising Johnson's decision, and calling Gans the best strategist known, always careful and never overconfident. Gans' step in the ring was compared to the spring in a wolf's snap. What had been called a show of "yellowstreak" by the New York papers in his loss to Erne was now definitively defended as a wise move after receiving a brunt to the eye. The press noted that in rematches Gans proved that he could knock out any man at any time he wanted. He was a hard hitter and had a perfect guard. The end of 1909 saw him acknowledged as having held two championship titles, lightweight and welterweight.

Gans served as advisor and chief second to his good friend, the great Sam Langford, when Langford beat middleweight champion Stanley Ketchel in a six-round non-title fight in Philadelphia on April 28, 1910. It was to be Gans' last time near the ring. A rematch in San Francisco for the middleweight crown was eagerly anticipated, and Gans was looking forward to attending this match in July. But after Langford's April fight, Gans' health needs were so pressing that he left humid Baltimore for Arizona, where the dry southwestern air might improve his deteriorating condition. He stayed the month of May in Phoenix where the soaring heat, between 102 and 120 degrees, pressed against his chest in suffocating waves. Relief from these furnace-like conditions came, when on June 9, a train took him away from the Salt River Valley of saguaro cactus and up and over the Mogollon Rim to the pine trees and cool, crystal air of Prescott, Arizona. Only a few miners, scattered through the surrounding hills, were left from the town's ore days, sifting the waters and sluicing the streambeds for flakes of gold and an occasional nugget. The old territorial capital's stock in trade now was its healthy, pollution-free air.

Doctors had established tuberculosis sanitariums among the sweet smelling pinion pines, drawing the afflicted from around the country who needed to give their "lungs a rest." Prescott was a national draw for those with tuberculosis. The most famous hospital was Pamsetgaaf Sanitorium which opened in 1903 on West Gurley and Willow Strand under the care of Dr. John W. Flinn from Montreal. The awkward sounding name was actually an acronym for the place, "Pure Air, Maximum Sunshine, Equitable Temperature, Good Accommodations and Food." His patients were many, from movie stars to miners.[35]

If there existed any chance for Gans' condition to improve, Prescott was his last hope. Here he and his partner looked forward to the time when the cool, dry air would restore him and he could return to Baltimore. The Mile High City was already familiar with Gans' achievements. The year before, Prescott hosted a huge boxing event that brought John L. Sullivan and Jake Kilrain out of retirement. The men, then in their fifties, engaged in a boxing exhibition that some spectators said was a show of nothing but flabby old men.[36] The preliminary event was none other than the film of the Gans-Herman fight, a full-length, 32-minute show. How sadly ironic that Gans would appear the next year in person in such ill-health.

Stately Victorian homes lined Senator Avenue, but because Gans was black, he would be taken to the modest section of homes on Virginia Street off Gurley where he and wife Martha J. resided with a friend, Mrs. Eliza Evans. From town center Gans could see Thumb Butte Mountain, an eroded mountain peak looming over the city. In the evening the town came to life along Town Square's Whiskey Row, a block of saloons in full operation since the territorial days.

According to the *Prescott Journal-Miner*, when Gans arrived in the city, he looked "pale, but optimistic, despite the fact that his health [was] broken."[37] He was not despondent. He declared he would "battle his threatened 'white plague' attack to a finish and be lively and prancing when his affliction gets the count."[38]

By the next week, the paper reported that his condition had improved and that Gans looked forward to attending the Johnson-Jeffries and the Ketchel-Langford fights in San Francisco in July. He was out of his bed for the first time, his appetite had improved, and he was generally experiencing relief in the piney mountains of the city. Gans was attended by a former Chicago physician, Dr. Harry T. Southworth. Both the doctor and his wife, Harriette Fay, were popular figures in Prescott. Dr. Southworth served as city health officer for many years.

Progress was slower than Gans had expected, forcing him to miss the fights for which he was chosen tutor emeritus. If his friends could have seen him, no one would have believed that he was only months removed from his former life in the ring. By the middle of July, Gans could dress himself and take short walks. But during the last few days of July his condition worsened.

He remained bedridden and became depressed. On July 28, 1910, a telegram was sent back to Baltimore with the grim news. Gans was "at the point of death" and he had "been in a semi-comatose condition, and no hope is held out for his recovery."[39] Gans wanted to return home. His wife tried to convince him to stay in Arizona, telling him that the city's clean, dry air would improve his condition and finally cure him if given enough time. She begged him to stay. But Gans was firmly determined to leave for Baltimore.

With his condition so fragile, he arranged to have Dr. Southworth travel with him. On the afternoon before he left Prescott, he told a reporter that he realized he could not survive for very long. "And believing that it was a matter of only a few weeks until the end came, he desired to close his earthly career at the old home and with those so near and dear to him."[40] He appreciated the kindness shown him while in Prescott, but it was time to go home.

On August 1, 1910, at 12:35 in the early morning, Gans arrived at the Prescott depot ready for his departure for Baltimore. Reporters there at the stroke of midnight quoted him as saying, "I know that I am going to die and feel that I am growing weaker daily. Several days ago I was walking around but the doctor ordered me to remain in bed. I want to see mother and the two children in Baltimore before I die. I made a mistake in not coming to Prescott in the beginning. I did not realize my condition. My last two fights broke down my constitution and made me an easy victim for consumption."[41] The wires sent word across the nation that the champion was going home. Reporters and huge crowds of fans waited patiently at every major train stop along the way to see the Old Master for the last time.

August 4, word circulated quickly that Gans' train had pulled into Chicago, and because he was expected to live only a few hours, he had been removed from his private car and taken along with his small entourage to the home of his former wife, Madge Gans. The press gathered and waited expectantly for the death knell. But like the fighter who would always summon the strength to rise on the count of nine, Gans refused to take the final count.

While physicians tried to persuade him to stay in Chicago, Gans insisted that they go to whatever ends possible to prolong his life so that he could make it to Baltimore to say goodbye to his family and friends. The doctors consented and reservations were made for him to board a train at 5:30 that afternoon. His physician said he believed the effort to reach Gans' old home would be fruitless, as it was "improbable the fighter would live longer than today, but a start would be made to please the patient."[42]

Journalists at the train station when two porters carried him out on a

The final days of the "Old Master." Porters carry Gans to his private train-car where he clung fiercely to life until he could reach his family in Baltimore. Weighing less than 100 pounds, Gans had been removed from the train in Chicago on his way home from Prescott, Arizona, August 4, 1910. He did not have the energy to sit up, and his accompanying physician, Dr. Harry T. Southworth, thought he would die that day. Gans demanded that he be allowed to complete his journey (Chicago History Museum, Photographer: *Chicago Daily News*, 1910).

stretcher to board the train snapped photos that would allow the world to see his pitiful, emaciated state. The germs of consumption had taken this world class athlete and reduced him to less than a hundred pounds. Tucked neatly into crisp white sheets, he wore his signature ivy cap. His dark eyes seemed only moments away from death and dwarfed his sunken face. The oxygen used to help him breathe seemed a pitiful aid.

Through sheer will and with the same fortitude that had seen him through so many battles, the Old Master made it to his life's final round in Baltimore on Friday afternoon, the 5th of August. He was able to see his family, settle his financial obligations, dictate his final wishes, and profess his everlasting faith. For five long days he was attended by his family, his children James, 16, and Julia, 15, friend "Kid" North, and the Rev. C. G. Cummings. Reporters waited at his mother's doorstep for news of his condition and telegrammed every detail to home papers. Late into the evening on Saturday, August 6, Dr. Southworth told reporters that the champion was "steadily losing strength," but that he was still alive. The doctor predicted that he would not expire on this night; "He is resting comparatively well, but his vitality is constantly decreasing."[43]

The next day *The New Times* reported, "The condition of Joe Gans, who is dying of tuberculosis at the home of his mother, was reported to be unchanged tonight. Only his closest friends are allowed to see him. Realizing that the end is fast drawing near, Joe sent for his attorney yesterday afternoon and drew up an assignment turning all of his property and belongings over to his wife, Martha J. Gans. His mother has also been provided for."[44] Gans paid Dr. Harry T. Southworth a $500 fee for accompanying him to Baltimore. He paid $1000 in expenses to bring him home. With the help of attorney Tom Smith, he deeded the Goldfield Hotel to his third wife for her to run.

Tuesday evening before Gans died, with halting breath he quietly sang, "I Am So Glad That Jesus Loves Me."[45] He expired at 8:08 on Wednesday morning of August 10 at home, and in the arms of his aging mother.

Word of Gans' death came immediately to the Goldfield, Gans' hotel. Bartender James Jackson, who had worked there from its beginning, pulled down the shades, took down the swinging doors, and locked the hotel. The lights stayed out until Monday, the only four days the place had ever been closed. The Goldfield was never again the same.

The papers reported that his doom had been sealed for at least a year.

For three days, thousands of people, black and white, "high in official life and lowly in the world," came to his mother's home on Argyle Street to give their condolences to the family and to take a final, sad look at the gentleman who brought such fame to himself and to his native Baltimore.[46] At 7:30 Saturday morning, the Reverend C. G. Cummings conducted a private service in his home with family and a few friends before taking him to lie in state at Whatcoat Methodist Episcopal Church, located at Pine and Franklin Streets. As had happened at his mother's home, a line of thousands formed outside the church to take a final look at their hero.

At 12:00 noon his family was seated at the front of the church. Reverend Cummings began the public service by inviting the choir, congregation, and all those gathered around the church to join in singing of the hymn "Nearer My God to Thee." Citizens later remarked that voices could be heard over Baltimore as though everyone in the city were singing the doleful hymn. There followed a scriptural reading, a prayer, and a solo by Mr. S. T. Hemsley. The Reverends Alfred Young and F. R. Williams remarked on his life. Several of Baltimore's social groups were represented and final rituals were performed by the Monumental Lodge, the I.B.P.O.E.W., and the Knights of Pythians. Gans' earthly remains lay in state the entire afternoon to accommodate the thousands of mourners who wished to pay their respects. Then came the long, slow journey to the Sharp Street Cemetery known as Mount Auburn, and Joe Gans was laid to final rest.

18

The Old Master's Legacy

Hamlet, Prince of Denmark, shuffled off his mortal coil with his dying words "and the rest is silence."[1] For the Old Master's legacy the rest would be music, science, and art, and how they all came together in Baltimore at his famous establishment. In 1906, Joe Gans returned to Baltimore with winnings from the Goldfield fight totaling $15,000, well over $2 million in today's dollars. Investing in real estate, he also became a pioneer hotelier, following the example of Tom Sharkey in New York. Although always a soft touch who spent freely, Gans was in the chips in 1907 and was able to build a hotel which he named "The Goldfield" in honor of his great battle. Its gala opening was celebrated October 29, 1907, with the crowd so large it spilled out onto the cobblestone street. The hotel became the first black-owned haven for ragtime musicians in Baltimore, or in the words of his contemporary H.L. Mencken, "the first black and tan club." It was also the club that first hired the musician who would carry ragtime into the Jazz Age.

Although Gans has in recent generations become an "invisible man," he was certainly an active participant in Baltimore society when he lived there. By 1908 he owned a $5000 car. He was said to be the first black man in the city to own an automobile. Gans was among the first to give the twentieth-century black American musicians a distinguished place to perform. Gans made and spent a small fortune in the last few years of his life, and this helped keep the fire lit at the Goldfield. Gans spent thousands of dollars on his hotel in what was called the Jonestown section at the corner of 200 Chestnut (later Colvin) and East Lexington. A slab of granite at the hotel's entrance announced with inlaid tile the "Goldfield Hotel." Inside the swinging bat-wing doors (doors that would swing all night long) was the lobby with a staircase rising to the second level where Gans stayed when he was in town. Through the lobby was the restaurant, furnished modestly with wooden tables and chairs. On the walls and behind the large mahogany bar hung oversized photos of Gans' many ring battles. One showed Gans helping Battling Nel-

Composer and musician Eubie Blake got his big break when Joe Gans hired him to play his ragtime music at the Goldfield Hotel. Blake wrote this "rag" for Joe Gans in 1908.

son to his feet after knocking him through the ropes at Goldfield. The hotel also had a rathskeller in the basement where Gans welcomed numerous visitors, friends, and any fighter who happened to be in town. Battling Nelson visited shortly after the Goldfield opened. It was the place to be whether you were a fighter, a fight fan, or just someone who loved the music and nightlife.

When Gans was alive the Goldfield was one of the liveliest spots in Baltimore, especially after fight-night or the burlesque shows at the nearby Monumental Theater, because that was where everyone could find the fun-loving, jovial Joe Gans. Everyone loved him. "Boxers, managers, handlers, agents, actors, vaudeville stars and thousands of sports fans made the Goldfield a sure port of call while in Baltimore."[2] After Gans returned from each winning fight in 1907 and 1908, his fans would give him a Cakewalk back at the hotel. This lively, high-stepping dance honoring a festive occasion demanded a talented piano player. It was here that the young Eubie Blake improvised popular tunes and gave a new twist to stately church songs, music that would become known as "rag time."

Another great fighter of the early twentieth century would pick up Gans' boxing and musical notes within a few years of the Old Master's prime. If imitation is the sincerest form of flattery, Jack Johnson certainly lavished Joe Gans with flattery both inside the ring and out. Johnson's footwork and punching came right out of Gans' bag of tricks. Jack Johnson's ascension to the heavyweight championship corresponded with the twilight of Gans' career. Johnson would visit the Goldfield Hotel whenever he traveled through Baltimore. Every night after his appearance on stage during one of his tours,

Johnson brought an entourage to the Goldfield and kept the place jumping into the early hours. It was said that those were the "good days." Johnson, obviously inspired by Gans' Goldfield, would later found his own nightclubs, one in Chicago, and another, the Club Deluxe in Harlem, which would later be renamed the Cotton Club. The Harlem club would later earn fame as the subject of a 1984 movie starring Richard Gere. Much to its credit, the Cotton Club would become a proving ground for jazz musicians, the leading hotbed for Jazz and the Harlem Renaissance, and less to its credit, a haven for gangsters.

That Joe Gans played an integral part in the founding of ragtime music, which gave its name to an entire era in American history, can be seen in the career of Eubie Blake, the premiere ragtime musician. Blake had been playing in Baltimore bordellos. His first big break came in 1907 when he was hired by Joe Gans. Because of Gans' celebrity, the Goldfield became a prominent entertainment venue for the wealthy, society types, politicians, and entertainers of all races from all over the world. As a performer in this prestigious hotel, Blake became acquainted with these important people, many of whom had a profound impact on his later career.

Blake composed many songs during his tenure with Gans. In addition to the hotel's namesake, "The Goldfield Rag," Blake wrote "The Baltimore Rag, "Tricky Fingers," "Poor Katie," and hundreds of other rags still played today. These tunes were heard in parlors, theaters, and saloons across the nation when they were printed on piano rolls for ease in playing. Blake's song "Wild About Harry" became a household ditty when Harry Truman used it in his presidential campaign.

One little girl who grew up in Baltimore listening to Eubie Blake was the legendary blues songstress Billie Holiday. She matched Gans to a degree in determination and grit, but unfortunately followed in the footsteps of Canadian boxer George Dixon with respect to excess and dissipation, becoming a drug addict in her later years. Billie's song about a beaten-down under class, "God Bless the Child," seemed a veritable socialist manifesto. Recent renditions of this song give it a happy turn, leaving out the sadness that gave it soul. In the movie based on Billie's life, we see young blacks casually lynched just as they were depicted in the stories that accompanied Gans' fights. Billie died penniless, although her songs made millions for the recording industry over the years. Gans' success in passing on the Goldfield Hotel to his designated heirs, by contrast, was a rarity among famous performers.

The music Eubie Blake created while at Gans' Goldfield Hotel was both off-beat and technically perfect, captivating the American public. Mechanically, ragtime is characterized by syncopation, a style carried into the twenties. This syncopation, where musical rhythms miss a beat, occurs in the melody usually played on the piano with the right hand against a regularly accented accompaniment by the left. It is as though the two hands are playing a game with each other while dancing to their individual tunes. It is interesting to note that "syncope" has two definitions: the loss of one or more sounds or letters in the interior of a word, and the loss of consciousness resulting from insufficient blood flow to the brain. Think of a left hook off a jab by a boxer, the timing of which can also be considered the art of syncopation.

Just as the element of unpredictability is key to ragtime, so it was essential when Muhammad Ali used a "syncopated" boxing strategy in his title-winning effort against George Foreman in Zaire. In the first round he turned the tables on Foreman by hitting him with a batch of right-hand leads that ruined the champion's timing and had him disoriented. Throughout the rest of the fight, Ali the dancing master tricked Foreman with the now famous rope-a-dope strategy that no one had predicted.

Gans left a legacy in ring style and technique that continues today. When author Mark Scott was a teenager boxing in the Golden Gloves, his trainer, Louie Munoz, would talk nostalgically about the days of Gans and the lost art of balance. One hotshot at the gym had a bad habit of stutter-stepping before launching his wicked left hook. Exasperated, Munoz donned the gloves on his leathery hands and climbed into the ring with the star left-hooker. They sparred lightly for a minute or so as the young star took it easy on Louie. Then came the wayward stutter-step, and quick as a flash, Louie's straight right crashed home to the point of the chin, wobbling the young star, proving a point. The right to the chin carried with it the wisdom of the ages.

As a child Mark watched the promotion for the upcoming Muhammad Ali fight. The excitement, the speed and grace, of the young Ali made anything Mark had seen before on the football or baseball fields seem boring by comparison. That night was born a love of boxing that continues to this day. A few years later Mark would begin an amateur boxing career, hoping to emulate the great Ali. One or two rounds in a real fight were all it took for him to know that Ali's moves were inimitable. After escaping with a narrow win, he realized he better listen to his trainers if he wanted to avoid getting hit. By following a regime much closer to that of the Old Master, Mark enjoyed an amateur boxing career without serious injuries.

In retrospect, virtually every move taught in boxing gymnasiums today owes a debt to the great Joe Gans. First the stance: the feet must be placed at 45-degree angles with the weight evenly balanced. A good trainer will make a novice move around the ring with his feet tied together by a rope, to combat the natural tendency to spread the stance. Only when a young fighter learns to move with balance can he block and deliver blows correctly. That Ali could do it from impossible angles was an anomaly in the annals of the ring. Gans invented proper footwork, as can be seen in his fight with Battling Nelson.

Once a novice can move around the ring, he can learn to punch, block, and slip. The young Ali was so tall and fast that he could pull away from punches and dance out of danger. This will get a novice fighter knocked out quickly. A boxer who can move in quickly will have a wide open target in the mid-rift and an exposed chin to tee-off upon with his best punches.

Gans perfected the art of moving only as much as necessary to slip a punch, all the while remaining in position to fire back. Some fighters of the modern era, such as Mike Ayala and Wilfred Benitez, slipped punches so well that they seemed to have a force field around their heads. This art of slipping punches is part of the legacy of Joe Gans.

When it comes to punching, the first thing a novice learns is the jab. Thrown correctly, it can cause quite a bit of damage. In Gans' fight with Nelson, for example, it is a hard, jarring jab in the 42nd round that spells the end for Nelson. A few moments after almost being decapitated by Gans' jab, Nelson deliberately fouls out. After that great fight, Gans devoted much of his time to giving back to his community.

In choosing to promote Eubie Blake's career, Joe Gans had done for Blake what Herford had done for him. He plucked a pearl from the Baltimore Harbor to give America one of its greatest treasures. In Gans and Blake, Baltimore had provided boxing and music, two great treasures of the twentieth century.

It is no small testament to the power of music that W.E.B. Du Bois began his masterful *The Souls of Black Folk* with written music that included both lyrics and the notes of the sheet music. The notes and half-notes, like hooks, jabs, and crosses of ringing melody, remind us of the integral part music played in Du Bois' conception of black America. As noted previously, Gans ended his life singing church music among throngs of friends and admirers. It is no stretch to say that a piece of the soul of the Old Master was destined to live on in the music of ragtime and jazz.

Joe Gans achieved his dream in his short and turbulent life and left a legacy shared by generations of Americans who may have never heard of him. He fought on in the shadow of death in order to make enough money to buy the Goldfield Hotel to insure his family's future, and in so doing, it helped to usher in the Jazz Age by promoting such future legends as Eubie Blake.

He was met by thousands of friends and fans when he made his final trip home to die, ending one of the most glorious chapters in sports history.

Gans' dream runs through the veins of inner city youth today who rise at 5 A.M. to do roadwork, with visions of big ring paydays lifting their spirits when their bodies scream for rest. It lives on in the rings and gymnasiums throughout the world, wherever boxers and other athletes perfect the artistry of their sports.

19

In the Words of Peers and Scholars

At the end of Gans' life the editor of the *Baltimore Sun* wrote that an earlier query had been sent to the paper asking, "What were the special features which made Gans so great a fighter? The answer was. "His ability to hit hard with either hand from short distance; his defensive work with feet, head, and body; his ring generalship; his ability to take punishment and not get rattled; his clean work in the ring and adaptability to any style of boxer."[1]

The Old Master's fellow boxers who saw him in action are lavish in their praise:

JOHN L. SULLIVAN: "Gans is easily the fastest and cleverest man of his weight in the world."

BOB FITZSIMMONS: "Gans is the cleverest fighter, big or little that ever put on the gloves."

MIKE "TWIN" SULLIVAN: "I realize that he is one of the greatest fighters that ever lived."

SAM LANGFORD: "Joe Gans was the greatest fighter of all time."

ABE ATTELL: "The greatest fighter of all time was Joe Gans."

HARRY LENNY, boxer and trainer: "There was never anybody like Gans and there probably never will be."[2]

Boxing historians love to opine on the characteristics of "greatness." More so than in any other field, historians are obsessed with who is the greatest of all time in the various weight categories and who is the best, pound-for-pound. During Gans' lifetime sportswriters and fellow boxers rarely covered one of his fights or spoke of him without applauding some aspect of the champion's technical genius. What follows are the views of premiere boxing experts and perspectives of scholars who typically have no occasion to comment on the sport. The interest taken by the latter group is remarkable for its rarity.

In comparison to other champions, little has been written about Gans since the Old Master's death. One current historian, however, has led the way in reviving Gans' remarkable legacy and elevating his stature. Monte Cox answers the important question: Was Joe Gans the greatest fighter of all time?[3] In a well-developed analysis, Cox rates Gans against the other all-time greats in ten categories that he considers essential for the purpose of comparison. The categories cover all aspects of boxing and include: punching power and effectiveness, speed and pace, defense, footwork, endurance, ability to take a punch, courage, and career record. Cox says of Gans that he was an iron man of the old timers, a "polished boxer-puncher" "who threw every punch perfectly, in combinations and with bewildering speed."[4]

When considering punching power and defense, Gans was judged by his peers and historians as unequaled, earning a "perfect score" on these points from Cox. Gans' record of more than 100 knockouts attests to the power and dead-on accuracy of his short jolts. And while all of the experts say that he was a "clever," "scientific" boxer, he proved to be a master of ring psychology. Anyone who has seen the film clip of the knockout of Kid Herman in Tonopah cannot fail to be amazed at how Gans in his wizardry plans the attack, corners his opponent, and draws him into the finishing blow, even turning to walk away as Herman falls to the canvas, knowing that he has landed the perfect punch. His speed with his hands and body stunned many opponents, leaving them confused and vulnerable. In the film clip with Battling Nelson (one is reminded of Ali), Gans dances around his prey, landing blow after forceful blow upon Nelson, blurring his senses, including the man's instinct to protect his head.

That Gans could fight with a broken hand in his long battle with Nelson and so disguise the fact from his opponent proves his resilience. Considering that Gans had a "weak constitution," was bothered by stomach problems most of his fighting life, and spent the last years of his career simultaneously battling both the best men and the most debilitating disease of the time, his power and endurance are truly mystifying. At times, Gans' remarkable defensive work with his mitts and elbows seemed more like offense. It was an elbow block of Jimmie Britt's jab that broke the San Franciscan's wrist and caused him to quit in their second bout. Gans' defensive guard was so impenetrable that he was virtually impossible to knock down. As Monte Cox has pointed out, if you omit the two battles he lost to Nelson when he was so very ill and the orchestrated loss to McGovern by his management, Gans only lost five fights in his long career.[5] His ring generalship was always noted in that he could control his opponent in ring center at close range, wasting little energy in either offense or defense. As Cox said, Gans was an expert at "stalking" and "baiting" his opponents.[6] His superb skills, offensively and defensively, awed writers of his day who described them as gems of "beauty."

Monte Cox's summary appraisal of the man is as follows:

Joe Gans was the transcendent master boxer, a greatly experienced ring general, one who had tremendous punching power with his perfectly thrown Joe Louis like punches. Gans was quick on his feet, and a master at blocking and counter-punching to vital points. Joe was an extremely intelligent fighter from a scientific point of view who could feint his opponents out of position, but could not be feinted. If one combines the masterful absolute boxing skills of an experienced ring stylist with the great speed of a marvelous athlete, the tremendous power of a natural puncher, along with proven toughness and endurance one has a nearly unbeatable fighter. That describes Joe Gans. The greatest of them all![7]

In addition to the technical aspects of boxing, we would add the ability to rise to a great occasion. As Gans proved in the Goldfield fight and on many other occasions, he could deliver at the moment of truth.

Some boxing historians complain that ratings are too often "subjective." Bill Gray's impressive system of ranking the greatest champions of all time uses a scientific, quantitative system when rating all of the fighters who held world titles. Gray's system is scientific enough, but it places Gans 27.[8] One of the reasons Gans ranks so low is because the numbers Gray uses in Gans' case are inaccurate. For example, he says that Gans defended his title once a year from 1902 to 1904. However, the record shows at least 10 official title defenses in those years and over 30 victories for Gans during this period.

How Would Gans Fare in the Ring Against Modern Fighters?

For *aficionados* of the *quadri-latero*, as they say on *Mundo del Box*, there are two questions that must be answered in determining how Gans would compare to a lightweight champion of another era. In deciding who is the greatest of all time, we must determine if Gans could have beaten a great fighter like Roberto Duran (generally considered the all time greatest lightweight) if he had lived in Duran's time. We must also determine if Duran could have beaten Gans if he had lived in Gans' time. As for the first question, if Gans had lived in the 1970s, had access to all the modern training equipment, and had not lived his fighting life with his hands tied by gambling interests and racism, he could have easily defeated Roberto Duran. A 15-round fight for Gans was a relatively short evening. Duran, although a great fighter, was easily frustrated, as was shown in his infamous "No Mas" capitulation against Sugar Ray Leonard. As for the other question, could

Duran have beaten Gans in 1906? Again the determining factor would have to be Gans' superior endurance. Duran, so used to overwhelming his opponents, would not have been able to last over 20 rounds with Gans.

It is always difficult to make comparisons across time and weight categories, but a good measure is the number of years the title was held along with the number of title defenses. A century later, Gans still toes the mark against the fighters who came after him.

Benny Leonard, also considered by many the greatest lightweight ever, only defended a handful of times in his long reign as champion. Sportswriters Robert Edgren and Grantland Rice both admired Gans over Leonard. (Edgren would say that had Gans been white, he would have been the most popular fighter of all time.) In a discussion of Leonard, it should be noted that while Nat Fleischer generally rates Gans as his number one pick in the lightweight division, he vacillated over the years as to whether or not Gans could defeat Leonard if both men were in peak condition. Current boxing historian Mike Casey takes Fleischer to task, "Gans had such a cool and calculating mind. Was he anything less of a wizard than Leonard? If anything, he was even more so, and I believe his lively and inventive brain would have given him the ability to adjust to any distance and any set of circumstances. The evidence is extremely weighty in favor of Joe Gans being the greatest lightweight that ever lived. He was most definitely one of the greatest pound-for-pound ring mechanics of them all. And let us never forget that he achieved much of what he did with one hand tied behind his back."[9]

Welterweight Sugar Ray Leonard, as well, only made a few successful title defenses during his career. The great Sugar Ray Robinson, who won the middleweight title five times, successfully defended only a total of three times during all five reigns. Gans defended his title 17 times.

A comparison of their records in title fights follows:

Gans	*Robinson*
1 win of the lightweight title	1 win of welterweight title
1 draw for the welterweight title	5 successful defenses of welterweight title
1 win of welterweight title	5 winning efforts of middleweight title
17 successful defenses of the lightweight title	5 losses of middleweight title
1 loss of the lightweight title	4 unsuccessful attempts at middleweight title
2 lost attempts	3 successful defenses of middleweight
19 total title-fight victories	15 total title-fight wins
3 losses (had TB in two, cut eye in other fight)	9 losses
1 draw	

In tribute to Sugar Ray Robinson was coined the phrase "best pound-for-pound." Ray was a dashing dancing master who could fire punches at angles that seemed to defy gravity. No stranger to organized crime, Ray was a tough-minded businessman who held his own with thuggish types named "Blinkey" and worse. After killing one opponent in the ring, he was pressed by a grand jury as to whether he knew he had his man in trouble. "Mister," Ray shot back, "my business is keeping those fellas in trouble."[10] Sugar Ray could punch as tough as he talked. But his defense did not compare with that of Gans. Robinson took many blows that Gans would have easily avoided.

Monte Cox has on several occasions compared Gans with Sugar Ray Robinson, and Gans always comes out on top in his evaluation of who was the greater fighter, pound-for-pound. The authors agree with Cox that Gans comes out on top in the analysis based purely on boxing skills, and would add that, for all the reasons stated in this book, Gans also surpasses Sugar Ray in historical significance.

Cox writes,

> In a head-to-head comparison with Ray Robinson, the most popular choice for greatest fighter of all time, Gans was equal in speed, skill and punching prowess and superior in his defense. Defensively Robinson relied primarily on his height, reach and footwork to avoid punches. When cornered he would duck, turn sideways and roll with punches but he was often hit cleanly by his opponents. Robinson was not clever when it came to eluding punches. In his '51 fight against Lamotta he was even hit by Jake's slow jabs. Gans, a master at stopping an opponent's leads, would never be hit by this kind of a punch. Gans' classic defense with glove and elbow blocking was much tighter and allowed him to stay in the pocket using angles to slip punches and his footwork was used to slide and counter. Joe Gans' defensive capability was far superior to Robinson, and his speed, power and athleticism is comparable. In terms of sheer talent Gans was every bit as good as Robinson, and technically, dare I say, better overall.[11]

Various accounts show Gans defended his title as few as 14 times, and as many as 17 times. This ambiguity relates to the peculiarities of the weigh-in process in his day. Managers often demanded a ringside weighing in of the contestants just before the hostilities were to begin. This would be in addition to the scaling the day before the fight. If both fighters "made the weight" the day before, but not the day of the bout, the fight would usually go on as scheduled but the championship would not be at stake, as with the case of Gans' Baltimore fight with Gardner. Gans' number of title defenses, whether 14 or 17, remains a record among the lightweight champions of history.

It should be noted that today many followers of pugilism are calling for a return to the day-of-fight weigh in. Fighters in the lighter categories will often dry out and starve themselves in order to make a weight 10 to 20 pounds less than their natural poundage. They hope to replenish their bodies sufficiently after the weigh in. This has at times proven dangerous, for example, when Ricardo Sandoval nearly died in defending his bantamweight crown in the early 1980s against Orlando Canizales. Later he stated that he had starved himself for weeks before the fight in which he was knocked out.

In comparison with the great Joe Louis, the level of competition and the number of fights that Gans won far exceeds that of Louis. Louis won his title after fighting just three years. In this time he faced tough competition in only one instance, the fight he lost against the German Max Schmeling.

Joe Louis, in addition to inspiring pride in the black community by his defeat of the Nazi representative of their so-called master race, also had a way with words. When one opponent said he would run from Louis, the latter replied, "He can run but he can't hide." On the war with Japan and Germany, Louis said simply, "We will win because we are on God's side."[12] Louis was certainly close to Gans in historical significance. But in the ring, Louis' skills were nowhere near the equal of Joe Gans.

Henry Armstrong, Hammering Hank, is often cited as one of the top fighters, or even the top, of all time. Armstrong overwhelmed opponents with his kamikaze windmill style for several years. But like all "face fighters" he soon wore out and became a punching bag.

Many boxing historians suggest that ring statistics alone don't tell the whole story of a fighter's greatness—that it is impossible not to recognize other, less tangible qualities that add to a man's record, such as a man's character or what he brings to the sport. Gans' mastery of the ring transcended the world of pugilism so much that sportswriters in the first half of the 20th century took entire pages of newspapers to remind their readers of Gans and how great a true athlete could be. It is quite regrettable that film technology was not sufficiently developed to capture the wealth of Gans' great performances in the ring. But the lack of film carried with it the need for top-rate sportswriters to provide telegraph reports in real time. The blow-by-blow descriptions written by the greatest and fastest pens of the day survive in newspaper accounts to tell us how the Old Master's fights looked from ringside.

Many of the great sportswriters of Gans' day and after wrote about what it was like to have seen the Old Master's talents. Tom "Tad" Dorgan of the *New York Evening Journal*, the boxing authority who is credited with giving Gans the moniker the "Old Master," asked his New York readers in 1911 to submit their choice for the greatest fighter of all time. The name they chose, over Sullivan, Jackson, Corbett, Dempsey, Fitzsimmons, Lavigne, or Griffo, was Joe Gans. In 1926 he asked the same question of San Francisco readers,

In the wake of the Gans-Nelson fight, Joe Gans took on super-human qualities, appearing invincible as king of all fighting men. Sportswriter and cartoonist Tad Dorgan depicts what it would look like if lightweight Gans fought against heavy-weight Jim Jeffries. Dorgan thought so much of Gans' ability that he believed his skill at defense would even the fighting odds. The caption reads, "How Gans the heavy-weight would block Jeff's drive and cut him with hooks and uppercuts" (illustration from *The San Francisco Examiner*, September 23, 1906).

sports who had seen Ketchel, Attell, Johnson, Dempsey and Jeffries; and once again, they picked Joe Gans, by two to one. Years later Dorgan said of Joe Gans' talent and character, "he was the greatest fighter I have ever seen; never wasting a move, nothing was an effort for him.... And he was the most modest fighter I ever met."[13]

Writing in 1942, Bill Moran of Nevada said, "There can be only one Greatest Fighter Who Ever Lived," and the "daddy of them all, the champion of all races, was a coffee-colored Baltimore boy named Joe Gans, who demonstrated with his two hands the perfect coordination that man is capable of developing between mind and muscle."[14]

Tom Mulvey of San Francisco, who was associated with boxing in California as long as Jim Coffroth, said that Joe Gans was his choice for the greatest man who ever wore boxing shoes. "I liked his style: it was so easy going. A master at blocking and a terrific man with a punch — when he hit he hit! He wasn't a splashing mauler. Everything was timed with Gans and everything went like clockwork. Taken all in all, I don't really believe that such a master in ring craft will ever live again."[15]

Perhaps the highest mark of a champion is not his statistical record at all, but exemplary sportsmanship and the will it takes, even against the crosscurrents of belief, to "fight the good fight." Referee Siler compared Joe Gans to a knight of the middle ages when he said of Gans' behavior in the ring with Battling Nelson: "He has shown forbearance; he has shown courtesy; and in the ring on Monday he displayed chivalry which is not unworthy of being classed with the superlative notions of the gentle men of the middle ages who wore spring suits of boiler plate and tilted at everything in sight for the defense of some fair lady. He failed to take advantage of technicalities; he aided his fallen foe and was assaulted even while his glove still maintained his friendly grasp on that of his adversary. He fought a good fight when crippled, and although fouled more than once, refrained from taking the advantage which the rules gave him."[16]

Nat Fleischer, as noted, embraced the racist attitudes of his day to some degree, but this did not prevent him from acknowledging the greatness of black fighters. In the late sixties, having had time to see fighters up until Muhammad Ali's day, he picked blacks as the greatest fighters in several divisions, including heavyweight, welterweight, and lightweight. Jack Johnson was his pick at heavyweight, Barbados Joe Walcott at welterweight, and Joe Gans at lightweight.

Ralph Ellison never mentions Joe Gans by name in his novel *Invisible Man*, but some of the scenes and images are straight out of his life story. The battle royal, the manipulative relationships between black and white, and the old, blinded boxer in the pages of the book prove how powerful a metaphor for life was boxing during the first half of the twentieth century.

H.L Mencken, premier scholar and chronicler of the late nineteenth and early twentieth century, states that Joe "was probably the greatest boxer who ever lived and unquestionably one of the gamest.... Joe became widely known as the most gentlemanly pugilist then on earth. His manners were those of a lieutenant of the guards in old Vienna, and many managers sent their white boys to him to observe and learn."[17]

As late as 1949 Henry Miller in his novel *Sexus* uses for dinner conversation the merits of Joe Gans and Jack Johnson. Jack Johnson obviously learned many a thing from Gans. Straight hitting, the stance with the feet always at 45-degree angles, and the emphasis on balance were all passed down from the Old Master. Jack Johnson's uppercut that he learned from Gans is what he used to dominate the heavyweight division for years and gave rise to the call from American sportswriters for a great white hope to redeem the white race.

Gans' superior boxing skills gave specific proof in the argument for equality, and from his work came language that could be sent across the telegraph wires, delivered from the pulpits, and echoed among the masses. Gans was no less important as a symbolic example to the social-political times than he was to boxing history.

Maybe shame is the answer to our original question as to why the great Joe Gans has been forgotten. Gans gave the lie to the stereotypes perpetrated about blacks in the early 20th century. With the passing of those generations who saw the marvel in action or read or heard about his accomplishments, just as with the razing of a building, it is easy to forget who lived there, the memory has vanished. It is only late in the 20th century that historians could look back and appreciate what Gans gave us.

In Gerald Suster's history of the lightweight division, *Lightning Strikes* written in 1994, he says of the Old Master, "Gans' memory remained an inspiration for all who came after him. He showed his own people that a black man could be a distinguished and dignified world champion. He introduced moves that many boxers were laboring to learn a generation or more later. With the aid of Tex Rickard, he demonstrated conclusively that there were megabucks in the lightweight championship. His life was unfortunate and he was the victim of the prejudice of his times: yet few could live up to the standards he set for the future."[18]

Joe Gans was such a dignified artist of the ring that he won the love of millions of Americans, even after the scandal of Chicago had linked his name with the fake fight with Terry McGovern. In Gans' own words, he was modest but in no way kow-towing or obsequious. In several interviews he promoted the virtues of "straight hitting," "clean-living," and "self-reliance." He calmly but insistently encouraged white fighters "to drop this issue of drawing the color line."

Finally, the all-time greatest boxing writer, Nat Fleischer, though he exhibited the prejudices of his time, states in his book about Benny Leonard, *Leonard the Magnificent,* "Merely to be compared to the Baltimore Negro was the highest compliment that could be paid to Leonard, for Gans truly was what they called him — The Master."[19] And yet the master scholar did great harm to the legacy of Joe Gans. By blemishing Gans' character as dishonest, Fleischer made him easy to relegate to the backwater of history, the scribe's weighty assessment coloring a line of subsequent histories deferring to his preeminent word. By painting Gans as cowardly, Fleischer rendered a service to those who wished to forget the truth of the world in which Gans prospered despite tremendous odds against him.

In this book we have presented the incredible accomplishments of Joe Gans, and cited several major literary works in which he apparently serves as a point of reference. A reader unfamiliar with boxing may fairly say at this point, "Surely you exaggerate the extent to which Gans has been forgotten."

In researching the book, Colleen made pilgrimages to the stomping grounds of the Old Master, hoping to find evidence of his memory. Our final chapter describes what she found.

20

Final Rounds

In Gans' day, a "distance fight" consisted usually of twenty rounds, rather than the fifteen fought in the film *Rocky* between Rocky Balboa and Apollo Creed. Rocky's seemingly impossible ambition was to be the first to "go the distance" with Creed. Gans in his day went twenty rounds and beyond in dozens of brutal contests, in addition to scoring his phenomenal knockouts. Sylvester Stallone's film arrived in 1976, just in time for the celebration of the American bicentennial, and Rocky gave a charge of hope to all Americans in a very democratic way. The history of American film is replete with inspirational heroes of the boxing ring. Stallone's film achievement celebrated Philadelphia, the city of brotherly love. In this book on Gans, our research kept bringing us back to the marvels of Baltimore.

From 1850 to the present, so many great artists and professionals have worked in Baltimore or called the city "home" that we cannot hope to list but a handful here. Edgar Allan Poe, Dashiell Hammett, and James Cain of the literary world hailed from the Monumental City. Thurgood Marshall, the first black Supreme Court justice, grew up there. Billie Holiday, as a child of Baltimore, grew up listening to Eubie Blake, whose career began at Joe Gans' Goldfield Hotel in Baltimore.

In 1910 when Gans' train made his final trip from the West, people came to the stations in droves to honor the champ. And when he was laid to rest in Baltimore, people flocked by the thousands from the city and all parts of the country to have a final moment with the Old Master.

Baltimore's adoration of the Master knew no bounds. Gans had been an ambassador of goodwill for his hometown. Early in his career the newspapers consistently refer to him as "the Baltimorean." Today it would be hard to find anyone who carries the banner of his or her city the way Gans did. And yet when Colleen visited his gravesite, no one could be found in the area who had ever heard of him. The graveyard was chained closed, overgrown with weeds, and dotted with plastic bags snagged on various thickets and headstones.

Above: Historic Mount Auburn Cemetery today, where Gans is buried. It was the first African American Cemetery in Baltimore (courtesy David W. Wallace, 2007).

Across the street from the cemetery a policeman sat in his car watching over the neighborhood. He too, had never heard of the man whose tombstone he could see if his eye had been trained on it. "Who's he?" he asked politely at the mention of Joe Gans.

"He" was a gentleman and a champion, a man who believed in a clean fight. He was no less than the greatest fighting machine who ever lived. The example Gans set by his embodiment of the Emersonian ideal of self-reliance still resonates today. One would think that Baltimore itself, Gans' hometown and long known as the Monumental City, would be a paragon of respect for the Old Master. Yet for years Gans' gravesite lay in an unkempt part of town, non-descript in a city known recently more for homicide and other crimes than for the majesty of its sports heroes. But even if Baltimore seems to have taken it on the chin in recent years, it remains the home of the Old Master.

During most of his short lifetime money flowed through Gans' hands. He was a gambler, enjoying his cards. Like many boxers who came from little means, he enjoyed looking his best. Winning boxers had the physiques and money to be able to wear whatever styles were popular at the time, expensive suits, shoes, even diamond-studded jewelry.

Throughout his life, when he spoke to the press, Gans was articulate and incomparably kind, when most boxers described their counterparts in mean-spirited ways. Gans was consistently described as "modest" in the press. Unlike the flamboyant Johnson who flaunted his wealthy, pleasure-filled lifestyle, Gans was a gentleman inside and out of the ring.

Gans won the sympathy of his fans and sportswriters when in the decline of life he absorbed punishment in the ring to insure financial stability for his family. He used his winnings to leave a powerful legacy in the Goldfield Hotel. Gans lived the American dream and epitomized American values, becoming a provider unafraid of hard work, and a success, rising from poverty and other setbacks by using his brain, his strength, and his determination. The authors consider Gans the greatest of all the American champions in a sense that encompasses more than just boxing. His efforts also paved the way for

Opposite bottom: The name "Gans," carved into the gravestone of Joseph Gans in Mount Auburn Cemetery, Baltimore, was recognized the world over when he died August 10, 1910. In 2005 the gravesite was restored by the Veteran Boxers Association of Baltimore. Carved into the stone after he was inducted into the International Boxing Hall of Fame in 1990 are the words: "World's Lightweight Champion 1902–1904 1906–1908." Even these well-meaning groups were misled as to Gans' title reign. His tombstone shows that he was not the champion from 1904 to 1906, echoing the notion that he had lost the title and had to regain it in the 1906 Goldfield fight (courtesy David W. Wallace, 2007).

Jesse Owens, Jackie Robinson, Jim Brown of the football Cleveland Browns, and all of the great black professional athletes of today. Indeed, Muhammad Ali in his autobiography acknowledges his debt to the old masters of the ring, dating back to the days of Joe Gans.

Gans achieved all of his great feats in the face of the Jim Crow segregation laws. These laws were named after a song by T.D. "Daddy" Rice, a comedian in the black-faced form of comedy in the nineteenth century. "Jump Jim Crow," the song, was a key initial step in a tradition of popular music in the United States that was based on the mockery of Africans. With time Jim Crow became a term often used to refer to blacks, and from this the laws of racial segregation became known as Jim Crow laws. Lyrics from the song include such affronts to decency as: "I went down to de river, I didn't mean to stay, But there I see so many girls, I couldn't get away."

As seen by the frequent references to lynching of "negro rapists," songs such as these kept the fear of "sexually ravenous blacks" at the forefront. A headline in the *San Francisco Examiner* during the week after the Goldfield fight asks, "What will be the End of the Dead-Earnest, Menacing Uprising of Atlanta to Crush Out with Guns, Ropes and Dogs, the Fearful Epidemic of Negro Crime Against Her Women?"[1]

Against a national backdrop of racism, Baltimore in Gans' time, and the Harlem renaissance of the '20s, helped bring a dream of black pride to fruition. In the sadness of the Old Master's death there was a golden moment when he returned to Baltimore and people were drawn for miles to bid him farewell. The moment was golden because all the townspeople: black, brown, and white came to celebrate the life of a people's champion, not just the first American-born black champion.

What if Joe Gans had not contracted tuberculosis and had lived a long life? He may have taken some of the public's attention away from Jack Johnson's provocative behavior. The easing of race tensions may have occurred much sooner with Gans emblematic of the black boxing champion, rather than Johnson with his golden smile or Ali with his Louisville lip. As with all tragedies, the question of what could have been will never be answered.

After Gans' death and during Johnson's reign, lynchings and other violence against blacks increased. In *Unforgivable Blackness*, Ward describes how Johnson, the only black champion in the year 1910, became such a lightning rod for white anger because of his brazen style and his flaunting of affairs with white women. If Gans had still reigned in 1910, with his gentlemanly manner, might he have served as a kind of elder statesman of the black pugilists? Would white outrage at black boxing superiority have been tempered by a modest, active champion like Gans? Sadly we will only know of the racial divisiveness that came in the wake of Johnson's title reign, which included continued segregation of the armed forces, the continued lynchings, and a host of other manifestations of racial persecution in the American twentieth century.

It has been a great misfortune and loss to American history that Gans was all but forgotten after World War II, "invisible" to generations coming after Ralph Ellison, Malcolm X, *et al.* Without Gans to lead the way, there would have been no straight-hitting boxing masters like Jack Johnson, Joe Louis, and Muhammad Ali. The Cotton Club and the Harlem Renaissance would have never had the Goldfield Club as a model upon which to build.

A little over a century ago, amid the manifest destinies, the crosses of gold, and flim-flam of the early days of the American 20th century, Joe Gans quietly developed the art of boxing and in the Goldfield Hotel helped provide for the future of American culture. His widow Martha kept the music alive and shared Gans' remarkable legacy at the Goldfield. In 1912 she married Ford Dabney, composer, orchestra leader, and proprietor of the Ford Dabney Theater and the Chelsea in Washington, D.C. Dabney's Syncopated Orchestra and his collaboration with Florenz Ziegfeld took the couple to New York. The Goldfield Hotel was eventually sold.

Sadly indicative of a society that thought the place not worth preserving, the Goldfield Hotel was demolished in December 1960. It had become a run-down apartment building over a grocery store, torn down to make way for an industrial park.[2] Gans mother's home on Argyle Street, where he spent the last few agonizing days of his life, has also been demolished. The adjacent block of row houses on the same street, however, stand abandoned, boarded up, awaiting the demolition crew, a sight frequently photographed as an example of the demise of inner city Baltimore. Maybe today, with a different eye, we might see their beauty.

In 1903, a year after Gans won the world lightweight championship, W.E.B. Du Bois wrote, "The problem of this century is the color line." Nowhere was the color line more pervasive and hard to overcome than in boxing. We hope that in future history courses on American blacks, the pioneering contributions of Gans in bridging the gap between the races will not be overlooked.

The authors hope to have done our part to resurrect the legacy of the great Joe Gans. In 1902 the Baltimore *Afro-American* bemoaned the fact that Joe Gans got more publicity than Booker T. Washington. Today, only dedicated boxing fans know the story of Joe Gans. Baltimore itself has not received much positive recognition in recent years. May Baltimore reclaim its status as a robust center of sport and art, and home of the Old Master.

In 1904 Joe Gans' title was stolen through a concerted effort on the West Coast. It is possible that the final demise of Joe Gans' reputation is largely attributable to Fleischer's hard words in 1938 about his "quitting" against Frank Erne and throwing the fight to Terry McGovern.

In *Hard Road to Glory*, Arthur Ashe is careful to denounce the throwing of a fight whenever he broaches the subject, because of the historical significance those who wrote before him placed on the fact. He writes of the Gans-McGovern fight, "Gans took a dive and lost in the second round to blows that observers declared would not harm an infant. It was obviously a fixed bout. He deserved the shame he felt, although he may have feared for his life just as Joe Walcott had before him."[3]

Later, Ashe writes of Jack Johnson's fight against Jess Willard, "Most boxing historians believe Johnson did indeed tank the bout—a disgraceful performance from a world champion in any sport."[4] Johnson, hounded by authorities on trumped up Mann Act charges of "transporting a woman across state lines for immoral purposes," had reasons similar to those of Walcott for his actions. It is a peculiar phenomenon that throwing a fight in American lore is considered much worse than almost any other kind of chicanery.

But somehow genius and artistry have charms to soothe the most savage, most virulent racism and cut through hypocrisy, even scapegoating. And if it was possible for Gans

Joe Gans died in the home that he provided for his mother in Baltimore on Argyle Street. Thousands of mourners came to pay their respects to the great champion during his last days. The block of row houses left on the street today awaits demolition (courtesy David W. Wallace, 2007).

to rise from the wretchedness of the Reconstruction and Jim Crow eras, take the fall for his crooked managers, live through the witch-hunt–like aftermath of the Chicago fight fix, regain his stolen title, and emerge a hero, what reason is there for anyone to think of impossibility?

Epilogue: Boxing's Continued Popularity

Many years after George Foreman's famous "Rumble in the Jungle" with Muhammad Ali, where big George lost his heavyweight crown, he was asked why he took such a risky fight as Ali. He replied, "One thing—five million dollars. Everyone should take a chance like that at least once in their lives."[1] So of course part of boxing's allure is the potential of great riches. In few places other than the ring can a poor-born child make $5 million in one night.

The authors are both among the staunchest fans of boxing, one being a former amateur boxer and the other the daughter of a Depression-era professional fighter. We acknowledge that boxing is one athletic endeavor where, when performed as intended, the result can be damage to the human brain. A left jab from even a mediocre professional can easily break a nose, cut an eye, or fill a mouth with blood. In one night's work the expert may have hundreds of such blows fired at his face like stabbing pistons. Once broken, a nose rarely sets back to its previous form, and loss of vision leaves a man to face the world in darkness. And yet every day throughout the world young men walk for miles, ride a bike or bus, or maybe a train with the hope of one day standing in ring center, fending off blows of a highly trained specialist in the destruction of the human face.

These facts cause many to feel that the sport should be banned. But boxing only thrives, its adherents growing more determined, when attempts are made toward its prohibition. Why is this?

In no other sport do the words, "self-reliance," "hard work" and "perseverance" have such relevance. The drive to excel, to be the best one can be in the prize ring is not subverted by politicians or thwarted by inept teammates. A boxer's achievement cannot be purloined by a hostile takeover, a crooked contract, or other misappropriation. The money fighters earn may be lost or stolen, but their accomplishments remain their own.

One Step Ahead of the Law

Boxing in Gans' day was, in fact, illegal in most venues where it was practiced. And so elaborate preparations were made by police and the fight crowd as to how to properly choreograph the arrests of the pugilists, while allowing the crowd to enjoy its collective self and make arrangements for the use of Thomas Edison's new invention of moving pictures. It is a shame that there are no rooms full of Gans' fight films. Despite the scarcity of footage of the Old Master, his moves have been passed down through the years. His art endures. Muhammad Ali's spectacular "floating like a butterfly" and "rope-a-dope" stratagems, by contrast, have not been copied by modern boxers.

When Gentleman Jim Corbett defeated John L. Sullivan to become the first heavyweight champion under the Marquis of Queensberry rules, boxing was illegal in every one of the United States. Fights were usually staged close to borders so that if necessary fighters could pick up and move to another locale quickly. On July 7, 1889, when the governor of Louisiana prevented the Sullivan-Kilrain fight, the parties moved the fight to Mississippi. When Sullivan fought Corbett, they fought on a barge in New Orleans harbor, to give the authorities the excuse that it was not in their jurisdiction. This was typical of the arrangements that allowed boxing to flourish in the 1890s. Private clubs like Baltimore's Eureka Athletic Club provided a venue for boxing matches where the law, strictly viewed, only prohibited "public displays of boxing." When the Eureka Club moved out of Baltimore City and to the outskirts of the county to avoid more strident rules imposed by city officials, one of the officials lamented the loss of revenue to the city in the way of $50 per event permits.

Gans' professional record cites several instances where a bout was scheduled but the police intervened. This was actually considered a *faux-pas*, bad form on the part of the police. The accepted way to handle the matter was that, prior to the fight, arrest warrants would be issued. The police serving the warrants typically watched the fights. After all, they were on police business. When the match was over, if no one had died in the ring or been critically injured, and the crowd had behaved, the boxers and managers would scram and the police would go on to other business.

Occasionally, as when Jack Johnson fought Joe Choynski, the fighters would actually be put in jail, a risk all pugilists faced and why few blacks were willing to fight in the South for fear that they might be jailed and lynched. And every now and then, a blow-hard politician made a speech about the immorality of professional pugilism and maybe got a few votes for his efforts.

Although the event itself was illegal, betting rules on prizefighting were scrupulously followed. As many permutations of results as could be imagined could be bet upon. "Three-to-one it won't go five rounds." "Gans within six rounds," they bet at even odds. "Four-to-one it won't go past seven." Men who killed for a living or cheated people every day in business would not even consider welching on a boxing bet. The infamy of such an act would stain their reputations for a lifetime. Professional boxing, like cock-fighting, was considered a sacred rite. In his novel *Cockfighter*, Charles Willeford explains the mentality of the followers of the sport. When the protagonist of the story loses everything he owns on one "hack," he is much more troubled by the implication that he would try to welch:

> "Please accept my apology, Mr. Mansfield. I don't know why, but I guess I expected an argument."
> Either he was plain ignorant or he was trying to make me angry. A handshake by two cockfighters is as binding as a sworn statement witnessed by a notary public, and he knew this as well as I did. For a long moment I studied his red face and then concluded that he was merely ill at ease on account of Dody's presence and didn't know what he was implying. But a bet is a bet.[2]

Later Willeford delivers the Cocker-Creed: "I am a full-time cockfighter. My goal in life was that little silver coin, not quite as large as a Kennedy half dollar. On one side of the medal there is an engraved statement: Cockfighter of the Year. To a noncocker, this desire might sound childish, but to a cockfighter this award is his ultimate achievement in one of the toughest sports in the world."[3] Mr. Willeford's description of this single-minded quest applies also to a fighter in quest of a title. As they used to say on the Wide World of Sports, boxing's appeal can be found in "the human drama of athletic competition, the thrill of victory, and the agony of defeat." Many times, this agony has included grim episodes of death.

Death in the Ring, in the American Living Room

In 1962 Emile Griffith and Benny "Kid" Paret fought a trio of unforgettable welterweight title bouts, all on national television. The two scrappers, like Barbados Joe Walcott before them, both hailed from Caribbean countries, Griffith from the Bahamas and Paret from Cuba. Their bodies were chiseled like black supermen, more muscular than professional body builders, the long powerful muscles of fighters, not weight lifters.

On three separate occasions, these cat-quick gladiators fought long punishing rounds for the American and world audiences. Griffith, a fearsome puncher at that time, won the first fight, coming from behind to starch Paret with a left hook. Paret took the second bout by decision.

The third fight between the two brilliant Caribbeans has haunted several generations of fight fans, as death was visited upon American living rooms. Before the fight an incident occurred at the weigh-in that would be debated for years. Paret called Griffith "maricon," faggot in Spanish. He also reportedly brushed behind Griffith in a sexually predatory gesture. As famed New York columnist Jimmy Breslin would later say, "He went looking for trouble and he found it."

That night Griffith fought like a man possessed and was well ahead in the middle rounds when a snapping left hook to the point of his chin dropped him, but he was saved by the bell. After a few more rounds, Griffith had regained control.

Whatever has been said about Griffith since that tragic night, by all accounts he was a very popular champion, and the loss of the second fight to Paret had sent him into depression. His determination to win the rubber match with Paret was absolute.

The last round of the third fight would spell the end of Benny Paret's life. As a horrified nation watched, Griffith hurt Paret with a combination, then backed him into a corner. Paret's left arm got caught behind the ring rope, and Griffith hit him with so many rapid-fire, concussive right-hand punches to the head that later, reporters would say they counted as many as 30 head shots within a few short seconds.

The calls for boxing's abolition had never been more shrill; Griffith would continue boxing and winning but was never again a knock-out puncher. The coverage of Paret's death-throes was merciless, as television and newspapers flooded the American psyche with images of the fallen, dead champion. Griffith seemed a broken man after that awful eve. One night, years later while walking the streets of New York, Griffith was beaten senseless by a gang of punks, resulting in his permanent brain damage.

In an effort at a modern redemption song, Griffith was recently introduced to Benny Paret's son. He asked wanly, a tentative smile on his old face, "Are you the son of 'the Kid'?" The two men embraced, and then together celebrated the life, not the untimely death, of the great welterweight.

Just as the saga of Joe Gans' fixed fight in Chicago sent shock waves through the boxing world in 1900, another drama of the lightweight division would shake pugilism to its core in the early 1980s. There have been few ring warriors in history who have exuded as much class as the Nicaraguan lightweight Alexis Arguello. In 1981 he defended his title against an exuberant youngster named Ray Boom Boom Mancini, who announced that he was fighting for the memory of his father, who by then suffered from *dementia pugilistica*. Boom Boom put up a heroic fight on national television, but was finally halted by the great Arguello. Afterward, Alexis paid tribute to Boom Boom and his father, and many hardened ring-siders had tears welling in their eyes.

A year later Boom Boom became lightweight champion when Arguello moved up to the 140-pound limit. One hazy November afternoon, as the world watched the national television coverage, Boom Boom defended his crown against a tough Korean named Doo-Koo Kim. Kim had a unique training regimen, consuming large amounts of Ginseng and scribbling "Victory or Death" on his walls.

Sparks flew from the opening bell. Boom Boom got nailed with awkward counters from the strangely wily Korean, and looked out on his feet at several points. The tide turned several times during the fight, with the outcome in doubt until the bitter end, when a super-human well of strength within Boom Boom was exerted in the 14th round and Kim, defenseless, took the last barrage of blows. His legs were still driving him forward until he pitched forward, face first to the canvas, never to regain consciousness.

The viewing public was shocked. For years boxing aficionados had referred to the 13th through the 15th stanzas of a fight as "the championship rounds." But after Kim's death, fights longer than 12 rounds were outlawed and network television ceded the live-fight market to cable and closed-circuit television.

Yet amid the death, the scandals, and the fringe criminal element of boxing, its popularity remains in tact. Consider it well, this martial art dating back to the time of Homer.

Whenever there is a loud hue and cry over a "fake fight" it is the underlying dignity of the sport that makes the indignation possible. The same people who cry havoc over a fixed match will yawn at the obvious hoax of professional wrestling, or the steroid-induced record breaking in professional baseball. The amazing aspect of boxing is not the crookedness, but rather the sense of integrity and sportsmanship that has survived over the years. For every thuggish personality, there are several famous gentleman-gladiators such as Alexis Arguello, Sugar Ray Robinson, and the Old Master, Joe Gans.

As the 20th century yielded its place to the 21st, boxing's popularity was again on a downward slope. But when the next clean-living, straight-hitting superstar like Joe Gans comes along, boxing will experience another renaissance.

Deaths in the ring before the age of television were more common, with the longer fights and the use of smaller gloves. At the turn of the century when the sport was under threat because of the number of deaths in the ring, enthusiasts went to great pains to show how boxing compared to other sports, particularly football. One of the first studies comparing the two was done during this time.[4] Ring deaths were fewer than those on the gridiron.

Boxing Is an Essential Piece of Americana

The boxing ring has inspired poets and great writers such as Joyce Carol Oates, Jack London and Ernest Hemingway. Boxers, themselves, have also shown a flair for the poetic. When told of a challenger's amazing speed, a taciturn Sonny Liston asked rhetorically whether the speedster was "fast enough to kiss a bullet?"

The extent to which boxing influences American culture can be seen in the proliferation of boxing idioms in the language. These expressions bespeak the heart of their generation. When the newspapers said that the fans had seen the "Real McCoy" after one of the "Kid's" great bouts, the phrase caught on in no small part because of the trickery that was so ingrained in the American experience during the gilded age.

When Gans' mother told him that the world is watching and to bring home the bacon, it stood for more than just providing for his loved ones. By ushering in a future filled with opportunity for black athletes of generations to come, Gans was, as he stated in his famous telegraph to his mother, "bringing home the bacon with lots of gravy on it."

Another idiom emanating from the world of boxing, and the cinema about the sport, that resonates for Americans is "going the distance." In the first *Rocky* movie this goal and its achievement inspired millions of Americans with the grit and determination displayed by Sylvester Stallone's character. He showed us that when you're down you're not out unless you think you are.

And of course there is the Garden. "Remember that night in the Garden.... I could have been a contender...." In Madison Square Garden stands a bronze statue of the ebony boxing master. When visiting Madison Square, one may remember Marlon Brando's famous soliloquy from *On the Waterfront*, Bogart from *The Harder They Fall*, or even Benny Paret's slow slide to death in his fatal bout against Emile Griffith. But the visitor should also point to the statue of Joe Gans and tell those who don't know, "That is Joe Gans, the greatest fighter who ever graced the ring."

Appendix:
Ring Record

The record does not reflect the number of Joe Gans' amateur fights. The professional record used by the press during Gans' lifetime begins with the year 1894. Win (W); Loss (L); Draw (D); Scheduled (SCH); No Decision (ND); Exhibition (EXB); Knockout (KO); Technical Knockout (TKO); Determined by Points (PTS); Disqualified on a Foul (F); Newspaper Decision (NewsD). Note: Pennsylvania allowed only newspaper decisions if the match resulted in anything but a knockout.

Date	Opponent	Site	Wins	Result	Rounds
1894					
	Dave Armstrong	Baltimore, Md.	W	KO	12
	Arthur Coates	Baltimore, Md.	W	KO	22
	Tommy Harden	Baltimore, Md.	W	KO	7
	George Evans	Baltimore, Md.	W	KO	3
	Dave Armstrong	Baltimore, Md.	W	KO	3
	Jack Daly	Pittsburgh, Pa.	W	KO	11
	Dave Horn	Baltimore, Md.	W	KO	2
	Bud Brown	Baltimore, Md.	W	KO	10
	John Ball	Baltimore, Md.	W	TKO	8
	Jack McDonald	Baltimore, Md.	W	TKO	7
	Dave Horn	Baltimore, Md.	W	TKO	11
	John Van Heest	Baltimore, Md.	W	TKO	9
1895					
Jan. 1	Samuel Allen	Baltimore, Md.	W	KO	3
Feb. 6	Fred Sweigert	Baltimore, Md.	W	PTS	10
Feb. 7	Samuel Young	Baltimore, Md.	W	KO	4
Feb. 11	John Coats	Baltimore, Md.	W	PTS	11
March 4	Max Wirsing	Baltimore, Md.	W	KO	3
March 6	Sol English	Baltimore, Md.	W	TKO	10 Halted
March 16	Howard Wilson	Baltimore, Md.	W	TKO	10 Halted
March 20	Harry Hunt	Baltimore, Md.	W	TKO	4
April 1	W. Edgerton	Baltimore, Md.	W	NewsD	6
April 18	Dave Armstrong	Baltimore, Md.	W	TKO	3
April 25	W. Edgerton	Baltimore, Md.	W	TKO	8

Date	Opponent	Site	Wins	Result	Rounds
May 4	Frank Peabody	Baltimore, Md.	W	KO	3
May 9	Howard Wilson	Washington, D.C.	W	PTS	10
May 20	Benny Peterson	Baltimore, Md.	W	KO	17
July 15	George Siddons	Baltimore, Md.	D	PTS	20
Oct. 21	Joe Elliott	Baltimore, Md.	W	KO	9
Nov. 18	Young Griffo	Baltimore, Md.	D	PTS	10
Nov. 28	George Siddons	Baltimore, Md.	W	KO	7

1896

Jan. 11	Benny Peterson	Philadelphia, Pa.	W	TKO	4
Jan. 17	Joe Elliott	Baltimore, Md.	W	KO	7
Jan. 28	Howard Wilson	Baltimore, Md.	W	TKO	8
Feb. 22	Jimmy Kennard	Boston, Mass.	W	TKO	6
March 12	Frank Erne	New York, N.Y.	SCH	No Show	
June 8	Jimmy Watson	Paterson, N.J.	W	KO	10
June 29	Tommy Butler	Brooklyn, N.Y.	W	PTS	12
Aug. 20	Jack Williams	Baltimore, Md.	W	KO	2
Aug. 31	Danny McBride	Baltimore, Md.	D	PTS	20
Sept. 28	John (Jack) Ball	Philadelphia, Pa.	W	KO	3
Oct. 6	Dal Hawkins	New York, N.Y.	L	PTS	15 Spect. said Gans won
Oct. 19	Jack Williams	Baltimore, Md.	W	KO	3
Nov. 12	Jerry Marshall	Baltimore, Md.	W	PTS	20
Dec. 14	Charles Rochette	San Fran., Ca.	W	TKO	4

1897

April 3	Howard Wilson	New York, N.Y.	W	KO	9
May 19	Mike Leonard	San Fran., Ca.	W	PTS	20
Aug. 24	John Coats	Baltimore, Md.	W	TKO	5
Aug. 24	Jerry Marshall	Baltimore, Md.	W	TKO	8
Aug. 24	Jack McCue	Baltimore, Md.	W	TKO	6
Aug. 24	Geo. Thomas	Baltimore, Md.	W	TKO	3
Aug. 24	August Stenzie	Baltimore, Md.	W	TKO	3
Aug. 30	Isadore Strauss	Baltimore, Md.	W	KO	5
Sept. 21	Young Griffo	Philadelphia, Pa.	D	PTS	15
Sept. 27	Bobby Dobbs	Brooklyn, N.Y.	L	PTS	20 Originally called a D
Nov. 6	Jack Daly	Philadelphia Pa.	W	NewsD	6
Nov. 29	Stanton Abbott	Baltimore, Md.	W	KO	5

1898

Jan. 3	Billy Young	Baltimore, Md.	W	TKO	2
Jan. 17	Frank Garrard	Cleveland, Ohio	W	TKO	15
March 11	Tom Shortell	Baltimore, Md.	W	TKO	6
April 11	Young Starlight	Baltimore, Md.	W	KO	3
April 11	Young Smyrna	Baltimore, Md.	W	TKO	4
May 11	Steve Crosby	Louisville, Ky.	W	KO	7
June 3	Joe "Kid" Robinson	Chicago, Ill.	W	KO	6

Date	Opponent	Site	Wins	Result	Rounds
July 1	Monk Brown	Baltimore, Md.	W	KO	6
July 26	James Obey	Baltimore, Md.	SCH		
Aug. 8	Billy Ernst	Coney Island, N.Y.	W	KO	11
Aug. 26	Young Smyrna	Baltimore, Md.	W	KO	15
Aug. 31	Tom Jackson	Eastern, Pa.	W	KO	3
Sept. 26	Herman Miller	Baltimore, Md.	W	PTS	4
Sept. 27	"Buck" Raynor	Baltimore, Md.	W	TKO	3
Sept. 27	William Hinton	Baltimore, Md.	W	KO	1
Sept. 27	Joseph Smith	Baltimore, Md.	W	KO	1 Smith (Middle-weight)
Sept. 28	James Martin	Baltimore, Md.	W	TKO	4
Sept. 29	Fred Sweigert	Baltimore, Md.	W	PTS	4
Sept. 30	Billy Duke	Baltimore, Md.	W	PTS	4
Nov. 4	Kid McPartland	New York, N.Y.	W	PTS	25
Dec. 27	Jack Daly	New York, N.Y.	W	PTS	25

1899

Date	Opponent	Site	Wins	Result	Rounds
Jan. 13	Young Smyrna	Baltimore, Md.	W	KO	2
Jan. 28	Martin Judge	Toronto, Canada	W	PTS	20
Feb 6	Billy Ernst	Buffalo, N.Y.	W	F	10
April 14	George McFadden	New York, N.Y.	L	KO	23 Gans sick
July 24	Jack Dobbs	Ocean City, Md.	W	KO	4
July 28	George McFadden	New York, N.Y.	D	PTS	25 Spect. said Gans won
Sept. 1	Eugene Bezenah	New York, N.Y.	W	KO	10
Sept. 15	Martin Judge	Baltimore, Md.	W	PTS	12 Police stopped
Oct. 3	Spider Kelly	New York, N.Y.	W	PTS	25
Oct. 7	Jack Daly	Philadelphia Pa.	D	NewsD	6
Oct. 11	Martin Judge	Baltimore, Md.	W	PTS	20
Oct. 31	Geo. McFadden	New York, N.Y.	W	PTS	25
Nov. 24	Steve Crosby	Chicago, Ill.	W	PTS	6
Dec. 11	George Ashe	Cincinnati, Ohio	W	PTS	15
Dec. 22	William McPartland	Chicago, Ill.	D	PTS	6

1900

Date	Opponent	Site	Wins	Result	Rounds
Feb. 9	William Sullivan	New York, N.Y.	W	TKO	14
March 23	Frank Erne	New York, N.Y.	L	TKO	12

For lightweight championship of the world
Gans is head-butted and suffered a severe cut over his eye

Date	Opponent	Site	Wins	Result	Rounds
April 2	Chicago Jack Daly	Philadelphia, Pa.	W	KO	5
May 25	Dal Hawkins	New York, N.Y.	W	KO	2
June 26	Barney Furey	Cincinnati, Ohio	W	KO	9
July 10	Young Griffo	Brooklyn, N.Y.	W	KO	8
July 12	Whitey Lester	Baltimore, Md.	W	KO	4
Aug. 31	Dal Hawkins	New York, N.Y.	W	KO	3
Sept. 7	George McFadden	Philadelphia, Pa.	W	NewsD	6
Oct. 1	George McFadden	Denver, Colo.	D	PTS	10 Press said Gans won

Date	Opponent	Site	Wins	Result	Rounds
Oct. 6	Joe Youngs	Denver, Colo.	W	PTS	10
Oct. 11	Alexander Johnson	Leadville, Colo.	W	KO	1
Oct. 11	"Kid" Robinson	Leadville, Colo.	W	KO	4
Oct. 16	Otto Sieloff	Denver, Colo.	W	KO	9
Oct. 19	Spider Kelly	Denver, Colo.	W	KO	8
Nov. 16	William Parker	Denver, Colo.	W	KO	4
Dec. 13	Terry McGovern	Chicago, IL	L	KO	2 Originally sch. Oct. 31

1901

Date	Opponent	Site	Wins	Result	Rounds
Feb. 12	Jack Daly	Baltimore, Md.	W	F	6
April 1	Martin Flaherty	Baltimore, Md.	W	KO	4
May 31	Bobby Dobbs	Baltimore, Md.	W	KO	7
July 15	Harry Berger	Baltimore, Md.	W	Gans failed to KO Berger in 6	
July 15	Jack Donahue	Baltimore, Md.	W	KO	2
July 15	Kid Thomas	Baltimore, Md.	W	Gans failed to KO Thomas in 6	
Aug. 23	Steve Crosby	Louisville, Ky.	D	PTS	20
Sept. 20	Steve Crosby	Baltimore, Md.	W	F	12
Sept. 30	Joe Handler	Baltimore, Md.	W	KO	1
Oct. 4	Dan McConnell	Baltimore, Md.	W	KO	3
Nov. 15	Jack Hanlon	Baltimore, Md.	W	KO	2
Nov. 22	Billy Moore	Baltimore, Md.	W	KO	3
Dec. 13	Bobby Dobbs	Baltimore, Md.	W	KO	14
Dec. 30	Joe Youngs	Philadelphia, Pa.	W	KO	4

1902

Date	Opponent	Site	Wins	Result	Rounds
Jan. 3	Tom Broderick	Baltimore, Md.	W	KO	6
Jan. 6	Eddie Connolly	Philadelphia, Pa.	W	KO	5
Feb. 17	George McFadden	Philadelphia, Pa.	W	NewsD	6
March 7	Jack Ryan	Allentown, Pa.	W	KO	3
March 27	Jack Bennett (Welterweight)	Philadelphia, Pa.	W	KO	5
May 12	Frank Erne *Gans wins lightweight title*	Fort Erie, Canada	W	KO	1
June 27	George McFadden	San Francisco, Calif.	W	TKO	3

Gans retains lightweight championship of the world (Not considered a TF by San Francisco Examiner)

July 24	Rufe Turner	Oakland, Calif.	W	KO	15

Gans retains lightweight championship of the world

Sept. 17	Gus Gardner	Baltimore, Md.	W	KO	5

Gans retains lightweight championship of the world

Sept. 22	Jack Bennett	Philadelphia, Pa.	W	KO	2
Sept. 25	Harry Duffy	New Britain, Ct.	W	TKO	2
Oct. 13	William McPartland	Fort Erie, Canada	W	KO	5

Gans retains lightweight championship of the world

Oct. 14	Dave Holly	Lancaster, Pa.	W	NewsD	10

Date	Opponent	Site	Wins	Result	Rounds
Nov. 14	Charley Seiger	Baltimore, Md.	W	KO	14
Dec. 19	Howard Wilson	Providence, R.I.	W	KO	3
Dec. 31	Charley Seiger	Boston, MA	W	PTS	10

1903

Jan. 1	Gus Gardner	New Britain, Conn.	W	F	11
	Gans retains lightweight championship of the world				
Jan. 31	Jack O'Brien	Philadelphia			
	Gans challenges the heavyweight (No record that O'Brien accepted)				
Jan. 31	Jack Donahue	Toronto, Canada	ND	6	
March 11	Steve Crosby	Hot Springs, Ark.	W	TKO	11
	Gans retains lightweight championship of the world				
March 23	Jack Bennett	Allegheny, Pa.	W	KO	5
May 12	Tom Tracey	Portland, Ore.	W	TKO	9
May 29	Willie Fitzgerald	San Francisco, Calif.	W	KO	10
	Gans retains lightweight championship of the world				
July 4	Buddy King	Butte, Mont.	W	KO	5
	Gans retains lightweight championship of the world				
Oct. 16	Joe Grim	Philadelphia, Pa.	W	NewsD	6
Oct. 20	Eddie Kennedy	Philadelphia, Pa.	W	NewsD	6
Oct. 23	Dave Holly	Philadelphia, Pa.	W	NewsD	6
Nov. 2	Jack Blackburn	Philadelphia, Pa.	D	NewsD	6
Dec. 7	Dave Holly	Philadelphia, Pa.	W	NewsD	6
Dec. 8	Sam Langford	Boston, Mass.	L	PTS	15
	Langford would later win Negro heavyweight title				

1904

Jan. 12	Willie Fitzgerald	Detroit, Mich.	W	PTS	10 (Fought at 135 lbs)
	Gans retains lightweight championship of the world				
Jan. 13	Clarence Connors	Mount Clemens, Mich.	W	KO	2
Jan. 22	Joe Grim	Baltimore, Md.	W	PTS	10
Feb. 2	Mike Ward	Detroit, Mich.	W	TKO	10 (Police halted)
March 25	Jack Blackburn	Baltimore, Md.	W	PTS	15
	Gans agrees to grant Blackburn a title fight after repeated challenges				
March 28	Gus Gardner	Saginaw, Mich.	W	PTS	10
April 21	Sam Bolen	Baltimore, Md.	W	PTS	15
May 27	Jewey Cooke	Baltimore, Md.	W	TKO	8
	(Some say this was a title fight)				
June 3	Kid Griffo	Baltimore, Md.	W	TKO	7
June 13	Sammy Smith	Baltimore, Md.	W	KO	4
June 27	Dave Holly	Philadelphia, Pa.	W	NewsD	6
Sept. 30	Joe Walcott	San Francisco, Calif.	D	PTS	20
	Some report as world welterweight championship; newspapers say Gans won				
Oct. 31	Jimmy Britt	San Francisco, Calif.	W	F	5
	Gans retains lightweight championship of the world				

Date	Opponent	Site	Wins	Result	Rounds
1905					
March 27	Rufe Turner	Philadelphia, Pa.	D	NewsD	6
Sept. 15	Mike "Twin" Sullivan	Baltimore, Md.	D	PTS	15
1906					
Jan. 19	Mike "Twin" Sullivan	San Francisco, Calif.	W	KO	15

For the welterweight championship of the world according to newspapers

March 17	Mike "Twin" Sullivan	Los Angeles, Calif.	W	KO	10

For the world welterweight title

May 18	Willie Lewis	New York, N.Y.	ND	6	
June 15	Harry Lewis	Philadelphia, Pa.	W	NewsD	6
June 29	Jack Blackburn	Philadelphia, Pa.	W	NewsD	6
July 23	Dave Holly	Seattle, Wash.	W	PTS	20
Sept. 3	Oscar Nelson	Goldfield, Nev.	W	F	42

Gans retains lightweight championship of the world

Oct. 25	Mickey Riley	Milwaukee, Wis.	EXB		4
Oct. 25	Geo. "Kid" Lavigne	Detroit, Mich.	EXB		3
1907					
Jan. 1	Kid Herman	Tonopah, Nev.	W	KO	8

Gans retains lightweight championship of the world

Jan. 16	George Green	Philadelphia, Pa.	EXB	3	
Sept. 9	Jimmy Britt	San Francisco, Calif.	W	TKO	6

Gans retains lightweight championship of the world

Sept. 27	George Memsic	Los Angeles, Calif.	W	PTS	20

Gans retains lightweight championship of the world

1908					
Jan. 3	Bart Blackburn	Baltimore, Md.	W	(KO)	3 (Blackburn laid down)
April 1	Frank Robson	Philadelphia, Pa.	W	KO	3
May 14	Rudy Unholz	San Francisco, Calif.	W	KO	11

Gans retains lightweight championship of the world

July 4	Oscar Nelson	Colma, Calif.	L	KO	17

Gans loses lightweight championship of the world

Sept. 9	Oscar Nelson	Colma, Calif.	L	KO	21

For lightweight championship of the world

1909					
March 12	Jabez White	New York, N.Y.	W	NewsD	10

Totals

181 fights (excluding amateur, exhibition, and no decision fights)
158 wins (of these, 110 were KOs)
15 draws
8 losses

It is estimated that Gans fought well over 200 fights during his lifetime. He won 5 fights by being fouled and lost to no one on a foul. Joe Gans is only one of ten fighters to score over 100 KOs.

Gans' Measurements

Height: 5 feet 6½ inches

Neck: 15½ inches

Biceps: 12 inches

Forearm: 11½ inches

Chest: 38 inches

Wrist: 6¾ inches

Thigh: 20 inches

Calf: 13 inches

Reach: 71 inches

Weight: 133

—*Baltimore Sun*, April 1, 1901

Gans was inducted into the Boxing Hall of Fame (instituted by the *Ring*, 1954) in the first group of inductees in 1954; into the Maryland Athletic Hall of Fame on February 19, 1973; and into the International Boxing Hall of Fame in 1990.

Chapter Notes

Chapter 1

1. Roger Simon and Angie Cannon, "An Amazing Journey: The Mirror of the Census Reveals the Character of a Nation," 18.

2. Ibid.

3. Francis J. Grimke, "The Atlanta Riot: A Discourse Published by Request." The Rev. Grimke was the pastor of the Fifteenth Street Presbyterian Church, Washington, D.C.

4. "Today's Big Fight," *Baltimore Sun*, September 3, 1906. The word *crepe* (variously written *crape*) denoted the black drapery of the late Victorian era hung ceremoniously to signify death and respectful mourning.

5. Harry C. Carr, "Study in Pathos is Face of Joe Gans," *Los Angeles Daily Times*, September 25, 1907.

6. Nat Fleischer, "Strays from the Narrow Path," *Black Dynamite*, Vol. 3, 151. For the next two decades, Fleischer continued to reiterate his view that Gans was a "quitter." Nat Fleischer and Sam Andre, *A Pictoral History of Boxing*, 246–247.

7. "Gans' Mother Tells Him to 'Bring Home Bacon,'" *San Francisco Examiner*, September 4, 1906. "Joe: the eyes of the world are on you. Everybody says you ought to win. Peter Jackson will tell me the news and you bring back the bacon."

8. Muhammad Ali, *The Greatest: My Own Story*, 322.

9. H.L. Mencken, "A Master of Gladiators (1907)" *Heathen Days*, 96.

10. "If you have ever boxed at all, you will remember that the simplest act, holding your gloves up in proper position, tires your arms within three rounds." Roger Kahn, *A Flame of Pure Fire: Jack Dempsey and the Roaring '20s*, 77. One can imagine the training needed to endure 42 rounds in a championship fight. To train for a 15-round fight, Jack Dempsey recommended a daily regimen of a "six mile run" and fifteen rounds or "fifteen three-minute intervals, of sparring, shadow-boxing, hitting bags, and skipping rope." Ibid.

11. The *New York Times* reported that not a "dissenting voice" had been heard since the decision was awarded for Gans (with the exception of those in the Nelson party). "Even losers in betting make no complaint, and numbers of them called on Gans after the fight and congratulated him." *New York Times*, "$25,000 to Throw Fight," September 5, 1906.

Chapter 2

1. Jack London used Jack Johnson's gold-toothed smile as an organizing metaphor for his journalistic reports of the Johnson fights, particularly the "Burns-Johnson Fight (Sydney)" and the "Jeffries-Johnson Fight (Reno, July 4)." Jack London, *Jack London Stories of Boxing*, James Bankes, ed., 145–187.

2. Harry C. Carr, "Study in Pathos is Face of Joe Gans," *Los Angeles Daily Times*, September 25, 1907.

3. Ralph Ellison, *Invisible Man*, 21.

4. Ibid., 22.

5. Geoffrey C. Ward, *Unforgivable Blackness: The Rise and Fall of Jack Johnson*, 24.

6. Ibid., 26.

7. Ibid., 24.

8. Nat Fleischer, *Black Dynamite, Vol. 3: Three Colored Aces*, 128–131. It has been variously reported that fight manager Al Herford either discovered Gans at a battle royal or placed him in these events after seeing him perform on the streets of Baltimore. Reports consistently place Gans' early battles at the Monumental Theater or Opera House, Fallsway and Baltimore streets.

9. "Something about Gans," *Baltimore Sun*, November 17, 1898.

10. Ibid.

11. "Our Yesterdays," *Baltimore Evening Sun*, January 6, 1955, with details reprinted from his obituary in the *Evening Sun* in 1930.

The "old-time boxing promoter" died at the age of 63 and was "credited with discovering, and for years managed, Joe Gans." After boxing was legislated out of public life and into private clubs, "Al and his brother Maurice organized the Eureka Athletic Club; sold 'memberships' at the gate, and hired a bum to read 'minutes of the previous meeting' at the start of weekly proceedings."

12. H.L. Mencken, "A Master of Gladiators," *Heathen Days*, 100.

13. Buck Washington fought as a stand-in for Kid Washington's opponent, who quit in the first round in the preliminary bout for the Joe Gans–Jewey Cooke fight, May 27, 1904. *Baltimore Sun*, "Like the Gans of Old," May 28, 1904.

14. Nat Fleischer, *Black Dynamite*, Vol. 3, 131.

15. Mencken, 105.

16. The name *Joe Gans* may have been adopted by more fighters than any other. Geoffrey Ward, *Unforgivable Blackness*, 15, lists: "Allentown Joe Gans," "Baby Joe Gans," "Cyclone Joe Gans," "Dago Joe Gans," "Italian Joe Gans," "Michigan Joe Gans," "Panama Joe Gans," and four other "Young Joe Gans." Thomas McGowan, a Scottish fighter in the thirties hailing from Lanarkshire (the same hometown as the legendary freedom fighter William Wallace) and father and trainer to world title holder Walter McGowan, permanently adopted the name Joe Gans. www.bbc.co.uk/scotland/sportscotland/asportingnation/0083/print.shtml.

17. Mencken, 100.

Chapter 3

1. In 1850 the population of New York City was 516,000 and Baltimore City was 169,000. Boston was the third largest city. www.demographia.com/db-uscityr1850.html.

2. Stanton Tierman, "Baltimore's Old Slave Markets," http://www.nathanielturner.com/baltimoreslavemarkets.htm.

3. Booker T. Washington, *Frederick Douglass*, 24.

4. Armond Fields, *James J. Corbett: A Biography of the Heavyweight Boxing Champion and Popular Theater Headliner*, 2.

5. James B. Roberts and Alexander G. Skutt, *The Boxing Register: International Boxing Hall of Fame Official Record Book*, 37. Tom Molineaux's birthplace is generally considered to be Georgetown, Md., although he was raised on a plantation in Virginia owned by Algernon Molineaux. He died touring Ireland in a boxing show at the age of 34, possibly of tuberculosis.

6. Nat Fleischer, *Black Dynamite: The Story of the Negro in Boxing*, 35.

7. Glenn O. Phillips, "Gans, Joseph 'Baby Joe' (1874–1900)," www.mdoe.org/gansjoe.html, 2004–2005. While there was some question surrounding his date of birth, Gans consistently acknowledged the year as 1874. Gans' death certificate noted his date of birth as September 1, 1874; however, in the hand of his wife Martha, his age at death is listed as 35 years, 9 months and 10 days. Maryland State Archives, cache of http://www.msa.md.gov/msa/speccol/sc5600/sc5604/html/images/joe_gans_death_cert.tif, accessed January 11, 2008.

8. Roger Simon and Angie Cannon, "An Amazing Journey: The Mirror of the Census Reveals the Character of a Nation, *U.S. News and World Report*, August 6, 2001, 8.

9. Francis F. Beirne, *The Amiable Baltimoreans*, 142–156.

10. *Fells Point, Out of Time*, a film documentary produced and directed by Jacqueline Greff, Baltimore, Md., 2004.

11. Baltimore's canned oysters were considered luxuries at America's early tables. Eastern aristocrat turned soldier's wife Martha Summerhayes, in her memoir *Vanished Arizona*, remembers bringing canned oysters from Baltimore to the army's wilderness outposts in the Arizona territory in the 1870s.

12. James B. Roberts and Alexander G. Skutt, eds., *Boxing Register*, 12.

13. Ibid., 44.

14. Eight world champions came from Baltimore. Thomas Scharf, *Images of Sports: Baltimore's Boxing Legacy 1893–2003*, 7.

15. Robert Lipsyte and Peter Levine, *Idols of the Game*, 24–30.

16. Christopher T. George, Monumentally Speaking: John Quincy Adams and "The Monumental City," n.d. www.baltimoremd.com/monuments/adams.html, accessed February 16, 2008.

Chapter 4

1. Alex Wade, It's a Knockout: Take a Ringside Seat for the Best View of New York, June 26, 2005, www.travel.independent.co.uk/americas/article, accessed July 17, 2007.

2. Mahonri Mackintosh Young's *Joe Gans* was sculpted during the 1930s. Young (1877–1957) was known for realistic portraiture of ordinary working people. In 1941 *Life* magazine called Young the "George Bellows of sculpture." Both artists admired the boxing master Joe Gans. Grandson of Mormon leader Brigham Young, Mahonri Young was born and raised in Salt Lake City. In 1950 he sculpted the figure of his venerable grandfather for the state of Utah's contribution to the National Statuary Hall Collection in the U.S. Capitol, Washington, D.C.

3. Geoffrey Ward, *Unforgiveable Blackness*, 429.

4. "This Was Joe Gans," *Boxing Illustrated/ Wrestling News*, August, 1960.

5. "Gans and the Corpses," *Baltimore Sun*, May 15, 1902.

6. Ibid.

7. John L. Sullivan (reported from San Francisco), "Stands Up for Boxing," *Baltimore Sun*, March 3, 1896.

8. "Fitz's Trouble with a Conductor;" "Pugilist Convicted of Manslaughter;" "Bunco O'Brien's Life Sentence;" *Baltimore Sun*, March 16, 1896.

9. George Bellows' *Both Members of This Club, 1909* is located in the National Gallery of Art, Washington, D.C. The black contestant is identified as "Joe Gans, lightweight champion for eight years." Painting is framed (52⅜ × 70⁵⁄₁₆), Chester Dale Collection, one of six Bellows oil paintings of boxing subjects.

10. "Eureka Athletic Club," *Baltimore Sun*, March 7, 1895. Management of Herford's Athletic Club included Hugo C. Bernstein, Lewis S. Cleveland, Edward Herford, Lewis Mandelbaum, Larry Etherich and William Eichberg.

Chapter 5

1. *New York Times*, "Straight Hitting Gets Boxers Plums: Champion Joe Gans Tells Why He Has Lasted So Long in the Prize Ring," February 2, 1908. "I owe my present position in the ring to my ability to hit straight more than to anything else." This is the definitive article where Gans assesses his own style.

2. A list of his early fights appeared in the *Baltimore Sun*, March 12, 1896. In an interview two years later, Gans stated that his first battle with David Armstrong was held on Bond Street for a purse of $2.80 in which he took home $1.40. His next battle was with D. Coates near the Lexington market. For that he was paid $8.00. "Something About Gans: The Self-Taught Colored Boxer who Defeated McPartland Last Friday Wants the Champion's Title; Gained His Skill Largely from Observation of Others," *Baltimore Sun*, November 17, 1898.

3. Bill Gray, *Boxing's Top 100*, 108.

4. "Gans Whips English," *Baltimore Sun*, March 7, 1895.

5. "Ruby Robert" Fitzsimmons, born in England in 1863, worked as a youth as a blacksmith after his family moved to New Zealand. His early professional fights took place in Australia, but he came to America when opportunities declined in his home country. He routinely fought heavier men over a career that spanned 27 years. James B. Roberts and Alexander G. Skutt, eds., *The Boxing Register: Inter-*

national Boxing Hall of Fame Official Record Book, 120–121.

6. Charles L. Convis, *True Tales of the Old West*, Vol. 9, 51.

7. "Straight Hitting," *New York Times*, February 2, 1908.

8. "Gans and Wilson Draw," *Baltimore Sun*, March 19, 1895. Gans would give Wilson his greatest exposure in their battle at the end of 1902 after Gans became world champion.

9. A committee called the "Maryland Game Protection Association" was formed in Ellicott City in Howard County, Md. "Protection of Game in Howard," *Baltimore Sun*, March 19, 1895.

10. "Gans Whips the Rosebud," *Baltimore Sun*, April 26, 1895.

11. "Elliott Knocked Out: Joseph Gans, the Clever Colored Man, Does it by a Strange Blow," *Baltimore Sun*, October 22, 1895.

12. "Death of Griffo," *Time*, December 19, 1927, http://www.time.com/time/magazine/article/0,9171,731305,00.html.

13. "Straight Hitting," *New York Times*, February 2, 1908.

14. "An Imitation Fight," *Baltimore Sun*, November 19, 1895.

15. Ibid.

16. Nat Fleischer, Ch. 11: "Joe Gans, 'The Old Master' (1874–1910)," *Black Dynamite*, Vol. 3, 134.

17. "Gans Knocks Out Siddons: The Dangerous New Orleans Lad Stays Nearly Seven Rounds," *Baltimore Sun*, November 29, 1895.

18. Ibid.

19. "Baltimore Boxers in Demand," *Baltimore Sun*, January 30, 1896.

20. "No More Sparring," *Baltimore Sun*, January 29, 1896.

21. Ibid.

22. "With the Boxers," *Baltimore Sun*, January 11, 1896, and "Another Victory for Gans," *Baltimore Sun*, January 13, 1896.

23. "Joseph Gans Won," *Baltimore Sun*, February 24, 1896.

24. "Gans in Quick Time," *Baltimore Sun*, May 13, 1902.

25. "Gans-Erne Fizzle: Buffalo Boy Backed Out and Herford is After a Match at $1000," *Baltimore Sun*, March 14, 1896.

26. "The Boxers: Gans Whips Watson," *Baltimore Sun*, June 9, 1896.

27. "The Boxers: Gans Whips Tommy Butler;" "Fitz Ready for Sharkey;" and "Where May Corbett and Sharkey Fight?" *Baltimore Sun*, June 30, 1896.

28. "The Boxers: Williams Still After Gans," *Baltimore Sun*, August 22, 1896.

29. "The Boxers: Both Clever Pugilists, but the Baltimorean Outpoints his Man," *Baltimore Sun*, September 1, 1896.

30. "Gans Lost to Hawkins: Battle at Bohemian Club Decided against the Baltimorean," *Baltimore Sun*, October 7, 1896.

31. "Jerry Marshall, Colored, of Australia, Challenges Gans for $500 a Side—Gans Accepts—Fitzsimmons May Fight Sharkey—Other Sporting News," *Baltimore Sun*, October 20, 1896, and "Another Victory for Gans," *Baltimore Sun*, November 13, 1896.

32. "Gans Whips Wilson," *Baltimore Sun*, April 5, 1897.

33. "Gans in Five Rounds: Puts Out the Game Isadore Strauss at the Eureka Athletic Club," *Baltimore Sun*, August 31, 1897.

34. "The Boxers: Gans and Griffo Draw," *Baltimore Sun*, September 22, 1897.

35. "Herford and Gans Angry," *Baltimore Sun*, September 29, 1897.

36. "Gans Whips Abbott," *Baltimore Sun*, November 30, 1897.

37. "Gans Whips Garrard," *Baltimore Sun*, January 18, 1898.

38. "Gans Defeats McPartland," *New York Times*, November 5, 1898.

39. Bill Moran, quoting Tad Dorgan in "The Greatest Fighter Who Ever Lived?" Reno *Nevada State Journal*, September 27, 1942.

40. "Strait Hitting Gets Boxers Plums: Styles of Other Fighters," *New York Times*, February 2, 1908.

41. George Bellows, *Both Members of This Club, 1909*, oil on canvas, National Gallery of Art, Washington, D.C., East Building, Ground Gallery.

42. "Gans Knocks Ball Out," *Baltimore Sun* (special dispatch from Philadelphia), September 29, 1896.

Chapter 6

1. "Gans in Quick Time: The Match that Failed," *Baltimore Sun*, May 13, 1902.

2. Erne beat Dixon on November 27, 1896, in a 20-round bout at the Broadway Athletic Club in New York, although many thought the bout should have been a draw (they had fought to a draw the previous year). "The referee, Sam Austin, evidently considered that Erne had out-pointed his dusky opponent with a good deal to spare." *San Francisco Examiner*, November 28, 1896.

3. Nat Fleischer says that Gans was close to getting a championship match with Kid Lavigne, and would have, had he not lost to McFadden in 1899. Ch. 12: "Strays from Narrow Path," *Black Dynamite*, Vol. 3, 145.

4. Evelyn Nesbit, *Prodigal Days*, 1934.

5. Melissa Haley, "Storm of Blows," Vol. 3, No. 2, "The Death of Andy Bowen," *Commonplace*, sponsored by the American Antiquarian Society and Florida State University Depart-

ment of History, January 2003. www.commonplace.org, accessed January 36, 2008.

6. "Gans and Erne," *Baltimore Sun*, March 23, 1900.

7. At that time there were only six world boxing titles: bantamweight, featherweight, lightweight, welterweight, middleweight, and heavyweight. By the 1920s there were eight categories, adding flyweight and light heavyweight.

8. Melissa Haley, "Storm of Blows," Vol. 3.

9. "Gans and Erne," *Baltimore Sun*, March 23, 1900.

10. The phrase "the Real McCoy" appeared in a San Francisco headline, "Choynski is Beaten by the Real McCoy," distinguishing from "a lesser boxer named Peter McCoy, who had fought in San Francisco days earlier." James B. Roberts and Alexander G. Skutt, eds., *The Boxing Register*, 182.

11. "Gans and Erne," *Baltimore Sun*, March 23, 1900.

12. Nat Fleischer, 151.

13. "Spear—barbed spear or iron hook for heavy fish or metal spur for a gamecock, slang to stand the gaff, something difficult to bear," *Dictionary by Webster*, 1936, s.v. "Gaff."

14. The "yellowstreak" was commonly reported in the newspapers of the time. An article in the *Washington Post* focused on the yellowstreak of a number of black boxers of the era. "Negro Pugilists Accused of Having Yellow Streak," *Washington Post*, June 13, 1909.

15. Comments made to author Mark Scott in gyms when he fought as an amateur.

16. Sam Langford, considered one of the ten greatest athletes of the first half-century, died penniless and blind in a Boston nursing home in 1956. The description of the photo in the boxing gym in Ralph Ellison's *Invisible Man*, 334, probably refers to Sam Langford. Battling Nelson, Gans' opponent in the first Great Fight of the Century "in later years worked for the Chicago Post Office, but when his eyes began to fail he was forced to live on a small pension aid from the Veteran Boxers Association. See J.J. Johnston and Sean Curtin, *Images of Sport: Chicago Boxing*, 24. Walcott Langford, a black fighter with no relation to Sam Langford or Barbados Joe Walcott, also went blind and broke, *Chicago Boxing*, 44.

17. "Gans is Whipped," *Baltimore Sun*, March 24, 1900.

18. Nat Fleischer, 151–152.

19. Nat Fleischer, 152.

20. "Gans is Whipped," *Baltimore Sun*, March 24, 1900.

21. "The New Champion: What He Told Harry Lyons," *Baltimore Sun*, May 14, 1902.

22. "Joe Gans is Married," *Decatur* (Ill.) *Review*, April 11, 1900.

23. www.streetswing.com/dancehistor-yarchives, accessed January 10, 2008.

24. Evelyn Nesbit, *Tragic Beauty: The Lost 1914 Memoirs of Evelyn Nesbit*, ed. by Deborah Dorian Paul, 98.

Chapter 7

1. A description of the living conditions of 1900 Chicago can be found at www.chipublib.org/004/chicago/1900.

2. *Chicago Tribune*, December 14, 1900. When the clergy "grew eloquent upon the possibility of young minds being corrupted by the sight of the pounding [Mayor Harrison] informed them that the fight was better calculated to develop morality than the Maze ever had been."

3. Ibid.

4. Lawyer Paul Harris and three other business owners in Chicago founded a club in 1905 that a century later had grown into a network of thousands of city clubs worldwide called Rotary International. In forming the original club as a reaction to the unethical business practices that existed at the turn of the century, Harris and his friends selected members who would honor ethical business practices and the motto "Service Above Self." Rotarians would eventually help draft the charter for and sit at the table of the United Nations. Women would become members of the club in 1987.

5. American Experience: Chicago, City of the Century; People and Events: World's Columbian Exposition of 1893: The Midway. PBS Online, 1999–2003. www.pbs.org/wgbh/amex/chicago/peopleevents/e_midway.html, accessed January 27, 2008.

6. "Notable Year for Pugilism: Fight Followers are Likely to Remember 1900 for Several Reasons; Crookedness Charged, Record-Breaking Number of Suspicious Bouts Causes Prohibitory Laws," *Chicago Tribune*, January 1, 1901.

7. Various rumors of "fix" accompanied fighters of the day. For the McCoy-Corbett story, see Armond Fields, 126 and the *Chicago Tribune*, "Notable Year."

8. Fields, 126.

9. Arthur Ashe, *Hard Road to Glory*, 9. A vitriolic editorial about Gans and Walcott, "Tale of Two Fighting Fakirs," by H.N. Pillsbury would be published in the *San Antonio Sunday Light*, April 29, 1906.

10. "Notable Year," *Chicago Tribune*, January 1, 1901.

11. The name of the secret Chinese society translated into "righteous harmony hand," mistakenly translated as "righteous harmony fist," or shortened to "boxers."

12. American servicemen, not to be out-trained elsewhere in the art of self-defense, were required to take classes in the 'manly' sport. In 1892 Tom Sharkey joined the U.S. Navy and served on the USS *Philadelphia*, where he took boxing instruction and fought gloved events with other sailors. On May 17, 1893, the British Navy sent its champion, Jim Gardner, to Honolulu, Hawaii, to fight Sharkey. "Sailor Tom" KO'd the heavier and more experienced fighter in 4 rounds. James B. Roberts and Alexander G. Skutt, eds., *The Boxing Register*, 216. "Smokers" continued on U.S. ships well into the twentieth century.

13. J.J. Johnston, *Chicago Boxing*, 19.

14. The newspapers were filled with reports of the Chicago fight, the arrests the next day, statements from the participants, and editorials. *Chicago Tribune, Chicago Times Herald, Baltimore Sun*, and the *New York World*, December 17, 1900.

15. "Gans Knocked Out," *Baltimore Sun*, December 14, 1900.

16. Ibid.

17. *Chicago Times Herald*, December 14, 1900, for the details of the colorful pageantry.

18. "Gans Knocked Out," *Baltimore Sun*, December 14, 1900.

19. "M'Govern Wins a 'Fake' Fight," *Chicago Times Herald*, December 14, 1900.

20. "Lynched Negro Testified for another Negro," *New Orleans Times Democrat*, March 24, 1900.

21. Ralph Ginzburg, *One Hundred Years of Lynchings*, 31–46.

22. Ibid., 49 and 68, respectively.

23. "Words of Warning to the Negro," *Chicago Broadax*, December 1, 1900.

24. "Attempted Suicide to Avoid Lynching," *Phoenix Anaconda Standard*, November 24, 1900.

25. Ginzburg, 145.

26. Mohammad Ali, *The Greatest: My Own Story*, 324.

27. Joyce Carol Oates, *On Boxing*, 95.

28. "Gans Knocked Out," *Baltimore Sun*, December 14, 1900.

29. Ibid.

30. "Loser on Fight Attempts Suicide," *Chicago Tribune*, December 14, 1900.

31. "Howl Over the Fight: Manager Herford Defends Gans and Himself, But Many Persons Cry 'fake,'" *Baltimore Sun*, December 15, 1900.

32. Ibid.

33. Ibid.

34. "Howl Over the Fight: Siler's View of It," *Baltimore Sun*, December 15, 1900.

35. Ibid.

36. "Herford in Baltimore," *Baltimore Sun*, December 17, 1900.

37. "Gans Knocked Out: How Baltimore Took It," *Baltimore Sun*, December 14, 1900.

38. "Howl Over the Fight: What Marias Thinks," *Baltimore Sun*, December 15, 1900.

39. "Howl Over the Fight: Denver Doesn't Want Gans," *Baltimore Sun*, December 15, 1900.

40. "Herford in Baltimore: Talk of Written Agreement," *Baltimore Sun*, December 17, 1900.

41. "Straight Hitting Gets Boxers Plums: Styles of Other Fighters," *New York Times*, February 2, 1908.

42. "Herford and Gans to Go to Chicago," *Baltimore Sun*, October 22, 1900.

43. "No Fights in Chicago if the Mayor Signs Resolution Passed by Council: Alderman Patterson Angry," *Baltimore Sun* (special dispatch from Chicago, December 17, 1900), December 18, 1900.

44. "McGovern's Earning Powers," *Baltimore Sun*, December 18, 1900. Six years later the *New York Evening World* investigated his earnings and reported that during McGovern's eleven years of fighting, he had gone through $203,000 of fight earnings. "Money M'Govern Made," *Baltimore Sun*, January 15, 1907. With his family penniless in 1907, McGovern would be the beneficiary of a charity boxing exhibition at Madison Square Garden on January 23, 1907. "With the Boxers: Many to Box at McGovern Benefit," *Baltimore Sun*, January 18, 1907.

45. Nat Fleischer, *Black Dynamite: The Story of the Negro in Boxing*, 144.

46. Ibid.

47. Arthur Ashe, *Hard Road to Glory*, 11.

48. Nat Fleischer, 171.

49. *Chicago Tribune*, December 20, 1900. "That Wonderful Little Fighter Terry McGovern," *The New York World*, December, 1900.

Chapter 8

1. One of Kelly's rare ring appearances as referee during the next four years was the fight between Jim Corbett and Tom Sharkey. *Baltimore Sun*, May 5, 2000.

2. Nat Fleischer, *Black Dynamite*, Vol. 3, Ch. 11: "Joe Gans, 'The Old Master,'" 136.

3. Nat Fleischer, *Black Dynamite*, Vol. 3, Ch. 11, 142.

4. "A Jig Time Prizefight: And the Hottest Ever Seen at the Broadway Club," *Baltimore Sun* (dispatch from New York, May 25), May 26, 1900.

5. "Gans in Third Round: The Fight which Knocked Dal Hawkins Senseless Last Under the Horton Law," *Baltimore Sun*, September 1, 1900.

6. Ibid. Jimmy Britt would be more suc-

cessful in years to come when he assumed Gans' title in a similar move by his manager and brother, Willus Britt.

7. "How Jeffries Stands," *Baltimore Sun* (from Richmond, Va., Aug. 31), September 1, 1900.

8. Nat Fleischer, *Black Dynamite*, Vol. 3, Ch. 12, "Strays from Narrow Path," 143.

9. "Flaherty is Beaten: Joseph Gans Takes Four Rounds to Undo the Lowell Man," *Baltimore Sun*, April 2, 1901.

10. Ibid.

11. "Gans Doesn't Do It: He Outclasses Them Easily," *Baltimore Sun*, July 16, 1901.

12. "Negro Rapist Hanged," *Washington Post*, July 13, 1901.

13. Michael McCurdy, ed. *Escape from Slavery: The Boyhood of Frederick Douglass in His Own Words*, 47.

14. Nat Fleischer, *Black Dynamite*, Vol. 3, 143.

15. Ibid., 155.

Chapter 9

1. "Now for Big Fight: Joe Gans and Frank Erne to Contest for Championship," *Baltimore Sun*, May 11, 1902. Various other attempts made by Herford to get a rematch for Gans with Frank Erne are reported in the *Baltimore Sun*. See "Herford and Gans Go to Chicago," October 22, 1900; "Herford's Hot Reply," February 13, 1902; and "Now Erne Must Fight: Herford for Gans Accepts Every Condition Offered," March 7, 1902.

2. "Now for Big Fight," *Baltimore Sun*, May 11, 1902.

3. Nat Fleischer, *Black Dynamite*, Vol. 3, Ch. 13, "Wins Lightweight Crown," 155.

4. "Now for Big Fight," *Baltimore Sun*, May 11, 1902.

5. "Gans in Quick Time: Baltimore Lightweight Now the World's Champion, Frank Erne Downed in 1.40," *Baltimore Sun*, May 15, 1902.

6. Ibid.

7. Ibid.

8. Ibid.

9. "The New Champion" *Baltimore Sun* (special dispatch from Al Herford, Buffalo), May 15, 1902.

10. "Gans and Rockefeller," *Baltimore Sun*, May 15, 1902.

11. "Joe Gans Wins," *Baltimore Sun*, September 4, 1906. The famous telegram from Gans' mother in Baltimore read at ringside, "Joe, the eyes of the world are on you. Everybody says you ought to win. Peter Jackson will tell me the news, and you bring back the bacon."

12. "Gans and the Corpses," *Baltimore Sun*, May 15, 1902.

Chapter 10

1. Nat Fleischer, *Black Dynamite*, Vol. 3, Ch. 13, "Wins Lightweight Crown," 155.

2. Ibid.

3. "Wasn't Hurt and Could Have Fought Twenty Rounds More," *San Francisco Examiner*, October 1, 1904.

4. Bill Moran, "The Greatest Fighter Who Ever Lived? This Writer Lauds Joe Gans, Old Master," *Nevada State Journal*, September 27, 1942.

5. "George McFadden Makes No Effort to Win Against Lightweight Champion Joe Gans," *San Francisco Examiner*, June 28, 1902.

6. "Exhibition May Be a Good One, But Public Fears Tactics of Baltimore Boxer," *San Francisco Examiner*, June 27, 1902.

7. "George McFadden Makes No Effort to Win Against Lightweight Champion Joe Gans," *San Francisco Examiner*, June 28, 1902.

8. Ibid.

9. Ibid.

10. Ibid.

11. David W. Maurer, *The Big Con: Story of the Confidence Man*, New York: Anchor Books/ Random House, 1940.

12. "Not in Gans' Class," *Baltimore Sun*, September 18, 1902.

13. "Chicago Club Bars Gans: Public is Against Champion Because of McGovern Fiasco," *Baltimore Sun* (special dispatch from Chicago), September 24, 1902.

14. "Ring Patrons Say Fitzgerald Has a Royal Chance to Win; Cite Gans' Fights with Erne and McFadden," *San Francisco Chronicle*, May 28, 1903.

15. "Many Willing to Pay Four to Win Ten," *San Francisco Chronicle*, May 29, 1903.

16. Willie Fitzgerald, "Gans Won an Honest Victory," *San Francisco Chronicle*, May 30, 1903.

17. "King No Match for Joe Gans: Lightweight Champion Had Him at His Mercy at Any Stage of the Game," *Butte Miner*, July 5, 1903.

18. Ibid.

19. "Walcott-Lafontise Go is the Next," *Butte Miner*, July 3, 1903. Walcott's quick defeat of Mose La Fontise in the third round, Friday evening on July 3, with Jack Johnson present as his second, was incorrectly cited as July 4 by Geoffrey Ward, *Unforgiveable Blackness*, 62. Gans' title defense was the more highly anticipated fight and was held on July 4.

20. "King No Match for Joe Gans," *Butte Miner*, July 5, 1903.

21. Nat Fleischer, *50 Years at Ringside*, 281–282, lists Jack Johnson as the number one heavyweight, Barbados Joe Walcott as the top welterweight, Joe Gans as number one light-weight, and Gans' contemporaries Terry McGovern as the top featherweight and George Dixon as best bantomweight.

22. "King No Match for Gans," *Butte Miner*, July 5, 1903.

23. "Are Titles in Danger? Gans to Show His Worth," *Baltimore Sun*, January 10, 1904.

24. Left Hook, *New York Morning Telegraph*, quoted in *Baltimore Sun*, "Is Gans in Danger?" January 11, 1904.

Chapter 11

1. Nat Fleischer, *Black Dynamite*, Vol. 3, 259.

2. Nat Fleischer, *Black Dynamite: The Story of the Negro in the Prize Ring from 1782 to 1938*, Vol. 5, Sockers and Sepia: A Continuation of the Drama of the Negro in Pugilistic Competition, 7.

3. Nat Fleischer and Sam Andre, *A Pictorial History of Boxing*, 300.

4. James B. Roberts and Alexander G. Skutt, eds., *The Boxing Register: International Boxing Hall of Fame Official Record Book*, 4th ed., 124–125.

5. Monte Cox, "Joe Gans Championship Years: Setting the Record Straight," *IBRO Journal*, No. 82, Summer 2004. This seminal research can be read online at coxscorner.tripod. com/ganschamp.html.

6. Bert Randolph Sugar, *Boxing's Greatest Champions*, 47.

7. Geoffrey C. Ward, *Unforgivable Blackness*, 161.

8. "Charges Local Boxer Deceived his Friends: Baltimorean Thinks Britt's Reputation Will Suffer When Truth Comes Out," *San Francisco Examiner*, February 18, 1906.

9. Charles Samuels, *The Magnificent Rube: The Life and Gaudy Times of Tex Rickard*, 107.

10. "Britt and Gans Ready," *Baltimore Sun*, October 31, 1904.

11. "The Runners at Pimlico: Over 900 Thoroughbreds Await Opening on Saturday," *Baltimore Sun*, November 1, 1904.

12. "Arrow is in $100,000 Event: Airship of Captain Baldwin of Oakland Qualifies for Contest for Big Prize by Second Flight at the World's Fair," *San Francisco Examiner*, November 1, 1904.

13. "Britt and Gans Ready," *Baltimore Sun*, October 31, 1904.

14. Ibid.

15. "Britt, Greatest Fighter of His Weight, Loses on Foul and Battles with Referee," *San Francisco Examiner*, November 1, 1904.

16. "Triumph Turned to Bitter Loss: Negro Hasn't One Chance in Million When the White Man Loses His Head," *San Francisco Examiner*, November 1, 1904.

17. Ibid.

18. Ibid.

19. "Gans Wins on a Foul," *Baltimore Sun*, November 1, 1904.

20. "Gans in Distress Welcomes the Illegal Blow," *San Francisco Examiner*, November 1, 1904.

21. Ibid.

22. Ibid.

23. Ibid.

24. Jimmy Britt, "Sorry He Couldn't Put Check on Self," *San Francisco Examiner*, November 1, 1904.

25. "McGovern Says Now that He is Very Anxious for a Fight with Britt," *San Francisco Examiner* (dispatch from New York, Oct. 31), November 1, 1904.

26. "Joe Gans Believes He Can Whip Britt: Sorry He Won on a Foul, but Says He Will Never Train Down Again to 133 Pounds Ringside, as He is Too Old," *San Francisco Examiner*, November 1, 1904.

27. Ibid.

28. Ibid.

29. "britt: Britt is Strictly a 133 Pound Pugilist: Says He's a Lightweight, and Will Refuse to Fight Outside His Class," *San Francisco Examiner*, November 8, 1904.

30. "ladies, Fair Sex Entertained at the Olympic Club: Britt Monologues at the Club Olympic," *San Francisco Examiner*, January 20, 1905.

31. W.W. Naughton, "Lightweight Laurels Belong to Boxer James Edward Britt," *San Francisco Examiner*, January 10, 1905.

32. Ibid.

33. "Crowd Hisses Fighters Clinched for 6 Rounds; McGovern and Nelson Displease Big Attendance at Bout; Champion is the Stronger; Spurred by the Taunts of the Spectators, the Dane Used Brooklyn Boy Severely in last Two Rounds," *New York Times*, March 15, 1906.

34. "Joe Gans Beaten: Referee O'Hara Calls It a Draw: The Crowd Lets Up a Howl," *Baltimore Sun*, September 16, 1905. (The *Sun* must have failed to note the dispatch sent from Philadelphia where it reported Gans' fight with Rufe Turner "Turner Better than Gans: Defeats the Champion, But Does Not Let Himself Out," March 28, 1905.)

35. "Charges Local Boxer Deceived His Friends: Baltimorean Thinks Britt's Reputation Will Suffer When Truth Comes Out," *San Francisco Examiner*, February 18, 1906. Britt's headline reply below Gans': "Britt Says Gans is Fool or Ill Advised."

36. Joe Gans, untitled, "From now on I shall fight on the level...." *San Francisco Examiner*, January 22, 1906.

37. Gunboat Smith, quoted by Peter Heller, *In This Corner*, 40–41.

38. Willie Ritchie, quoted by Peter Heller, *In This Corner*, 21.

Chapter 12

1. "Billy the Kid's Exploit," *National Police Gazette*, May 21, 1881; "Billy LeRoy, the Bandit," *National Police Gazette*, June 18, 1881; Thomas F. Daggett, *The Life and Deeds of Billy LeRoy alias The Kid, King of America Highwaymen*, published in 1881 by Richard K. Fox. See: J.C. Dykes, *Billy the Kid: The Bibliography of a Legend*, 11–12.

2. Stories are legion about managers who left their boxers destitute. Even after Jack Dempsey had beaten Jess Willard to win the heavyweight title and had taken a purse of $27,000, he was still broke. As his manager Doc Kearns explained, he had needed money to move around with, pay bets, and money to entertain the writers with. Roger Kahn, *A Flame of Pure Fire*, 100–104.

3. F. Daniel Somrack, *Images of Sports: Boxing in San Francisco*, 83. That Gans went west to avenge his first loss in the ring in October of 1896 is reported in the *Baltimore Sun*, November 4, 1898.

4. "Gans Wins in a One-Sided Match: Rochette, the Local Boxer, Completely Outclassed by the Baltimorean," *San Francisco Examiner*, December 15, 1896.

5. Herbert Ashbury, *The Barbary Coast—An Informal History of the San Francisco Underworld* (rpt. of Benjamin Estelle Lloyd, *Lights and Shades of San Francisco*, San Francisco, 1876), 101.

6. Ibid.

7. Earp's side of the Sharkey-Fitzsimmons story, *San Francisco Examiner*, December 10, 1896.

8. "Gans and M'Fadden Draw: But the Baltimore Negro Had the Best of It," *Baltimore Sun*, October 3, 1900.

9. Armond Fields, *James J. Corbett: A Biography of the Heavyweight Boxing Champion and Popular Theater Headliner*, 67.

10. The play appeared in New York City on September 29, 1911, as *The Birth Mark* and in Minneapolis on July 15, 1911, as *Her Brother's Clothes. Jack London Stories of Boxing*, James Bankes, ed., 14.

11. T. Allston Brown, *A History of New York Stage: From the First Performance in 1732–1901*, 650–652.

12. Armond Fields, 85.

13. "Kid M'Coy Married Again: Divorced from Former Wife Thrice. New One an Actress," *Baltimore Sun*, January 19, 1904.

14. Felicia Feaster, "The Wizard of Oz (1925)," Turner Classic Movies, articles online. www.tcm.com/thismonth/article.jsp?cid=1380

86&mainArticleId=138084, accessed February 18, 2008.

15. "McFadden's Claim on Gans" *Baltimore Sun* (from letter sent to the sporting editor of the *Sun*, dated September 29, 1902), October 1, 1902.

Chapter 13

1. "Decision over Gans: Sam Langford Gets It in a Fifteen-Round Bout," *Baltimore Sun* (special dispatch from Boston), December 9, 1903.
2. ESPN survey online, ESPN.com, accessed June 15, 2007.
3. Gans had been ill for the Langford match in early December. See "Decision Over Gans," *Baltimore Sun*, December 9, 1903. Gans missed a match with Blackburn scheduled December 21 due to illness. See "Boxing and Wrestling," *Baltimore Sun*, January 6, 1904. Temperatures on the East Coast, falling below the zero-degree mark, were responsible for many deaths, including that of Terry McGovern's two-year-old daughter who died of pneumonia.
4. Charles A. Dana, quoted by Arthur Ashe, *Hard Road to Glory*, 11.
5. Rex Lardner writes about Walcott in *The Legendary Champions*, 170.
6. "Says That Gans Had Skill, But Walcott Was Aggressor," *San Francisco Examiner*, October 1, 1904.
7. "Wasn't Hurt and Could Have Fought Twenty Rounds More," *San Francisco Examiner*, October 1, 1904.
8. Barbados Negro Declares He Fought with Broken Left Arm," *San Francisco Examiner*, October 1, 1904.
9. "Gans Outpoints Walcott, But Referee Calls It Draw: Ruling Makes Crowd Frown," *San Francisco Examiner*, October 1, 1904.
10. *The Joe Louis Story*, 1953.
11. "English Fighter Beaten by Gans," *New York Times*, May 28, 1904. "Like the Gans of Old: He Never Gave Jewey Cooke the Slightest Chance," *Baltimore Sun*, May 28, 1904.
12. W.W. Naughton, "And Now Gans is the Idol of Boxing Patrons," *San Francisco Examiner*, January 23, 1906.
13. Alexander Johnson, *Ten And Out*, 300–301.
14. David L. Hudson, Jr., and Mike H. Fitzgerald, Jr., *Boxing's Most Wanted*, 209.
15. "McCoy Gets into a Street Brawl," *Chicago Tribune*, December 29, 1900.
16. Charles Convis, *True Tales from the Old West*, Vol. 9, 56.
17. "Wasn't Hurt," *San Francisco Examiner*, October 1, 1904.
18. "Novel Challenge," *Philadelphia Enquirer*, January 31, 1903.

19. Charles E. Van Loan, "One Thirty Three Ringside," Paul D. Staudohar, ed., *Boxing's Best Short Stories*, 237.

Chapter 14

1. Charles Samuels, *The Magnificent Rube: The Life and Gaudy Times of Tex Rickard*, 96.
2. Ibid., 66.
3. George Graham Rice, *My Adventures with Your Money*, 99.
4. Samuels, 98.
5. Ibid., 102.
6. Ibid., 98.
7. Tracy Callis, "Battling Nelson: Always Battered, Seldom Beaten," *wail! The CBZ Journal*, February 2006.
8. Ibid.
9. Samuels, 109–110.
10. Ibid.
11. Ibid., 101.
12. Ibid., 103.
13. Ibid., 103–104.
14. Rice, 114.
15. "Today's Big Fight: Crowds Flock to Goldfield to Take Their Places Beside the Ring," *Baltimore Sun*, September 3, 1906.
16. Rice, 116.
17. Ibid., 104.
18. "Today's Big Fight," *Baltimore Sun*, September 3, 1906.
19. John D. McCallum, *The Encyclopedia of World Boxing Champions*, 230.
20. "Today's Big Fight," *Baltimore Sun*, September 3, 1906.
21. Ibid.
22. Ibid.
23. "Joe Gans Wins," *Baltimore Sun*, September 4, 1906.
24. Every major paper covering the fight quoted this telegram from Gans' mother in their sporting pages the next day, September 4, 1906.
25. "Joe Gans Wins," *Baltimore Sun*, September 4, 1906.
26. Ibid.
27. Ibid.
28. Ibid.
29. Arthur Ashe, *Hard Road to Glory*, 13.
30. Samuels, 129.
31. Ibid., 103.
32. Rice, 131.

Chapter 15

1. Geoffrey Ward, *Unforgivable Blackness*, 6.
2. "Consumption Can be Cured," *Albuquerque Morning Journal*, July 3, 1910.
3. "To Fight White Death," *Baltimore Sun*, September 19, 1902. The first complete study

of tuberculosis in Baltimore was done by a third year medical student from Johns Hopkins University who visited the homes and workplaces of 190 consumptives, everyone who had visited the hospital's dispensary. Her visits were recorded in the *American Journal of Nursing* in 1902. During her visits she instructed the residents in methods of disinfecting the home, concerns regarding expectoration and matters of personal health.

4. Ibid.

5. Ibid.

6. Ibid.

7. "To Check 'White Death,'" *Baltimore Sun*, March 11, 1903.

8. "Figure on White Death: Exposition at M'Coy Hall," *Baltimore Sun*, January 14, 1904.

9. Ibid.

10. "Smallpox Case," *Baltimore Sun*, January 9, 1904.

11. "Open-Air Cure: Sleeping Out in a Tent in Zero Weather," *Baltimore Sun*, January 9, 1904.

12. "Turner Better than Gans," *Baltimore Sun* (special dispatch from Philadelphia), March 28, 1905.

13. "Joe Gans Beaten," *Baltimore Sun*, September 16, 1905.

14. "Divorce Denied to Gans: Pugilist Fails to Make Out a Case at Baltimore," *Washington Post*, February 7, 1906.

15. W.W. Naughton, "If Gans Triumphs He'll Hold Two Championships," *San Francisco Examiner*, January 16, 1906.

16. Diane Yancey, *Tuberculosis, Twenty-First Century Medical Library*, 59–60. See also: Jean and Rene Dubos, *The White Plague*, 1952; Katherine Ott, *Fevered Lives: Tuberculosis in American Culture Since 1870*, 1999; and Frank Ryan, *The Forgotten Plague*, 1993.

17. "To Neglect a Cold," *Albuquerque Morning Journal*, July 31, 1910.

18. "El Reposo Sanitorium, Ranch and Health Resort Sierra Madre, Calif.," *Albuquerque Morning Journal*, July 31, 1910.

Chapter 16

1. Harry C. Carr, "Study in Pathos," *Los Angeles Times*, September 25, 1907.

2. Ibid.

3. Ibid.

4. Charles A. Dana, "The Negro Domination in the Field of Fistic Sport," *New York Sun*, 1895.

5. Nat Fleischer, *Black Dynamite*, Vol. 3, 22.

6. Jack London, "Jeffries-Johnson Fight," *Jack London Stories of Boxing*, James Bankes, ed., 187.

7. Ibid.

8. London, 183.

9. "Put up a Poorer Fight than Herman," *San Francisco Examiner*, September 10, 1907.

10. H.L. Mencken, *Heathen Days*, 96–97.

Chapter 17

1. "Graney Declares Gans Was Offered $25,000 to Fake with Battling Nelson: Well-known Referee Says a Friend of the Champion Advised Him to Take the Money and Double-Cross the Sure-Thing Gamblers, But Gans Refused," and "Gans Admits He was Offered $25,000 to Lose to Nelson," *San Francisco Examiner*, September 7, 1906.

2. It was reported that Battling Nelson showed up at the Goldfield Hotel in what seemed to be their first meeting after the fight. Apparently, Nelson had been told by his manager that Gans was going to "lay down." Nelson asked Gans why he didn't take the dive, explaining that they could have fought again later and it would have saved them both from the protracted ring battle. Elton C. Fax, "Incident at the Goldfield," *Maryland*, Vol. 12, 34–37.

3. Jim Jeffries was to receive $1500 to referee the fight. However, he had called the Burns-O'Brien bout a draw and received such criticism that he decided against serving as a referee for any future boxing matches. "Today's Big Ring Fight: Now Joe Gans and Herman Will Clash at Tonopha: The Crowds are Pouring In," *Baltimore Sun*, January 1, 1907.

4. Ibid.

5. "Gans Sends Mother $6000: She Wires Back to Pugilist, 'Thanks; Keep Stepping, Joe,'" *New York Times*, January 1, 1907.

6. "Gans, Only Gans: The Fight at Tonopah is His All the Way Through," *Baltimore Sun*, January 2, 1907.

7. "Gans is Well Received: Tells New York that He Will Whip Jimmy Britt Quickly," *Baltimore Sun*, January 16, 1907.

8. Ibid.

9. "Another Fight Scandal on Coast," *New York Times* (from Los Angeles, Aug. 9), August 10, 1907.

10. "Today's Big Ring Fight," *Baltimore Sun*, January 1, 1907.

11. W.W. Naughton, "Britt Sure He is Stronger than Gans and Will Thus Win: Native Son Has New Stunt in Training," *San Francisco Examiner*, September 5, 1907.

12. C.E. Van Loan, "Britt Only Lands Two Dangerous Blows and These in First Round," *San Francisco Examiner*, September 10, 1907.

13. C.E. Van Loan, "At All Times Outclassed and At the Mercy of the Baltimorean," *San Francisco Examiner*, September 10, 1907. There was no question that Gans had been the rightful titleholder.

14. "Joe Gans Wins," *Baltimore Sun*, September 10, 1907.

15. C.E. Van Loan, "Local Fighter a Beaten Man after Second Round," *San Francisco Examiner*, September 10, 1907.

16. Ibid.

17. Harry C. Carr, "Study in Pathos is Face of Joe Gans," *Los Angeles Daily Times*, September 25, 1907.

18. Ibid.

19. Ibid.

20. Ibid.

21. "Miller's Big Benefit: Many Star Boxers Perform for the Old Fighter: Gans Gets Great Ovation," *Baltimore Sun*, January 4, 1908.

22. "Gans Still Champion," *Baltimore Sun*, May 15, 1908.

23. Film footage of the 17th round. *History of Boxing: 1906–1955*. (The film incorrectly identifies this fight as the Goldfield fight.)

24. Ralph Ellison, *Invisible Man*, 8.

25. William Shakespeare, *Hamlet*, Act V, Scene 2, line 359–360.

26. "Joe Gans Knocked Out: Down at Joe's Hotel," *Baltimore Sun*, July 5, 1908.

27. Ellison, 278.

28. "Gans Knocked Out: Battling Nelson Finishes Him in Twenty-First Round, Never Had Chance to Win," *Baltimore Sun*, September 10, 1908.

29. "Gans, After a Merciless Beating: Nelson Again Batters Down the 'Old Master,'" *San Francisco Examiner*, September 10, 1908.

30. "Gans Puzzles Sports: Former Negro Champion Wins from Jabez White on Points," *Baltimore Sun*, March 13, 1909.

31. Ibid.

32. "Joe Gans in Poor Health," *New York Times* (from Denver, March 29), March 30, 1909.

33. "Cross and Stone in Tame Bout," *New York Times* (from Baltimore, Oct. 28), October 29, 1909.

34. "Joe Gans Will Be Great Asset to Jack Johnson," *Washington Post*, December 26, 1909.

35. Florence B. Yount, M.D., "A Century of Medicine," *Echoes of the Past: Tales of Old Yavapai*, Vol. 2, 89.

36. Katherine J. Gernand Nicolay, "Tuberculars Have Positive Cultural Effect on Prescott," *Days Past*, Prescott, Ariz.: Sharlot Hall Museum, January 15, 2006.

37. Ryan Flahive, "Prescott's Pugilistic Production: The Sullivan-Kilrain Exhibition of 1909," *Days Past*, Prescott, Ariz.: Sharlot Hall Museum, April 17, 2005.

38. Ibid.

39. "Joe Gans Slowly Sinking," *New York Times* (from Baltimore, Aug. 6), August 7, 1910.

40. Gans arrived in Prescott on June 9, 1910. There were three reports in the local paper regarding his stay in Prescott: *Prescott Journal-Miner*, June 10, June 18, and August 2, 1910 (courtesy Sharlot Hall Museum, Prescott, Ariz.).

41. "Joe Gans Going Home to Die," *Albuquerque Journal*, August 2, 1910.

42. "Gans on Last Lap Home," *Washington Post*, August 5, 1910.

43. "Joe Gans Slowly Sinking," *New York Times*, August 7, 1910.

44. "No Change in Gans' Condition," *New York Times*, August 8, 1910.

45. "Joe Gans," obituary. Baltimore *Afro American*, August 13, 1910.

46. Ibid.

Chapter 18

1. William Shakespeare, *Hamlet*, Act V, Scene 2.

2. "'Swinging Doors' Recalled on Last Visit to Goldfield," *Baltimore Sun*, December 6, 1960.

Chapter 19

1. "Joseph Gans," obituary. *Baltimore Sun*, August 11, 1910.

2. Quotes from the boxing greats who knew Gans are taken from the research of Monte Cox, "Joe Gans, The Old Master: Was He the Greatest of Them All?" online publication by the IBRO, *Journal* No. 83, September 2004. Twin Sullivan's statement comes from a letter he wrote to the *San Francisco Examiner*, January 22, 1906.

3. Monte Cox, "Joe Gans, The Old Master: Was He the Greatest of Them All?" and Cox's Corner Profiles, "Joe Gans, The Old Master....' He Could Lick Them All on Their Best Day!'" www.coxscorner.tripod.com/gans.html.

4. Ibid.

5. Ibid.

6. Ibid.

7. Ibid.

8. Bill Gray, *Boxing's Top 100*, 108.

9. Mike Casey, "Joe Gans: Secrets of the Old Master," February 11, 2007. www.boxingscene.com, accessed February 11, 2008.

10. Herb Boyd, *Pound For Pound: A Biography of Sugar Ray Robinson*, 89. New York: Amistad/HarperCollins, 2005.

11. Monte Cox, "Joe Gans, The Old Master: Was He the Greatest of Them All?"

12. Robert Sylvester, *The Joe Louis Story*, Robert Gordon, dir., Miracle Pictures, 1953.

13. Bill Moran, quoting Tad Dorgan in "The Greatest Fighter Who Ever Lived? This Writer Lauds Joe Gans, Old Master," *Nevada State Journal*, September 27, 1942.

14. Ibid.

15. International News Service, New York, September 30, 1919.

16. Referee Siler is quoted by Francis J. Grimke in his sermon, "The Atlanta Riot: A Discourse Published by Request." Washington, D.C., Oct. 7, 1906.

17. H.L. Mencken, "A Master of Gladiators," 104.

18. Gerald Suster, *Lightning Strikes*, 27.

19. Nat Fleischer, *Leonard the Magnificent*, 2.

Chapter 20

1. *San Francisco Examiner*, "What Will be the End of the Dead-Earnest, Menacing Uprising of Atlanta to Crush Out with Guns, Ropes and Dogs, the Fearful Epidemic of Negro Crime Against Her Women?" September 20, 1906.

2. "'Swinging Doors' Recalled on Last Visit to Goldfield," *Baltimore Sun*, December 6, 1960.

3. Arthur Ashe, *Hard Road to Glory*, 12.

4. Ibid., 25.

Epilogue

1. *Champions Forever*, 2000.

2. Charles Willeford, *Cockfighter*, 29.

3. Ibid.

4. "Deaths in the Ring: Statistician Gets in His Work on Finished Pugilists," *Baltimore Sun*, November 3, 1905. The "statistician," whose work appears to be the first of its kind reported in America, was Prof. Edwin G. Dexter of the University of Illinois. The list of deaths goes back to 1758.

Works Cited

Ali, Muhammad. *The Greatest: My Own Story*. New York: Random House, 1975.

Ashbury, Herbert. *The Barbary Coast: An Informal History of the San Francisco Underworld*. New York: Knopf, 1933.

Ashe, Arthur. *Hard Road to Glory*. New York: Amistad, 1988.

Baum, L. Frank. *The Wonderful Wizard of Oz*. Chicago: Geo. M. Hill, 1900.

Beirne, Francis F. *The Amiable Baltimoreans*. Baltimore: Johns Hopkins University Press, 1951.

Brown, T. Allston. *A History of New York Stage: From the First Performance in 1732–1901*. Vol. 2. New York: Dodd, Mead, 1903.

Burroughs, Edgar Rice. "The Mucker." *Story Cavalier Weekly*, 1914. Reprinted in book form, New York: Ace Books, 1974.

Callis, Tracy, Chuck Hasson, and Mike Delisa. *Images of Sports: Philadelphia's Boxing Heritage 1876–1976*. Charleston, S.C.: Arcadia Publishing, 2002.

Casey, Mike. "Joe Gans: Secrets of the Old Master," February 11, 2007, http://www.boxingscene.com.

Connell, Richard Edward. "A Friend of Napoleon," *Apes and Angels*. 1924. Reprint, Freeport, N.Y., London: Library Press, 1970.

Convis, Charles. *True Tales of the Old West*, Vol. 9. Carson City, Nev.: Pioneer Press, 1998.

Cox, Monte. Best of the Century, n.d. http://members.tripod.com/coxscorner/index.html.

_____. "Joe Gans Championship Years: Setting the Record Straight," *IBRO Journal*, No. 82, Summer 2004.

_____. Joe Gans, the Old Master ... He Could Lick Them All on Their Best Day! n.d. http://coxscorner.tripod.com/gans.html.

_____. "Joe Gans, The Old Master. Was He the Greatest of Them All?" *IBRO Journal*, No. 83, September 2004.

Du Bois, William Edward Burghardt. *The Souls of Black Folk*. Chicago: A.C. McClung, 1903.

Dubos, Jean, and Rene Dubos. *The White Plague*. New Brunswick, N.J.: Rutgers University Press, 1952.

Dykes, J.C. *Billy the Kid: The Bibliography of a Legend*. Albuquerque: University of New Mexico, 1952.

Ellison, Ralph. *Invisible Man*. New York: Signet, 1953. Reprint, New York: Vintage/Random House, 1995.

Fax, Elton C. "Incident at the Goldfield," *Maryland*, Vol. 12, 34–37.

Fields, Armond. *James J. Corbett: A Biography of the Heavyweight Boxing Champion and Popular Theater Headliner*. Jefferson, N.C.: McFarland, 2001.

Flahive, Ryan. "Prescott's Pugilistic Production: The Sullivan-Kilrain Exhibition of 1909." *Days Past*, Prescott, Ariz.: Sharlot Hall Museum, April 17, 2005. http://www.sharlot.org/archives/history/dayspast/text/2005_04_17.

Fleischer, Nat. *Black Dynamite: The Story of the Negro in Boxing.* New York: C.J. O'Brien, 1938.

_____. *Black Dynamite: The Story of the Negro in the Prize Ring from 1782 to 1938, Vol. 3, Three Colored Aces.* New York: C.J. O'Brien, 1938.

_____. *Black Dynamite. The Story of the Negro in the Prize Ring from 1782 to 1938, Vol. 4, Fighting Furies: Story of the Golden Era of Jack Johnson, Sam Langford and Their Contemporaries.* New York: C.J. O'Brien, 1939.

_____. *Black Dynamite: The Story of the Negro in the Prize Ring from 1782 to 1938, Vol. 5, Sockers and Sepia: A Continuation of the Drama of the Negro in Pugilistic Competition.* New York: C.J. O'Brien, 1947.

_____. *50 Years at Ringside.* New York: Fleet Publishing, 1958.

_____. *Leonard the Magnificent: Life Story of the Man Who Made Himself King of the Lightweights.* Norwalk, Conn.: O'Brien Suburban Press, 1947.

_____. *The Ring Record Book and Boxing Encyclopedia.* New York: The Ring Book Shop, Inc., 1942. Citations are to the 1961 edition.

Fleischer, Nat, and Sam Andre. *A Pictorial History of Boxing.* Secaucus, N.J.: Bonanza Books/Citadel, 1959.

Fried, Ronald K. *Cornermen.* New York: Four Walls Eight Windows, 1991.

George, Christopher T. Monumentally Speaking: John Quincy Adams and "The Monumental City," n.d. http://www.baltimoremd.com/monuments/adams.html.

Ginzburg, Ralph. *One Hundred Years of Lynchings.* Baltimore: Black Classic Press, 1962.

Gray, Bill. *Boxing's Top 100.* Barnesville, Ohio: Blue Lightning Press, 2006.

Greff, Jacqueline, prod./dir. *Fells Point, Out of Time.* Documentary, Baltimore: 2004.

Greig, Murray. *Goin' the Distance: Canada's Boxing Heritage.* Toronto: Macmillan, 1996.

Grimke, Francis J., "The Atlanta Riot: A Discourse Published by Request." Washington, D.C., Oct. 7, 1906. Facsimile of the first edition, Georgia Room, main library, University of Georgia: http://fax.libs.uga.edu/F294xA8xG8/#.

Grombach, John V. *The Saga of the Fist: The 9000 Year Story of Boxing in Text and Pictures; The Saga of Sock.* Cranbury, N.J.: A.S. Barnes, 1949. Reprint, London: Magdalen House, 1977. Citations are to the Magdalen House edition.

Haley, Melissa. "Storm of Blows, III: The Death of Andy Bowen," *Common-place*, Vol. 3, No. 2, American Antiquarian Society and Florida State University, Department of History, January 2003. www.common-place.org.

Hedin, Robert, and Michael Waters, eds. *Perfect in Their Art: Poems on Boxing from Homer to Ali.* Carbondale: Southern Illinois University Press, 2003.

Heinz, W.C., ed. *Fireside Book of Boxing.* New York: Simon and Schuster, 1961.

Heller, Peter. *In This Corner: 42 World Champions Tell Their Stories.* New York: Da Capo Press, 1973.

Hietala, Thomas R. *The Fight of the Century: Jack Johnson, Joe Louis and the Struggle for Racial Equality.* Armonk, N.Y.: M.E. Sharpe, 2002.

Hudson, David L., Jr., and Mike H. Fitzgerald, Jr. *Boxing's Most Wanted: The Top 10 Book of Champs, Chumps, and Punch-Drunk Palookas.* Washington, D.C.: Brassey's, 2004.

Johnston, Alexander. *Ten And Out: The Complete Story of the Prize Ring in America.* New York: Ives Washburn, 1927.

Johnston, J.J., and Sean Curtin. *Images of Sport: Chicago Boxing.* Charleston, S.C.: Arcadia, 2005.

Kahn, Roger. *A Flame of Pure Fire: Jack Dempsey and the Roaring '20s.* New York: Harcourt Brace, 1999.

Lardner, Rex. *The Legendary Champions*. New York: American Heritage, 1972.

Lipsyte, Robert, and Peter Levine. *Idols of the Game: A Sporting History of the American Century*. Atlanta: Turner Publishing, 1995.

London, Jack. *Jack London Stories of Boxing*. Edited by James Bankes. Dubuque, Iowa: William C. Brown, 1992.

McCallum, John D. *The Encyclopedia of World Boxing Champions: Since 1882*. Radnor, Pa.: Chilton Book, 1975.

McCurdy, Michael, ed. *Escape from Slavery: The Boyhood of Frederick Douglass in His Own Words*. New York: Knopf, 1994.

Mencken, H.L. "A Master of Gladiators (1907)," *Heathen Days: 1890–1936*. New York: Knopf, 1943, 96–106. Page references are to this edition.

Mencken, H.L. *The Mencken Bibliography*. Compiled by Betty Adler. Baltimore: Johns Hopkins Press, 1961, 157. Second supplement compiled by Vincent Fitzpatrick, 1971, 157, "A Master of Gladiators, 1907," *The New Yorker*, Vol. 18, April 1942, 18–20.

Miler, Thomas. *The Sweet Science Goes Sour: How Scandal Brought Boxing to Its Knees*. Vancouver, B.C.: Greystone Books, 2006.

Miller, Henry. *Sexus: The Rosy Crucifixion, Book One*. New York: Grove Press, 1987.

Naughton, W.W. *Kings of the Queensberry Realm*. Chicago: Continental, 1902.

Nesbit, Evelyn. *Tragic Beauty: The Lost 1914 Memoirs of Evelyn Nesbit*. London: John Long, 1914. Reprint, United States: Deborah Dorian Paul, 2006.

Nicolay, Katherine J. Gernand. "Tuberculars Have Positive Cultural Effect on Prescott," *Days Past*, Prescott, Ariz: Sharlot Hall Museum, January 15, 2006. http://www.sharlot.org/archives/history/dayspast/text/2006_01_15.shtml.

Oates, Joyce Carol. *On Boxing*. Garden City, N.Y.: Dolphin Doubleday, 1987.

Ott, Katherine. *Fevered Lives: Tuberculosis in American Culture Since 1870*. Cambridge, Mass.: Harvard University Press, 1999.

Remnick, David. *King of the World: Muhammad Ali and the Rise of an American Hero*. New York: Random House, 1998.

Rice, George Graham. *My Adventures with Your Money*. Boston: R.C. Badger, 1913.

Roberts, James B., and Alexander G. Skutt. *The Boxing Register: International Boxing Hall of Fame Official Record Book*. Ithaca, N.Y.: McBooks Press, 2006.

Roberts, Randy. *Papa Jack: Jack Johnson and the Era of White Hopes*. New York: Free Press, 1983.

Ryan Frank. *The Forgotten Plague*. Boston: Little, Brown, 1993.

Samuels, Charles. *The Magnificent Rube: The Life and Gaudy Times of Tex Rickard*. New York: McGraw-Hill, 1957.

Scharf, Thomas. *Images of Sports: Baltimore's Boxing Legacy 1893–2003*, Charleston, S.C.: Arcadia, 2003.

Simon, Roger, and Angie Cannon. "An Amazing Journey: The Mirror of the Census Reveals the Character of a Nation," *U.S. News and World Report*, August 6, 2001, 10–18.

Smith, Mona Z. *Becoming Something: The Story of Canada Lee; The Untold Tragedy of the Great Black Actor, Activist, and Athlete*. New York: Faber and Faber, 2004.

Somrack, F. Daniel. *Images of Sports: Boxing in San Francisco*. Charleston, S.C.: Arcadia, 2005.

Staudohar, Paul D., ed. *Boxing's Best Short Stories*. Chicago: Chicago Review Press, 1999.

Stevens, Robert C. *Echoes of the Past: Tales of Old Yavapai*, Vol. 2. Prescott, Ariz.: Yavapai Cowbelles, 1964.

Stocker, Joseph. *Arizona: A Guide to Easier Living*. New York: Harper and Brothers, 1955.

Sugars, Burt Randolph. *Boxing's Greatest Fighters*. Guilford, Conn.: Lyons Press, 2006.

Summerhayes, Martha. *Vanished Arizona: Recollections of the Army Life of a New England Woman*. Lincoln: University of Nebraska Press, 1979.

Suster, Gerald. *Lightning Strikes: The Lives and Times of Boxing's Lightweight Heroes.* London: Robson Books, 1994.

Torrence, Ridgely. *Granny Maumee, the Rider of Dreams, Simon the Cyrenian: Plays for a Negro Theater.* New York: Macmillan, 1917. Reprinted in electronic form by Questia Media American: www.questia.com.

Ward, Geoffrey C. *Unforgivable Blackness: The Rise and Fall of Jack Johnson.* New York: Vantage Books/Random House, 2006.

Washington, Booker T. *Frederick Douglass.* London: Hodder and Stoughton, 1906. Facsimile of the document reprinted in electronic form by Tuskegee University Libraries: http://docsouth.unc.edu/neh/doug1906/menu.html.

Willeford, Charles. *Cockfighter.* Black Mask Online, Disruptive Publishing, 1962.

Yancey, Diane. *Tuberculosis, Twenty-First Century Medical Library.* Brookfield, Conn.: Twenty-First Century Books, 2001.

Films

Champions Forever (2000)

Cinderella Man (2005)

Fells Point, Out of Time (2004)

History of Boxing: 1906–1955 (1990)

The Joe Louis Story (1953)

Mandingo (1976)

On the Waterfront (1954)

The Outlaw Josie Wales (1976)

Raging Bull (1980)

Rocky (1976)

The Seven Faces (1929)

When We Were Kings (1997)

The Wizard of Oz (1925)

The Wizard of Oz (1939)

Newspapers

Albuquerque Journal

Anaconda Standard (Phoenix, Ariz.)

Baltimore Afro American

Baltimore Sun

Broadax (Chicago)

Butte (Mont.) *Miner*

Chicago Record Herald

Chicago Times Herald

Chicago Tribune

Daily Northwestern (Oshkosh, Wis.)

Decatur (Ill.) *Review*

Fort Wayne (Ind.) *News*

Goldfield (Nev.) *Sun*

Houston (Texas) *Post*

Los Angeles Times

Memphis (Tenn.) *Press*

Nevada State Journal (Reno)

New Orleans Times Democrat

New York Herald

New York Police Gazette

New York Sun

New York Times

New York World

Philadelphia Inquirer

Prescott (Ariz.) *Daily Miner*

San Antonio (Texas) *Sunday Light*

San Francisco Examiner

Washington Post (D.C.)

Index